RUNNING FOR FREEDOM

Critical Episodes in American Politics

Consulting Editor
Robert A. Divine
University of Texas at Austin

Years of Decision: American Politics in the 1890s
R. Hal Williams

Reform and Regulation: American Politics from Roosevelt to Wilson,
Second Edition
Lewis L. Gould

From Margin to Mainstream: American Women and Politics Since 1960
Susan M. Hartmann

Running for Freedom
Civil Rights and Black Politics in America Since 1941

[handwritten annotations:]
human rights
legal power - union
political - jobs
justice color blind   grassroots - house
unaware of race   party —
opportunity uncovered   electoral —
with color   — ~~Disability Bill~~
Justice

Steven F. Lawson
University of South Florida

McGRAW-HILL, INC.
New York St. Louis San Francisco Auckland Bogotá Caracas
Hamburg Lisbon London Madrid Mexico Milan Montreal New Delhi
Paris San Juan São Paulo Singapore Sydney Tokyo Toronto

This book was set in Caledonia by the College Composition Unit
in cooperation with Ruttle Shaw & Wetherill, Inc.
The editors were Christopher Rogers and Lauren G. Shafer;
the production supervisor was Stacey B. Alexander.
The cover was designed by Gayle Jaeger.
R. R. Donnelley & Sons Company was printer and binder.

Cover photo: From top to bottom: AP/Wide World, © Matt Herron/Black Star (3),
© Arnold Zann/Black Star.

RUNNING FOR FREEDOM
Civil Rights and Black Politics in America Since 1941

1 2 3 4 5 6 7 8 9 0 DOH DOH 9 5 4 3 2 1 0

ISBN 0-07-556975-2

Library of Congress Cataloging-in-Publication Data

Lawson, Steven F., (date).
    Running for freedom: civil rights and black politics in America since
1941 / Steven F. Lawson.
        p.   cm.
    Includes bibliographical references.
    ISBN 0-07-556975-2
    1. Afro-Americans—Civil rights.   2. Afro-Americans—Politics and
government.   3. Civil rights movements—United States—History—20th
century.   4. United States—Politics and government—1933-1945.   5. United
States—Politics and government—1945-   I. Title.
E185.61.L38   1991
323.1'196073—dc20   90-33515

For Nancy Ann Hewitt

About the Author

Steven F. Lawson is professor of history at the University of South Florida in Tampa. He has received fellowships from the National Endowment for the Humanities, the American Council of Learned Societies, and the National Humanities Center. He has served as an adviser to the television documentary series, *Eyes on the Prize*, and has participated as an historical consultant on voting rights cases. His publications include *Black Ballots: Voting Rights in the South, 1944–1969* (1976), which was awarded the Phi Alpha Theta best first-book prize; *In Pursuit of Power: Southern Blacks and Electoral Politics, 1965–1982* (1985); and numerous articles and essays on the civil rights movement and politics.

Contents

FOREWORD *viii*

PREFACE *x*

1. World War II and the Origins of the Freedom Struggle *1*

2. Ballots, Boycotts, and the Building of a National Agenda *31*

3. Surging Protest, Shifting Politics *66*

4. Reenfranchisement and Racial Consciousness *105*

5. The New Black Politicians: From Protest to Empowerment *146*

6. Progress and Poverty: Politics in a Conservative Era *183*

7. In Search of Legitimacy *222*

8. Still Running for Freedom *261*

BIBLIOGRAPHIC ESSAY *272*

INDEX *298*

Foreword

The resurgence of political history is one of the most intriguing developments in recent American historical scholarship. In the years immediately following World War II, historians tended to dismiss the study of past politics as mundane and old-fashioned as they focused on cultural, psychological, ethnic, and intellectual approaches to the American experience. But the enduring importance of political events, brought home to scholars as well as journalists by the tumultuous events of the 1960s and the devastating Watergate scandal, led historians to examine the political past anew. Many borrowed ideas and techniques from social scientists to probe into such new areas as voting behavior, party fluctuations, and the role of ethnocultural factors in politics. Others relied on more traditional studies of campaign rhetoric and the impact of charismatic leaders on the political process. The result was a new flowering of political history.

Critical Episodes in American Politics is a series of interpretive volumes designed to bring new scholarship to bear on some important periods and themes in American political history. Departing from the original attempt to provide chronological coverage, the series now emphasizes significant topics that helped shape the course of American political development in the twentieth century. Employing different techniques and approaches, each of the authors focuses on a distinctive pattern of past political behavior to show how it contributed to the evolution of modern American democracy.

In this volume, Steven Lawson offers a sweeping view of the impact of the civil rights movement on postwar American politics. He shows how blacks, once a passive group largely denied political participation, adopted tactics of protest and confrontation to gain access to the polls and then used this new freedom to make significant political gains. By focusing on both the national movement and grassroots activism, he establishes the close connection between what happened in Washington and in local communities across the country. Professor Lawson also underscores the ironies of this political transformation—the way in which the solidly Democratic South voted overwhelmingly Republican in presidential elections as well as the fact that the median black family income relative to white declined just as black political activity increased. The story he tells is one of victories and defeats, of long-overdue political gains and frustrating setbacks. Ranging from A. Philip Randolph's threatened march on Washington on the eve of American entry into World War II to Jesse Jackson's stirring presidential bids in the 1980's, the author provides insights into the continuing dilemma facing American society in the last decade of the twentieth century—how to enable black Americans to enjoy the full benefits of citizenship in a democratic society.

paternalism

Robert A. Divine

Preface

In the more than two decades since the civil rights movement achieved some of the most momentous reforms of the twentieth century, scholars have produced a rich body of literature detailing the battle for racial and political equality. Initially, most of the works focused on the activities of major civil rights organizations and leaders and their efforts to enact national legislation, gain presidential support, and win litigation before the federal courts. In general, they concentrated on the responses of government institutions and officials to demands for social change. More recently, a second generation of scholarly studies has shifted the emphasis away from powerful leaders, interest groups, and agencies to indigenous mass movements, seeking to discover their unique structures, ideologies, strategies, and tactics. From this perspective, black protest and politics are not viewed primarily as a struggle for obtaining civil rights laws in the national arena but for liberating black communities at the grass roots level.

As scholarly inquiry has refocused the vision of this struggle "from the bottom up," it is appropriate to consider how efforts at the local level intersected with those on the national stage. Both national civil rights campaigns aimed at legislation and litigation and community organizing directed toward consciousness raising were part of a larger process of empowerment. In an interactive way, the civil rights movement altered local black institutions and shaped national goals; in turn, the actions of the federal government and established civil rights groups transformed local communities in the process of expanding freedom.

An interpretive synthesis, this book examines the freedom struggle and black political development since the beginning of World War II. Moving along two tracks, the national and the local, this study attempts to gauge the connections between the two.

x

Pressure from below ultimately pushed the federal government to challenge disfranchisement. Northern blacks, whose votes swung the balance of power in close national elections, demanded that lawmakers remedy the plight of blacks deprived of their rights in the South. The urgency of a response became greater as southern blacks, prevented from registering their discontent at the polls, used nonviolent civil disobedience to spark crises forcing the national government to come to their aid. In organizing against racism, the civil rights movement mobilized blacks for political action and prepared the way for extensive black participation in the electoral process following passage of the 1965 Voting Rights Act.

The franchise figured prominently in the thinking of both white officials and black protesters, though in different ways. White leaders saw the ballot as a means of promoting orderly social change during a period when black protests and hostile white reactions to them threatened civic peace and the legitimacy of democratic institutions. Blacks considered the franchise less as an implement of social cohesion and more as a weapon for destroying racist institutions and encouraging liberation. In pursuit of group power, African-Americans marshaled their forces to elect candidates of their own race, a preference that has highlighted the conflict between proportional representation and color-blind politics, between affirmative action and traditional notions of political equality.

Since 1941, the political system has been opened up to active minority participation, gradually though sometimes dramatically, and black Americans are working through it to acquire the advantages long denied them. Consequently, they have come to rely much less on the tactics of agitation and confrontation employed so effectively during the civil rights struggle and to depend more on the process of bargaining and compromise associated with professional politics. As a result, increased electoral power at the local level and influence at the national level generally have come at the expense of mass-based activism. Many black leaders have made the transition from the civil rights battlefield to the electoral arena, but they have had to heed the realities of practical politics. Furthermore, despite considerable progress, the political system has only partially settled black grievances, especially those related to economic deprivation. Race has not disappeared as a divisive element, and polarization of the electorate often stands in the way of further resolution of critical problems.

Whatever these limitations, the quest for freedom over the past half century released blacks from serving as passive objects of white domination and forged them into active agents striving to shape their own political destinies. Much of this story necessarily focuses on the South, where the civil rights movement originated and tested its most innovative political strategies. Yet the problems of racial inequality and political powerlessness were not confined to any one region, but were national in scope. Though they did not have to reacquire the ballot as was the case in the South, northern blacks nonetheless had to struggle to mobilize their communities to compete successfully for electoral office and obtain political legitimacy. In doing so, they joined black southerners in trying to redefine the meaning of success and to infuse American politics with a greater dose of democratic participation. The words of Jesse Jackson both underscore this point and provide the title for this book:

Winning is new people running.
Winning is also new voters.
Winning is more young voters.
Winning is providing hope....

We're not just running for an office.
We're running for freedom.[1]

ACKNOWLEDGMENTS

I would like to acknowledge my debt to the many scholars of civil rights history and black politics upon whose fine works I have drawn. Fortunately these fields have attracted many top-notch researchers, and their insights have contributed greatly to my own interpretive study. The bibliographical essay that appears at the end of the book is not only a guide for students but is also an expression of appreciation to the many authors from whom I have benefited. In addition to reading the works of other scholars, I also had the unique opportunity to listen to their ideas as an adviser to the production of the film documentary series *Eyes on the Prize, I* and *II*. Henry Hampton, the executive producer, gathered together an insightful

[1]"Jesse Jackson on Winning," *New York Times,* May 5, 1984, 10.

group of civil rights scholars whose lively meetings turned into the most stimulating seminars I have ever attended. At those sessions I learned a great deal from Henry and the Blackside staff, and from Professors Vincent Harding, Clay Carson, David Garrow, Darlene Clark Hine, Paul Gaston, Aldon Morris, and the other participants too numerous to name in so short a space.

Books need free time to develop and get written, and I thank the University of South Florida for granting a yearlong sabbatical allowing me to do so. I took my leave as a fellow at the National Humanities Center in Research Triangle Park in North Carolina. There I found more than arboreal splendor and an environment conducive to contemplation and writing; I encountered a resident staff whose hospitality made hard work a joy. My colleagues in the "Horseshoes Seminar"—Jack Greene, Charles Townshend, Tom Cogswell, Phil Mitsis, and Mike Holt—stimulated my thinking and kept me laughing. While in North Carolina I further enjoyed the warm company of Eugene Goodheart, Kate Townshend, Judith Bennett, Cynthia Herrup, Jacqueline Hall, Robert Korstad, Joe Sinsheimer, Val Rogers, Lorna Chafe, and Jean Anne Leuchtenburg. Both in the Tar Heel State and elsewhere I have had the good fortune to spend time with the two Bills: William Chafe and William Leuchtenburg. Besides friendship, they have provided me with models of historical synthesis that combine scholarly breadth with elegance of style.

My return to USF after such a wonderful year was made less difficult through the camaraderie of Louis Pérez, Robert Ingalls, Kelly Tipps, Georg Kleine, Tom Dilkes, Giovanna Benadusi, Fraser Ottanelli, Sylvia Wood, and Peggy Cornett. I am grateful to Mark Stern of the University of Central Florida for sharing the fruits of his research with me. At McGraw-Hill, I thank my editor, Christopher Rogers, for his good sense, light touch, and his choice of outside reviewers, Darlene Clark Hine, Michigan State University; Gary W. Reichard, Florida Atlantic University; and George C. Wright, University of Texas at Austin; who were extremely encouraging and perceptive. I also appreciate the careful editorial assistance of Niels Aaboe, Lauren Green Shafer, and Ester Moskowitz. One person merits special praise. Robert Divine first conceived of the idea for this book and allowed me free rein to develop and complete it. For more than a decade, he has been a faithful supporter, and I am proud to be associated with his series.

Most of all, I am indebted to Nancy Hewitt. Without her generosity of spirit, sharp intellect, and unflagging patience, this book would have been much more difficult, if not impossible, to write. Reserving a paragraph for her alone only partially expresses my gratitude. I hope I can do more for her in the many years ahead that we spend together.

Steven F. Lawson

Chapter 1

World War II and the Origins of the Freedom Struggle

For African-Americans, the ultimate aim of politics, either protest or electoral, has been liberation. Seeking emancipation from the bondage of white supremacy, disfranchised southern blacks challenged the political system for admission, even as they hoped to transform it by their participation. Civil rights proponents have long believed that blacks could not be free without obtaining the right to vote. At the turn of the century, W. E. B. Du Bois set the standard for rejecting racial solutions that excluded the exercise of the franchise. Attacking Booker T. Washington for his strategy of postponing black participation at the ballot box, Du Bois insisted that the right to vote was intimately connected to first-class citizenship. Without it blacks would never command respect, protect themselves, and feel pride in their own race. To Du Bois, a scholar of the freedom struggle after the Civil War, Reconstruction provided vivid evidence that black elected officials could transform the lives of their constituents. From this experience they derived the historical lesson, summarized by Eric Foner, that "it was in politics that blacks articulated a new vision of the American state, calling upon government, both national and local, to take upon itself new and unprecedented responsibilities for protecting the civil rights of individual citizens."

The long history to obtain the right to vote suggests that reenfranchisement was considered the decisive first step toward political equality. Civil rights proponents expected participation at the polls to yield the kinds of basic benefits that groups exercising the

1

franchise customarily enjoyed. Yet for black Americans, much more was at stake. With their systematic exclusion from the electoral process, the simple acquisition of the vote constituted an essential element of liberation from enforced racial subordination. The political scientist Charles V. Hamilton, who studied the voting rights struggle both as a participant and a scholar, found this passion for the ballot very understandable. "White America had spent so much effort denying the vote to blacks," he observed, "that there was good reason to believe that they must be protecting some tool of vast importance. Perhaps it was reasonable to put so much emphasis on the one fundamental process that clearly distinguished first-class from second-class citizens."

VICTORY AT HOME AND ABROAD

Going off to war in the months after Pearl Harbor, black GIs might very well have pondered the connection between politics and freedom. They had many reasons to wonder about the principles of the democratic creed and their promise of first-class citizenship for all. Like their white counterparts they remembered December 7, 1941, when Dorrie Miller, a black sailor, performed heroic deeds that would win him the Navy Cross; but they also carried with them the memory of Sikeston, Missouri, where on January 25, 1942, a black prisoner named Cleo Wright was taken out of the local jail and cruelly burned and lynched by a white mob. Unlike Japan and its Axis partners, which were eventually defeated on the battlefield and forced to accept unconditional surrender, the killers of Cleo Wright were never brought to justice. Helping to combat fascism abroad, black fighting men and the families they left behind also demanded unconditional surrender from the forces of racism at home. Blacks failed to persuade the American government to wage total war in their behalf, but they did lay the groundwork for continuing the battle in the decades to come.

This determination to stand up for their rights, strengthened by the Second World War, grew out of both disillusionment and optimism. In response to Woodrow Wilson's pledge during World War I to make the world safe for democracy, blacks had followed the advice of Du Bois to "close ranks [and] while this war lasts, forget our special grievances." Rather than freedom, the end of the war pro-

**Dorrie Miller receiving the Navy Cross from Admiral Chester Nimitz.
Miller was later killed in action. (U.S. Navy, The National Archives)**

duced bloody race riots and a continuation of Jim Crow practices.
At the same time, African-Americans refused to plunge into despair
and experienced instead a heightening of racial consciousness. The
Harlem Renaissance and the black nationalist movement spearheaded by Marcus Garvey explored the roots of black identity and
helped forge renewed racial solidarity. A. Philip Randolph organized workers into the Brotherhood of Sleeping Car Porters and
not only fought for economic benefits from employers but also challenged racial discrimination within the trade union movement. In
addition, the National Association for the Advancement of Colored
People (NAACP), an interracial organization founded in 1909, kept
alive the battle for equal rights by lobbying Congress to enact an
antilynching bill and petitioning the Supreme Court to outlaw
disfranchisement measures such as the white primary.

The Great Depression provided unexpected opportunities for
black advancement. Franklin D. Roosevelt's New Deal extended
economic relief to the one-third of the nation that was ill-housed,
ill-clothed, and ill-fed, which included blacks as well as poor
whites. Blacks profited from these programs because of their poverty, not because of their race; in fact, many New Deal agencies,
especially in the South, were administered to preserve prevailing

racial practices that maintained blacks in a subordinate position. Despite the perpetuation of racial discrimination and the unwillingness of President Roosevelt to fight for special civil rights measures, African-Americans welcomed federal assistance. "Any time people are out of work, in poverty, have lost their savings," Du Bois remarked, "any kind of a 'deal' that helps them is going to be favored."

Blacks showed their appreciation by abandoning their traditional allegiance to the Republican party of Abraham Lincoln and hopping aboard the Roosevelt bandwagon. This realignment was facilitated by appointments of blacks to federal posts, a sufficient number to convene an informal "black kitchen cabinet" in Washington. Whites sensitive to racial concerns headed several New Deal agencies and worked to see that relief was distributed more fairly. Furthermore, Roosevelt's selections to the Supreme Court after 1937 paved the way for a constitutional revolution that augured well for NAACP attorneys preparing a legal assault upon racial discrimination. Most of all, the President's wife, Eleanor, nurtured the growing attachment African-Americans felt toward the Roosevelt administration. Mrs. Roosevelt's commitment to civil rights was far greater than her husband's, and she served as an ally in the White House to see that complaints of black leaders received a hearing in the Oval Office. This combination of racial gestures and economic rewards led the majority of the black electorate to vote for Roosevelt beginning in 1936.

On the eve of World War II, blacks stood poised to consolidate their gains and press ahead for full equality. Their political agenda included an end to job discrimination, which helped keep black unemployment at a high 11 percent in 1940; legislation to empower the federal government to prosecute lynchers and to abolish the poll tax on voting imposed by eight southern states; the destruction of the lily-white Democratic primary; and the abandonment of the principle of "separate but equal" that actually produced segregated and unequal treatment in the armed forces, public education, and public accommodations. As the prospect of war increased, black aspirations collided with the reality of pervasive discrimination in a country where mobilization for war came first.

National defense took priority over racial equality in the armed services. As the nation inched closer to the side of the Allies and prepared to join them in war, the Army maintained its customary policy of segregation, the Navy recruited blacks only as messmates, and the Marines and Army Air Corps generally excluded them. When pressed by black leaders for integration of the military, in the fall of 1940, President Roosevelt refused to alter practices that had "been proved satisfactory over a long period of years." Instead, he directed the utilization of "the services of negroes...on a fair and equitable basis." To do otherwise, he and his advisers believed, would risk upsetting white soldiers and would lower their morale, thereby jeopardizing the war effort.

The attempt to make the system of racial separation operate more equally failed to solve the problem. Black GIs assigned to military bases in the South encountered segregation both on and off the bases. Conforming to the law and customs of the surrounding communities, the military enforced segregation in recreation clubs, theaters, and post exchanges. In one camp, a sign on a chapel announced religious services for "Catholics, Jews, Protestants, Negroes." When they received passes to travel into town, black soldiers rode on segregated buses and used Jim Crow facilities. With the population of many towns swollen with servicemen, an intolerable strain was placed on public transportation and accommodations. Crowded transit systems often led to pushing and shoving between black and white passengers, frequently ending in violence. In July 1942, a black Army private in Beaumont, Texas, refused to vacate his seat in a section of a bus reserved for whites. After his arrest, he was shot by white patrolmen while in their custody. Racial incidents such as this were becoming increasingly commonplace throughout the South that year, culminating in a riot in Alexandria, Louisiana, in which 28 blacks were wounded and nearly 3,000 arrested.

Among the black soldiers encountering wartime discrimination was Jackie Robinson. Having attended the University of California at Los Angeles before entering the service, Robinson excelled in basketball, track, baseball, and football, a sport in which he was named as a college All-American. However, these accomplishments did not guarantee him an easy time in the Army. When military officials attempted to keep him out of Officers' Candidate School at Fort Riley, Kansas, he successfully complained and gained admission to the program. Despite his athletic prowess, Robinson was

barred because of his race from playing on the baseball team at the
Army training camp. In protest, he refused to join the football team,
which was open to blacks. In 1944, Lieutenant Robinson again challenged unfair racial treatment. While stationed at Ford Hood, Texas,
he steadfastly refused to follow a bus driver's order that he sit in the
back of the vehicle with the other black passengers. Subjected to a
military court-martial for his defiance of local segregationist customs,
the former All-American athlete was found innocent.

Black civilians also encountered blatant racial prejudice as they
sought employment in wartime industries. Blacks had been especially
hard hit by the depression, and as the economy geared up for war
production after 1940, they looked forward to taking their places in
the booming factories. They had to wait in line, however, behind
millions of unemployed white workers who were the first choice of
employers. When African-Americans showed up looking for work at
aircraft plants, they were informed that "the Negro will be considered only as janitors and in other similar capacities." Of 100,000 aircraft workers in 1940, only 240 were black. In related electrical and
rubber industries, black employees constituted a meager 1 percent
and 3 percent of the work force. The federal government, which let
out war contracts and could have challenged discriminatory hiring
practices, collaborated with employers in reinforcing them. According to the policy of the United States Employment Service, "white
only" requests for defense labor would be filled in conformity with
"the social pattern of the local community."

That whites did not intend the war to alter race relations was
demonstrated in several other ways as well. Though the process of
storing blood plasma was developed by a black scientist, Dr.
Charles Drew, the Red Cross refused to mix donations of whites
and blacks in their blood banks. In Tennessee, those blacks who
wanted to fight for their country experienced difficulty in getting
enlisted by all-white selective service centers. Refusing to appoint
blacks to sit on draft boards, the governor of the state explained:
"This is a white man's country. The Negro had nothing to do with
the settling of America." In neighboring Mississippi, to avoid any
suggestion that the war against totalitarianism overseas was meant
to affect the status of blacks at home, the state legislature ordered
the deletion of all references to voting, elections, and democracy in
textbooks used in black schools.

Despite these racist setbacks, most blacks supported the war effort and responded to the global conflict as did other patriotic Americans. One survey revealed that 66 percent of blacks considered that they had a great stake in the outcome of the war and 43 percent felt that they would be better off than before. Though daring victories of nonwhite Japanese over Caucasians early in the war inspired admiration in many blacks, the majority realized what would happen if the Axis powers emerged victorious. "If Hitler wins," the NAACP pointed out, "every right we now possess and for which we have struggled here in America for three centuries will be instantaneously wiped out." At least if the Allies triumphed, black Americans would be free to continue fighting for their democratic rights. Desiring full participation as American citizens, they had no real difficulty choosing which side they were on.

Nevertheless, blacks remained sorely troubled by the discrimination they encountered at home. Their loyalty was not at issue, but as one knowledgeable observer declared, many blacks displayed a "lack of enthusiasm for a war which they did not believe is being fought for true democratic principles." Lloyd Brown, a black soldier stationed in Salina, Kansas, who was refused service at a restaurant that admitted German prisoners of war, poignantly expressed his disappointment: "If we were *untermenschen* [subhuman species] in Nazi Germany they would break our bones. As 'colored' men in Salina, they only break our hearts." That the price of a fascist victory would cost more than an Allied one was acknowledged by African-Americans; yet this awareness did not bring contentment. No greater slogan of despair over the gap between the democratic creed and discriminatory practice existed than in the sardonic statement popular at the time: "Here lies a black man killed fighting a yellow man for the protection of a white man."

Cynical yet hopeful, African-Americans used the war to pursue their own political aims. While blacks sought to defend their country on foreign battlefields alongside other American citizens, they also intended to open up a second front for freedom at home. Wartime ideology extolling the virtues of the "four freedoms" and denouncing the doctrines of Aryan racism was not lost upon blacks. On January 16, 1943, a black newspaper, the *Baltimore Afro-American*, published a "Draftee's Prayer," a poem that tersely summed up the twin goals black soldiers fought for:

So while I fight
Wrong over there
See that my folks
Are treated fair.

Black leaders agreed and seized the opportunity to turn America's lofty pronouncements to their advantage. Shortly after Pearl Harbor, Walter White, the executive secretary of the NAACP, asserted that "declarations of war do not lessen the obligation to preserve and extend civil liberties here while the fight is being made to restore freedom from dictatorship abroad." These sentiments were echoed in the pages of the *Pittsburgh Courier*, a black newspaper that mounted a campaign for the "double V," victory at home and overseas. In this way, the black press not only reflected the increasing militancy of its readers, but also reinforced black support for the war against the Fascists. Not willing to postpone their egalitarian demands as they had during World War I, blacks planned to attack "the principle and practice of compulsory segregation in our American society."

This new assertiveness on behalf of full equality had its most powerful expression in the March on Washington Movement (MOWM). Organized by A. Philip Randolph, the militant trade union leader, the MOWM represented both the exclusiveness of racial pride and the integration of blacks into the mainstream of American life. The group barred whites from participation not out of prejudice but because, as Randolph explained, an all-black movement would promote "faith by Negroes in Negroes." The main goals of the movement were the desegregation of the armed forces and the elimination of discrimination in employment by government contractors. To gain these ends, Randolph proposed a mass march on Washington by some 75,000 to 100,000 blacks to take place in June 1941. Though this proposal had the endorsement of established black groups such as the NAACP, the MOWM derived its power from the black masses rather than middle-class reformers, who generally worked for change through the courts and legislatures. In this way, the MOWM foreshadowed the successful protest tactics of the later civil rights movement.

The MOWM timed its efforts well. The prospect of tens of thousands of blacks descending on the nation's capital as the United States prepared for war disturbed the President. Concerned about tarnishing the nation's image as well as hampering attempts to rally support for the Allies, Roosevelt tried to get Randolph to halt the demonstration. Unsuccessful, the chief executive agreed partially to meet the movement's demands. Issuing Executive Order 8802, the President created the Fair Employment Practice Committee (FEPC) to investigate and publicize cases of employment discrimination. However, he left the policy of segregation in the military basically unchanged. Not getting all that he wanted, Randolph nevertheless called off the march, convinced that he had won an important political victory and confident that the movement would continue to apply pressure for social change. The MOWM did function throughout the war, but it never reached the same level of influence as it had during this first confrontation with the President.

Rising black militancy stimulated the growth of existing civil rights organizations. Foremost among them, the NAACP kept up the pressure to lower racial barriers along the color line. Although this oldest of civil rights groups had thrown its weight behind the MOWM, it preferred to operate in the traditional arenas of litigation, legislation, and lobbying. The national association's staff of dedicated attorneys prepared suits against white Democratic primaries in the South, segregation of passengers on interstate buses, and unequal educational facilities. The NAACP functioned as a clearinghouse for complaints from black soldiers and civilians experiencing discriminatory treatment and directed them to the attention of officials in Washington. It prodded the Justice Department to investigate and prosecute perpetrators of lynching and other forms of violence and joined with white liberals and labor unions in petitioning Congress and state legislatures to lift poll tax restrictions on the ballot. As a reflection both of its increased activism and the rising expectations of blacks, NAACP membership soared from 50,000 in 1940 to over 450,000 in 1946. Of these new recruits an estimated 15,000 black GIs signed up while they were still in uniform.

In addition, black activism spawned the formation of new protest groups. Most important for the future was the creation of the Congress of Racial Equality (CORE) in 1942. Like Randolph's March on Washington Movement, CORE believed in the tactic of direct action to spotlight racist problems and bring them to an immediate resolution; in contrast to MOWM, however, the group welcomed white participation. Founded in Chicago by pacifists committed to the principle of nonviolence, its interracial membership initiated sit-in and picketing campaigns to desegregate public accommodations in northern cities. These innovative techniques led to the desegregation of restaurants and movie theaters in Detroit, Los Angeles, Denver, and Chicago, and they caught on with black college students, such as those at Howard University, who successfully integrated several restaurants in Washington, D.C.

As blacks actively confronted Jim Crow and pushed for their rights, they often came into sharp conflict with hostile whites. The friction did not result as much from legal battles in the courts and in legislatures and along picket lines as from the increasing daily contact between blacks and whites in the overcrowded communities the war had produced. The influx of blacks into urban areas in search of jobs brought them into direct competition with older white residents and newer white migrants for employment, housing, and recreational facilities. By 1943, 50,000 southern blacks and 500,000 whites had swarmed into Detroit to find work. Instead, many of them found substandard housing and high rates of tuberculosis and infant mortality. These deplorable conditions fell hardest upon blacks, and when attempts were made to provide some measure of relief whites resisted them. On June 20, 1943, this explosive situation finally erupted in a bloody race riot over a fracas at an amusement park, and after the smoke cleared 34 blacks had been killed, 700 injured, and $200 million in property destroyed. Only the intervention of federal troops restored peace to the "Motor City." By the end of the year, another 241 racial disturbances in forty-seven cities had broken out, though none as severe as in Detroit.

With violence spreading throughout American cities, civil rights leaders became alarmed. Following a riot in Harlem, New York City's black newspaper, the *Amsterdam News*, warned that only by making blacks "feel that they are part of this country" would the violence cease. The way to achieve that, most black leaders believed, was to continue to press for the "double V" but to do so through peaceful channels. The NAACP called upon its chapters to step up the campaign for racial equality in the courts, legislatures, and ballot boxes, thereby removing potentially incendiary conflicts from the streets. This preference for seeking social change in a deliberate and orderly fashion diminished support for the tactics of direct mass action. After 1943, the once popular MOWM received criticism from the black press as "just Ku Kluxism in reverse" for its all-black policy, and a poll of black newspaper readers showed that 70.6 percent opposed the March on Washington Movement. Established civil rights leaders and their organizations did not retreat from the goal of securing full equality, but their strategy of measured militancy helped defuse the appeal of more confrontational approaches toward achieving that end.

To combat racial discrimination, they increasingly put a premium on attracting sympathetic whites. Before the war, white liberals thought primarily in economic rather than racial terms. They figured that the New Deal's recovery programs would lift blacks out of poverty along with whites and improve black chances of gaining acceptance for civil and political equality. However, the end of the depression had not significantly extended first-class citizenship. Wartime ideals and the persistence of racism exposed by the 1943 riots persuaded liberal whites to assign a higher priority to civil rights. Fighting Hitler's atrocities abroad shifted the focus of racism at home from an economic to a moral issue, prompting liberals to try to prove that their society did not behave like Nazi Germany. Accordingly, they joined with blacks to set up interracial committees in scores of communities to open up better lines of communication and avoid the type of situation that engendered racial violence. The increasing presence of whites in the civil rights movement after 1943 had a further moderating effect on black militancy and reinforced those who favored the tactics of cooperation over confrontation, legalism over disruption, the ballot over direct action. The most prominent of all white liberals, Eleanor Roosevelt, endorsed this approach in contending that blacks should strive for complete equality but they should "not do too much demanding [or] try to bring those advances about any more quickly than they were offered."

Mrs. Roosevelt's husband had the power to influence the pace of racial change, and he chose to act cautiously. According to the historian Harvard Sitkoff, President Roosevelt held a paternalistic view toward racial affairs, believing that the "Negro" was "an unfortunate ward of the nation to be treated kindly and with charity as a reward for good behavior." Ordinarily preferring gradualism and education to promote racial toleration, FDR felt even more inclined toward those methods at a time when winning the war was his chief concern. Though he disapproved of any racial prejudice that lowered black morale, he also took into account the position of southern white politicians who opposed any change in the racial status quo and whose legislative support for war appropriations he greatly needed. Black voters had joined the New Deal Democratic coalition, but their political clout remained weaker than that of Dixie politicos. In offering encouraging words to African-Americans, "Dr. Win-the-War" Roosevelt never forgot that while the overseas conflict lasted "the long-range problems of racial and minority-majority antagonism cannot be settled.... [T]he war must be won first."

The experience of the Fair Employment Practice Committee demonstrated this point. Created by Roosevelt to head off the proposed June 1941 march on Washington, the FEPC was authorized to investigate discrimination in defense-related employment but lacked the power of enforcement. Instead of coercion it relied on publicity and persuasion to expose and alter biased practices. Reflecting the President's philosophy, committee members believed that winning the war should take precedence over the pursuit of racial equality. One commentator summed up their thinking: "For the government to terminate an important war contract by reason of the contractor's indulgence in discriminatory employment would be highly impractical."

Unable to compel compliance and unwilling to alienate powerful employers, the FEPC achieved mixed success. Of 8,000 complaints submitted to the committee, two-thirds were dismissed without merit and only one-fifth were settled in the South. Employers and unions, which were also covered under the executive order, ignored 35 of 45 compliance decrees. For example, the railroad brotherhoods and southern railway lines signed an agreement restricting employment opportunities for blacks and then disregarded an FEPC order against it. The government did not dare take action that might provoke a crippling strike by a powerful union and also antagonize the white South. In contrast, the President sometimes backed the committee when the political risks were not so great. In Philadelphia, a strike by a dissident union faction in protest of an FEPC ruling upgrading black jobs on streetcars triggered President Roosevelt's decision to send in federal troops to resume normal operation of the transit system. In this instance, a stronger rival union supported the black position, and the residents of the "City of Brotherly Love" did not threaten a political revolt over the settlement. Even the lukewarm record of the FEPC proved too much for southern members of Congress, who succeeded in 1944 in enacting a provision that paved the way for the committee's legislative funding to be cut off two years later.

Although blacks did obtain some benefits from the FEPC, their main economic gains resulted from labor shortages during the war. As millions of whites marched off to battle and industrial production expanded, blacks helped plug the labor-power holes on the home front. Black employment rose by over 1 million; the number of unemployed dropped from 937,000 to 151,000; union membership doubled; and the percentage of blacks in defense work climbed from 4.6 to 8.3. African-Americans found jobs in factories where employers had initially resisted hiring them. Under the strain of war, the number of black employees increased from 6,000 to 14,000 in shipyards and from zero to 5,000 in aircraft plants. The federal government itself gave black employment a big boost, increasing its rolls from 60,000 to 200,000 Afro-American workers. On the down side, most of the blacks entering the labor force took jobs at low levels as janitors and custodians. Consequently, blacks made up only 3.6 percent of craftsmen and foremen; 2.8 percent of clerical and sales personnel; and 3.3 percent of professional and technical staff. Concentrated in low-paying jobs, black families on the average earned about half the income of whites. Nevertheless, the improvements in their economic condition whetted black appetites for more and raised expectations that opportunities would continue to grow once the war ended.

African-Americans also beefed up their political muscle as a force for freedom. In the North, where voting booths were open to blacks, both the Democratic and Republican parties courted them. In 1940, the GOP presidential candidate, Wendell Wilkie, campaigned hard for the black vote and made slight inroads in a losing effort. In lining up behind Roosevelt's third-term bid, the black electorate moved the victorious President to grant them concessions. Black support spurred FDR to add an antidiscrimination clause to the Selective Service Act, appoint Colonel Benjamin O. Davis as the first black (brigadier) general, select blacks as civilian aides in the War Department and Selective Service, and establish an Army Air Corps training school at Tuskegee Institute. Four years later, though the Democrats did not draft a strong civil rights plank for their platform, FDR personally called for a permanent

FEPC and elimination of restrictions on the ballot. Again, the black electorate responded enthusiastically.

Because black support for the President was much stronger than for the Democratic party as a whole, the minority vote seemed very much up for grabs once the popular chief executive was no longer a candidate. In 1940, 67 percent of Afro-American voters had backed the President, though only 42 percent considered themselves Democrats. After the election in 1944, both Democrats and Republicans took note that a shift in the black vote in eight states would have defeated Roosevelt's reelection for a fourth term. Given their strategic location in major urban centers in northern states rich in Electoral College votes, blacks looked forward to wielding the balance of power in close presidential races in the future.

Meanwhile, in the South, where blacks remained largely disfranchised, wartime developments lifted hopes for change. In 1944, the Supreme Court's *Smith v. Allwright* decision struck down the Democratic white primary. Victory in these preliminary contests ordinarily determined the winners in subsequent general elections in the one-party South, and hence the destruction of the white primary would remove a major obstacle to black participation in the region. The assault on the primary had begun two decades earlier. In 1923, after the Texas Legislature officially barred blacks from participating in Democratic primaries, the NAACP mounted a legal challenge that had great significance for blacks in the Lone Star State as well as for those in the rest of the South where the exclusionary practice also flourished.

Initially, the NAACP convinced the judiciary of its argument, but these triumphs neither settled the issue nor did they gain for blacks the right to vote. In 1927 and again in 1932, the Supreme Court ruled that a state could not officially authorize racial discrimination in the fashion of Texas without violating the Fourteenth Amendment of the Constitution. However, in a pattern that would become increasingly common in the face of rising black protest, southern officials resisted attempts to dismantle segregation and disfranchisement by countering with measures purporting to conform with the law while at the same time managing to evade it. In this instance, the Texas Legislature obeyed the court's pronouncement by repealing its white primary regulation, thereby leaving the state Democratic party free to adopt rules denying blacks access to its internal affairs. Previously the high tribunal had struck down the white primary because the state had deliberately created and maintained it, but the court had left open the question of whether a political party, operating as a private association, could deny blacks participation in its activities. Presented with another case in 1935, the Supreme Court decided that a political party had the constitutional right to fix its own qualifications for membership and therefore could legally exclude blacks if it so desired. In *Grovey v. Townsend* the justices argued that the conduct of a primary was strictly a private party matter and was immune from the guarantees of the Fifteenth Amendment, which forbade interference with the right of blacks to vote in general elections open to the public.

Before they could overcome this judicial blow to reenfranchisement, blacks first had to settle some differences that had hampered their legal battle. The main problem concerned the conflict for control of the case between local blacks and the NAACP, headquartered in New York City. Run in a hierarchical manner, the national association insisted on maintaining tight supervision of its programs from the top down. This style irritated some black attorneys and other leaders in Texas, who believed they should play a greater role in shaping policies and legal strategies directly affecting their community. They also wanted the NAACP to make a greater effort in recruiting black lawyers whenever possible to try suits and to rely less heavily on whites. These tensions had produced unfortunate results. Against the wishes of the NAACP, which considered the attempt premature, a group of black Texans had initiated the *Grovey* case and suffered a severe setback to the cause of black voting rights.

Following this debacle, the NAACP sought to remedy the difficulties. Under the leadership of Charles Houston, the dean of Howard Law School, and his protégé, Thurgood Marshall, the national association assembled a talented staff of black attorneys and labored to work more closely and harmoniously with blacks in the local areas from which the legal challenges arose. This interaction between national and grassroots forces became the hallmark of the burgeoning civil rights struggle. In the wake of *Grovey*, the NAACP organized black Texans into a mass movement for first-class citizenship. Its state convention created a Democratic Primary Defense Fund, which galvanized black churches, civic leagues, fraternities, and business groups behind a fund-raising campaign to finance a new court suit. "Brother, have you spared that dime for your liberation and freedom?" asked a black newspaper, and the response was generous. As Darlene Clark Hine has observed: "The white primary became a rallying cry for black Texans and assisted them in developing black solidarity." In addition to contributing money and generating publicity, local blacks furnished the plaintiff to contest the white primary. Represented by Marshall, a Houston dentist and NAACP member named Lonnie Smith filed litigation against S. E. Allwright, a state election official who had refused to allow him to cast a ballot in the 1940 Democratic primary.

On this fourth attempt to wipe out the offensive and highly resilient discriminatory electoral procedure, African-Americans finally triumphed. Drawing upon a recent opinion in a case brought by the federal government against voting fraud in a Louisiana primary, on April 3, 1944, the Supreme Court reversed *Grovey*. The justices held that where a primary was an integral part of the electoral process, as was the circumstance in Texas, blacks were entitled to the protection of the Fifteenth Amendment, which sheltered their right to vote from racial discrimination. Smith not only won for himself the right to participate in the crucial Democratic primary, but he greeted his victory as a second emancipation for blacks throughout the South. The Houston dentist gleefully commented that this ruling would affect the political history of the country more than any case since the infamous *Dred Scott* decision before the Civil War. If the joy of victory caused this happy plaintiff to exaggerate somewhat, many could still agree with the assessment of an NAACP attorney that the "Supreme Court released and galvanized democratic forces" which one day would transform the political life of the South and the nation.

Toward this end, suffragists had also aimed their attack at another troublesome obstacle to black voting: the poll tax. Confined to the South, this financial requirement differed from state to state but generally discouraged the poor of both races from going to the polls. In fact, it worked a greater hardship on whites than on blacks, as long as the white primary and the racially biased administration of literacy tests operated to chase southern blacks away from the ballot box. Encouraged by Roosevelt's New Deal, progressive southerners tried to find ways of extending economic and political democracy to the region. Consequently, in 1941 they formed the National Committee to Abolish the Poll Tax, composed of labor, liberal, and civil rights groups. Actively cooperating with the

NAACP and the Congress of Industrial Organizations (CIO), the anti-poll-tax alliance lobbied national lawmakers to enact a measure repealing the restrictive levy in federal elections.

America's entry into World War II provided proponents of abolition with fresh ammunition for their attack. Reformers claimed that the disfranchising effects of the tax hurt public morale, and they compared the decline of free elections in Fascist-dominated Europe with the shrinking of the electorate in the poll tax South. Twice during the war, the repeal advocates convinced the House of Representatives to support their proposal, only to suffer defeat in the Senate. Though whites stood more to gain than did blacks from elimination of the tax, southern foes warned their constituents of the dangerous racial consequences of legislative repeal. "If the [anti]poll tax bill passes," Senator Theodore Bilbo of Mississippi contended, "the next step will be an effort to remove the registration qualification, the educational qualification of the negroes. If that is done we will have no way of preventing negroes from voting."

Despite such fears, pressure from the progressive, interracial coalition encouraged Congress to take some limited but positive action to soften the burden of the poll tax. In 1942, lawmakers exempted soldiers from having to meet poll tax requirements to vote in national elections. Reformers also made some progress at the local level. In 1945, Georgia abolished its franchise tax entirely, and at the war's end most of its neighbors in the region released their returning veterans from having to pay for casting a vote. Even with these wartime changes, most blacks remained disfranchised. Southern officials discriminated against black soldiers seeking to claim their poll tax exemption, and the majority of blacks continued to encounter insurmountable suffrage barriers, such as literacy tests. Yet the easing of poll tax restrictions, together with the Texas white primary ruling, had a liberating impact. Between 1940 and 1947, the proportion of southern blacks enrolled to vote climbed from 3 percent to 12 percent.

Taking advantage of these opportunities, blacks marshaled their forces at the local level to convert votes into power. To stimulate both greater registration and political involvement, grassroots organizations offered citizenship classes, conducted poll tax payment drives, and initiated challenges to discrimination within state Democratic parties. In one imaginative move that would be copied in the 1960s, black activists in South Carolina, in cooperation with the

NAACP, formed a statewide Progressive Democratic Party (PDP), which attempted to unseat the regular Democrats at the 1944 national convention. Though unsuccessful, the PDP still managed to stimulate political activity, and by 1948, more than 35,000 blacks voted in the regular Democratic party primary, a figure ten times greater than the turnout four years earlier.

The South Carolina campaigns received the enlightened guidance of three members of the state's black middle class. Segregation had produced unequal treatment and inferior public facilities for nonwhites, but it had also provided blacks with opportunities to develop separate religious, economic, and civic institutions under their exclusive control. Having achieved a measure of independence within their business and professional spheres, some of them attempted to gain for the majority of blacks the right to participate in governing their own communities. The Reverend James Hinton held a managerial position with Pilgrim Life Insurance Company, a black-owned enterprise, and headed the Palmetto State's NAACP Conference. He was joined by Osceola McKaine, a native of Sumter and a World War I veteran who had established a successful restaurant business in Belgium before returning home shortly after the onslaught of Hitler's army. Rounding out the trio, John McCray provided valuable leadership as editor of the *Lighthouse and Informer*, a black newspaper in Columbia that editorialized against racial injustice and for first-class citizenship. As Hinton, McKaine, and McCray showed, middle-class blacks did not have to confine their egalitarian impulses to seeking change exclusively through the courts. They worked tirelessly to organize South Carolina blacks behind a variety of grassroots activities to regain the precious ballot snatched away in the late nineteenth century. McKaine, also an editor of the *Lighthouse and Informer*, saw the black masses aroused by the war against fascism and responsive to the renewed efforts to advance their political fortunes. In his view, the creation of the PDP marked a revolutionary beginning "to give the disinherited men and women of both races in South Carolina some voice in their government, [and] some control over their destinies."

To reinforce their local drives, black leaders requested federal assistance. They usually met with disappointment. An organizer of the South Carolina PDP held the national Democratic party "as responsible as the state party for the denial of membership to Negroes in that it tolerates discrimination in the South." This policy would not change so long as white voters constituted the foundation of the Democratic party in the South and their elected representatives played a key role in determining the outcome of legislation desired by the President. Based on this political calculation, Roosevelt's Justice Department refused to follow up *Smith v. Allwright* with criminal prosecutions against suffrage violators. When Senator Lister Hill of Alabama, a legislative ally of President Roosevelt, heard that such legal action was contemplated in his home state, he warned the White House that it would "be a very dangerous mistake." Worried about a political revolt at the polls in Dixie and concerned about getting along with the southern-influenced Senate Judiciary Committee, the Justice Department backed off with the President's blessing. For similar reasons the chief executive declined to give more than lip service in favor of congressional measures designed to repeal the remaining poll tax requirements in the South.

While Roosevelt attempted delicately to balance the political wishes of southern whites and blacks, demographic forces were in motion that would eventually upset that equilibrium. During the war southern blacks voted with their feet and migrated northward, more than doubling the number of their race living above the Mason-Dixon line. Increased urbanization was propelled by changing labor patterns on the farm. The extension of mechanized agriculture, especially the use of the tractor, during the decade of the 1940s pushed blacks off the farm and sent them to northern cities in search of jobs. Remembering the plight of friends and relatives left behind, they intended to use their unfettered ballots to select candidates favoring civil rights measures. Some 750,000 blacks journeyed from rural areas to cities within the South, and there they usually encountered a less restrictive application of suffrage requirements. Moreover, the urban environment afforded wider social space to develop racial solidarity and community organizations for political and economic emancipation. Away from the tight regulations imposed by the plantation economy, they were more readily exposed to the wartime promises of democracy and became more determined to challenge enduring forms of racial discrimination. These demographic changes were a precondition for the building of a movement to transform race relations in the postwar South.

The tempo and direction of that change would be determined by the interconnected efforts of federal officials and local black communities across the South. Civil rights groups, including national associations and their local chapters, as well as civic, fraternal, and religious organizations initiated the struggle to eradicate racial barriers, mobilize the black masses to confront these obstacles, and apply ongoing pressure on white officials to demolish them. In cities and towns throughout the region, blacks were joining together to transform their own lives economically, politically, and psychologically, seeking to liberate themselves totally from the bonds of oppression. The process of struggle could free blacks spiritually and forge racial pride and solidarity, but their liberation would not be completed without allies in Washington helping them crack potent southern white opposition and enacting their goals into law.

World War II was the seedtime of the racial and legal metamorphosis that was to sweep over the South. The war propelled a growth of racial consciousness and a burst of militancy that foreshadowed the assault on Jim Crow. It provided new economic and political opportunities and at the same time underscored the failure of the nation to allow African-Americans to take full advantage of them. Having caught a glimpse of a better life and frustrated by the resistance to achieving it, blacks did not intend to retreat. They had already seen some of the old hurdles tumble in the courts, and their nascent political influence had pressured the President into supporting limited reforms. By V-J Day, black troops had fought together with whites on an emergency basis in the European theater of war, and planning for integration had begun in the Navy. Surveys showed that the more contact whites had with blacks in the military and in the workplace the more likely they were to oppose segregation. Buoyed by these initial advances and imbued with egalitarian wartime ideology, African-Americans looked ahead with great expectations for the future.

A TROUBLED PEACE

Black veterans marched at the forefront of those demanding unconditional surrender from the forces of fascism at home. Having fought for their country and demonstrated their worth on the battlefield, they returned to their communities intent on challenging the racist practices they had temporarily escaped from. On May 19, 1945, before shipping out of Okinawa, Private Herbert W. Seward expressed the view of many of his black buddies in a letter to the *Pittsburgh Courier*:

Our people are not coming back with the idea of just taking up where they left off. We are going to have the things that are rightfully due us or else, which is a very large order, but we have proven beyond all things that we are people and not just the servants of the whiteman.

By reading black newspapers and letters from home they had kept track of the many incidents of racial discrimination and abuse that blacks experienced during the war. The "majority will return home," Walter White of the NAACP predicted, "convinced that whatever betterment of their lot is achieved must come from their own efforts."

One such veteran was Jackie Robinson. Having played on an integrated baseball squad in college, Robinson was determined to crack the color line that barred blacks from the major leagues. While playing professional ball with the Kansas City Monarchs in the Negro Leagues in 1945, he was spotted by the Brooklyn Dodgers' owner, Branch Rickey, who wanted to integrate the country's national pastime. Displaying the same fierce pride that pushed him

World War II veteran Jackie Robinson integrated major league baseball and became a star with the Brooklyn Dodgers. (UPI/Bettmann Newsphotos)

to protest wartime discrimination, Robinson readily accepted the challenge. "I'm ready to take the chance," he declared in anticipation of his task. "Maybe I'm doing something for my race." After playing a season in the minor leagues, in 1947, Robinson joined the Dodgers and succeeded in opening up one of America's most cherished institutions to blacks. Indeed, Robinson served as an enormous source of pride for all African-Americans looking for expanded opportunities and equal rights in the postwar years.

At the same time, black southerners directed much of their energy toward extending the right to vote, which they considered the essential weapon in gaining and protecting the rest of their civil rights. Many black GIs had barely taken time to remove their uniforms before they marched to local courthouses to register to vote. In Birmingham, Alabama, about a hundred ex-soldiers paraded in double file through the main street of the city, ending up at the registrars' office. Veterans like these reasoned that as long as blacks did not determine who governed them, they would continue to be victimized by racial discrimination. One discharged soldier from Georgia thought that conditions would be better in the future. "Now that the war has been won," he wrote, "the most difficult job ahead of us is to win the peace at home. 'Peace is not the absence of war, but the presence of justice' which may be obtained, first, by becoming a citizen and registered voter. If you become a registered voter we may be able to win the peace." Black leaders concurred. The *Pittsburgh Courier* predicted "that once Negroes start voting in large numbers... the jim crow laws will be endangered and the whole elaborate pattern of segregation threatened and finally destroyed."

Southern officials tried to block this chain of events at the first step, resorting to a variety of racist subterfuges to perpetuate black disfranchisement. Even after the destruction of the white primary, registrars were able to exclude blacks from the suffrage by administering literacy tests for prospective voters. In the hands of bigoted clerks these examinations were manipulated to prevent qualified black applicants from enrolling and were interpreted to allow illiterate whites to pass. White registrars accomplished this biased feat by asking only blacks the meaning of highly technical clauses in state and federal constitutions or by asking them such absurd questions as "How many bubbles are there in a bar of soap?" One Mississippi official frankly admitted that he "didn't care which way the

[Negroes] answered those questions, it wouldn't come up to his satisfaction."

Mississippi had long been a leader in reducing blacks to second-class citizenship. Combining the white primary, literacy tests, and the poll tax, with terror and coercion thrown in for good measure, the Magnolia State had created a "closed society." Blacks lived at the bottom of a rigid caste structure, held down by a separate and unequal educational system, dependent upon white-controlled economic institutions for survival, and disciplined to remain in place by official and private acts of violence. Generations of white supremacists had sternly taught Mississippi blacks that participation in civic life was folly. Not surprisingly, in 1944, out of 350,000 adult black Mississippians only 2,500 had managed to register to vote.

However, for several years after World War II the idea that "politics is white folks' business" was challenged by a small but determined group in the Magnolia State. In 1944, a small circle of middle-class blacks from Jackson, led by T. B. Wilson, the secretary of the local NAACP chapter, formed the Mississippi Progressive Voters League. Designed to stimulate black enrollment, the league attempted to educate black citizens to recognize the importance of the suffrage. This task was made a bit easier after *Smith v. Allwright*. Until that ruling, Wilson explained, blacks "were indifferent, disinterested, but when we worked up this case of registering and voting them because the Supreme Court decision gave us to understand that we could vote, then they began to register." In addition, like most other southern states, Mississippi exempted veterans from payment of the poll tax for voting. Their racial and political consciousness heightened by the war, black veterans in Mississippi attempted to exercise their franchise rights.

In doing so, they ran up against Senator Theodore "The Man" Bilbo. An outspoken bigot whose storehouse of invectives was plentiful enough to smear racial, religious, and ethnic minorities alike, Bilbo had few peers to match the virulence of his antiblack tirades. In the midst of his reelection campaign in 1946, he encouraged white Mississippians to keep the ballot boxes shut to the growing number of blacks who were seeking to register. "The Man" unabashedly suggested to the registrars that if "there is a single man or woman serving...who cannot think up questions enough to disqualify undesirables then write Bilbo or any good lawyer, and there are a hundred good questions which can be furnished." Bilbo was

confident that the Magnolia State's brand of racial justice would not
pose a hazard to these biased attempts. "How many registrars do
you think can be convicted here in the state of Mississippi?" he
asked rhetorically. If such chicanery did not do the trick, the senator informed his audiences: "You and I know what's the best way
to keep the nigger from voting. You do it the night before the election. I don't have to tell you more than that." Apparently getting
his not too subtle message, one county clerk refused to register a
black veteran because "niggers don't vote in this county." To add
injury to insult, the rejected ex-GI was abducted and flogged by
white vigilantes as he left the courthouse. Given these potent lessons in repression, fewer than 1 percent of adult blacks registered
to vote, and a majority of white electors cast their ballots to return
Bilbo to the Senate.

Meanwhile, Bilboism did not go unchallenged. Aided by the
NAACP and sympathetic whites in the North, the Progressive Voters League compiled affidavits documenting the racist nature of the
senator's demagoguery. Sufficient evidence was accumulated to
convince the Senate to send a special committee to conduct public
hearings in Jackson on the charge that Bilbo's election was tainted
with fraud and corruption. Because the five-member investigation
team contained a Democratic majority including three southerners,
and because it was chaired by Allen Ellender, an avid defender of
white supremacy in Louisiana, blacks did not expect a favorable report. Instead, they hoped to expose how disfranchisement operated
in Mississippi and to arouse northern senators to block Bilbo from
taking his seat.

On December 2, 1946, blacks journeyed from all over the state
to puncture the myth of their contentment with race relations in
Mississippi. They jammed the hearing room to testify before a
mixed gallery of friends, hostile whites, and the national press.
With veterans in the forefront, they braved the danger of possible
retaliation from angry whites resentful of the unfavorable publicity
the proceedings trumpeted throughout the country. An observer
compared the plight of the black witnesses to that of a "pedestrian
in any typical American city or community, attempting to cross the
street with a green light and the law in his favor but who, nevertheless, is seriously injured or killed in the process."

For three days courageous black veterans recounted their frustrated attempts to enroll and vote. They detailed stories of threats,

beatings, and police brutality. The testimony revealed that the registrars misused the literacy exam to prevent them from qualifying to vote. Amazingly the registrars themselves corroborated the damaging testimony. One official admitted that he had told a black not to cast his ballot, because "in the southern states it has always been a white primary, and I just couldn't conceive of this darkey going up there to vote." The candor of this testimony prompted an NAACP representative on the scene to remark: "Sometimes I think Jesus Christ must be ill at ease in Mississippi."

Although these revelations proved that blacks were disfranchised on racial grounds, the Ellender committee voted to exonerate Bilbo of any personal guilt. Instead, the Democratic majority blamed the blacks' failure to vote on the white primary tradition and on lethargy. However, the challenge was not over. As the NAACP had hoped, when the matter reached the Senate floor, in early January 1947, a bipartisan coalition of Republicans and northern Democrats succeeded in postponing consideration of Bilbo's credentials. Suffering from jaw cancer, the Mississippi senator agreed temporarily to withdraw his claim to his seat while he sought treatment for his ailment. This solution turned out to be permanent: on August 21, "The Man" died.

Incipient black militancy in Mississippi yielded limited short-run returns, but it raised promising expectations for the long run. Although Bilbo had departed, the white supremacist system lived on. When John Stennis replaced Bilbo, only the cruel rhetoric and not the underlying policy of disfranchisement changed. Behind the Magnolia Curtain, blacks continued to encounter most of the old difficulties and a few new ones in trying to vote. Yet blacks benefited from having stood up to Bilboism. The public hearings demonstrated rising political awareness, especially among younger blacks. Despite persistent obstacles in front of ballot boxes, nearly 20,000 blacks added their names to registration lists in the decade after the war's end. This modest increase revealed the development of tiny chinks in the armor of the closed society. White politicians who justified their racial policy on the basis that African-Americans were content with their lot had that explanation graphically disputed by black veterans and their friends who defied white hostility to appear in Jackson. As a matter of fact, the Senate investigation documented only part of the rising tide of black protest. A former soldier not called to testify about his own encounter with Bilboism,

Medgar Evers later became state field secretary of the NAACP and worked tirelessly to organize blacks against racial discrimination and disfranchisement. In that capacity, working alongside a new breed of blacks, he helped breathe life into the civil rights movement in Mississippi until additional recruits and allies were mobilized.

Black Mississippians were not alone in their struggle to obtain the franchise. Throughout the postwar South, blacks campaigned to break down suffrage barriers. The NAACP, while concentrating its energies in the courts, was among the groups promoting the use of the ballot. After *Smith v. Allwright,* many of its branches created citizenship schools to teach blacks how to fill out registration forms properly and to answer typical questions that the clerks posed. The national association made cash awards to those who took up this work; in 1947, for example, the organization presented a prize to its chapter in Monroe, Louisiana, for having conducted a drive that added over 600 names to the voter lists. Assistant secretary Roy Wilkins expressed the value to blacks in creating these voter education classes: "The issue of civil rights is politics. If we are to win the fight for civil rights we must use our political strength."

African-Americans also organized voter leagues to supplement the efforts of the NAACP. These groups solicited support from various organizations in the black community—civic, fraternal, religious—and thus they recruited many individuals outside of the national association's orbit of influence. In 1946, an Atlanta All Citizens Registration Committee was formed because "previously NAACP registration drives had failed to reach the masses." Within four months, this committee assisted in bringing out some 18,000 blacks to sign up to vote. In Winston-Salem, North Carolina, an alliance of blacks and organized labor succeeded in electing a black to the city council. In Richmond, Virginia, a similar coalition supporting the election of a black veteran to the state legislature only narrowly failed. Elsewhere, in union halls, business establishments, farm groups, and small county associations, men and women gathered to plan suffrage crusades. Joining them, representatives of the Southern Conference for Human Welfare (SCHW), an interracial group of New Deal liberals formed in 1938, carried on voter registration drives throughout Dixie. In addition, from church pulpits ministers urged their congregants to go to the polls. During the Atlanta registration drive, the Reverend Martin Luther King, Sr., preached for the cause of enfranchisement, thereby providing a role model for his son to follow.

The situation in Winston-Salem especially illustrated new possibilities for black political advancement stirred by the war. A drive by Local 22 of the Food, Tobacco, Agricultural and Allied Workers, a CIO affiliate, to gain a collective bargaining agreement with R. J. Reynolds Company boosted union membership among blacks and stimulated efforts to challenge racial discrimination within their community. This interracial union chapter, with Communists actively in the lead, mobilized working-class blacks to take part in the freedom struggle that had been waged haltingly in the past by a small middle-class segment of blacks associated with the NAACP. By 1947, CIO and NAACP voter registration campaigns had succeeded in enrolling ten times the number of blacks eligible to vote three years before. "I didn't take registration seriously until the union came in and we began to talk about...the importance of voting," one newly signed-up registrant commented. In 1947, Kenneth Williams, a black minister, won election to the Winston-Salem Board of Aldermen largely on the strength of this emergent Afro-American electorate. The efforts of Local 22 and its allies in heightening racial and political consciousness greatly impressed a visiting black journalist, who reported: "I was aware of a growing solidarity and intelligent mass action that will mean the dawn of a New Day in the South. If there is a 'New Negro', he is to be found in the ranks of the labor movement." Ultimately, however, much of the hope for this trade union path toward racial equality was dashed by the rising anti-Communist reaction that gripped the United States during the Cold War era (see Chapter 2).

Attempts to increase black political involvement throughout the South produced substantial dividends. Within a decade after *Smith v. Allwright*, over 1 million blacks, about four times the number in 1944, had qualified to vote. As Everett C. Ladd, Jr., noted, blacks were transformed "from 'blanks' to participants in city politics." Black voters sometimes held a balance of power in close elections and increasingly helped defeat the most racist of candidates. Commentators noted that where blacks voted in sizable numbers treatment by police improved; black patrolmen were hired; and health, education, and recreational facilities were constructed. Streets in black neighborhoods in those areas were paved. Osceola McKaine, who after the war served as a field representa-

tive of the SCHW, reported from his travels: "The Negro masses
are becoming keenly aware that the questions of jobs and schools
are essentially political questions and these are the things that interest them most." The greater turnout at the polls also encouraged
blacks to seek political office in the South, and for the first time in
the twentieth century nearly a dozen blacks in the South were
elected to posts as aldermen, county supervisors, and members of
city councils.

SEEDTIME OF REFORM

The struggle to expand the vote following World War II was a prelude to the civil rights struggle that mushroomed in the years after
the landmark *Brown v. Board of Education* school desegregation
case. The blatant discrimination in registration procedures that had

Blacks in Charleston lining up to vote in the 1948 Democratic party
primary. (UPI/Bettmann Newsphotos)

been shockingly revealed to the public and a virtual reign of terror to preserve disfranchisement underscored the need for a second reconstruction in which the national government intervened in the South. As one black journalist explained: "Each time the United States Supreme Court outlaws one of these 'Negro stoppers' a new one is invented. It is clear that sooner or later the federal government will have to step in." It would not be too long before politics combined with principle: In a little more than a decade Washington lawmakers would enact four civil rights measures to extend the suffrage to southern blacks.

Just as vital as federal intervention was local assertiveness. Voter registration activities at the grassroots level paralleled the development of the "new Negro," the African-American unafraid to stand up for his or her rights in the face of grave danger. The over 1 million blacks who registered to vote demonstrated that politics was no longer for whites only. Enrollment drives often brought suffrage reformers into direct confrontation with representatives of the racist system in the South and sustained a protest tradition upon which more militant action would be built in the future. It required courage, pride, and emotional strength for blacks living in Dixie to enter courthouses and run the gauntlet of registrars likely to reject their applications and sheriffs anxious to punish them for having made the attempt in the first place. The lessons learned by the civil rights workers of the late forties and early fifties proved valuable to the "new abolitionists" of the 1960s. They taught that the right to vote could be obtained if the federal government intervened to destroy the white stranglehold over the registration process and civil rights groups rallied the mass of blacks behind the ballot. By virtue of this interdependent relationship, the national government changed the law while the civil rights movement erected a support network emboldening blacks to transform their local communities. Although suffragists were only slightly successful in the 1940s, most of them were still around to see a majority of southern blacks enfranchised within a generation.

The World War II era furnished the staging ground for the black revolution. It revitalized black solidarity, tested innovative protest tactics, and moved the federal government closer to the side of racial equality. Wartime urban migration and improved economic opportunities laid the basis for later social and political changes. The war loosened some of the old chains of subservience imposed by the southern caste system and freed blacks in hundreds of locales throughout Dixie to join together to overthrow Jim Crow. What the historian Nancy J. Weiss concluded about Franklin D. Roosevelt and the New Deal should be extended to the years that followed: "The growing interest of blacks in politics, their involvement in the Democratic party, and their new sense that the political process could be responsive to their needs became essential underpinnings of the drive for civil rights." Along two fronts, black soldiers and veterans and their families and friends steered the United States toward living up to its democratic political principles.

Chapter 2

Ballots, Boycotts, and the Building of a National Agenda

While black southerners struggled to clear racial obstacles in the path of the right to vote, their allies in the North applied increasing pressure to move the federal government behind the cause of civil rights. The Supreme Court had taken the lead in beginning to dismantle barriers blocking equal access to public education, housing, and the ballot box, but neither the President nor Congress had taken very firm steps in that direction. Roosevelt's FEPC lacked the necessary administrative authority to combat discrimination in employment, and during World War II the chief executive generally refrained from engaging in controversies over racial issues that would offend white segregationists and threaten national unity. Similarly, southern lawmakers succeeded in strangling congressional attempts to punish lynchers, repeal the repressive poll tax requirement for voting, and preserve the Fair Employment Practice Committee. The anti-Fascist rhetoric of wartime notwithstanding, in the absence of sufficient political leverage, appeals to moral conscience were not enough to guarantee first-class citizenship for African-Americans.

The proponents of civil rights did not lack political resources. Though a majority of black southerners remained disfranchised in the decade following *Smith v. Allwright*, northern blacks could exercise the franchise as a strategic weapon to combat racial discrimination. Precipitated by World War II, the migration of blacks to the urban centers of the North and Far West in search of defense jobs placed them in a favorable position to tip the balance of power in tight elections. Where this critical mass of voters existed, even blacks themselves managed to win election. This incipient strength placed two blacks in the House of Representatives—Adam Clayton Powell of New York City and William Dawson of Chicago—as well as a sprinkling of officials in local positions. Yet black influence derived from something more than actual minority-group representation, which was meager. Rather it rested in its potential to sway white politicians—to reward friends and punish enemies, the most basic axiom in politics.

THE TRUMAN ADMINISTRATION AND CIVIL RIGHTS

President Harry S. Truman had to factor in such political calculations in finding the right political equation for dealing with African-Americans. The successor to FDR, Truman inherited the New Deal's black converts to the Democratic party. However, in 1945, it was not clear whether this newfound partisan allegiance of blacks was a personal or an institutional one. Would it survive Roosevelt's death or would the black electorate return to its historical Republican mooring? Though the majority of blacks remained faithful to the party of Roosevelt in the November 1946 midterm legislative elections, the GOP recaptured some of FDR's black followers on its way toward securing control of the Eightieth Congress. Charles Houston, the noted attorney and legal adviser to the NAACP, expressed the disaffection of many blacks several months before the elections: "The president may do this and he may do that as leader, but if he cannot produce, well, there is no such thing as gratitude in politics." In December 1945, Houston had evidenced his own frustration with the lack of presidential leadership in civil rights by resigning as a member of the increasingly ineffective FEPC.

A practical politician, President Truman was prepared to heed these warning signals. Much of his early attitudes toward race were grounded in political considerations. As a border-state senator from Missouri during the late 1930s and early 1940s, Truman had supported, without much enthusiasm, abolition of the poll tax and passage of an antilynching bill. About the latter, he admitted to a southern colleague and opponent of the measure: "All my sympathies are with you, but the Negro vote in Kansas City and St. Louis is too important." At the same time, Truman backed legislation to fund the FEPC and spoke out for giving "the Negroes the rights that are theirs." His moderate positions on race made him acceptable to both southern and northern Democrats as the compromise candidate to replace the more controversial Henry A. Wallace as Roosevelt's running mate in 1944.

As President, he quickly received an education about racial injustice that deeply affected his thinking. In 1946, vicious attacks on returning black servicemen in the South generated widespread notoriety. "My God! I had no idea that it was as terrible as that!" the chief executive exclaimed after learning that Isaac Woodward, still in uniform, had been severely beaten and blinded while passing through South Carolina en route home. Together with a bloody race riot in Columbia, Tennessee, and mounting violence and threats of attack against blacks who sought to exercise their newly won suffrage rights, these events shocked Truman.

He responded by appointing a special committee to investigate the deteriorating condition of civil rights and devise remedies for its improvement. The moral concerns that prompted the formation of this group were reinforced by sound political considerations. The defeat of the Democrats at the polls in the 1946 congressional election charted the President's declining political health and brought a prognosis of doom for the party's presidential nominee two years hence. The once robust Roosevelt coalition appeared to be dying in the wake of Truman's inability to solve the postwar reconversion problems of inflation, shortages, and labor conflict as well as growing racial tensions. The establishment of the President's Committee on Civil Rights provided one way for Truman to resuscitate the ailing Democratic alliance in time to achieve a reelection victory.

This strategy was put to a stiff test after the committee issued its report in October 1947. *To Secure These Rights* urged greater federal involvement in promoting racial equality. It endorsed removal of the poll tax and other discriminatory obstacles to voting, creation of a Civil Rights Division in the Department of Justice, and desegregation of the armed forces, interstate transportation, and government employment. These suggestions broke new ground in establishing a reform agenda and alarmed southern white politicians. Already troubled by their perception that Roosevelt's New Deal had tilted the axis of Democratic power away from the rural South to an urban North teeming with ethnic and racial minorities, many southerners resented the Truman committee's assault upon the racial status quo.

Their complaints forced the President to move circumspectly. Despite delivering an unprecedented special message on civil rights to a joint session of Congress in February 1948, Truman failed to press lawmakers to consider particular measures based on the committee's recommendations. He did not want to provoke a southern revolt in the upcoming presidential election, and the prospect of a southern filibuster against any civil rights legislation would prove even more divisive to party unity. Furthermore, southern legislative support for his Cold War economic and military policies toward the Soviet Union commanded a higher priority than did passage of civil rights bills, however worthy they might be.

Yet the Cold War offered a double-edged sword for racial advancement. Having recognized the difficulties in challenging the white South, Truman could not afford to risk the political consequences of ignoring rising black militancy. Since World War II, blacks in and out of the South had begun mobilizing for first-class citizenship, prepared to force the United States to live up to its democratic ideals. This also came at a time when the country was venturing into a fierce propaganda battle with the Soviet Union for allies in global struggle. Committed to the United Nations, President Truman did not want domestic racial conflicts to diminish his diplomatic efforts in the international arena. In this context, the attempt by Mississippi blacks to unseat the racist Senator Theodore Bilbo not only demonstrated a growing collective consciousness against oppression at the local level, but also focused national and world attention on the gap between democratic pronouncements and the reality of bigotry. Recognizing such predicaments, the President's Committee on Civil Rights declared in 1947: "An American diplomat cannot argue for free elections in foreign lands without meeting the challenge that in sections of America qualified voters do not have access to the polls."

Black protest leaders sought to exploit Truman's vulnerability on this point. In its traditional, legalistic manner, the NAACP petitioned the United Nations to consider a list of grievances against American racial practices. In a less conventional way that prefigured future campaigns against racial discrimination, A. Philip Randolph called upon blacks to apply pressure through civil disobedience. In early 1948, the "father" of the March on Washington tangled with Truman over an issue he had first brought up with Roosevelt seven years earlier and had failed to resolve: desegregation of the military. During a period when Truman sought increased military measures to combat Soviet aggression, Randolph urged the President to promulgate an executive order abolishing segregation in the armed forces or he would counsel black youth "to resist a [Selective Service] law, the inevitable consequences of which would be to expose them to un-American brutality so familiar during the last war." Although black leaders divided over Randolph's threatened action, a survey revealed that 71 percent of draft age blacks supported the proposed boycott.

The danger of black insurgency was not confined to Truman's defense program; it menaced the political fortunes of the President. The black electorate gave some indication of rallying around the candidacy of Henry Wallace, who criticized Truman for responding too aggressively in seeking to contain the Soviet Union in foreign affairs and for not acting forcefully enough to repel racial discrimination at home. As early as May 1946, a poll showed that 91 percent of black voters favored Wallace as the Democratic nominee in 1948. Since then the President had appointed a pioneering civil rights committee and presented Congress with a pathbreaking legislative reform agenda. Nevertheless, Wallace carried a strong appeal for black voters. In late 1947, he campaigned throughout the South, audaciously addressed integrated audiences that included many of the region's newly enfranchised blacks, and spoke out in favor of racial equality. Up North, a special congressional election in a Bronx district in New York City with a large black population resulted in the victory of a pro-Wallace candidate.

These political rumblings did not exactly catch Truman by surprise. In November 1947, one of his key advisers, Clark Clifford, had counseled the President to concentrate on appealing to the liberal elements of the Democratic coalition, particularly blacks and labor union members, to ensure his reelection the following year. "Unless there are new and real efforts," Clifford predicted, "the Negro bloc... will go Republican." A strong civil rights stand might disturb the Democratic South, but Clifford suggested that the former Confederate states would not bolt the party of their forebears.

Initially, however, Truman responded cautiously to this advice. Unwilling to confront the southern wing of his party any further, the President backed away from pressing his bold civil rights initiatives in Congress. True, the chief executive had some very good tactical reasons for backing off, given the likelihood that a southern filibuster would kill reform bills as well as stall passage of those pertaining to Cold War remilitarization. But Truman did not face the same legislative hurdle with respect to desegregation of the armed forces. In that case, he could have dealt with the matter by executive decree; this he refused to do. Moreover, he displayed excessive timidity in failing to endorse his own committee's civil rights recommendations as part of the Democratic party's platform. Instead, he planned to run on the Democrats' mild 1944 plank vaguely worded in support of granting minorities equal rights under the Constitution.

Once again, strong political forces knocked the President off dead center and moved him to the left. At the Democratic National Convention in July 1948, party liberals engineered an end run around the Truman-controlled Platform Committee and won a floor fight for a stronger resolution on civil rights. Though stopping short of pledging an end to segregation in the military, it did promise "equal treatment in the service and defense of our nation" as well as "the right to equal opportunity of employment." Hubert H. Humphrey of Minnesota, a leader of the liberal upstarts, eloquently captured the spirit behind the proposals: "The time has arrived for the Democratic Party to get out of the shadow of states' rights and walk forthrightly into the bright sunshine of human rights."

Embracing the revised platform rhetoric was not sufficient. With Randolph still intending to lead a mass draft-evasion movement and with Henry Wallace running on an independent Progressive party ticket, Truman took the kind of concrete action on civil rights he had hesitated to implement previously. Shortly after the Democratic convention adjourned, the President signed two executive orders establishing a nondiscriminatory fair employment policy for the federal government and creating a committee to promote equal opportunity in the armed forces, with the ultimate aim of eliminating segregation. He also convened a special session of Congress to act on his party's civil rights proposals, but southern lawmakers succeeded in blocking them.

These assorted efforts precipitated a revolt by white southerners, contrary to Clifford's predictions. After staging a walkout

Protesting discrimination in the military, A. Philip Randolph heads a
picket line at the 1948 Democratic National Convention. (UPI/Bettmann
Newsphotos)

from the Democratic National Convention, a band of southern dis-
sidents formed the States' Rights party and nominated Governor
Strom Thurmond of South Carolina for President. These Dixiecrats
condemned federal tyranny and reaffirmed their allegiance to the
principle of racial segregation. Rather than pushing Truman to
mend his political fences in the South, this uprising produced the
opposite effect. It reinforced the President's determination to secure minority backing in the North. According to this line of thinking, the "Negro votes in the crucial states will more than cancel out
any votes he may lose in the South."

Not only might this strategy neutralize southern losses, but it
could also undermine black support for Truman's main rivals in the
North. The Republican nominee, Governor Thomas E. Dewey of
New York, ran on a platform that declared its opposition to racial
segregation in the military, a declaration omitted from the Democratic manifesto. Furthermore, Henry Wallace's Progressive party

denounced all forms of segregation and gained the endorsement of such prominent blacks as Charles Houston, W. E. B. Du Bois, and Paul Robeson. To secure black votes against his opponents, Truman emphasized his civil rights accomplishments during his first term and, in a symbolic gesture, swung his campaign through Harlem, the first President to do so. He hammered away at the Republican-controlled Eightieth Congress for doing nothing to pass his civil rights proposals. At the same time, he attacked Wallace for permitting Communists to collaborate with his Progressive party, a charge designed to appeal to black civil rights leaders wary of Communist infiltration of their own organizations.

Truman's maneuvering paid off in his reelection. As his counselors had forecast, the loss of five deep South states to the Dixiecrats was more than offset by the huge margins Truman piled up among black voters in the urban North. He captured 69 percent of the black ballots cast in twenty-seven major cities, and in California, Illinois, and Ohio, black votes made the critical difference in his victory. Indeed, his share of the black electorate exceeded that of FDR, and as Nancy Weiss has pointed out, Truman managed to use the civil rights issue "as a means to transform black Roosevelt supporters into black Democrats." The incumbent's pro-civil-rights record along with Dewey's lackluster campaign and the unwillingness of most blacks to "waste" their votes on a Wallacite third-party bid, especially one tainted with the stigma of Red radicalism, solidified black fidelity to the New Deal coalition.

The cementing of black loyalty to the Democratic party as an institution, rather than to a single leader, depended on more than the attraction to civil rights. Though the vote of the cohesive black bloc grew out of racial concerns, class issues also shaped it. In casting a ballot for the Democratic presidential nominee, blacks were endorsing the party that brought economic relief from depression, sponsored measures to increase employment, and defended labor unions from restrictive assaults. The scant evidence that exists for the New Deal era suggests that lower-income blacks, like their white counterparts, were more inclined to back the Democrats than were those higher on the economic scale. This pattern persisted during the Truman years. Donald R. McCoy and Richard T. Reutten have noted that whereas nearly all black newspapers supported Dewey in 1948, reflecting the higher socioeconomic status of their publishers, the lower-income readers of these publications sided overwhelmingly with Truman. For most African-Americans, who were still not afforded equal economic and citizenship rights, race and class interests coincided.

The election of 1948 established civil rights as a key issue on the agenda of presidential politics. Three out of the four political parties had endorsed the extension of racial equality. Black delegates attended the Democratic convention in comparatively small but record numbers and contributed to passing the minority civil rights plank. Blacks were also represented in prominent ways in the Progressive party campaign, and the GOP, the former home of the majority of the black electorate, created a National Council of Negro Republicans to lure them back.

Yet the growing visibility of the civil rights issue did not mean that black Americans, especially those residing in the South, were about to achieve their goal of first-class citizenship through electoral politics. Southern segregationists continued to retain key positions within the Democratic party and in Congress, ready to shred any legislative proposal on civil rights that appeared. Though the chief executive owed blacks a big debt for his reelection, he lacked the substantial commitment necessary to tackle powerful conservative congressional forces against civil rights. For Truman, the Cold War and national security took precedence over domestic reform, and he hesitated to antagonize the southern lawmakers whose support he needed. Besides, Truman's policy of global containment fueled excessive anti-Communist sentiment in the United States. Zealous "Red baiters" equated any challenge to the status quo with un-Americanism. Even liberal and labor organizations such as the NAACP and the CIO hunted for suspected Communists in their ranks. No matter how hard they tried to achieve the requisite purity, civil rights groups still came under attack from segregationists who considered advocates of racial equality soft on communism. This fear of social change and the attempts of politicians to capitalize on it created an inhospitable environment for civil rights activism.

To crack the entrenched opposition to racial equality required a public zeal that did not yet exist. In fact, the majority of whites did not embrace the cause of civil rights. In March 1948, a Gallup Poll that asked whether Americans favored Truman's moderate civil

[handwritten annotations:] opens gate to more public stance for anti-racist views   1948 - 56% would not say they support approaches even

rights program found out that 56 percent did not. Northerners were more likely than southerners to express sympathy, but most of them remained poorly informed about the issue.

THE ELECTION OF DWIGHT D. EISENHOWER

The election of Dwight D. Eisenhower in 1952 did not place a forceful advocate of civil rights in the White House, yet neither did it bring in someone totally unsympathetic to the principle of desegregation. The Republican President did not intend to turn back the civil rights clock to the days before the Truman administration. However, events were pushing ahead the timetable for racial equality and creating new standards of measurement to gauge presidential performance. Faced with this accelerated schedule, Eisenhower moved forward, but did so too cautiously to keep in step with the quickened rate of black expectations.

President Eisenhower began his first term in office without having accumulated any political debt to blacks. The overwhelming share of the black vote, 73 percent, had gone to Eisenhower's Democratic rival, Adlai E. Stevenson. The former Illinois governor exceeded Truman's ratio of the minority vote by recovering the backing of black Wallacites. The newly expanded southern black electorate in Louisiana, South Carolina, Kentucky, and Arkansas provided the margin of victory for Stevenson in those states. The majority of blacks stuck with the Democratic party even though its platform did not retain the strong language of 1948 and its vice presidential nominee was Senator John Sparkman of Alabama, who had opposed Truman's civil rights program.

Unlike 1948, the black vote did not save the Democrats from defeat. The popularity of General Eisenhower among whites throughout the nation more than canceled out the impact of the black vote. The black electorate could play a decisive role in swinging the outcome of elections only when, as the *Pittsburgh Courier* noted, "the balance between the two major political parties is so even." Such was not the case in 1952. Eisenhower captured 55.2 percent of the popular vote and 442 electoral votes. His winning electoral column included 57 votes from the South, 18 more than the Dixiecrats had gathered four years earlier.

Despite the fact that Eisenhower had made inroads into Dixie and gained endorsements from popular figures such as Governor James F. Byrnes of South Carolina, he entered the White House with a civil rights agenda in mind. The Republican platform had differed from the Democrats' chiefly in its unwillingness to propose federal measures to combat employment discrimination, preferring instead to rely on state authority. Otherwise, the GOP advocated federal action to eliminate lynching, poll taxes, and segregation in Washington, D.C. Eisenhower had also assured black leaders that he would strive to end discrimination in federal employment under his direct control, continue desegregation of the armed forces, and in a campaign address in Harlem, he invited blacks to join his crusade "based upon merit and without respect to color or creed." / *At use of phrase nationally visible*

However, there were definite limits to Eisenhower's plans for obtaining racial equality. Committed to a view of government that emphasized persuasion over coercion in shaping social and economic relations, Eisenhower wanted to give state, local, and private sectors broad discretion in resolving conflicts in public policy. He believed that problems of race were deeply embedded in the fabric of southern society and could not be easily removed. Still, he considered white southern politicians as law abiding and responsible, and he had faith in their willingness over time to abandon discriminatory racial practices. Consequently, the chief executive would not compel white southerners hastily to change their long-standing racial customs. Gradualism rather than speed characterized his approach. Eisenhower consistently declared in public what he confided to his personal diary at the beginning of his term: "I believe that Federal law imposed upon our states in such a way as to bring about a conflict of the police power of the states and the nation, would set back the cause of progress in race relations for a long, long time."

COMMUNITY MOBILIZATION AND THE MONTGOMERY BUS BOYCOTT

While the cause of civil rights inched along slowly under Truman and Eisenhower in the national arena, southern blacks and a handful of sympathetic whites in their home communities struggled to set themselves free. Civil rights leaders viewed electoral politics as a prime instrument for achieving racial gains. Political exclusion had pinned a twentieth-century badge of subordination on black southerners, which enfranchisement promised to remove. Without a free and unfettered right to vote, the constitutional guarantee of full citizenship would remain elusive. Given the history of their official exclusion from the governing process, indeed their legitimacy as participants in government denied, blacks sought to enter politics as a fundamental act of liberation. The vote could be wielded as a tool of protest, a means of asserting dignity and pride, a source of personal and group autonomy. "There's one thing the Negro has that the white man wants but can't get unless you give it to him," a black Floridian remarked. "That's your vote. He can offer you a million dollars for your vote, but he can't get it unless you give it to him."

These symbolic qualities were not the only rewards attributed to the suffrage. The ballot had a practical side that offered a way to improve the daily living conditions of those deprived of basic public services most white Americans took for granted: paved streets, regular sanitation disposal, adequate police and fire protection, and access to recreational facilities. The vote would convert blacks into constituents, providing them with an opportunity to elect representatives whom they could hold directly accountable at the polls for delivering material benefits. This classic view of civic democracy did not take into account the pervasiveness of race and caste as features that would retard black political influence, but it did conform to the conventional American creed of self-help and equal opportunity for advancement. In sharing and promoting this ideal, black suffragists attached their cause to republican principles and portrayed their foes as undemocratic and un-American.

Whatever the merits of their argument, black southerners still had to overcome numerous barriers to their entry into politics. Federal law had eliminated the white primary, but poll taxes, literacy tests, intimidation, and fear induced by centuries of discrimination kept most blacks disfranchised. With federal involvement growing but unreliable and southern resistance firm, blacks assumed increased responsibility for marshaling their resources against discrimination. According to Henry Lee Moon, an NAACP official who closely monitored this heightened political activity, "the real drive to register and get out the vote is essentially a grass-roots movement with local Negro leadership."

The postwar voter and citizenship education campaigns, discussed in Chapter 1, demonstrated the need for collective action. Civil rights groups in concert with voter leagues and sympathetic labor union locals, especially those in the CIO, waged intensive efforts to sign up black registrants and bring them out to the polls on election day. These organizations were necessary to arouse black consciousness to the efficacy of voting, counsel blacks on how to meet the suffrage requirements they faced, and sustain encouragement and support for those willing to break from the past when politics was the exclusive domain of whites.

These endeavors initially worked best in urban areas of the South. In the cities blacks had greater access to education, economic opportunities, and cultural institutions, all of which encouraged civic participation or preparation for it. Even the barriers that still existed there were not erected as high as in the rural black belt where African-Americans were isolated, economically dependent on whites, and vulnerable to reprisals. In 1947, when Richmond, Virginia, blacks mounted a successful voter registration drive, the city's leading newspaper acknowledged: "We do have a democratic tradition which holds that American citizens are entitled to vote and to hold office. So we may as well accustom ourselves to [it]." In Atlanta, Georgia, blacks extended their political influence by forming a coalition with wealthy businesspeople to elect a white mayor, William B. Hartsfield, in 1949. Four years later, this biracial alliance, which cut across class lines, succeeded in electing Dr. Rufus E. Clement, the black president of Atlanta University, to the board of education, turning aside his white opponent.

However, other attempts at forging interracial coalitions based on shared economic experiences ran into trouble. Issues of political ideology divided people with common class grievances, as the situation of tobacco workers in Winston-Salem revealed. Following the Second World War, the R. J. Reynolds Company undertook to roll back the gains that Local 22 of the CIO had made in unionizing black and white workers. In 1947, after management refused to agree to demands for a wage increase, the union went out on strike. The company, supported by the local newspaper, attempted to undermine the walkout by shifting the focus from collective bargaining to Communist infiltration of the union. Indeed, Communists did occupy top positions in Local 22, which left the organization susceptible to charges that it was operating as an agent of a foreign power and using blacks to foster subversive aims. In the highly charged Cold War climate, the company succeeded in attacking the union for its Communist affiliations, but it could not triumph without assistance from the national CIO, which was also engaged in eliminating Communists from its ranks. Whereas the company was attempting to squelch unionization, the CIO merely wanted to establish a non-Communist affiliate. However, "if purging communist leadership also led to a destruction of the legitimate battle to organize the unorganized and achieve social justice," William H. Chafe has argued, "any victory would be hollow." Arrayed against the combined forces of union and management, Local 22 collapsed.

Its defeat under this anti-Communist assault seriously affected the shape of the black freedom struggle in Winston-Salem and in other areas to which progressive unions might have expanded. Blacks continued to play a role in the political life of the North Carolina city, but they lost the kind of civil rights militancy that the union had energized during its heydey in the 1940s. As Nelson Lichtenstein and Robert Korstad have shown, Winston-Salem became a "model of racial moderation." Politics consisted mainly of registering to vote and turning out at the ballot box on election day, with a deemphasis on protest activities and community organizing. Even the NAACP felt the negative effects, as its membership dwindled during the 1950s to less than 500. Political affairs were run by a select group of white and black leaders, with the mass of black residents increasingly relegated to the background in vital decision-making.

Nevertheless, civil rights activism did not disappear from the South. As a matter of fact in cities such as Montgomery, Alabama, the expanding political clout of the black electorate raised expectations for the possibilities of social change. In the "cradle of the Confederacy" blacks counted for between 7 and 8 percent of the registered voters by 1955, a figure slightly above the statewide average. Even with this relatively small ratio of voters, in 1953 blacks had helped ensure the election of a white city commissioner running against the political establishment. This victory encouraged blacks to make demands on local officials, and several individuals who had actively engaged in political organizing following the demise of the white primary led the way. Edgar D. Nixon, a representative of the

International Brotherhood of Sleeping Car Porters and a driving force in the NAACP, obtained a noteworthy 42 percent of the vote in a losing contest for a seat on the county Democratic Executive Committee. Jo Ann Robinson, an English instructor at Alabama State College, headed the Women's Political Council, which served not only to get out the black vote but also to petition the city commission to redress black complaints. Nixon and Robinson were often joined by Rufus A. Lewis, a businessman who chaired the Citizen's Steering Committee.

Buoyed by their growing political confidence, black leaders met with modest success. With the lone commissioner blacks had helped to elect in their corner, they persuaded white officials to increase the number of black police officers and improve bus service in black neighborhoods. Civil rights proponents also pressed demands for appointment of a black to the Parks and Recreation Board and for the elimination of certain humiliating policies related to bus transportation. Particularly irksome were the requirements that black passengers first pay their fares at the front door and board through the back door and that they remain standing when seats were available in the white but not the colored area. The limits of their political strength became manifest when the city rejected their requests for change, and in 1955 their white ally on the commission went down to defeat for reelection, beaten by an opponent who injected explicit racial appeals into the campaign.

Thus, black progress remained at a standstill and black political influence appeared on the decline when Rosa Parks was arrested on December 1, 1955. A seamstress, a former secretary of the local NAACP branch, and a recent participant in interracial workshops at the Highlander Folk School in Tennessee, Mrs. Parks refused to vacate her seat for a white passenger on a crowded bus. A spontaneous action only in the sense that the exact details were not planned in advance, her defiance reflected long-standing personal involvement in civil rights activities as well as the natural extension of political efforts by fellow blacks to challenge racism in Montgomery. Consequently, Parks turned to E. D. Nixon for assistance in bailing her out of jail, and he, along with Jo Ann Robinson, hatched plans for a boycott of the buses. The Women's Political Council took the lead in spreading word of the proposed strike by cranking out some 40,000 handbills on a mimeograph machine borrowed by Robinson.

Once plans for the boycott were set in motion, black ministers, including Dr. Martin Luther King, Jr., were tapped to assume direction of the protest activities. The recruitment of the clergy brought an important dimension to the struggle. A network of independent churches provided a base from which to mobilize the black masses in a way that middle-class–oriented civil rights groups, civic leagues, and political clubs had failed to accomplish. Though ministers like Dr. King's father in Atlanta had used their pulpits on behalf of voter registration drives, they had rarely before undertaken a project that rallied blacks on such a large, community-wide scale against racial discrimination.[1] So long as most black Montgomerians were barred from participating in the electoral process as voters, they resorted to mass protest to achieve their political aims.

Blacks who participated in the yearlong boycott were transformed by the struggle. Reverend King and the Montgomery Improvement Association (MIA), which he directed, came to realize the intransigence of the segregationist forces opposing them and modified their demands accordingly. Originally they had accepted the concept of segregation on the buses and merely sought more courteous treatment and a system that did not force them to relinquish their seats to whites when the black section was filled. Then, the city refused to negotiate, black leaders were arrested, and King's home was dynamited. These acts of resistance stiffened the MIA's resolve, and the organization decided to settle for nothing less than complete desegregation of the buses. Mass meetings sustained the minister-leaders and their congregants behind this evolving goal. The inspiring sermons of the charismatic Dr. King and the singing of gospel songs filled with messages of freedom reinforced group solidarity and the determination to persevere. Nevertheless, collective action alone was not enough to destroy Jim Crow, and victory came only after the Supreme Court, on November 13, 1956, voided segregation on public buses.

The lessons that emerged from the Montgomery bus boycott had profound significance for the battle to obtain civil and political rights. Indeed, it showed that the two were inextricably linked. Acquisition of the ballot by itself did not bring power, nor did the piecemeal dismantling of the limbs of Jim Crow. Even after the buses were desegregated blacks in Montgomery faced sporadic vi-

---

[1]In 1953, the Reverend T. J. Jemison had led a seven-day bus boycott in Baton Rouge, Louisiana, which ended in a compromise. A small number of seats were reserved for whites in the front and for blacks in the rear of the buses, but those in between were open to all.

The Montgomery police fingerprint Rosa Parks after her arrest for failing to vacate her seat on a segregated bus. (AP/Wide World Photos)

olence against their enjoying this right, and most continued to meet obstacles in enrolling as voters. Unless black southerners devised new techniques in mounting grassroots protest, thereby dramatically exposing their plight to the rest of the country, the white South would not voluntarily yield. As J. Mills Thornton has observed: "In the end, the bus boycott teaches that segregation could have been disestablished only in the way in which it was disestablished: by internal pressure sufficient to compel intervention from outside the South." The Supreme Court set the lead in this direction; it remained for the President and Congress to follow.

MASSIVE RESISTANCE AND EISENHOWER MODERATION

The high tribunal's monumental decision in *Brown v. Board of Education* (1954) presented new opportunities for and challenges to the quest for black political equality. Though the ruling applied to the desegregation of public schools, it carried far-ranging implications. Richard Kluger has written that the opinion "represented nothing short of a reconsecration of American ideals." The Court removed the legal sanction a prior bench of justices had conferred on the doctrine of white supremacy in *Plessy v. Ferguson* nearly sixty years before. "Separate but equal" no longer bore legitimacy, and blacks could pursue their full rights of citizenship armed not only with morality but with the law. Yet racial justice did not arrive so simply. The Supreme Court left implementation of *Brown* in the hands of southern federal judges and instructed them to proceed with "all deliberate speed." Whatever that phrase signified, it did not mean "soon." Given some leeway, the southern states attempted to push compliance back for as many tomorrows as possible.

The South embarked on massive resistance to preserve segregation in the schools and black subordination in political affairs. State legislatures passed interposition resolutions "nullifying" *Brown* and enacted pupil placement laws assigning students and teachers to segregated schools according to nonracial criteria. Members of Congress from Dixie issued manifestos denouncing the landmark judicial opinion as unconstitutional and pledging to seek to reverse it. Organizations calling themselves "White Citizens Councils" arose to buttress the efforts of politicians to concoct supposedly legal means to preserve the status quo. However, this middle-class group of solid citizens—the "uptown Ku Klux Klan"—frequently resorted to illegal or extralegal methods of keeping blacks in their place. As employers they fired "uppity" blacks; as creditors they denied loans to blacks or foreclosed their property; and if all else failed the "uptown Ku Klux Klan" retaliated physically.

White supremacists also waged a fierce battle to destroy the NAACP, the group that had successfully litigated the *Brown* case. Charging the organization with subverting the established system of segregation, southern lawmakers tried to drive it from the region. In 1956, Alabama demanded that the NAACP register with the state as an outside corporation and turn over its membership lists. When the association refused to do so for fear of subjecting its members to racial intimidation, Alabama prohibited the NAACP from operating and tied it up in the courts for nearly a decade be-

fore the group legally could function again. The South hatched
a variety of additional schemes to put the organization out of business. Virginia passed antibarratry legislation aimed at hindering
the NAACP from initiating or sponsoring lawsuits against segregation. Louisiana barred teachers from advocating integration of the
schools, and South Carolina banished NAACP members from public employment. States such as Florida wielded the weapon of anti-
Communism against the association, targeting the NAACP as a
subversive organization and establishing a legislative committee to
investigate its activities. Although managing to survive, the group
suffered considerable damage. In order to defend itself from attack,
the NAACP had to divert precious resources away from the main
battle against Jim Crow and disfranchisement.

Under this counterassault the drive toward racial equality sputtered. School desegregation moved ahead at a trickling pace and was
mainly confined to a handful of cities around the southern periphery;
the deep South shouted "never!" White opposition had a similarly
chilling effect on the advancement of blacks into electoral politics.
Though the rate of black voter registration had begun to slow before
Brown, new recruits were harder to sign up as tensions escalated over
the segregation issue. The White Citizens Councils in Mississippi and
Louisiana did their best to keep black applicants off the voter rolls and
connived to purge many of those who had managed to get on. In
Ouachita Parish, Louisiana, of the 4,000 blacks who had registered
through September 1956, only 1,000 remained after Council-inspired
challenges. The head of the Mississippi Council facetiously explained
the thinking of the disfranchisers: "Why, it'd be like giving the vote to
these children of mine, you give the vote to my children and you
know who they'd elect for President? Elvis Presley!" Not surprisingly,
between 1952 and 1956 only 215,000 additional blacks succeeded in
enrolling to vote in the South, leaving 75 percent without the ballot.

Southern blacks had fallen short of reaching their registration
potential for several reasons. The voter leagues and the NAACP
had merely skimmed the surface. Blacks located in the urban areas
of the upper South and in the largest cities in the heart of Dixie
made up the biggest proportion of the new voters. However, in rural sections of the black belt, African-Americans with little school-
ing and money were unable and unwilling to register. In these areas they had trouble developing independent leadership because
the tiny group of professionals remained tied to white purse strings.

School boards threatened to fire teachers who exhibited signs of militancy, and banks refused to extend credit to businesspeople and farmers who tried to organize suffrage drives. If economic pressure did not work, registrars managed to apply literacy tests in such a biased manner that hardly any blacks could pass. And whites were not hesitant to use old-fashioned brute force.

Although the issue of school desegregation became the storm center of political controversy between white and black southerners following *Brown*, the acquisition of the suffrage continued to loom large as a source of contention between the races. Each side saw much at stake in the outcome. White extremists raised the bugaboo of racial amalgamation that supposedly would follow black political participation. Blacks "desire a much shorter detour, via the political tunnel," Judge Tom Brady, the founder of the White Citizens Councils, claimed, "to get on the intermarriage turnpikes." Whether or not most white southerners actually feared racial politics entering into their bedrooms, they were concerned that black ballots would lead to a basic rearrangement of power and prestige in society. This view received support from blacks themselves. One commentator declared: "... desegregation would be much further along if Negroes in the South could vote more nearly in proportion to their potential voting population." In effect, both groups exaggerated the importance of the suffrage as a springboard to equality, but each correctly understood that without the extension of the franchise blacks remained vulnerable to rulers not of their own choosing and whites could not be held strictly accountable for the racist policies they imposed.

The key question was how to achieve enfranchisement. As black southerners struggled against resistance from below, they looked to the federal government for support. Once before—during the Reconstruction period following the Civil War—the national government had provided protection for the right to vote from racial discrimination, but ultimately retreated in the face of southern obstructionism. This time African-Americans called for a Second Reconstruction with staying power. During the 1950s they had to rely on a President whose views on race were paternalistic and who preferred to keep Washington out of the internal affairs of the states. This left the job to Congress, a body dominated by a conservative coalition in which southerners routinely pounced on reform measures. Thus, the prospects for assistance from above appeared dim, but they were not hopeless.

Most civil rights leaders and scholars have disapproved of President Eisenhower's handling of racial affairs. Roy Wilkins, the executive director of the NAACP during the Eisenhower years, summed up the perspective of his colleagues: "President Eisenhower was a fine general and a good, decent man, but if he had fought World War II the way he fought for civil rights, we would all be speaking German today." This judgment has been echoed by nearly every historian who has studied this period: "Eisenhower and his subordinates," Robert F. Burk concluded, "had displayed a consistent pattern of hesitancy and extreme political caution in defending black legal rights."

The strength of this criticism lies primarily in the failure of the President to take a firm moral stand in support of *Brown*. When asked whether he endorsed or merely accepted the desegregation ruling, Eisenhower replied: "I think it makes no difference whether or not I endorse it," though he added that he would "do my very best to see that it is carried out in this country." Yet for southern black children it made a critical difference whether the President, especially one as popular as Eisenhower, affirmed their moral, as well as legal, right to attend desegregated schools. The chief executive delayed that possibility by refusing to throw his considerable weight behind the integration process, which, in turn, allowed the momentum to pass to those advocating massive resistance in the South. Ironically, he repeatedly preached the value of education in changing the hearts and minds of individuals, but he distinctly failed to use his presidential pulpit to instruct white southerners about their moral duty to obey the law. Furthermore, he offered scant encouragement to blacks who struggled peacefully to persuade white segregationists to abandon Jim Crow according to the voluntaristic principles Eisenhower espoused. Thus, despite the urging of Martin Luther King, Jr., the President remained silent during the yearlong Montgomery bus boycott.

Even with these failings, Eisenhower's record was not without significant accomplishments. He fulfilled his campaign pledge to work for desegregation of the nation's capital in a variety of ways. Without much fanfare, the White House facilitated the desegregation of local movie theaters, hotels, and municipal agencies. The chief executive placed Vice-President Richard M. Nixon in charge of the President's Committee on Government Contract Compliance, and although this agency, like the FEPC before it, lacked enforcement power, it persuaded the transportation company serving

the District of Columbia to hire more black bus drivers and street-
car operators and convinced the local telephone company to end
segregation in its offices. Moreover, following *Brown*, Eisenhower
pressed the District of Columbia to desegregate its schools and
likewise ordered several southern military bases to desegregate
their educational and service facilities.

These deeds reflected a growing working relationship between
the White House and one of black America's premier politicians,
Adam Clayton Powell. Along with William L. Dawson of Chicago,
Powell sat in the House of Representatives, occupying the highest
national elected office held by blacks since Reconstruction. Whereas both belonged to the Democratic party, they displayed very different styles. A product of Chicago's political machine, Dawson
usually placed organizational interests above racial goals. For example, in 1952, he assumed a major role in working out a compromise
on the civil rights plank of the party platform that represented a
weaker version than that of 1948. In contrast, Powell had been an
active protest leader in New York City, had a well-deserved reputation as a political maverick, and had voiced sharp criticism of
party leaders, particularly Adlai Stevenson, for hedging on civil
rights during the 1952 campaign.

With Eisenhower installed in the Oval Office, Powell aimed his
sights at the Republicans and found a receptive target. The New
York congressman brought the issue of segregated military installa-
tions to public attention, and he met with presidential counselors
to arrange a satisfactory settlement. Powell added to his influence
within GOP circles by the publication in *Reader's Digest* of his
highly complimentary article about the President's civil rights
achievements. Writing in 1954, he lavishly praised Eisenhower for
quietly launching a "revolution" that would mean "an era of greater
promise for Negro citizens." Nor did Powell's flattery diminish
because the chief executive refused to support the congressman's
periodic attempts to attach desegregation riders to school construction bills. This rejection did not smart so much, for Powell did not
find any stronger support for his amendment among Democratic
leaders.

Powell further manifested his independence by bolting to
Eisenhower for President in 1956, opening the possibility of large
numbers of blacks following him. Some of Eisenhower's advisers
recognized the political dividends to be earned from closer administration identification with Powell and the cause of civil rights.

Congressional representatives William L.
Dawson, on the left, and Adam Clayton Powell,
standing in front of the nation's Capitol, were
known for contrasting styles of political
leadership. (UPI/Bettmann Newsphotos)

They rewarded the congressman with donations to defray the costs of his campaign for reelection. In a less pecuniary vein, Republican officials believed that their party had a "wonderful story to tell," and recommended publicizing more extensively to black audiences the President's favorable record on civil rights.

The possible payoff from doing so was high. In 61 legislative districts outside the South, blacks held the balance of power in the 1954 congressional elections that produced thirty-two Democratic and twenty-nine Republican victories. In 25 of these constituencies, GOP candidates won with a ratio of less than 55 percent of the vote, while in 14 of those districts the Democrats triumphed in similar fashion. An exchange of fifteen seats from the Democratic to the Republican side would furnish the GOP with a majority in the House. A shift of two seats in the Senate would achieve Republican dominance of that body. With the political importance of this in mind, in 1956, Vice-President Nixon told a campaign audience that he awaited the day "when American boys and girls shall sit side by side, at any school...with no regard paid to the color of their skin."

Eisenhower weighed these considerations against the potential for boosting Republican votes in the South. He hoped to build upon the four southern states he had garnered in 1952. The *Brown* decision, identified with Chief Justice Earl Warren, an Eisenhower appointee, posed a dilemma for a GOP southern strategy, but the President had reduced this liability by persistently declining to speak out forcefully for school integration. Furthermore, he refused to permit his party's 1956 platform to state more than an acceptance of the Court's desegregation ruling. At the same time, Ike set out actively to court white southern ballots, especially in the states of the upper South, where Democratic attachments were less solid.

These overtures certainly dismayed black voters, but they also had reason to question the Democrats' commitment to civil rights. Concerned with recovering their earlier presidential losses among whites in the South, the Democrats attempted to soft-pedal the civil rights issue. Their nominee, Adlai Stevenson, sounded very much like Eisenhower in offering his opinion that "only 'gradual' means would satisfactorily settle the school crisis and other problems affecting equal rights for all Americans." In fact, Roy Wilkins found little to choose between in either the Democratic or Republican platforms. Expressing displeasure with both, he sarcastically observed: "The Democratic plank smelled to heaven; the Republican plank just smelled." In addition, the prominence of obstructionist southern lawmakers in the Democratic party annoyed blacks. Referring to James Eastland, the powerful chairman of the Senate Judiciary Committee, Clarence Mitchell, the NAACP's Washington lobbyist, called the segregationist senator from Mississippi a "stinking albatross around the neck of the Democratic Party." This appraisal was reinforced by Congressman Powell, who urged black voters to repudiate "Eastlandism."

Bombarded by mixed signals emitted by both partisan camps, the black electorate stuck with the Democrats while displaying some movement toward the Republicans. Though Stevenson received between 60 and 65 percent of the black vote, Eisenhower's portion rose more than 5 percent from its 1952 level. In Harlem, his share climbed by 16.5 percent, and in Chicago it jumped 11 percent. In the South, where the Democratic party stood most strongly for white supremacy, blacks exhibited the sharpest reversal from past form. Eisenhower increased his share of the black vote by 25 percent, thereby allowing him to win Tennessee and Kentucky. In the urban South, where most enfranchised blacks resided, the GOP incumbent won a majority of nonwhite votes in Atlanta, New Orleans, Memphis, and Richmond. Whereas blacks might cast a mild civil rights protest vote by favoring Eisenhower, most stayed with the Democratic party, probably in recognition of the New Deal and Fair Deal economic programs from which they benefited. Nevertheless, Roy Wilkins conjectured that the "Republicans could have wrapped up at least 65 percent of the Negro vote...if they had early and emphatically backed the [*Brown*] decision."

Although Eisenhower succeeded once again without the majority of the black electorate behind him, his improved showing encouraged the Republican administration to proceed with pushing ahead its civil rights agenda. As usual, Eisenhower moved cautiously for both philosophical and political reasons—five southern states, one more than in 1952, supported his reelection bid. But he intended to obtain legislation from Congress, something neither Roosevelt nor Truman had been able to do.

His legislative program centered on expanding the suffrage and drawing blacks into the political mainstream. The chief of the Justice Department's Civil Rights Section, Arthur Caldwell, aptly reflected the President's viewpoint. "The heart of the whole problem of racial discrimination," he asserted, "lies in determined efforts to prevent the Southern Negroes from participation in local government through the use of the vote." In contrast with his attitude toward school desegregation, Eisenhower embraced the franchise as a proper sphere of federal intervention. He considered the right to vote as the foundation of constitutional republicanism, with specific guarantees for its protection from racial bias spelled out in the Fifteenth Amendment. Besides, the chief executive emphasized the suffrage because it suited his gradualistic approach toward racial equality. As blacks gained access to the ballot box, he reasoned, they could quietly and methodically remove the barriers that confronted them. Accordingly, this deliberate process would reduce tensions by allowing time for white southerners to change their hearts and minds slowly but surely. Furthermore, especially in light of the inroads the Republicans had made among the black electorate in 1956, the President and his political aides looked forward to bringing newly enfranchised blacks into GOP ranks.

The vehicle for the Eisenhower administration's designs became the Civil Rights Act of 1957. This measure had originated two years earlier after the attorney general, Herbert Brownell, became alarmed by rising violence against southern blacks. During 1955, two black Mississippians had been murdered while engaging in voter registration activities, and a fourteen-year-old youth, Emmett Till, was kidnapped and killed by two Mississippi whites for allegedly making an improper remark to a white woman. Along with Brownell, sympathetic White House aides worried about a "dangerous racial conflagration" brewing in the South. At the same time, the Montgomery bus boycott indicated the determination of black southerners to wage, albeit nonviolently, a prolonged struggle against Jim Crow. In April 1956, Brownell responded to the potential for disruption caused by black protest and white resistance by proposing to Congress a four-part civil rights measure. This omnibus bill created a Commission on Civil Rights, upgraded the Civil Rights Section into a division within the Justice Department, and empowered the attorney general to initiate civil proceedings to enforce school desegregation and voting rights suits.

The President hesitated to embrace his attorney general's broad proposal. His cabinet divided over the matter, FBI Director J. Edgar Hoover warned about Communist influence in the civil rights movement, and the chief executive appeared reluctant to offend his white southern allies. At first, he agreed to approve only the two least controversial provisions, those establishing a Civil Rights Commission and a Civil Rights Division. However, in the heat of his campaign battle for reelection in 1956, he adopted the entire package as his own. Passed by the House, the bill died in the Senate in the clutches of Senator Eastland's Judiciary Committee.

Following Eisenhower's presidential victory, the administration revived the civil rights measure with all four sections intact. That did not last for long. A combination of presidential moderation and Democratic party factionalism shaped the final version of the bill. Never enthusiastic about the item authorizing the Justice Department to seek court orders for school desegregation, the chief executive virtually withdrew his support for it. In one memorable instance, he publicly confessed that he "didn't completely understand" the proposal. In contrast, he did not waver in his support for the suffrage recommendation. "This was the overriding provision of the bill I wanted set down in law," he told a prominent southern senator, and added: "With his right to vote assured, the Negro could use it to help secure his other rights."

The President found a powerful ally on the Democratic side of the congressional aisle. Majority Leader Lyndon B. Johnson of Texas also wanted a measure restricted to the suffrage that avoided the pitfalls of the more emotionally charged issue of school desegregation. The Texas senator was at the stage of his career when he was trying to shape a national reputation to distinguish himself from his segregationist southern colleagues. Although opposed to civil rights legislation earlier in his tenure as a lawmaker, he was never a diehard segregationist and most recently had refused to sign the Southern Manifesto condemning the *Brown* decision. With presidential ambitions possibly in his mind, he was now ready to advance a step further.

The majority leader sought to fashion a bill that would be acceptable to both liberal and conservative wings of his party, one which northern Democrats could claim as a victory for civil rights and southerners could accept as least objectionable. This last concern was particularly important. Though Johnson hoped to enhance his image in the North he retained strong roots in and affection for the South. In fact, he wished to save the region from its worst instincts, as his legislative aide explained: "The South is now completely without allies. In this situation, the South can stave off disaster only by appealing to those men who wish to see a civil rights bill enacted but who are willing to listen to reason." In serving as a broker between the two opposing camps of congressional Democrats, Johnson would improve his own chances for higher office, build party unity, and strengthen the Democrats for competing in upcoming national elections.

Driven by Johnson's skillful parliamentary maneuvering, Congress produced a moderate civil rights law. After the House passed the original four-part version of the bill, the Johnson-led Senate sliced the school desegregation feature, leaving the sections on the Civil Rights Commission, Civil Rights Division, and voting rights litigation. With these features intact, Johnson made a gesture to keep his fellow southerners from waging a filibuster against them. He engineered passage of a proviso that required voting rights infractions in certain cases to be tried before a jury. Until this point, Eisenhower had approved of Johnson's handiwork, but he balked at adding the jury trial proviso. In this instance he joined liberals in both parties who believed that reliance upon southern white juries for enforcement would severely weaken the bill. In the end, Johnson forged an alliance of southerners, Democratic moderates from the North and West, and conservative Republicans to approve the disputed item. After adopting some modifications acceptable to the President, Congress passed the bill and Eisenhower signed it into law.

The first civil rights act in eighty-two years owed its passage to a variety of sources. The Eisenhower administration sponsored the original measure and then cooperated with Johnsonian Democrats to mold it into a right-to-vote law. Southerners refrained from sabotaging the proposal through a filibuster because they could live with a bill restricted to the franchise. Though liberal lawmakers and civil rights advocates expressed great disappointment in the final outcome for its omission of school desegregation, they still took some satisfaction in securing this "half-loaf." Senator Hubert Humphrey of Minnesota remarked to Roy Wilkins: "Roy, if there's one thing I have learned in politics, it's never to turn your back on a crumb." At the very least, the NAACP and its allies had a bill aimed at expanding black voter registration, which they regarded as a significant advance. Moreover, they had a legislative precedent to build upon for the future.

THE TUSKEGEE STRUGGLE

Ultimately the success or failure of the act would be judged by its performance at the local level. The struggle for enfranchisement in Macon County, Alabama, offers a look at the interrelationship between federal policy and grassroots social change. With a unique history and social structure of its own, the county nevertheless shared many of the same experiences as hundreds of localities throughout the black belt of the South.

Located in the southeastern portion of the state, about forty-five miles from Montgomery, the county had a black population exceeding 80 percent. Its county seat of Tuskegee also had a substantial black majority, many of whom came to teach or study at the famous institute founded by Booker T. Washington in the 1880s. Many of the town's residents were employed at the Veteran's Administration Hospital built in 1923, and some had arrived as soldiers for training at the Army air field during World War II. In the postwar era, the size of the black middle class in Tuskegee swelled, and blacks held a majority of the white-collar jobs in the town. The presence of a rising black bourgeoisie centered in Tuskegee, however, could not obscure the existence of widespread poverty, especially in the rural areas of the county. In 1960, 15 percent of Macon County blacks earned $6,000 or more, a stark contrast to the 64 percent with incomes of less than $3,000.

Since the days of Booker T. Washington, when whites had cooperated in establishing Tuskegee Institute, relations between the races had been paternalistic. Whites and blacks took pride in the school as a model for racial advancement as long as it developed within a rigidly segregated environment. Early in the twentieth century a leading white politician explained how things worked: "The very best representatives of the white race, from its beginnings until now, have controlled the destinies of the town... and by the grace of God, will continue that control to the end." This "model community" depended on accommodation on the part of blacks in return for civility from whites in order to maintain this customary power relationship. Yet the pattern of interaction inherited from Washington's era contained the seeds of its own destruction. Given the space to develop their own educational and economic institutions, to lift themselves up by their bootstraps as Washington had prescribed, black Tuskegeeans demanded the full citizenship rights to which their advancement into the middle class entitled them.

To leaders of this upwardly mobile group no badge of inferiority seemed more irksome than did their exclusion from the ballot. No one had worked harder to achieve the goal of black political enfranchisement than Charles G. Gomillion. A sociologist at the institute, he was one of less than a hundred blacks in Macon County to have registered to vote by 1939. Two years later, he converted the Tuskegee Men's Club into the Tuskegee Civic Association, admitted women, and embarked on a concerted campaign to rally blacks to challenge their treatment as second-class citizens. Gomillion based his approach on the concept of "civic democracy," by which he meant that all citizens, regardless of color, had "the opportunity to participate in societal affairs, and benefit from or enjoy public services, in keeping with their interests, abilities, and needs." Without the chance for color-blind political participation, Gomillion reasoned, blacks would continue to suffer from discrimination in the allocation of resources for essential municipal services, such as health and education. Until black Tuskegeeans exercised the power of the ballot, white officials could afford to ignore their requests for equal treatment.

However cordially white rulers behaved out of a sense of paternalism toward blacks, the whites did not intend to be held politically accountable to blacks. Instead, the whites had devised a series of hurdles to prevent blacks from registering to vote. In addition to the standard poll tax restriction, the three-person county election board administered a harsh literacy test to black applicants that whites did not have to endure. The panel used its discretion to fail blacks no matter how educated they were. If blacks pressed on and refused to give up, they often could not find the board in session to risk another try. When in operation the registrars processed black applications at a snail's pace and confined waiting blacks to cramped quarters, making it uncomfortable for them to show up at the courthouse. According to Alabama law, registrars could require applicants to bring a voucher to identify them as a proper resident of the area, and in Macon County the board insisted that a black could not vouch for more than two registrants per year.

In 1945, the Tuskegee Civic Association, in cooperation with the NAACP, decided to bring the election board to court. William P. Mitchell served as the plaintiff. An employee of the VA hospital and executive secretary of the Civic Association, Mitchell had been doggedly and unsuccessfully trying for years to register. The case dragged on for two years and became moot when local officials belatedly "discovered" that Mitchell had been registered in 1943, though he had never been informed of that fact. The situation improved for a stretch of time in the late 1940s after Herman Bentley, a newly appointed member of the registration board who held a populistic commitment to political democracy, broke from tradition and agreed to sign up nonwhites. After more than 400 blacks added their names to the rolls, the other two members of the board put a halt to further progress by boycotting meetings, thereby hamstringing the panel from functioning.

This upsurge in black political participation frightened white officials. In 1950, blacks, now 30 percent of the electorate, wielded their balance of power to defeat the incumbent sheriff and replace him with a more sympathetic white candidate. The landmark *Brown* decision in 1954 and the bus boycott in nearby Montgomery the following year highlighted the threat that rising black activism posed for white supremacy. In response, Macon County officials fought back. Led by State Senator Samuel M. Engelhardt, Jr., they slowed down black registration by removing Bentley from the board and, in 1957, devised a scheme to eliminate nearly all black voters from Tuskegee. Through an imaginative redrawing of the town's boundary lines, the state legislature carved black neighborhoods out of the city, leaving the black electorate disfranchised in municipal elections and not plentiful enough to exert much influence in the county.

Whatever illusions middle-class blacks in Tuskegee may have retained about the fairness of paternalistic whites operating within a segregated system were shattered by the flagrant gerrymander. In response, the Civic Association organized a boycott—a selective buying campaign—against local white merchants. Though lay political leaders like Gomillion led the protest, ministers played an important role in mobilizing masses of blacks who regularly attended church but remained outside the sphere of Civic Association influence. The protest against the gerrymander succeeded in connecting middle-class blacks in the town with impoverished rural blacks in the surrounding county. Paralleling the situation in Montgomery, the Tuskegee boycott welded a community into a palpable force for political change. Years of voter education and litigation by the Civic Association had paved the way, but the experience of collective action rallied ordinary individuals as well as college teachers and professionals into agents of political participation. Gomillion's civic democracy came alive, as mass meetings provided an inspirational forum to build morale, share information, and maintain discipline.

Also like its Montgomery counterpart, the boycott did not force whites to capitulate to black demands; the federal government did. In 1960, the Supreme Court finally declared the gerrymander unconstitutional and restored black voters to the city's political boundaries. In *Gomillion v. Lightfoot*, Justice Felix Frankfurter denounced Alabama's peculiar "essay in geometry and geography" that impaired black voting rights under the guise "of the realignment of political subdivisions."

Macon County blacks had learned at firsthand that protest had to be reinforced by federal intervention in order to achieve equal citizenship rights. Besides the gerrymander battle, the Tuskegee Civic Association was directly involved with obtaining national legislation to erase suffrage discrimination. During the debate over the 1957 Civil Rights Act, Charles Gomillion and William Mitchell traveled to Washington to tell their stories of voter discrimination by county registrars. New York City's *Amsterdam News*, a black newspaper, declared that "nothing could throw the spotlight so brilliantly on the shame and hypocrisy of southern legislators than the fight the Negroes are now waging in Macon County . . . for constitutional rights to register and vote." Following passage of the 1957 law, Senator Paul Douglas, a liberal Democrat from Illinois, advised Mitchell to "continue to assemble the facts that will help to make the case for the next forward steps."

This Mitchell did by turning over to the Justice Department the voluminous records of suffrage bias he had carefully compiled over the years. As a result, one of the first suits the federal government initiated under the 1957 law pertained to Macon County. However, the Civic Association suffered a setback in 1959, when a federal judge ruled that the statute did not apply to the situation at hand. Because the members of the registration board had resigned, the government had no party to sue.

In the meantime, county residents themselves provided dramatic testimony of the trouble they experienced in attempting to exercise their political rights. In December 1958, the United States Commission on Civil Rights convened public hearings in Montgomery to investigate franchise abuses. The testimony it heard, which was recorded for broadcast on national television news pro-

grams, came across as a vivid morality play. Blacks stepped forward
to testify, with both passion and dignity, to the affronts they had
suffered in trying to accomplish what should have been a simple act
of signing up to vote. Instead, property owners, taxpayers, veterans, college graduates, and VA hospital employees explained how
the members of the registration board frequently went into hiding,
how they engaged in work slowdowns, and how they failed applicants on the literacy tests without ever notifying them of the reason. "I have come up to the other requirements to make myself a
citizen," a black Macon County farmer declared. "I would like to be
a registered voter; they ought to give that to me. It's like I want to
become a part of the government activity."

In contrast, the civil rights commissioners and television view-
ers saw local officials refuse either to testify under oath about their
behavior or to furnish suffrage files that had been subpoenaed. One
of Macon County's registrars, Grady Rogers, invoked his constitutional right against self-incrimination and further denied that the
commission had the authority to probe into his activities. Faced
with this lack of cooperation, the panel obtained the vital information through a court order. The records its investigators subsequently examined convinced the commissioners that the federal
government would once again have to intervene to correct widespread voting discrimination. Released in 1959, the agency's report
catalogued the obstructionist practices manipulated by Alabama
registrars against black applicants and recommended that Congress
empower the President to dispatch federal registrars to enroll qualified black voters in the South.

Though civil rights advocates like William Mitchell wholeheart-
edly endorsed such a proposal, national lawmakers refrained from going so far. The alliance between the Eisenhower administration and
Johnson Democrats that had succeeded in 1957 triumphed again three
years later. Despite objections from liberals in both parties and from
civil rights lobbyists, in 1960 Congress passed a voting rights law that
retained judicial supervision over the suffrage process. Instead of federal registrars, legislators authorized court-appointed referees to resolve difficult franchise cases. This procedure was substantially weaker
than the one proposed by the Civil Rights Commission because it continued to rely on litigation that had proven to be slow and cumbersome in furnishing a cure for chronic discrimination.

Nevertheless, a provision of the new law immediately benefited Macon County blacks. Allowed to sue state officials when a county registration board ceased functioning, the Justice Department succeeded in obtaining a federal court injunction against prevailing voter bias in the county. In 1961, Judge Frank M. Johnson of Alabama, whose rulings on race made him one of the most liberal federal judges in the South, reviewed the copious documents gathered by the Justice Department in cooperation with the Tuskegee Civic Association and had no trouble finding ample evidence of bias. Consequently, he ordered the registration board to cease its discriminatory practices and to take positive action to speed up its work schedule, enroll qualified applicants, and report back to him on a regular basis. Within a short period, black registration more than doubled to nearly 2,500. After so many years of determination and frustration, William Mitchell was elated. "We had not even thought of such an all-inclusive decree," he jubilantly remarked.

A MEASURE OF PROGRESS

The struggle to obtain the ballot, the prerequisite for blacks to compete in the electoral system, moved forward with some success during the 1950s. Compared with the more emotional issue of school desegregation, reenfranchisement drew greater support from northern politicians and less opposition from southern officials. By lining up behind two voting rights measures in 1957 and 1960, the Eisenhower administration proferred bipartisan legitimacy to the civil rights agenda initiated by President Truman. Clearly on the defensive, white southerners, particularly in the rural black belt and in some major cities, continued to probe how they could keep black political participation to a minimum. In fact the laws were too weak to overcome all the difficulties that remained, but they did establish a crucial precedent for renewed federal intervention against racial discrimination in the South. Eisenhower also set a pattern that would guide his successors: federal intrusion in state control over racial matters would proceed cautiously, with cooperation rather than coercion the standard. Intervention did not necessarily mean invasion, and only as a last resort, as Eisenhower did in Little Rock in 1957, would a president send troops into the South to enforce federal court rulings.[2] Voluntarism backed up by litigation and administrative pressure were the preferred techniques.

For civil rights activists this approach dictated a strategy that increasingly emphasized confrontation. Only by challenging racism directly could they produce the kind of disorder and crisis that would bring federal intervention on their side. Events had already demonstrated that the civil rights movement needed to operate along two tracks—the national and the local. Without pressure from below neither the stimulus for change nor the group solidarity to propel the struggle would exist. Without assistance from above, the weapons to shatter entrenched local resistance would be missing. Blacks in Montgomery and in Macon County had shown the truth of this proposition. Combining mass action, litigation, and lobbying, African-Americans were defining their goals, mobilizing their communities around them, and drawing in national allies on their side.

[2]After a federal court decreed the desegregation of Little Rock's Central High School, Governor Orval Faubus blocked the order by deploying the Arkansas National Guard to keep out nine black students. Having initially remarked that he could foresee no circumstances that would compel him to send military forces into the South, President Eisenhower changed his mind in order to uphold the primacy of national authority. Consequently, he federalized the National Guard and dispatched paratroopers from the 101st Airborne Division to implement the law and preserve order while the students attended the school.

Chapter 3

Surging Protest, Shifting Politics

The initial ferment of black discontent in the 1950s left white supremacy challenged but unbroken. Although innovative boycotts succeeded in rallying black communities against segregation and disfranchisement, they failed to crack Jim Crow or destroy the virtual white monopoly over public affairs. Along with litigation and lobbying, sustained protests in Montgomery, Tuskegee, and scattered cities throughout the South managed to engage the federal government against racial discrimination. However, the combination of local black activism and national involvement had not yet created sufficient force to overcome massive white resistance to extending political power to blacks. Despite passage of the 1957 Civil Rights Act, by the end of the decade slightly less than three in ten adult black southerners had qualified to participate in the electoral process.

CRUSADERS FOR CITIZENSHIP

The bus boycott struggle had produced a new and potentially powerful institutional weapon to gain first-class citizenship. In 1957, the Southern Christian Leadership Conference (SCLC) was formed to coordinate local black protest movements that emerged to challenge racial bias in the South. Black ministers directed the organization. In the past the clergy had often provided conservative racial leadership, stressing otherworldly rewards for those who patiently suffered their fate in the here and now. Following World War II, a new breed of preacher arose, emphasizing Christian virtues of brotherhood, equality, and justice as principles to be attained on earth as well as in heaven. From pulpits in Montgomery, Birmingham, and Mobile, Alabama; Baton Rouge, Louisiana; Atlanta, Georgia; Nashville, Tennessee; and Tallahassee, Florida, these ministers activated the machinery of the black church and the language and symbols of the Bible to lead their congregants in battles against racism.

In effect, the SCLC functioned as "the political arm of the black church." It attempted to supplement the traditional civil rights work of the NAACP with its own brand of activism. Unlike the older group which preferred to achieve political change through legislation and the courts, the SCLC focused on direct action techniques to obtain that goal. Drawing upon their recent experiences in attacking Jim Crow, the founders of the conference chose nonviolent resistance as their primary means of combating white supremacy. This meant that the black masses would be mobilized in their local communities to confront directly the sources of their oppression. More than any other institution, the black church could provide an independent base from which to stage demonstrations and furnish the moral and social support necessary to nurture collective action. Thus, the SCLC fused religious traditionalism—the cultural heritage of the church—with political progressivism.

Though many strong-willed and independent-minded ministers created the SCLC, Martin Luther King, Jr., stood out to lead it. His compelling oratory and his courage in the face of violence during the Montgomery bus boycott thrust him into the national limelight. He had a special ability to give voice to the immediate concerns of ordinary black folks and to place their goals and aspirations within a larger national and international movement for freedom. As one of those people who sat in the mass meetings in Montgomery and heard him preach later recalled: "I mean, he was talking about what we oughta have, and what we oughta be, and what the situation oughta be in the South, and what kind of country we oughta live in." Along with many others, that listener found inspiration in King's powerful message to his audience: "If you will protest courageously, and yet with dignity and Christian love, when the history books are written in future generations, the historians will have to pause and say, 'There lived a great people—a black people—who injected new meaning and dignity into the veins of civilization.'"

King's political strategy developed from both secular and religious influences. An intellectual with a doctorate in theology from

Boston University, King studied the philosophical tracts of Henry David Thoreau, Karl Marx, Friedrich Hegel, and Reinhold Niebuhr, among others, which provided him with a framework for action in which struggle was necessary to liberate oppressed people everywhere. From Mahatma Gandhi, whose ideas he became better acquainted with through advisers such as Bayard Rustin, Dr. King adopted the philosophy of nonviolent resistance to evil. But, perhaps above all, he owed his personal resolve to challenge racism, actively yet peacefully, to Jesus of Nazareth. In his darkest moments of despair, King turned to Christ for strength in confronting the hardships of racial tyranny. In late January 1956, his arrest and the receipt of numerous threats against his life left him sorely troubled. One evening, in the quiet of the midnight hour in the kitchen of his home, he heard the voice of Jesus consoling him: "Martin Luther, stand up for righteousness. Stand up for justice. Stand up for truth. And lo I will be with you, even unto the end of the world."

This total commitment to nonviolence as a religious and ethical principle did not make King politically softminded. Though often speaking about converting the hearts and minds of white supremacists through the example of Christian love, suffering, and forgiveness on the part of blacks, he always understood that this transformation would not occur merely by persuading whites voluntarily to abandon discriminatory practices. Instead, he backed up his moralistic appeals with practical acts of coercion. Ecumenical arguments alone would never lead blacks to freedom; the application of power was essential to changing racist behavior and the underlying institutions that supported it. "When King spoke of 'converting' the oppressor," Adam Fairclough has argued, "he was thinking of a long-term historical process rather than an immediate personal response."

King and the SCLC aimed one of their first efforts at exerting political pressure on the Eisenhower administration and Congress to pass the Civil Rights Act of 1957. Joined by A. Philip Randolph, the architect of the 1941 March on Washington Movement, and Roy Wilkins of the NAACP, King convened a "Prayer Pilgrimage" in the nation's capital "to give thanks for progress to-date, and pray for wiping out the evils that still beset us." For months the SCLC chief had pressed Eisenhower to condemn racist violence against blacks in a major address delivered in a southern city. Repeatedly rebuffed, King informed him that if "you, our President, cannot come South, we shall have to lead our people to you." On May 17, 1957, in commemoration of the third anniversary of the *Brown* decision, nearly 30,000 people gathered to hear King call for the passage of legislation guaranteeing the ballot, which, he declared, would clear the way for the attainment of the other basic rights blacks sought.

Though the convocation came off smoothly, it took final shape in a manner different from that originally conceived. While King prepared to practice the new politics of mass mobilization, Adam Clayton Powell and leaders of the NAACP implemented the old-fashioned politics of power brokerage. The close relationship between the New York City congressman and the Eisenhower administration paid off for the President. Powell, as well as Roy Wilkins, opposed the march as a means of applying pressure on the chief executive. Rather, they favored the protesters directing their full force at Congress, urging it to pass civil rights legislation. Along with NAACP representatives, Powell succeeded in steering attention away from the President as a target of the demonstration. Administration officials breathed a sigh of relief that they had avoided "the damaging effects of a spectacular effort designed to criticize the president." Consequently, in his address Dr. King denounced the lawmakers of both parties who "so often have a high blood pressure of words and an anemia of deeds."

At this early stage in his career, King had limited effectiveness as a national political leader. However significant the Washington demonstration may have been in rallying tens of thousands of blacks in protest against racial discrimination, it had little impact on the eventual enactment of the civil rights bill. Furthermore, it had no immediate impact in persuading the President to make even a symbolic gesture that would recognize the legitimate concerns of civil rights advocates. In June 1957, the Reverend King managed to meet with Vice-President Richard Nixon, who affirmed his personal support for civil rights; nevertheless, the President himself refused to confer with black leaders despite their repeated requests for an appointment. Not until June 1958 did the chief executive hold his first and only conference with a delegation of black leaders. On this occasion they discussed voting rights enforcement, but reached no agreement on the need for stronger implementation by the federal government of the 1957 statute.

By then, King and the SCLC had launched their own project within the South designed to register the majority of disfranchised blacks. They hoped to build upon the momentum of the bus boycotts and galvanize the black electorate as an active force in regional and national politics. "The time has come to broaden the struggle for Negroes to register and vote," the SCLC declared, "for the simple reason that until this happens, we cannot really influence the legislative branch of government." In the past the NAACP, civic leagues, unions, and the churches had conducted voter registration drives. The SCLC sought to link these traditional efforts with its emerging direct action program. The passage of the 1957 Civil Rights Act offered the prospect of federal judicial support for the suffrage, but King believed the effectiveness of the remedy would "depend in large degree upon programs of sustained mass movement on the part of Negroes." According to the SCLC's president: "History has demonstrated that inadequate legislation supported by mass action can accomplish more than adequate legislation which remains unenforced for lack of a determined mass movement."

On February 12, 1958, the birthday of Abraham Lincoln, the Southern Conference embarked on a project to help emancipate blacks from the "strong fear and deep antipathy toward having anything to do with politics." The Crusade for Citizenship hoped by 1960 to enroll an additional 3 million black southerners as voters, doubling the number already on the books. Toward that goal, it planned to coordinate mass registration campaigns through community-based civic organizations and churches. Workshops, clinics, and rallies were conducted in cities throughout the South— Montgomery, Birmingham, Memphis, Atlanta—where SCLC had strong affiliates. Not only would prospective registrants learn how to satisfy suffrage requirements, but they also would learn about the strategy of direct action that SCLC espoused. At the very least, the Crusade intended to gather specific complaints of voter discrimination and turn them over to the federal government.

These ambitious designs went largely unrealized. As a fledgling organization the SCLC lacked the funds and experience to implement such a massive enterprise. Budgeted for $200,000, the Crusade failed to raise more than a quarter of that amount. Inadequate finances placed an economic burden on the Crusade's overworked staff. Ella Baker, who nearly single-handedly managed the operation, received little support from the agency's ministerial leaders.

Baker did not lack the talent or experience to perform the job, for she had served as field secretary and director of branches for the NAACP. However, she was the lone female on the SCLC's administrative staff, and she suffered from the slights of paternalistic male preachers, who did not view women as equal partners and whose powerful egos made it difficult to impose strict organizational discipline upon them.

Even without these internal problems, the SCLC encountered a nearly insurmountable task. The rise of massive white resistance following the *Brown* ruling, though directed mainly at halting school desegregation, thwarted civil rights activities of any kind. Southern officials employed literacy tests and other restrictive registration methods to retard black electoral participation. In the face of suffrage discrimination and in a hostile environment that punitively discouraged minority voting, the SCLC had little chance of reaching most disfranchised southern blacks. Instead of the 3 million new voters that the SCLC targeted, only 160,000 blacks signed up to vote between 1958 and 1960. Still, the group did compile a list of suffrage grievances and presented them for investigation to the United States Civil Rights Commission and the Justice Department.

In addition, the SCLC received scant help from the NAACP. Under assault by southern state governments, the association's activities were suspended or severely limited in several areas. Besides, the NAACP viewed the formation of the Southern Conference with misgivings, fearful of the competition it would provide for funds and publicity. During this same period the National Association, despite its hardships, inaugurated a campaign to register 3 million southern blacks. It, too, fell far short of the mark. Neither conventional registration drives nor those linked to direct action worked against the firm obstacles erected by the white South. Beset by serious internal and external difficulties, by 1960 King and the SCLC had failed to rally the black masses behind the ballot.

With the efforts of the SCLC and the NAACP stymied, the movement for first-class citizenship needed a boost. Blacks had barely penetrated the wall of white supremacy, and fresh troops and ideas were needed to scale over it. The federal government had provided some welcome judicial and legislative relief, but Washington expected southern blacks and whites to resolve their problems largely at the local level.

Civil rights leaders recognized that they did not have sufficient power to win by themselves; yet, at the same time, they understood the importance of blacks joining together to fight for their own freedom. The adoption of boycotts as a response to discrimination had evidenced this. A useful means of forging collective action, they nevertheless possessed limited political advantages. A boycott had the effect of withdrawing blacks from participation in economic and civic life until white businesses or local officials capitulated. Civil rights proponents needed additional techniques that would actively engage blacks in directly confronting white racist practices, particularly those from which they were excluded. Through such encounters they would dramatically expose the source of their oppression, bring the evil to the surface, and exert moral pressure to eradicate it. In the process, people would have to break laws they considered unjust and go to jail for their convictions. By doing so they would ultimately transform themselves, their communities, and their nation.

On February 1, 1960, southern blacks took a critical step in forging those new tactics. Students in Greensboro, North Carolina, shook up the freedom struggle, provided a powerful nonviolent weapon, and furnished fresh, youthful people to deploy it. By sitting down at a segregated Woolworth's lunch counter that would not accommodate them and demanding equal service, four black undergraduates at North Carolina Agricultural and Technical State University energized a sagging protest movement. Within two months their action sparked similar demonstrations in some 60 cities throughout the South, involving thousands of high school and college students, and by year's end protests had sprouted in over 200 cities. What King's Crusade for Citizenship had failed to do for direct action over a span of two years was achieved virtually overnight. These sit-ins spawned wade-ins, kneel-ins, stand-ins, and freedom rides, all designed to bring together ordinary folks to challenge racial oppression head on. The result of these dynamic efforts did not always lead immediately to integration or equality; however, they did help liberate those who participated in them. "I felt as though I had gained my manhood," Franklin McCain, one of the original Greensboro four, declared, "not only gained it, but had developed quite a respect for it."

Many cities throughout the South proved ready to be ignited by these young activists. In Greensboro, for example, the roots of protest were sunk deep. The NAACP had maintained an active chapter since the 1930s, and in 1943, Ella Baker had established an NAACP Youth Group in the city, an organization two of the original sit-in demonstrators subsequently joined. The local black high school also served as a training ground for black insurgency. Several teachers inspired their students to think about the history and culture of African-Americans as a struggle for freedom and to relate their own lives to that quest. "I had to tell youngsters," one instructor remarked, "that the way you find things need not happen....I don't care if they push and shove you, you must not accept [discrimination]." This lesson received positive reinforcement from the pastor of the Shiloh Baptist Church, which some of the students attended. During the 1950s, their minister had been active in civil rights affairs and only recently had succeeded in leading a drive to double the membership of the NAACP chapter.

Furthermore, the young protesters lived in a city in which blacks had gained a measure of access to the electoral process. The heightened political assertiveness that blacks displayed after World War II surfaced early in Greensboro. In 1949, two black candidates for the city council made it through the primary, only to lose in the general election. Following this contest the Greensboro Citizens Association, a black civic league interested in improving municipal services in their community, mounted a voter registration drive that led to the election of its president, Dr. William Hampton, to the council in 1951. Although Hampton ran reasonably well in white precincts, he scored much more impressively in black districts. In unprecedented fashion, black voters united as a solid bloc behind a candidate of their own race. In previous years they had split their votes among various white contestants, but, as one black politician later explained, "You don't help a black by putting his name on the ticket and then voting for six white candidates because you are scattering your vote."

This modest electoral success did not fulfill rising black expectations. During the 1950s, the single council seat occupied by a black as well as the selection of a black to the school board did not alter traditional patterns of racial inequality. Instead, what William H. Chafe has termed "sophisticated American racism" prevailed in Greensboro. Following the *Brown* decision, white leaders permitted only token desegregation of the schools, closed recreational facilities rather than integrated them, and steered black college grad-

uates away from white-collar employment. They did so with
civility, not brutality, thereby projecting an image of progress. Outnumbered by whites, the lone blacks on the council and the school
board had no leverage to reverse this course. Ironically, their very
presence on these panels served to legitimize the discriminatory
policies the majority adopted. Thus, the Woolworth sit-in represented both continuity with the black community's past and a significant departure from the electoral and judicial strategies that had
stalled in obtaining racial justice.

The creative energy of the sit-ins flowed into the formation of
the Student Nonviolent Coordinating Committee (SNCC). Con-
vening in Raleigh, North Carolina, in April 1960, recent protest
veterans sought to establish an organization that offered new political leadership. James Lawson, who had been active in the development of the Nashville sit-in movement, expressed the participants' disdain for "middle-class conventional, half-way efforts to
deal with radical social evil." They wanted to replace the NAACP's
emphasis on litigation with the nonviolent power of "a people no
longer the victims of racial evil who can act in a disciplined manner
to implement the Constitution." Toward this end, SNCC founders
shared the vision of an interracial beloved community preached by
Dr. King and SCLC. Indeed, Lawson and others had been inspired
by the Montgomery bus boycott and the exercise of grassroots direct action.

Yet if the iconoclastic committee rejected the tactics of the
NAACP, it also eschewed any formal affiliation with the SCLC. Part of
this independence resulted from a need for self-preservation, a desire not to become absorbed within another organization, and a
preference for retaining maximum flexibility of action. But the
choice of autonomy reflected an even deeper wish to break with the
style of leadership exhibited by Dr. King. Though SNCC's philosophy of nonviolent civil disobedience dovetailed with the SCLC's,
the student group had doubts about organizing a mass movement
around a single charismatic personality. It adopted instead a decentralized organizational structure, stressed group decision-making,
and encouraged the emergence of leadership from indigenous black
communities. In effect, SNCC echoed the criticism of Ella Baker,
who had become disenchanted with the SCLC. Miss Baker, as she
was affectionately called, argued that a "prophetic leader" like Dr.
King ultimately stifled the opportunity for people to tailor unique
programs to suit their own particular needs.

The perspectives that separated the two groups did not deter the students from cooperating with Dr. King. The SCLC president had earned a national reputation for his civil rights activities, which gave him contacts with important political figures that they did not have. By the autumn of 1960, King had moved from Montgomery to his birthplace of Atlanta, where he copastored the Ebenezer Baptist Church with his father. In the "City Too Busy to Hate," as the mayor referred to it, black students from Morehouse College, King's alma mater, initiated sit-in demonstrations to desegregate downtown eating establishments. Moderate white and black leaders, including "Daddy" King, disapproved of the continuing protests, but the demonstrators persuaded a reluctant Martin, Jr., to join them. In doing so not only did they receive prominent help for their local struggle, but they also set off a chain of events that reverberated nationally and connected black politics with the White House.

On October 19, 1960, Dr. King joined some seventy-five demonstrators in seeking to integrate the cafeteria at Rich's Department Store, where blacks were welcome to spend their money but not to eat. The protest ended in the arrest of King and the others for trespassing. Detained for several days, all but Dr. King were finally released. Earlier in the year, the Atlanta minister had been arrested for driving without a valid Georgia license, issued a fine, and placed on one year's probation. As a result of his current arrest, a county judge ruled that King had violated his probation and sentenced him to four months of hard labor at the state prison.

Although the harsh sentence was not anticipated, the arrest fitted in with a larger plan the student demonstrators had formulated. The incident came in the midst of the presidential contest between John F. Kennedy and Richard M. Nixon, an opportunity the civil rights forces hoped to exploit. One of the organizers of the protest at Rich's recalled that it was deliberately timed "so as to influence the election." The student activists expected that King's arrest "would create enough of a national uproar in the black community," and they intended to put the candidates on the spot concerning their positions on civil rights. "I did not have a preference, believe it or not, between Nixon or Kennedy," recalled Lonnie King, a student activist who was not related to the imprisoned minister.

This neutral stand was hardly surprising. As a Republican member of Congress, senator, and vice-president, Richard Nixon had antagonized liberals on the issue of anti-Communism, but on racial matters he backed reform. One of the few top-level officials in the Eisenhower administration to endorse the *Brown* ruling, the vice-president strongly supported the 1957 civil rights legislation and used his position as presiding officer of the Senate to assist in passage of the measure. Nixon also chaired the President's Committee on Government Contracts, which investigated charges of racial discrimination in federally related employment and sponsored education campaigns to further equal opportunity. He had conferred with Martin Luther King on a couple of occasions during the 1950s and earned praise from the civil rights leader for making "a real impression on the Negro."

As might be expected of a Democratic senator from Massachusetts, John F. Kennedy had routinely supported proposals to relieve the plight of blacks in the South. He voted for civil rights legislation in 1957 and 1960, and spoke out firmly for acceptance of the *Brown* verdict. Yet, Carl Brauer has noted, Senator Kennedy approached civil rights issues as "a moderate by conviction and design." Unwilling to address racial matters as a category of special concern, he considered them an expression of larger social and economic problems. The senator acted more for political reasons than out of any moral obligation and did just enough to court the black electorate in his home state. At the same time, he spent much effort in wooing the white South. In 1957, Kennedy voted for Lyndon Johnson's jury trial amendment to the civil rights bill, a deed that angered liberals and delighted southern conservatives. His pragmatic approach to civil rights questions won for his presidential bid the early endorsement of Governor John Patterson of Alabama, who thought Kennedy "would probably be more understanding of our situation down here" than any other possible Democratic candidate.

That same practical outlook guided Kennedy in his pursuit of the presidency. As the Democratic nominee he selected Harris Wofford, a white attorney with the U.S. Commission on Civil Rights, and several prominent blacks for his campaign staff. One of them, Louis Martin, the editor of the *Chicago Defender*, convinced the opportunistic Congressman Adam Clayton Powell, who had flirted with the Eisenhower administration for the preceding half-dozen years, to join the Kennedy bandwagon. Along with the perennial Democratic stalwart, Congressman William Dawson of Chicago, Powell very effectively spoke in northern black ghettos on Kennedy's behalf. Wofford also introduced Kennedy to Dr. King, who came away from the meeting with a favorable impression of the Democratic aspirant. Still, King considered Nixon a loyal supporter of civil rights, and he declined to endorse either candidate.

The influential black presence in the Democratic camp partially offset Kennedy's choice for vice-president, Senator Lyndon B. Johnson of Texas. Apparently chosen to appeal to Democratic voters in the South, this grandson of a former Civil War Confederate received a low rating among party liberals and blacks for weakening civil rights legislation. Nevertheless, while Johnson soothed southern audiences with his down-home stories, he also reassured blacks "that I have done my dead best to make progress in the field of civil rights."

Nixon followed a similar route. Like Kennedy he ran on a strong civil rights platform that pledged firm executive leadership, promised new legislation to combat suffrage and employment discrimination, backed legal and technical assistance for school desegregation, and upheld the right of sit-in demonstrators to assemble peacefully. Also like his Democratic rival, Nixon labored to improve his standing with southern whites. The GOP nominee campaigned vigorously in the deep South, where he counseled gradualism and urged justice for blacks not as a moral imperative but as a means of undermining Communist exploitation of racial tensions for propaganda purposes. Furthermore, by not appearing in Harlem, as Eisenhower had done, and by appointing few blacks to important and visible roles in his campaign, Nixon avoided offending the white South. One prominent black who joined Nixon's staff, E. Frederic Morrow, an assistant in the Eisenhower White House, bitterly complained that he did not receive any specific assignment or support.

The political balancing acts of both candidates suffered a severe jolt from the arrest of Dr. King in October, just as the student activists had hoped. The nominees reacted very differently, however. Treading lightly at first, Senator Kennedy decided to work for King's release on bail through Georgia's Democratic governor, Ernest Vandiver, and his state campaign director, Griffin Bell. When negotiations stalled, Harris Wofford and Louis Martin came up with the idea of having Kennedy telephone a worried Mrs. Coretta King to express his concern for her husband's safety. This sympathetic gesture did not free the celebrated prisoner, and the candidate's brother and closest adviser, Robert Kennedy, wrestled with the thorny question of whether to take additional action. Initially he had been angry with Wofford for his attempt to involve the senator directly in the King affair, fearing an adverse southern white response. Also concerned with black ballots, he quickly changed his mind, interceded with the Democratic county judge presiding over the case, and obtained King's release on bail. "I called him," Robert Kennedy told Wofford, "because it made me so damned angry to think of that bastard sentencing a citizen to... hard labor for a minor traffic offense and screwing up my brother's campaign."

In contrast, Nixon remained publicly silent during this episode. Privately he believed that King had received a "bum rap," but that it would be improper for him as a lawyer to communicate with the judge. Perhaps he was more interested in political calculations. Nixon refused to heed the plea of a prominent black Republican in Atlanta to make a statement in support of King, telling him "He [Nixon] would lose some black votes, but he'd gain white votes." Still, seeking to walk a fine tightrope, he had the Justice Department draft a statement for President Eisenhower's release, calling the sentencing of King "fundamentally unjust" and directing the attorney general "to take all proper steps" to free him. When Eisenhower declined to authorize such a statement, Nixon lost the opportunity to neutralize Kennedy's efforts on King's behalf.

The Democrats turned the King incident to their advantage. The civil rights leader commended Senator Kennedy for his courage and remarked: "There are moments when the politically expedient can be morally wise." With less than two weeks before the election, the Kennedy campaign distributed nearly 2 million pamphlets, entitled *The Case of Martin Luther King*, in black communities throughout the nation, publicizing the matter. One of the endorsements Kennedy obtained came from Dr. King's father, a Baptist minister who originally had intended to vote against the Democrat because of his Catholic religion. "I've got all my votes and I've got a suitcase and I'm going to take them up there and dump them in his lap," the Reverend King, Sr., declared. Likewise, the younger King's closest friend and colleague in the SCLC, Ralph David Abernathy, remarked: "I earnestly and sincerely feel it is time for all of us to take off our Nixon buttons."

Approximately 68 percent of the black electorate agreed by casting their votes for Kennedy. The Democrats won by less than

120,000 popular votes, three-tenths of 1 percent of the total, and by eighty-four electoral votes. This razor-thin victory highlighted the significant role played by African-Americans in determining the outcome. In several key northern states rich with electoral votes—Illinois, Michigan, New Jersey, and Pennsylvania—black votes made the difference. In the South, blacks helped put the Kennedy-Johnson ticket over the top in South Carolina and Texas. Nixon carried only three states in the region, Florida, Tennessee, and Virginia, two fewer than Eisenhower did in 1956. Nationwide, Kennedy needed strong black support to offset the 52 percent majority Nixon rolled up among white voters. Had not the senator succeeded in regaining 7 percent of the black vote that went to Eisenhower four years before, Richard Nixon would have entered the White House in 1960.

This key segment of the electorate returned to the Democratic party for a variety of reasons. With the popular Eisenhower out of the race, the proportion of black Democratic support again reached its previously high 1952 level. Because Kennedy's civil rights record going into the contest appeared no stronger than Nixon's, the Democratic nominee's intervention in the King controversy attracted blacks who were inclined to vote Republican or, at the very least, retained the loyalty of black Protestants who opposed Kennedy on religious grounds. But the King incident does not explain the entire matter. In King's home city of Atlanta, Nixon outpolled Kennedy in black districts, though his 54 percent marked a slip of twelve points from Eisenhower's share in 1956. Just as important as civil rights, economic considerations steered blacks into the Democratic column. Kennedy benefited from the recession in the last year of the Eisenhower term. The recession hurt economically vulnerable blacks and strengthened their attachment to the Democratic Party, which promised financial relief from hard times.

THE KENNEDY ADMINISTRATION AND CIVIL RIGHTS

As in 1948, black ballots contributed significantly in electing a Democratic President, but the prospective rewards remained unclear. Kennedy had delivered ambiguous messages during his campaign. His gesture toward King, his appointment of black advisers, and his pledge to exert strong executive action to remove discrimination in such areas as housing suggested that a great leap foward was about to take place on the civil rights front in Washington. Yet Kennedy had also led the white South to believe that, as Carl Brauer has noted, "he would not favor a reinstitution of Reconstruction." These soothing words had aided Kennedy in securing 50.5 percent of the popular vote in the South, a rise of nearly three points from Stevenson's total in 1956. In all likelihood Kennedy would have done even better in this bastion of Protestant fundamentalism had his religion, much more than civil rights, not been an issue. Furthermore, even if President Kennedy desired to push for new legislation to combat racial bigotry, he faced a Congress in which southern Democrats wielded disproportionate influence through their control of potent committees, their deployment of the Senate filibuster, and their alliance with conservative Republicans to thwart reform measures.

Caught between rising black electoral strength and entrenched southern white political power, President Kennedy ventured circumspectly in the field of civil rights. Like his predecessor, the President opted to concentrate on extending the suffrage to blacks and drawing them into the political mainstream. Where African-Americans "are given their rights to participate in the political process," Kennedy asserted, "they do it as free individuals...giving their considered judgment on what is best for their country and what is best for themselves and what is best for the cause of freedom." In the tradition of Eisenhower he placed his faith in the courts to ensure equal voting rights for southern blacks. However, Kennedy instructed the Department of Justice, headed by his brother, Robert, to enforce the Civil Rights Acts of 1957 and 1960 more vigorously than had the previous Eisenhower administration. Combining executive and judicial action, the Kennedys hoped to satisfy civil rights proponents without unduly antagonizing southern lawmakers in Congress.

This approach was threatened by rising civil rights militancy in 1961. In May, "freedom rides," aiming to desegregate interstate bus terminal facilities, encountered vicious attacks by southern white extremists. Integrated buses carrying passengers recruited by CORE and SNCC were assaulted and burned outside of Birmingham, Alabama. In Montgomery, a white mob beat the riders as they departed from their bus. Later a bloodthirsty crowd surrounded a church and menaced its congregants gathered inside to hear Martin Luther King voice his support for the protesters. Despite the fact that the Supreme Court had outlawed segregated terminals serving interstate travelers, the Kennedy administration tried to defuse this crisis by urging a cooling-off period during which the civil rights forces would suspend their offensive against Jim Crow. The White House desperately wanted to avoid sending in federal troops to the South for fear of reviving memories of post-Civil War Reconstruction, but the demonstrators refused to comply. In the end, Kennedy dispatched civilian federal marshals to restore peace in Alabama, and the attorney general worked out an agreement with the governor of Mississippi to provide protection for incoming riders before subjecting them to arrest. Finally, the Justice Department obtained a decree from the Interstate Commerce Commission, banning segregated facilities in interstate transportation.

The Kennedy administration attempted to reduce the possibility of provoking further racial confrontations that would again drag the federal government into a clash with state officials. Seeking to channel black protest in a "safer" direction, the Kennedys encouraged voter registration activities. Suffrage drives were a regular feature of American life and civil rights organizations, such as the NAACP and SCLC, had incorporated them as an essential part of their programs. In contrast to the highly publicized and confrontational sit-ins and freedom rides that often generated violence, voter registration drives promised peaceful, nonconfrontational efforts to place the names of blacks on the suffrage lists. Besides keeping the President from having to dispatch federal troops to Dixie in Reconstruction era fashion, a voter registration strategy might enhance the fortunes of the reformist wing of the Democratic party. Additional black voters presumably would support at the national level the party that enfranchised them, and their ballots would also serve to select more moderate officeholders in the South.

The Voter Education Project (VEP) grew out of this convergence of politics and principle. In the wake of the freedom rides, the Kennedy administration believed that "it would be valuable if some of the present energy were channeled into this vital [registration] work." The Justice Department had already begun to file suffrage litigation and invited civil rights groups to work in this area and collect evidence of ongoing discrimination. Kennedy aides with contacts in liberal philanthropic foundations arranged to obtain fi-

nancing for nonpartisan voter registration activities. Under the auspices of the Southern Regional Council, a private interracial agency
based in Atlanta, nearly a million dollars were raised to conduct
voter education projects. The council hired Wiley Branton, a black
civil rights lawyer from Arkansas, to direct the enterprise and elic-
ited participation from the major civil rights organizations—the
NAACP, SCLC, SNCC, CORE, and the Urban League, an organization specializing in housing and employment programs.

Bringing these groups together was a significant political
achievement. Though in agreement with Dr. King's assertion that
"if we in the South can win the right to vote it...will give us the
concrete tool with which we ourselves can correct injustice," they
regarded each other warily. The NAACP viewed itself as the premier organization in the fight for black enfranchisement. Tena-
ciously guarding its terrain, the national association looked suspiciously at rival organizations that had recently arrived on the scene.
The NAACP particularly worried about competition from SCLC,
whose president, Dr. King, exhibited considerable success as a
fund-raiser and organizer of affiliates throughout the South. Because money was usually a scarce resource for civil rights groups,
each agency needed to stand in the center of public attention and
earn credit for accomplishments that would attract new supporters
and financial contributions. SNCC and CORE posed an additional
problem for the NAACP, which feared that their direct-action orientation would foster troublesome, diversionary operations pointed
away from the goal of suffrage. Placing its commitment to the ballot
first, the NAACP cast aside its misgivings and joined the coalition.

From a different perspective, SNCC also worried about signing
up with the VEP. Born out of the sit-in movement and weaned on
the freedom rides, the group's members suspected that white liberals and established civil rights leaders wanted to raise the child in
their own image. For its part, SNCC was ready to stand among
adults and pursue its goals militantly. Though some considered the
VEP as a clever means of sidetracking protest, the young activists
decided to join the project. The fresh infusion of outside funds for
voter registration would save the group the money necessary to
continue mass action demonstrations. Moreover, persuaded by
Robert Parris Moses, a soft-spoken, intense, and compelling field
secretary from New York City, SNCC viewed voter registration as
a potentially radical means of transforming the political and social

lives of southern blacks and whites. "In many ways," one SNCC staffer explained, "it seems to me that the voter registration project is even more significant than other forms of protest. The problem is being attacked at its core. A new sense of human dignity and self respect is being discovered."

Whatever reservations SNCC, the NAACP, and the rest of their civil rights comrades harbored, they agreed that the federal government would try to shelter them from racist harm. Without spelling out their intentions, Justice Department officials, who helped arrange for the creation of the VEP, pledged the cooperation of the Kennedy administration in implementing the project. The civil rights representatives attending planning sessions in 1961 left thinking that they could turn to Washington for staunch protection against violent attacks and other forms of harassment from white supremacists. Wiley Branton inferred that "the Justice Department would take all steps necessary to protect federal or constitutional rights" which embraced "the elementary matter of protection."

The Justice Department held a different view. Attorney General Kennedy and his staff wanted to keep the federal government out of the law enforcement business for political and constitutional reasons. They hesitated to ship troops or marshals into Dixie for fear of alienating powerful southern lawmakers whose cooperation the administration needed to pass its legislative program. Furthermore, they argued that the Constitution left law enforcement in local hands, and they did not want to discourage local responsibility by taking over police powers. Besides, federal lawyers insisted that the national government did not maintain its own police force and that the Federal Bureau of Investigation did not function in that capacity. They envisioned a cooperative partnership between national and state authorities, based on goodwill and mutual trust, and exercised through voluntary compliance rather than coercion. If disputes arose that threatened the constitutional rights and safety of the voter registration workers, the Justice Department preferred to assist them through the courts, not with armed force.

Robert Kennedy had deliberately chosen his top assistant in charge of civil rights enforcement to reflect this viewpoint. He did not want a crusader in the post, and so picked a negotiator. The attorney general passed over Harris Wofford, who had strong civil rights credentials, in favor of Burke Marshall, who had virtually none. Kennedy did not desire someone for the job who had a passionate commitment to racial equality. He explained that he wanted instead a "tough lawyer who could look at things... objectively." Intending to administer existing suffrage laws more forcefully than before, Kennedy desired the head of the Civil Rights Division to appear neutral and not too closely identified with the civil rights movement. Accordingly, he hoped that the image of evenhandedness would make it easier to deal with southern segregationists, such as James Eastland of Mississippi, who chaired the Senate Judiciary Committee. Marshall fit the bill and said he intended "to make the federal system in the voting field work by itself through local action, without federal court compulsion."

The two-front attack initiated by the Voter Education Project and the Justice Department helped boost political participation in the South. From 1962 to 1964, the VEP accounted for some 287,000 new black registrants, about half of the increase. The Department of Justice supplemented these efforts by filing approximately fifty voting rights suits. Overall, during this period the proportion of southern black registrants jumped from 29.4 percent to 43.1 percent, the steepest rise since 1952 [see Table 1]. The bulk of the new voters generally came from urban areas in which hostility to black suffrage was less than in the rural black belt and the unusually repressive cities like Birmingham, where white extremists resorted to bombs to restrict ballots.

These accomplishments exacted a high price. The failure of the federal government to furnish protection for civil rights workers hampered their effectiveness and engendered their bitterness. Field staff from SNCC and CORE dug themselves into the most hard-core–resistant locales in Mississippi, Alabama, Louisiana, and Georgia and met verbal threats, violence, and intimidation by the police. The supposedly safe act of canvassing potential registrants door-to-door and accompanying them to the courthouse often converted suffrage drives into direct-action confrontations. The local law enforcement officers the Justice Department depended on to keep the peace themselves violated the constitutional rights of registration workers. At the mercy of sheriffs who interpreted the law from the grip of a billy club or the handle of a gun, the suffragists pleaded with the Kennedy administration for assistance.

In response, they received sympathy rather than protection. If the FBI appeared on the scene it was not to make arrests but to jot down their observations. In pursuit of interstate car thieves, kidnappers, and bank robbers, the bureau worked closely with local

Table 1   Black Voter Registration in the South, 1944–1964[a]

	1940	1947	1952	1960	1962	1964
Alabama	0.4	1.2	5.0	13.7	13.4	23.0
Arkansas	1.5	17.3	27.0	37.3	34.0	49.3
Florida	5.7	15.4	33.0	38.9	36.8	63.8
Georgia	3.0	18.8	23.0	29.3	26.7	44.0
Louisiana	0.5	2.6	25.0	30.9	27.8	32.0
Mississippi	0.4	0.9	4.0	5.2	5.3	6.7
North Carolina	7.1	15.2	18.0	38.1	35.8	46.8
South Carolina	0.8	13.0	20.0	15.6	22.9	38.7
Tennessee	6.5	25.8	27.0	58.9	49.8	69.4
Texas	5.6	18.5	31.0	34.9	37.3	57.7
Virginia	4.1	13.2	16.0	22.8	24.0	45.7
Total	3.0	12.0	20.0	29.1	29.4	43.1

[a]Estimated percentage of voting-age blacks registered.

SOURCE: David Garrow, *Protest at Selma* (New Haven, Conn.: Yale University Press, 1978), 7, 11, 19.

law enforcement officials, including those in the South, and did not want to jeopardize this cooperation by interfering with traditional racial practices. "You couldn't find those bastards," Timothy Jenkins, a student activist complained about federal agents in general: "All the force, all the demonstrations of force and intimidation... were on the side of the local authorities who wore badges and suits, and they had the ostensible perquisites of the state. Our part of the state was invisible—the federal state."

The Justice Department's reliance on the courts did not help the situation. The Kennedy administration had appointed to federal benches in the South a handful of judges who steadfastly resisted its efforts to enforce suffrage laws and shield individuals who peacefully engaged in voter registration activities. Judges like William Harold Cox of Mississippi publicly belittled the claims both of Justice Department lawyers and black litigants who appeared before him. These judges won appointment, because the President as a matter of courtesy, had to clear their names with the Democratic senators from their home states. The potential choices were narrowed even further, for the candidates had to pass through the nomination roadblock set up by Chairman Eastland's Judiciary Committee. Not all of Kennedy's selections behaved poorly, but too frequently the obstructionist jurists presided in precisely those areas where registration workers faced the greatest hazards.

SNCC'S ENCOUNTER WITH MISSISSIPPI

The experiences of SNCC in Mississippi demonstrated the challenges to black political development. In the deep South, the civil rights activists struggled to organize blacks in local communities to liberate themselves from oppressive white domination. They saw voter registration not as an end in itself but as the means for black people to obtain power to secure control of their lives. According to Bob Moses, the architect of much of SNCC's suffrage strategy, the real issue was "not only do you gain the right to vote but you begin to change all the other educational values." The ballot could open the way for blacks to determine their own leaders and change the conditions that exploited them. Indeed, to the young radicals politics was the key to rearranging economic and social relations. Lawrence Guyot, a SNCC field-worker in Mississippi, explained his group's message: "There is a relationship between your not being able to feed your children and your not registering to vote."

The key to political organizing in the black belt was first to overcome fear. In the Mississippi delta area, blacks had to muster sufficient courage to make an attempt to register. During the late 1950s and early 1960s, several blacks had been killed in retaliation for their political activities, and their deaths served as a vivid reminder for others who might follow them. Short of murder, white supremacists kept blacks in line through economic intimidation. Plantation owners fired "troublemakers" and stores cut off their credit. In August 1962, Mrs. Fannie Lou Hamer filled out a voter registration form and was fired from her job on a Ruleville plantation immediately after she refused to withdraw her application. The SNCC workers who entered these dangerous areas were also subjected to an array of threats, arrests, and brutality. They grappled with their personal fears even as they joined with those they were trying to mobilize to do collectively what was so difficult to do alone. "To go with friends and neighbors," SNCC field secretary Charles Cobb remarked, "made the attempt less frightening and reduced the chances of physical assault at the courthouse, since cowards don't like to openly attack numbers." Still, the struggle

**Bob Moses along with other SNCC workers on a voter registration
campaign in Mississippi. (Danny Lyon/Magnum)**

against fear, no matter how successful in persuading blacks to defy
racial discrimination, did not confer the right to vote.

While laboring to extend political power at the grassroots level,
SNCC fully realized that without federal intervention it could not
break the hold of white control over local electoral institutions. In
addition to its campaigns of community organizing, SNCC fought
the interconnected battle of mobilizing Washington on its side. The
group's staff operated in the rural sections where voter registration
was certain to arouse racial confrontation. SNCC planned the national dimension of its strategy to focus attention on what was happening in this "other America." Amzie Moore, the longtime fighter
for civil rights who had first brought Bob Moses to the Magnolia
State, sought to "expose the conditions in Mississippi with reference to people voting...to uncover what is covered." The civil
rights activists counted on newspaper and television reporters to
record their plight and influence public opinion in their favor,
thereby pressuring the Justice Department to furnish the necessary
protection.

Greenwood, Mississippi, sorely tested SNCC's strategy. In
LeFlore County, of which this Delta town was the county seat,

blacks comprised 64 percent of the population but only 9 percent of the registered voters. In June 1962, SNCC assigned Sam Block to launch a voter education drive in the area. A native Mississippian, the twenty-three-year-old Block had been deeply influenced by the murder of Emmett Till seven years before, which made him realize that one day he had "to do something." After graduating from high school, he left for college in Missouri, joined the Air Force, and returned home during the time of the freedom rides. He became involved with SNCC through his neighbor, Amzie Moore. Block entered Greenwood alone, without a car, money, or a place to stay. He made contacts wherever people congregated—in pool halls, laundromats, and grocery stores. Through his painstaking canvassing for voter registration he "learned that there were a lot of frightened people in Greenwood. They knew local blacks were being killed in LeFlore County... and nothing was being done about it."

The SNCC organizer began to whittle down some of this fear. He received help from blacks who had been involved with voter education attempts in the past. Holding meetings in fraternal halls and churches, he taught those in attendance freedom songs that "served as a drawing card... that seemed to make people want to come back." A local resident expressed the sentiments of many who participated in these sessions: "We have been living in fear, afraid to do something. It is time to do something. The time is now." Having taken the initial step of rallying ordinary, yet heroic black folks, Block could barely move ahead. The applicants he accompanied to the courthouse failed to pass the literacy tests unfairly administered by the registrars, and the SNCC field-worker was ordered by the sheriff "to pack your goddamn bags" and get out of town. He stayed despite constant harassment, arrests, and violent attacks.

When SNCC sent in reinforcements, white resistance grew even stiffer. In October 1962, county officials cut off the distribution of surplus food to some 22,000 residents, contending that the program was too expensive to operate. Block and his companions correctly viewed this action as a reprisal for their voter registration efforts and worried that without the commodities program impoverished black sharecroppers could not survive. In response, SNCC conducted a national food and clothing drive to help the beleaguered farmers get through the winter. In addition to keeping blacks from starving and suffering cold, the drive stimulated their interest in registering to vote. Lawrence Guyot, who was working with Block, recalled how the county government unwittingly assisted SNCC in graphically demonstrating to disfranchised blacks the connection between politics and economics. "It's easy to sell political involvement," he asserted, "when you have that kind of activity by an identifiable political apparatus."

White supremacists provided more brutal lessons about the dangers of voter registration and, hence, confirmed the importance of the ballot. In February and March 1963, whites initiated a reign of terror against SNCC. Arsonists attempted to burn down its headquarters, and unidentified assailants fired shotgun blasts into a car carrying three voter registration workers, seriously wounding one of them. Vigilantes torched several black businesses, burning them to the ground, and aimed gunfire into the homes of two black youths active in the suffrage drive. These attacks spurred the civil rights troops to launch a series of marches in protest of the violence. Direct action and voter registration, which for many SNCC activists originally seemed unrelated, fused in Greenwood. For two weeks, national television cameras spotlighted peaceful demonstrators under siege by the police and their snarling dogs.

As blacks filled the Greenwood jail, they once again exhorted the federal government to intercede on their behalf. Some approached Washington with ambivalent feelings. James Forman, executive secretary of SNCC and one of those arrested, considered "the presence of the federal government as an instrument to be used over the state governments of the South," and expected the Justice Department to protect voter registration workers. At the same time, he doubted federal commitment and believed that suffrage drives would "expose the dirt of the United States and thus alienate black people from the whole system." In part, SNCC had staged the demonstrations, in anticipation of arrests, to force federal authorities to intervene or else "prove the government was not on [its] side, and thus intensify the development of a mass consciousness among blacks." The VEP, which funded voter registration activities in Greenwood, seconded SNCC's request for federal protection. The agency considered such intervention essential if its projects were to be sustained in hostile southern battlefields.

The Justice Department applied just enough pressure to defuse the crisis, but not with sufficient vigor to satisfy black activists. It stubbornly refused to provide personal protection and relied instead on the preferred techniques of litigation and negotiation. The Justice Department petitioned the federal district court for an order releasing the imprisoned protesters and enjoining local officials from interfering with the suffrage campaign. Behind the scenes, John Doar, an attorney in the Civil Rights Division, persuaded Greenwood authorities to free the jailed demonstrators, and in turn, the department dropped the suit that would have permanently restrained town officials. Having restored some peace to Greenwood, the Justice Department backed off for fear of inflaming white passions anew.

Though the voter registration campaign proceeded, the civil rights forces made little progress in actually enrolling black voters. By mid-1963, some 1,300 blacks in Greenwood had taken the literacy test to register, but officials refused to notify them of the results. Faced with such meager gains and the unwillingness of the federal government to protect the constitutional rights of the fieldworkers, later that year the VEP reluctantly suspended funding for its projects in Mississippi and concentrated its efforts where the returns were higher. Despite these disappointments, such suffrage campaigns as that in Greenwood had a significant political impact. Many of the blacks who encountered the civil rights activists had taken a crucial step toward liberation. They had moved, as a Georgia SNCC organizer reported, "into freedom of the mind, and it is now theirs for life, even if they should never succeed in their efforts to persuade a semi-literate, hostile registrar to put their names on the roll." She succinctly summed up what the movement meant for the political future of the blacks it touched: "They have learned to live with fear, and to advance."

To underscore this point, the civil rights forces in Mississippi devised a novel strategy to turn disfranchised blacks into active political participants. Since 1962, the Council of Federated Organizations (COFO) had coordinated voter registration activities in the state. The NAACP, SNCC, CORE, and SCLC put aside some of their philosophical differences and organizational rivalries to focus their energies on combating the fierce opposition to black suffrage. Out of this cooperative venture the idea for a "freedom vote" emerged. COFO designed a mock election to accompany the regularly scheduled gubernatorial contest in 1963. The parallel balloting would be open to all black adults, especially the 95 percent who had been excluded from the normal electoral process.

COFO aimed the freedom vote in two directions. By casting ballots in this symbolic election, black Mississippians would send a message to the federal government that they wanted to vote and needed outside help to shatter the racial blockades that hampered them. "The freedom ballot will show," declared Bob Moses, one of the prime movers behind it, "that if Negroes had the right to vote without fear of physical or economic reprisal, they would do so." Yet civil rights activists wanted to achieve much more than Washington's assistance. As director of COFO, Moses envisioned the campaign as part of SNCC's enduring attempt to organize black communities around their perceived needs, in pursuit of their own goals, in behalf of their own emancipation, apart from white control. In holding this independent election, blacks would strike a blow for their political legitimacy. Rejected by white registration officials according to their definitions of political eligibility, black Mississippians intended to demonstrate that they were qualified to vote and seek power on their own terms.

Eighty thousand blacks, nearly four times the number of those registered, vividly staked their claim for recognition as first-class citizens. They marked their ballots in makeshift polling places in locations throughout their communities. In a unified manner they voted for the freedom ticket of Aaron Henry, the black president of COFO who ran for governor, and his running mate, Ed King, the white chaplain at Tougaloo College. Though considered illegitimate by official white standards, these voters and their candidates collectively constructed the machinery to continue agitating for equal political rights and representation. "The Freedom Vote gave Negroes an opportunity to build an organization in every nook and cranny of the State," Henry remarked. "We have an organization now in Mississippi that once we get the vote, we'll be able to direct it."

MARTIN LUTHER KING, JR., THE SCLC, AND THE CRISIS AT BIRMINGHAM

While SNCC strived to mobilize people around the right to vote in rural areas, the SCLC shaped its protest around broader issues of segregation and discrimination in a city notorious for its repression of blacks: Birmingham, Alabama. Over the years, this steel city had been the scene of numerous bombings and acts of violence against civil rights activists and, most recently, the freedom riders. The commissioner of public safety, Eugene "Bull" Connor, ruled the police with an iron fist and believed that civil rights protesters were Communist dupes who deserved the harsh punishment they received.

The local movement for first-class citizenship was led by the Reverend Fred Shuttlesworth, a founding member of the SCLC. Pastor of the Bethel Baptist Church, Shuttlesworth also headed the Alabama Christian Movement for Human Rights, a group that originated in the mid-1950s after Alabama officials banned the NAACP from the state. Under Shuttlesworth's lead, the organization had attempted to desegregate schools, buses, and government offices in Birmingham. In retaliation against these efforts, the Reverend Shuttlesworth's home and church were bombed, and the minister and his family were attacked and beaten by a mob. Undaunted by threats, Shuttlesworth continued to challenge the city's system of racial apartheid. "I always believed that the minister is God's first line soldier," he remarked bravely. "I should say I'm a battlefield type general like Patton, I guess."

Against this pattern of intimidation, Dr. King, the Reverend Shuttlesworth, and their associates used mass-action strategies to bolster growing, but still underdeveloped, black political influence. In 1962, approximately 12,500 blacks had signed up to vote, about 10 percent of those eligible. This small bloc of voters joined with white reformers in an attempt to unseat the reactionary Connor. Businesspeople and other civic leaders believed the racial violence encouraged by Connor and his henchmen had a harmful effect on the city's economic fortunes and hoped to put a stop to it. They arranged for a referendum to change the form of city government from a three-person commission to a mayor and seven-member council, thereby reducing Connor's power. The measure passed with solid black support, and in the spring of 1963, the coalition of white moderates and blacks defeated Connor's mayoral bid. Instead of accepting his loss at the polls, Connor began litigation challenging the validity of the new government and its newly elected officials. Meanwhile, he retained control over the police.

On April 3, the day after the disputed election, the SCLC orchestrated sit-in demonstrations to desegregate downtown eating facilities and to press for the hiring of black store clerks. These protests had a twofold purpose: to win concessions for Birmingham blacks as part of the ongoing community struggle led by Shuttlesworth and to force the federal government to combat Jim Crow throughout the region. King deliberately picked Birmingham because of the potential for its police, under Connor's command, to respond brutally to protests. To arouse the conscience of the nation, the SCLC deployed nonviolent marches to provoke the expected response from Connor's men. King did not seek to create bloodshed so much as he attempted to dramatize publicly, for newspapers and television to record, the vicious white resistance to racial equality. "You see a policeman beating somebody and with water hoses," Reverend Shuttlesworth declared, "that's news, that's spectacularism."

The protests did elicit white violence. High-pressure water hoses and trained attack dogs were turned on peaceful demonstrators, many of whom were children the SCLC had recruited into the movement. Bombs exploded at the hotel where King was lodged and at his brother's home. These blasts sparked outraged blacks to take to the streets in retaliation, hurling rocks and bottles at the police. Before the city fell into this grip of violence, local civic leaders and federal officials had quietly negotiated with King to forge order out of chaos. The President sent Assistant Attorney General Marshall to mediate between a committee of white businesspeople and black protesters. They hammered out a compromise that called for the desegregation of eating facilities and the gradual hiring of black sales personnel, but left intact the segregation of most public accommodations and the criminal charges brought against black demonstrators, including King. Subsequently, the newly installed mayor, whose election had been upheld by the courts, established a biracial community affairs committee, and the city council repealed its municipal segregation ordinances.

Although much remained to be done, Birmingham witnessed significant change. The demonstrations strengthened the local movement by fostering racial solidarity and provided tangible evidence that collective action enhanced the influence of blacks in shaping public affairs. To extend the gains derived from direct action protests, civil rights groups mounted voter registration drives to build up budding black electoral clout. By 1964, the proportion of registered blacks had doubled to 20 percent. However far their struggles carried them, they still needed federal support to overcome Jim Crow and disfranchisement. Like their counterparts in Greenwood, blacks in Birmingham continued to face calculated vigilante violence. The culmination of such brutality in Birmingham occurred on September 15, 1963, with the bombing of the Sixteenth Street Baptist Church and the tragic deaths of four young girls worshiping inside.

Meanwhile, the Kennedy administration had continued to venture cautiously in the civil rights field. The President delayed issuing the executive decree on residential desegregation he had promised during the presidential campaign until November 1962. Even then, he limited the order to homes subsidized by federal loans, which left most of the housing market uncovered. Shortly before, the administration had demonstrated its unwillingness to exercise federal might unless given no other choice. Facing a direct threat to a federal court order admitting James Meredith to the University of Mississippi in September 1962, the President finally mobilized sufficient military force to combat racist interference with desegregation. Like Eisenhower in his handling of the Little Rock crisis, Kennedy hesitated to send federal troops to the South, preferring instead to persuade the state to enforce the desegregation ruling voluntarily. On October 1, only after Governor Ross Barnett refused to negotiate in good faith and failed to guarantee Meredith's safety did the President move in the Army. This intervention came belatedly after a riot had broken out, resulting in two deaths and over 300 injuries.

The following year, Kennedy showed that he could learn from his mistakes. On June 11, 1963, the administration won a well-publicized battle with Governor George Wallace to desegregate the University of Alabama. With the Mississippi disaster in mind, the President acted more firmly in dealing with Governor Wallace. Carrying out a carefully orchestrated plan, the Kennedy administration dispatched Deputy Attorney General Nicholas Katzenbach and federal marshals to escort two black students, Vivian Malone and James Hood, whose admission had been ordered by the federal judiciary. After Wallace blocked their entry by standing in the schoolhouse door, the President federalized the state National Guard. The six-hour standoff ended when the Alabama governor stepped aside and allowed integration at the Tuscaloosa campus to proceed peacefully.

In the end, President Kennedy went further than his Republican predecessor, Dwight Eisenhower, in pursuing racial equality. The political pressure of protest had pushed the chief executive to embrace at least the more moderate goals of the civil rights movement. The disruptive Birmingham demonstrations convinced the chief executive that the racial situation in the South had reached a dangerous phase. The crises provoked by civil rights protesters sparked widespread racial confrontations throughout Dixie and even threatened to consume the North. Worried by the escalating violence and the increasing possibility of black retaliation, the President introduced the legislative program he had postponed since entering the White House. The events of the previous two years compelled him to recognize the morality of the civil rights struggle. On June 11, he informed a nationwide television audience that the extension of equal rights to all Americans was an issue "as old as the scriptures and... as clear as the American Constitution." Conflicts in Birmingham and elsewhere, he warned his listeners, required legislation "if we are to move this problem from the streets to the courts." The chief executive's proposals attacked segregation in public accommodations and schools, created a Community Relations Service to mediate racial disputes, authorized cutting off federal funds to local agencies practicing discrimination, and expanded judicial power to speed up voting rights cases. The administration's civil rights measures were timed to restore peace to southern battlegrounds by removing the conditions that had spawned protest. Nonetheless, soothing words alone could not stop violence: only a few hours after the president's address, the NAACP's Medgar Evers was assassinated by a white supremacist in Jackson, Mississippi.

FREEDOM VOTES, FREEDOM SUMMER

The Kennedy administration saw its preferred solution to civil rights controversies taking shape in scattered communities throughout the South. In a number of cities, such as Atlanta, Georgia; Tampa, Florida; and Norfolk, Virginia, businesspeople had responded to civil rights turbulence by seeking ways voluntarily to desegregate public accommodations and municipal facilities. These civic leaders recognized that explosive race relations made poor business sense. Seeking to attract outside investments and commercial enterprises to their areas, they took measures to reduce the kind of negative publicity that would tarnish their cities' images, as it had that of Little Rock and Birmingham. A politician such as Mayor Ivan Allen

On August 28, 1963, following introduction of
the civil rights bill in Congress, approximately
250,000 blacks and whites marched on
Washington to stage a massive rally for jobs
and freedom. The demonstration was
highlighted by two contrasting speeches. An
angry SNCC chairperson, John Lewis,
complained that the progress of civil rights
was moving too slowly, while Martin Luther
King, Jr., pictured above, recited his optimistic
"I Have a Dream" speech for an integrated
America. (UPI/Bettmann Newsphotos)

of Atlanta went so far as to support the Kennedy civil rights bill, but
this kind of expression by local white moderates was rare. More
frequently, they tried to maintain local control over the amount
and pace of desegregation in order to forestall federal intervention.
Consequently, they accepted sufficient changes to keep their cities
relatively quiet and out of the headlines, yet without guaranteeing
full equality for blacks.

Also without much fanfare, blacks followed the electoral path to first-class citizenship. In 1964, in Tuskegee, Alabama, a small group of white liberals joined with Charles Gomillion's Macon County Democratic Club, an offshoot of the Tuskegee Civic Association, to elect a biracial slate to city and county offices. By then blacks constituted a majority of the registered voters in Macon County and split about evenly with whites in Tuskegee. With blacks assuming majority status as voters, Gomillion and his associates favored a gradualist approach in sharing power with whites. They wanted to avoid raising the specter of black domination and hoped to show that the two races could cooperate in governing responsibly. Gomillion hoped this policy would serve as a model for encouraging "whites elsewhere to be willing to appoint or elect qualified Negroes, even in places where Negroes were less numerous than in Macon County." The outcome of elections in his own bailiwick did not disappoint the Tuskegee sociologist. An interracial coalition elected Gomillion to a seat on the board of education, along with three other blacks who won countywide positions. In the city, two blacks gained posts on the municipal council. At the same time, whites retained control of both county and city governments and held the key offices of sheriff and mayor.

This landmark election in Macon County revealed the growing complexity of black politics as the majority of African-Americans obtained the vote. Gomillion's strategy had run into serious opposition from within the black community. A group of younger blacks who had come of age during the birth of the civil rights movement in the 1950s challenged the sixty-five year-old Gomillion and his prescription for racial advancement. These insurgents decried the "pace of social change in Tuskegee [as] unconscionably slow" and argued for the election of as many black candidates as possible. This intraracial split reflected different class as well as ideological perspectives. The Gomillion wing articulated distinctly middle-class values and spoke mainly for the professionals and staff of the Tuskegee Institute and the Veterans Administration Hospital. The challengers, many of whom taught at Tuskegee, also came from the middle class but directed their attention to the problems of lower-income and impoverished blacks in the city and the rural sections of the county.

As long as most blacks experienced racial disfranchisement in common, class divisions remained in the background. Nevertheless, class divisions did exist and had already begun to surface in Mississippi as well. The 1963 freedom vote campaign had encountered opposition from some of the state's 27,000 blacks who had managed to register to vote. They resented SNCC's efforts to develop political consciousness among the masses of blacks, which, if successful, might eventually undermine their own leadership. These middle-class blacks had succeeded by playing according to white electoral rules; they considered voting a privilege that should be extended to those, like themselves, who passed the literacy test, as long as it was applied equally. When members of the black middle class opposed racial discrimination they usually did so through "respectable" civil rights groups like the NAACP, which stressed litigation, and not through organizations like SNCC, which they considered disruptive and likely to stir up white hostility. Thus, as Neil R. McMillan has pointed out, in rallying the black masses against white supremacy, civil rights organizers were also challenging "traditional [black] elites once thought to be the natural leaders of their people by the people themselves."

Because racial oppression was so harsh in Mississippi, the civil rights movement generally had been able to submerge class divisions beneath black solidarity. The NAACP had joined SNCC in designing the freedom vote campaign, and one of its leaders, Aaron Henry, had led the insurgent gubernatorial ticket. Following the 1963 mock election, COFO planned a massive voter registration drive for the next summer, climaxing in a challenge to the state Democratic party delegation at the presidential nominating convention in Atlantic City. The project was fashioned to spotlight national attention on the blatantly racist means by which white Mississippians excluded blacks from the suffrage. The planners of the 1964 "Freedom Summer" invited northern white students into the state to expose them to the dangers blacks experienced every day. White Americans hardly noticed the deaths of black people, Bob Moses candidly admitted, but "they would respond to a thousand young white college students" suffering brutality at the hands of Mississippi racists. Like the nonviolent provocation King practiced in Birmingham, the use of white students did not cause the violence; rather it served to dramatize the terror that already existed. It would take blood spilled by whites, COFO cynically though realistically reasoned, to prompt federal intervention.

Months before Freedom Summer was scheduled to begin, the assassination of John F. Kennedy had placed in the Oval Office a new President, though not a new policy. Upon taking over in November 1963, Lyndon B. Johnson threw his support behind Kennedy's civil rights bill and, together with a coalition of liberal lawmakers and civil rights, labor, and religious groups, had waged a long, fierce struggle that succeeded in obtaining a stronger measure than the one originally proposed.[1] However, the new law did not help the political insurgents in Mississippi. Though it accepted a sixth-grade education as evidence of literacy for the purpose of voter registration, the statute continued to leave enforcement with the judiciary, a procedure that proved cumbersome and inadequate. Furthermore, the act failed to address the improper application of literacy tests, which in the past had allowed illiterate or semiliterate whites, but not blacks, to register. Above all, nothing in the legislation directed the administration to provide protection for civil rights volunteers engaged in Freedom Summer.

The murder of three young civil rights workers, James Chaney, Michael Schwerner, and Andrew Goodman—one black and two whites—on June 21, 1964, finally forced some intervention from Washington. President Johnson ordered the FBI, which previously had been ineffective if not uninterested in pursuing civil rights offenses, to launch an intensive manhunt to apprehend the killers. The bureau set up an office in Mississippi and with assistance from paid informers inside the Ku Klux Klan arrested nineteen men, including a sheriff and deputy sheriff, for commission of the crime. Nevertheless, the Justice Department declined to provide day-to-day protection for the suffragists who remained in the field to suffer the usual assortment of intimidating tactics: beatings, bombings, arson, and at least three additional homicides.

This racist reign of terror against the freedom fighters did not prevent COFO from organizing blacks into a potent political force. Though relatively few managed to register to vote during the sum-

---

[1] In addition to the provisions originally offered by the Kennedy administration in 1963, the 1964 Civil Rights Act prohibited employment discrimination based on race and sex and created an Equal Employment Opportunity Commission to implement it. The law passed after the Senate shut off a filibuster that lasted for fifty-seven days. President Johnson signed the bill into law on July 2.

mer campaign, a great many more participated in the formation of the Mississippi Freedom Democratic Party (MFDP). Protesting their exclusion from the process by which state Democrats selected their delegates to the national convention, the Freedom Democrats erected an alternative structure to challenge them. While predominantly black, the reform organization was open to members of both races and included Ed King, the white clergyman who had run with Aaron Henry in the 1963 COFO mock election. In the style of SNCC, which heavily influenced its creation, the MFDP was the product of grassroots organizing constructed from the bottom up. Unlike the conservative regulars, the group pledged to support Lyndon Johnson as the Democratic party's presidential nominee as well as his liberal Great Society platform.

President Johnson counted on widespread black support for his candidacy. Since his early career as an opponent of Truman's civil rights program and his middle years as a proponent of lukewarm civil rights legislation, the Texan had grown into a staunch advocate of racial equality. As he climbed higher up the ladder of electoral success, away from the constraints of his southern segregationist constituency, he developed an increasing sense of moral obligation to extend first-class citizenship to blacks. His ethical and political convictions meshed with his regional loyalty. A complex man, he believed a resolution of racial problems would liberate his native South, white as well as black, from the burdens of outmoded discriminatory institutions that retarded its economic progress. In the absence of the race issue and the reactionary politics it spawned, Johnson envisioned southern Democratic politicians falling in step behind his reform leadership.

In customary fashion, the President attempted to build a broad consensus for his nomination in 1964. The northern, liberal wing of his party backed him solidly, but the South posed some difficulties. Upset with the passage of the 1964 Civil Rights Act and with the expensive social welfare programs that Johnson was preparing for his Great Society, many white southerners were unenthusiastic about their native son. Instead, they seemed to prefer the Republican nominee, Senator Barry Goldwater of Arizona, who had voted against the civil rights law and whose conservative economic views were more compatible with theirs. To stem these potential losses and achieve the biggest possible electoral victory, Johnson came to the convention seeking unity.

The challenge of the MFDP endangered Johnson's plan for a well-ordered convention. Joseph Rauh, a prominent white liberal attorney with connections to organized labor, presented the case for recognition of the Freedom Democrats as the legitimate representatives from Mississippi. He contended that they had been illegally barred from participation in the selection of delegates by the regular party organization and questioned their lily-white rivals' loyalty to the reform principles of the national party. The Freedom delegation backed up its legal right to the convention seats with powerful moral arguments. The most striking presentation came from Fannie Lou Hamer of Sunflower County, the home district of Senator Eastland. She recounted with great emotion the brutality and pain she had suffered from Mississippi law enforcement officials while working for civil rights. In stirring testimony before the Credentials Committee and recorded by television cameras for a national audience, Mrs. Hamer painted a graphic picture of the outrages happening so frequently in Mississippi and asked her listeners: "Is this America? The land of the free and the home of the brave?"

In this conflict, President Johnson mixed his moral concern for the plight of Mississippi blacks with his political passion for consensus. He hastily arranged a press conference to preempt live coverage of Mrs. Hamer's powerful testimony and put forces in motion to work out a compromise on the Freedom challenge that would appeal to blacks, their liberal allies, and moderate white southerners. He let the reformers know that he would choose Hubert Humphrey, the liberal senator from Minnesota, as his running mate if the latter could settle the dispute without a divisive credentials fight. With the help of Rauh, Walter Reuther, the head of the United Automobile Workers, and Walter Mondale, Humphrey's protege who sat on the Credentials Committee, the Minnesota senator hatched a plan acceptable to the majority of convention delegates. It extended two at-large seats to the MFDP and named Aaron Henry and Ed King to occupy them. The rest of the Freedom Democrats could attend the convention as nonvoting guests. Those state regulars who swore allegiance to the national party would officially represent Mississippi and cast its forty-four votes. Furthermore, looking ahead, the Democrats agreed to draw up guidelines to eliminate racial discrimination in delegate selection to the next national nominating convention.

The compromise preserved party harmony at the convention, but it satisfied neither Magnolia faction. Most of the white regulars refused to sign the loyalty pledge and returned home to vote for Goldwater. The Freedom Democrats also rejected the agreement. Believing that they had morality as well as legality on their side, they would not accept a token assignment of two seats while the regulars controlled the votes of the entire delegation. They had not risked their lives merely for a symbolic victory and further resented the fact that Democratic leaders, not the MFDP representatives, had specifically chosen the two delegates for them. For many of the civil rights organizers, particularly those in SNCC, this whole episode had a souring effect on their relationship with white liberals. They felt sold out by the administration and its allies, who presumed to know what was best for them and to dictate a solution accordingly. They also lost trust in their lawyer, Joseph Rauh, and black leaders, such as Martin Luther King and Bayard Rustin, who favored the arrangement for practical reasons—as a first step toward eventual reform and the best bargain they could get. Despite their loss of faith, most of the Freedom delegation returned home and campaigned for Johnson and future recognition by the Democratic party.

The convention challenge also produced serious internal strains within the civil rights movement in Mississippi. As John Dittmer has concluded, the Atlantic City affair marked "the beginning of the end of the COFO partnership and the emergence of class conflict as a major destructive force." The debate over whether to accept the administration's offer split the MFDP delegation. Urban middle-class blacks, about one-fifth of the group, tended to favor the compromise in opposition to the largely rural, poor delegates who rejected it. The latter contingent won the opening skirmish, but when the Freedom Democrats returned home the feud continued. Within the state, blacks who were associated with SNCC's increasingly radical vision of grassroots organizing struggled with more traditional elements allied with the NAACP for control over the future course of black politics.

THE TRIUMPH OF LBJ

President Johnson may have abandoned the most militant blacks at the convention, but he had no intention of ignoring the black elec-

In 1965, the Mississippi Freedom Democratic
party contested the election of that state's
congressional representatives. The three
Freedom Democratic candidates who journeyed
to Washington in hopes of replacing the
regulars were, from left to right, Annie Devine,
Fannie Lou Hamer, and Victoria Gray. The
House denied their claim. (UPI/Bettmann
Newsphotos)

torate. With Barry Goldwater enticing white voters away from the
Democratic party in the South, the President recognized the growing importance of the black vote in carrying Dixie. After Lawrence
O'Brien, a top political adviser, returned from traveling through
the region during the campaign, he reported to Johnson that "victory in at least four of the states and possibly in six hinges upon the
percentage of Negro voters who go to the polls." Because the chief
executive would probably garner at least 90 percent of the black
vote, the Democrats had to concentrate on getting out the vote.
State party leaders like those in Mississippi had discouraged black
participation, so it remained for the national organization to mount
a suffrage campaign. Under the direction of Louis Martin, the Demo-

cratic National Committee sponsored such drives, which, according to Martin, "are better than they ever have been and better than we thought they ever would be." This effort did not prevent Goldwater from capturing five southern states, including Mississippi, but it did help Johnson win the rest of the former Confederacy. Everywhere else, except Goldwater's Arizona, the President triumphed and racked up huge margins among black voters. They went to the polls in approval, as the *Afro-American* newspaper commented, for one whose record "proves his compassionate concern for people, irrespective of race, creed or color."

Johnson's triumph over Goldwater cemented black voters more solidly than ever before behind the Democratic party. The trend that started with Franklin Roosevelt, was pushed along by Truman, momentarily interrupted by Eisenhower, and renewed by Kennedy reached landslide proportions under Johnson. As the black electorate grew in influence, so too did its success in shoving civil rights to the front of the national political agenda. In the South, where the majority of blacks still could not vote, protest and community organizing served as the most potent weapons for influencing politics. In different ways, Martin Luther King and the more radical activists in SNCC and CORE recognized that mobilizing blacks from below pressured the national government to act from above. This pincer movement had trapped and wounded Jim Crow, which though kicking and screaming nonetheless refused to die.

Chapter 4

Reenfranchisement and Racial Consciousness

THE SELMA MOVEMENT AND THE VOTING RIGHTS ACT OF 1965

The distance between Oslo, Norway, and Selma, Alabama, spanned more than an ocean and thousands of miles. For African-Americans it represented the difference between dignity and degradation. The winner of the 1964 Nobel Peace Prize, Dr. Martin Luther King, Jr., returned to the United States after obtaining his prestigious award in Oslo and journeyed to Selma in hope of eliminating the gap between the honorific treatment he had received abroad and the lack of respect blacks were accorded at home. Specifically, he sought to do something about the continuing denial of their right to vote. Throughout the former Confederate states, approximately 57 percent of eligible blacks remained off the suffrage rolls; in Alabama, the figure was a more shocking 77 percent; and in Dallas County, where Selma was the county seat, only 335 blacks out of a total population of 15,000 were registered. With this in mind, on January 2, 1965, Dr. King told an audience gathered at Selma's Brown Chapel AME Church what was at stake in the demonstrations the SCLC was about to launch. "When we get the right to vote," he predicted, "we will send to the state-house not men who will stand in the doorways of universities to keep Negroes out, but men who will uphold the cause of justice."

King's plans capped the twenty-year struggle to reenfranchise black southerners. Since the outlawing of the white primary in 1944, civil rights groups and the national government had attempted to remove discriminatory barriers impeding black suffrage. Though a combination of litigation, legislation, and voter registration campaigns had yielded much progress, the majority of southern blacks still were disfranchised and were likely to stay so unless state and local officials lost their stranglehold on the enrollment process. Like most of the gains made during the civil rights era, the expansion of black ballots depended upon the power of the federal government in reinforcing the efforts of blacks at the local level, who were already fighting for first-class citizenship.

President Johnson intended to throw his considerable political weight behind renewed efforts to secure the right to vote. The chief executive shared civil rights advocates' faith in the ballot as the ultimate weapon in promoting racial advancement. Once blacks voted in large numbers, he believed, "many other breakthroughs would follow as a consequence of the black man's own legitimate power as an American citizen, not as a gift from the white man." This thinking reflected the willingness of liberals like Johnson to use the federal government to attack racist obstacles in the South, but it also mirrored the more conservative view of the right to vote as a self-help vehicle for uplifting an oppressed group.

In addition to these philosophical considerations, Johnson, the consummate politician, recognized the pragmatic benefits that reenfranchising blacks would bestow. In achieving his landslide victory in 1964, the President had lost the votes of five states in his native South—Alabama, Georgia, Louisiana, Mississippi, and South Carolina. In each of these states, the black enrollment figure was under 39 percent. If the Johnson administration found a way to dismantle discriminatory suffrage procedures, it could boost black registration to offset the Republican inroads Barry Goldwater had made into Democratic ranks in the South. After the election, an official of the Democratic party reported "that the first step toward getting out a big Democratic vote is to increase [black] registration."

Having already succeeded in obtaining passage of the 1964 Civil Rights Act, Johnson could not afford to rest on his laurels. This landmark legislation continued to leave voting rights enforcement in the hands of the judiciary. Previous experience had proven the courts inadequate in repelling white southern obstructionists. Besides, in the past registrars had not been deterred from signing up white illiterates while excluding those who were black, and the force of any criterion that preserved some standard of literacy would fall disproportionately on the thousands of undereducated blacks who remained disfranchised.

To correct flaws in the existing legislation, both federal agencies and civil rights groups recommended a new approach. On several occasions, most recently in 1963, the United States Commission on Civil Rights suggested that Congress grant the President authority to appoint federal enrollment officers to register qualified blacks. SNCC went even further. Based on its efforts in the impoverished, black-belt South, the organization advocated the complete abolition of literacy tests as a requirement for voting. Either the country must eliminate these qualifications or, as Bob Moses argued, provide blacks with "the right to learn how to read and write *now.*" Indeed, in several cases, an unusually progressive federal judge in Alabama, Frank M. Johnson, had ordered the enrollment of black illiterates as voters. Because illiterate whites had managed to register in the past, he decreed that blacks under similar circumstances did not have to prove their ability to read and write in order to qualify to vote.

After his election, in November 1964, President Johnson began seriously to consider his options. Although some White House advisers suggested that the administration forgo proposing any new voting rights legislation for a year, until the South had time to adjust to the recently enacted Civil Rights Law, the chief executive forged ahead. After ordering the Justice Department to prepare a new suffrage measure, on January 4, 1965, Johnson delivered the annual state-of-the-union address and affirmed his desire to "eliminate every remaining obstacle to the right and opportunity to vote."

In the meantime, Dr. King marshaled civil rights forces in Selma to guarantee swift and effective federal action. The unofficial capital of the Alabama black belt, Selma had served as an arsenal and naval foundry for the Confederacy. In 1865, Union forces torched the town, and memories of the Civil War and Reconstruction still burned in the minds of local whites. This section of the state had backed the Dixiecrat challenge in 1948, and the attitude of many white officials toward blacks was summed up by James A. Hare, a Dallas County judge. "Your Negro," he asserted, "is a mixture of African types like the Congolite who has a long heel and the blue-gummed Ebo whose I.Q. is about 50 or 55." James G. Clark, the Dallas County sheriff, practiced the "Bull" Connor brand of law enforcement, showed little patience for civil rights protesters, and seemed genuinely to enjoy roughing them up. Sporting a green helmet adorned with an eagle and a Confederate flag and dressing in the style of the World War II general George S. Patton, Clark led his deputies in poking demonstrators with electric cattle prods, beating them with clubs, and dispersing them with tear gas.

This stronghold of segregation and police-state tactics offered an inviting setting for King and the SCLC to wage a major assault against political disfranchisement. From his previous encounter with Connor in Birmingham, the Nobel laureate had learned that the application of nonviolent pressure would provoke intemperate, racist lawmen to commit acts of brutality. The SCLC's strategy depended on blacks behaving with restraint in the face of such vicious attacks and on television cameras and journalists recording the confrontation so as to prick the conscience of an outraged nation. Injuries and fatalities would very likely accompany this struggle, but King was seeking drama, not bloodshed. By carefully stage-managing events at Selma, by combining disruption with prudence, he hoped to appeal to the larger audience of the public and the more specific one of the President and lawmakers in Washington, D.C.

King's troops marched along the trail blazed by SNCC and local black activists in Selma. In 1963, two SNCC field-workers had established a beachhead in the town and conducted a voter registration drive that led to the formation of the Dallas County Voters League (DCVL). This indigenous association was headed by Reverend Frederick Reese. A high school teacher and Baptist clergyman, Reese felt strongly that black educators should take an active role in the freedom struggle. Dependent on white school boards and county administrators for their livelihood, many teachers had refrained from becoming actively involved in the movement. Reese believed that his colleagues had both a personal and professional obligation to seek to become registered voters and challenge those who tried to thwart them; otherwise, they could not properly fulfill their responsibility of instructing their pupils in exercising the duties of citizenship.

Amelia P. Boynton joined Reese as a prime mover behind the creation of the Voters League. The widow of the county's black agricultural extension agent, Mrs. Boynton was an independent businesswoman who operated an employment and insurance agency in

Selma. Along with her husband, she had actively taken part in civil rights efforts and was especially concerned with efforts to increase black voter registration. Herself an enrolled voter, Boynton was well aware of the discriminatory treatment most blacks suffered. She knew of one official who could barely pronounce the words "constitutionality" and "interrogatory" on a literacy test administered to a black teacher. After the applicant interrupted the clerk to read the words correctly, "the registrar turned red with anger" and flunked her. Boynton had originally invited SNCC into the county to aid the DCVL in mobilizing blacks against such injustices.

Spearheaded by Reverend Reese and Mrs. Boynton, the league sponsored voter registration workshops to encourage blacks to enroll. In the autumn of 1963, together with SNCC, it held a "Freedom Day" rally at the county courthouse that spurred more than 300 blacks to make an attempt to sign up to vote. Instead, the applicants met resistance from the board of registrars and from Sheriff Clark and his deputies, who tried to prevent the would-be enrollees from receiving food and water as they stood for hours waiting on line to enroll. Throughout the following year, SNCC continued to organize voter registration drives in Dallas County but met with scant success.

At the same time, the federal government tackled the registration problem in its usual fashion. Justice Department lawyers had filed suits to restrain Clark from interfering with voter registration activities, and in November 1963, they won a ruling barring county registrars from using the literacy test to discriminate against black applicants. However, this decree failed to deter officials from engaging in biased practices against prospective black voters, and additional legal action to stop them proved unsuccessful. To make matters worse, a local judge issued an injunction blocking the Voters League from conducting mass meetings. By 1965, after several years of frustrating litigation, less than 400 Dallas County blacks had managed to register to vote. Acknowledging this failure, Attorney General Nicholas Katzenbach complained of "the inadequacy of the judicial process to deal effectively and expeditiously with a problem so deep-seated and so complex."

The inability of the federal courts to remedy unfair registration practices was matched by the unwillingness of the executive branch to protect suffrage workers from harassment. Adhering to the policy of his predecessors, Johnson refused to deploy federal marshals to Dallas County to safeguard voter registration workers from the menace of Sheriff Clark and his deputies. The chief executive preferred to leave law enforcement under the control of local authorities, barring a total breakdown of public order. In a similar manner, the Justice Department refused to instruct FBI agents to offer relief when they saw the constitutional rights of suffragists under attack. For example, on Freedom Day, October 7, 1963, the FBI merely observed and took notes as peaceful protesters were pushed around and arrested by Sheriff Clark and his men on the steps of the U.S. courthouse. Observing this scene firsthand exasperated Howard Zinn. "For all the good the federal officials did," the historian and adviser to SNCC bitterly commented, "[Alabama Governor] George Wallace might have been President of the United States."

Despite the racist intimidation and the failure of the national government to check it, blacks in Selma refused to retreat. SNCC had helped galvanize the community behind the struggle for political empowerment and set in motion forces for liberation that could not be easily turned back. SNCC's executive secretary, James Forman, celebrated Freedom Day as "the day when a century of Southern fear and terror...had not been able to stop the forward thrust of a people determined...to be free." Nevertheless, SNCC's efforts had sputtered, and local black leaders called in civil rights reinforcements. Their immediate goal was to secure help in registering residents of their own and surrounding counties; nonetheless, in late 1964, when the Dallas County Voters League invited King and the SCLC to Selma, it opened the way for the enfranchisement of the majority of blacks throughout the South.

The second day of the new year brought King to Selma to shape the kind of crisis that would force the federal government to crack white southern interference with black voting. During January and February 1965, the SCLC mobilized blacks in a march to the courthouse, where they would petition to register. At first, a moderate white faction in Selma, represented by the city's director of public safety, Wilson Baker, kept Sheriff Clark and his troops in line. This group, which had taken over political control of the city, believed that brutal suppression of black protest would generate unfavorable publicity and endanger new opportunities for business and civic development. "[T]he social, economic, and industrial complexion of this community," the editor of Selma's newspaper commented, "has suddenly and simultaneously arrived at a point from which there can be no turning aside." Restraint more than racial reform was uppermost on their minds, as Baker declared in referring to the demonstrators: "If we can only get the bastards out of town without getting them arrested, we'll have 'em whipped." Patience, however, was a virtue Clark did not possess, and he soon ordered the arrest of scores of peaceful black protesters.

His tough posture did not deter Selma's blacks; it only united them further. When usually cautious middle-class African-American teachers joined Reverend Reese on a march to the courthouse, they raised black solidarity to a new height. Though the educators did not wind up in jail, on February 1, Martin Luther King, Jr., did. Imprisoned for four days, King directed his aides from his cell to pressure President Johnson "to intervene in some way." Upon his release, he met personally with the chief executive and received assurances that a voting rights bill was in preparation.

Meanwhile, the SCLC attempted to hasten delivery of this promised congressional legislation. In mid-February a night march in neighboring Perry County resulted in the first fatality of the Selma suffrage campaign. In conjunction with the Perry County Civic League, the SCLC had convened a mass meeting and attempted to conduct a peaceful rally, only to come under siege from city, county, and state police. While trying to shield his mother from a beating by a state trooper, twenty-six-year-old Jimmie Lee Jackson was shot in the stomach and later died. Several reporters, including Richard Valeriani of the National Broadcasting Company, were also injured in the melee, thereby ensuring that this police riot received unfavorable publicity from the national media. A series of protests continued throughout the month, and King pledged, "We are going to bring a voting bill into being in the streets of Selma."

In the aftermath of Jackson's shooting, the SCLC began to conceive of dramatically expanding the demonstrations into a march from Selma to Montgomery, fifty miles away. Following the murder, blacks in Perry County discussed the possibility of carrying Jackson's body to Montgomery and depositing it on the steps of the state capitol. "We had to do something," Albert Turner, one of the local leaders recalled, "to point out to the nation the evils of the system." After Jackson's burial, the SCLC picked up on the idea and planned a mass march from Selma to Montgomery to begin on Sunday, March 7. With King having returned to Atlanta that day, one of his aides, Hosea Williams, and the chairman of SNCC, John

Bloody Sunday

Lewis, led 600 protesters over the Edmund Pettus Bridge toward the capital city. Before they could get across, however, state troopers and Clark's posse charged into the procession, lobbed tear gas canisters, and clubbed and chased the marchers back to town. Mrs. Boynton, who had previously been roughed up by the sheriff, was knocked unconscious in the assault. "The horses... were more humane than the troopers; they stepped over fallen victims," she wryly remarked.

This display of raw aggression finally provided the SCLC with the provocative incident it needed to mobilize public opinion and secure federal intervention. Television cameras vividly recorded the events of "Bloody Sunday," and the American Broadcasting Company interrupted its network premier showing of the film *Judgment at Nuremburg*, the story of the Nazi war trials, to present footage of the Fascist-style behavior here at home.

Throughout this period, King and other civil rights leaders held several meetings with the President and urged him to introduce legislation immediately to outlaw literacy requirements for voter registration and to authorize the assignment of federal registrars. Johnson intended to support a suffrage measure, but he had several options from which to choose, including taking the slow route of a constitutional amendment. The escalating racial conflict in Selma prompted the chief executive to scuttle any proposal that did not move swiftly to dismantle discriminatory registration barriers. A

Alabama state troopers, wearing gas masks, attack John Lewis on "Bloody Sunday" in Selma. (UPI/Bettmann Newsphotos)

growing coalition of lawmakers in both political parties called for quick congressional action, and outside of Dixie, civil rights sympathizers held a wave of protests in support of the Selma marchers. In the nation's capital hundreds of marchers demanded that Washington come to the aid of the suffragists, and a contingent from SNCC dramatically mounted a sit-in at the Justice Department to push it in the same direction. Meanwhile, the demonstrations in Alabama and the national outcry they engendered pushed President Johnson to accelerate his legislative timetable, dictated the selection of the most potent legislative option, and created the favorable political climate to guarantee its passage.

Even before the President had an opportunity to move forward, King and his followers precipitated a new crisis. They rescheduled the pilgrimage to Montgomery for March 9, despite the issuance of a federal court decree postponing it. King had not violated a federal judicial order before, but in this instance he was ready to proceed to show that racist violence could not be used to derail the civil rights movement. President Johnson sent to Selma his personal emissary, LeRoy Collins, former governor of Florida and director of the federal Community Relations Service, who carried on negotiations separately with the marchers and the state police and successfully defused the crisis. Accordingly, the protesters walked to the end of the bridge, knelt in prayer, and turned back, while the troopers calmly monitored the situation. This peaceful resolution did not prevent a group of whites from killing one of the returning marchers, the Reverend James Reeb, a white minister from Boston. Brutally beaten while he walked the streets of Selma, Reeb soon died from his wounds.

After federal Judge Frank M. Johnson lifted his ban, the parade finally began on March 21, two weeks after Bloody Sunday. By that time, Governor George C. Wallace refused to furnish protection for the marchers, forcing Johnson to federalize the Alabama National Guard for that purpose. Their presence generally deterred violence but could not prevent one further slaying of a white civil rights volunteer, Mrs. Viola Liuzzo of Detroit, as she rode in her car with a black companion en route to Montgomery to pick up returning marchers. The deaths of Liuzzo and Reeb especially shocked northern whites, including the President.

In the meantime, this renewed round of demonstrations produced the long-awaited presidential proposal on voting rights. On March 15, in a magnificent address to a joint session of Congress

televised to an audience of 70 million Americans, Johnson praised
the Selma demonstrators as freedom fighters and admonished Congress to allow "no delay, no hesitation, no compromise with" passage of remedial legislation to aid their cause. In one eloquent and
memorable moment, he adopted the language of the civil rights
movement and promised, "We shall overcome." Two days later,
the administration measure reached the halls of Congress.

The Selma struggle had developed along two different fronts.
Local movement leaders in Dallas County desired above all to un-
clog the registration process in their community. As its top priority,
the DCVL hoped to place blacks on the voter lists and welcomed
any action that brought significant modifications in biased registration procedures. When a federal judge instructed the enrollment
board to cease administering literacy tests and to start processing
black applicants at a speedier rate, the Voters League considered
it a substantial step toward reaching its major goal. In contrast,
the SCLC looked beyond the immediate arena and focused on obtaining national legislation to enfranchise blacks throughout the region. King and his aides argued "that if Selma Negroes gained [the
right to vote] under special court order or through community
agreement...this would not satisfy SCLC." Nevertheless, the
grassroots goal and the broader civil rights aim remained inter-
twined in support of extending the ballot; only the tactics differed.
In the end, the voting rights bill, forged as a result of the Selma
campaign, gave each side what it desired.

Johnson's suffrage plan took the forceful approach recommended by civil rights proponents. Instead of a constitutional
amendment, the chief executive asked Congress simply to pass legislation that suspended literacy tests, authorized the attorney general to dispatch federal registrars and observers to recalcitrant
counties, and empowered the Justice Department to clear in advance changes in state electoral rules that might unfairly burden
black voters. Johnson's lawyers had designed these provisions to
enforce suffrage expansion through the administrative machinery of
the executive branch rather than by the judiciary, where equal voting rights had been stalled for so long. Consequently, the measure
contained an automatic triggering mechanism devised to snare only
those states and localities that employed a literacy test and in which
less than a majority of those eligible had registered to vote or
had voted in the presidential election of 1964. As a result of this

formula, Alabama, Georgia, Louisiana, Mississippi, South Carolina, Virginia, and sections of North Carolina would come under federal supervision.

Introduced in March, the voting rights bill encountered relatively little difficulty in Congress, and by early August it had become law. The final version followed closely the outline of Johnson's recommendation and also adopted a provision allowing the affected jurisdictions to escape coverage once they proved to the federal district court in Washington, D.C., that they had not employed a discriminatory test or device for the previous five years. In addition, the lawmakers issued a finding that the poll tax infringed upon the right to vote, and they directed the attorney general to initiate litigation, which resulted the following year in the removal of the levy in the four southern states that still required it in nonfederal elections. (The Twenty-fourth Amendment, ratified in 1964, had eliminated the franchise fee in all national elections.)

This landmark legislation emerged in such powerful shape for a variety of reasons. The President displayed a strong commitment to the bill and exercised firm leadership in guiding it through the legislature. His aides worked diligently to round up key votes and keep supporters in line at critical moments. Johnson helped win over to his position the Senate Republican leader, Everett Dirksen of Illinois, which guaranteed bipartisan backing for the administration's version of the measure. The President's task was made easier because of the favorable climate of opinion created by Reverend King's handling of the Selma episode. Southern whites found it increasingly difficult to defend the brutal opposition to black suffrage in Alabama, and their congressional representatives failed to mount their customary fierce challenge to the legislation. A Gallup Poll taken during the march to Montgomery reported that 76 percent of the nation favored a voting rights bill; in the South a surprising 49 percent of the sample indicated approval compared with 37 percent in opposition. Democratic Representative Hale Boggs of Louisiana summed up the sentiment of forty of his colleagues from the South who voted for the legislation: "I . . . support this bill because I believe the fundamental right to vote must be a part of this great experiment in human progress under freedom which is America."

The Voting Rights Act resulted in the reenfranchisement of the majority of southern blacks. Within four years after its passage, approximately three-fifths of southern black adults had registered to vote. The most striking gains occurred in the deep South, where resistance to the suffrage had been most harsh. In Mississippi, black registration leaped from 6.7 percent in 1964 to 59.4 in 1968. Similarly, black enrollment in Alabama jumped from 23 percent to 53 percent. In Dallas County, the scene of the Selma demonstrations, the number of registered blacks soared from less than 1,000 to over 8,500 within months after the suffrage law took effect.

The combination of federal power and grassroots activism helped generate the stunning rise in black political participation. The suspension of literacy requirements removed the major obstacle to black registration, and most of the new voters were signed up by local officials who complied with the law. In hard-core areas where blacks still encountered difficulty in securing the ballot, federal examiners intervened to place the applicants' names directly on the rolls. The greatest opportunities for success occurred when federal registrars operated in localities that also experienced voter registration drives. The presence of civil rights organizations laid the basis for progress by building solidarity among blacks and providing them with the strength to confront those risks involved in challenging white segregationists. The freedom movement bound people together in collaborative projects and broke down some of the helplessness they felt when facing the burdens of discrimination alone. As Mary King, a SNCC staff member, has written about political organizing in Mississippi: "If blacks failed individually they succeeded collectively, because of the learning and experience gained."

However potent the law, the federal government expected the civil rights groups themselves to register the bulk of disfranchised blacks. "Legislation is not self-implementing," the NAACP's Roy Wilkins acknowledged. "There is work to be done." The new law challenged civil rights proponents to undertake a "tedious, unglamorous task" that required "more recruits, more money and more dedication." After 1965, all of those resources were in short supply as the days of large demonstrations and widespread national support for the civil rights movement drew to a close.

To register additional voters, the Southern Regional Council once again formed a Voter Education Project. From 1966 to 1968, this second VEP funded and coordinated over 200 suffrage drives throughout the South. Not only did it help underwrite the costs of well-established groups like the NAACP in conducting enrollment campaigns, but the Atlanta-based group also injected money into the efforts of local civic associations, many of which had been spawned or nurtured by the civil rights movement. These projects attempted to empower blacks, individually and collectively, who had not previously felt a sense of political worth. To combat generations of political helplessness, they embarked on programs of basic education to teach lessons fundamental to expressing first-class citizenship. Vernon Jordan, the director of VEP, explained the problem: "Too many of these people have been alienated from the political process for too long a time... and so we have to... teach them what a local government is, how it operates, and try to relate their votes to the things they want."

RISE OF BLACK POWER

Heightened racial consciousness, instilled through the freedom struggle and boosted by the Voting Rights Act, swelled even further with the emergence of "black power." A concept that embodied racial pride and solidarity, it partially grew out of the positive experiences of the freedom struggle. The collective engagement of blacks against Jim Crow and disfranchisement through boycotts, sit-ins, freedom rides, voter registration drives, and other political activities fostered self-respect and a feeling of political efficacy. Men and women, boys and girls, who had long been relegated to the sidelines of southern politics, became active agents in reclaiming first-class citizenship and in transforming the structures of oppression. The Montgomery bus boycott, for example, did more than withhold "patronage from the bus; it... [restored] dignity to the patrons," as Joseph Lowery, an SCLC official, noted. He explained, "prior to the bus boycotts, the determination of our freedom rested with the courts. With the bus boycott, *we* determined it."

The notion of black power also arose from some of the negative consequences of the civil rights struggle. Resistance to racism spawned it, and disillusionment with white liberals nurtured it. The failure of the federal government to protect civil rights workers and the willingness of liberal whites to compromise the Mississippi Freedom Democratic Party's convention challenge in 1964 outraged many black activists. Furthermore, within the South, the constant exposure to violence and harassment faced by black and white civil rights organizers produced enormous tensions between them. Under these circumstances, even the most well-meaning white volunteers were perceived by their black comrades as guilty of paternalism. Middle-class, college-educated whites who journeyed to the South for a march or a voter registration campaign often had superior skills and resources compared to the blacks they worked beside. Their efforts, no matter how unself-conscious or helpful, were sometimes perceived as perpetuating white dominance. "Look at these fly-by-night freedom fighters bossing everybody around," a black SNCC member bitterly commented during the 1964 Mississippi Freedom Summer about white students who could soon return to their comfortable northern campuses.

The black power slogan first gained notoriety in June 1966, on a march initiated by James Meredith to mobilize black Mississippians to register to vote in the wake of passage of the Voting Rights Act. Soon after the pilgrimage through the Magnolia State had begun, Meredith, whose admission to the state university had sparked a riot in 1962, was shot and wounded. Rising to take up his cause, leaders of SCLC, SNCC, and CORE set out to complete the trek. Along the way, Stokely Carmichael, the chairman of SNCC, pointed out the new direction toward which many blacks were turning. At a stop in Greenwood, Mississippi, he declared that blacks should concentrate on gaining political control over their own communities. Deemphasizing integration and moral appeals to the consciences of whites, Carmichael proclaimed: "The only way we gonna stop them white men from whippin' us is to take over. We been saying freedom for six years and we ain't got nothin'. What we gonna start saying is Black Power."

Stokely Carmichael was a movement veteran who had grown up in New York City. A senior at the prestigious Bronx High School of Science when lunch counter sit-ins swept the South in 1960, Carmichael joined in demonstrations against Jim Crow. The following year he rode the buses as a freedom rider, was arrested in Mississippi, and served a jail sentence in the state prison at Parchman. In the early sixties, Carmichael attended Howard University and together with several other students formed the Nonviolent Action Group (NAG), an affiliate of SNCC. As a student he was influenced by his reading of Marx and by contact with Malcolm X, the influential Black Muslim minister, whom he invited to speak at Howard. His campus views matured and grew more militant by virtue of

From left to right, Floyd McKissick of CORE, Martin
Luther King, Jr., of SCLC, and Stokely Carmichael
of SNCC on the last leg of the Meredith march into
Jackson. (Bob Fitch/Black Star)

his experiences on SNCC battlefields in the Mississippi delta and
the Alabama black belt. In May 1966, the articulate and charming
twenty-four-year-old Carmichael became chairman of SNCC, replacing John Lewis and signaling a change in direction of the organization toward black nationalism.

The chant of black power voiced both cultural and political aspirations. More of a rallying cry than a systematic program, black
power expressed the dual message of racial unity and group self-
determination. Heavily influenced by his activities as a SNCC field-
worker in Mississippi and Alabama, Carmichael saw the key to liberation in the political organizing of black communities. His
personal experiences in the South found reinforcement in his identification with the African struggle against European colonialism.

Moreover, Carmichael's reading of America's multiethnic history taught him the necessity for minority groups to develop "their own institutions with which to represent their communal needs within the larger society."

In collaboration with Charles V. Hamilton, a political scientist who had taught at Tuskegee Institute, Carmichael attempted to clarify his views by publishing *Black Power: The Politics of Liberation in America*. Combining the moral outrage and toughened perspective of an embittered SNCC veteran with the scholarly analysis of an academic social scientist, this 1967 book rejected integration and criticized the values of white middle-class society as "antihumanist" and "racist." Denying that black power was merely "racism in reverse," the authors argued that blacks had no intention of turning whites into second-class citizens on the basis of their skin color. Instead, Carmichael and Hamilton espoused self-determination and self-identity as the goals of black power: "full participation in the decisionmaking processes affecting the lives of black people, and recognition of the virtues in themselves as black people." Acknowledging the predominance of race throughout American history, they contended that blacks could not end discrimination on a color-blind, individual basis but could only do so by organizing their own communities around common group concerns. For the present, they ruled out coalitions with whites, including some former allies; however, once blacks had developed independent bases of political and economic power, Carmichael and Hamilton held open the possibility of creating biracial alliances based on mutual interest. Yet if the authors intended their message to be interpreted as problack rather than antiwhite, they refused to soothe white sensibilities by guaranteeing that the outcome of black power would be nonracist. "The final truth," they asserted without apology, "is that white society is not entitled to reassurances, even if it were possible to offer them."

The rhetoric of black power produced divisions within the civil rights movement, but its substance evoked widespread appeal among blacks. Julian Bond, the communications director of SNCC, considered black power the logical outgrowth of the freedom struggle. He traced its lineage "from the courtroom to the streets in favor of integrated facilities, from the . . . backwoods roads in quest of the right to vote, from the ballot box to the meat of politics, the organization of voters into self-interest units." Dr. King, who participated with Carmichael on the Meredith march, disapproved of the antiwhite connotations of the phrase and the inflammatory remarks that frequently accompanied it. However, he applauded attempts "to build racial pride and refute the notion that black is evil and ugly." As King had expressed many times, most recently in Selma, the ballot offered a critical tool for exhibiting pride and achieving equality. Blacks of more radical persuasions shared this view. Malcolm X, the charismatic black nationalist leader whose ideology differed in most respects from King's, agreed with him that if blacks were fully permitted to exercise their constitutional right to vote they "would sweep all of the racists and segregationists out of office... [and] would change the entire political structure of the country."

The controversial black power concept had a mixed impact on black political development. On the one hand, it helped to splinter the civil rights coalition and hastened the decline of two of its most innovative components, SNCC and CORE. Having started out firmly committed to interracial cooperation, they became increasingly disillusioned with white liberals and the prospect of blacks gaining their freedom under white leadership. To the extent that whites had a continuing place in the movement, it was to work within their own communities to combat racist attitudes. As these two groups applied black power principles to their organizations and white participation dwindled, they lost considerable institutional and financial backing. Increasingly isolated from mainstream civil rights groups as well as from whites, by the end of the decade SNCC had virtually disappeared and CORE was in serious disarray. Their deterioration deprived blacks, especially in the South, of the kind of imaginative leadership that had rallied many local communities to organize for freedom. Much work remained to be done in registering voters and summoning them to political action, and the departure of these important organizations from the scene made those tasks more difficult.

On the other hand, burgeoning racial pride among African-Americans was instrumental for black political mobilization. Following successful completion of the legislative struggle to obtain the suffrage, political activists had to convert the disfranchised into actual voters. Collective action had demonstrated the power of an oppressed group to reshape its political world, and the racial esteem that developed convinced blacks that politics was as much their business as whites'. Traditionally, individuals with little income and education had a low rate of political participation. Con-

centrated disproportionately at the bottom end of the socioeconomic scale, blacks nonetheless became politically involved at a
level above that predicted from their backgrounds. "Organization,
with an emphasis on group consciousness and a sense of group efficacy," according to one political scientist, accounted for the difference. In Mississippi, where the black registration figure soared in
the years following passage of the Voting Rights Act, a black observer touring the Magnolia State remarked upon the transformation in this way: "It is so good to realize that we are casting aside
the feelings of inferiority and shame and realizing what a strong
people we are."

The expanded electoral mobilization of blacks further stimulated their interest in competing for public office. This was especially true in areas with a large number of blacks among the eligible
voters, where the chances of electing a black candidate seemed
high. Just as acquisition of the ballot furnished a necessary step toward advancing first-class citizenship, so did the election of blacks
serve as a badge of equality. The running of black candidates both
reflected racial pride and presented a stimulus to further black
political mobilization. The election of a black to a post in a rural
county in Mississippi, the winner asserted, "will give the Negro
race the feeling...like they can progress, and this in itself [will
make] more people run for public office."

As southern blacks began competing for a growing number of
political positions, they were most successful at the local level. Because blacks remained a clear minority of the state and national
electorates, their greatest chances for success came in those towns
and counties in which they constituted a majority of the voting-age
population. A decade after enactment of the Voting Rights Act law
nearly 50 percent of black elected officials held municipal government posts. The largest number of black officials sat on city councils, and about three-fifths of those were in small towns with a population of less than 5,000. This same pattern held true for southern
black mayors, approximately 66 percent of whom presided over
municipalities with under 5,000 residents.

A raised racial consciousness accounted for much of the support
for turning whites out of office and replacing them with blacks;
however, part of the explanation stemmed from practical political
considerations. In most places in the South, especially where blacks
were in the majority, few whites were initially willing to support

black candidates or enter into alliances with them. Without white collaboration, blacks had little choice but to go it alone. In Greene County, Alabama, in the rural black belt, a leader of the group of blacks who took control of the government explained the futility of constructing an interracial coalition: "We wanted the government to be polka dot, but the whites wouldn't cooperate, so we had to make it all chocolate."

In a similar manner, blacks constituted a majority of the population in Lowndes County, Alabama, and sought to branch out on their own. After the 1965 Selma-to-Montgomery march, Stokely Carmichael had remained in Lowndes County to help in the political mobilization of the black community. Under the tutelage of SNCC, local blacks formed the independent Lowndes County Freedom Organization (LCFO) to compete against the white-dominated Democratic party. "To me," John Hulett, LCFO's chairman remarked, "the Democratic primaries...are something like a gambler who carries a marked card around in his pocket and every now and then has to let somebody win to keep the game going." Choosing the black panther as its insignia, an emblem of fierce racial pride, at the end of the decade LCFO succeeded in electing Hulett to the most critical county office of sheriff.

These triumphs were repeated elsewhere. In Hancock County, Georgia, blacks comprised about 75 percent of the residents and had only recently made inroads in challenging total white domination of their government. In 1964, local black leaders formed the Hancock County Democratic Club to promote voter registration and political education. A combination of civil rights organizing and the passage of the 1965 Voting Rights Act succeeded in enfranchising a majority of Hancock's black electorate. In 1966, this paid off in the election of three blacks to county posts, and two years later blacks captured two of the three seats on the powerful county commission.

Much of the success of black political efforts here could be attributed to John McCown. A civil rights veteran, he had worked with the SCLC and the Georgia Council on Human Relations. In Hancock he built upon the previous voter registration drives of the County Democratic Club and expanded its endeavors to secure federal poverty program benefits for blacks. Riding the crest of expanded black enrollment, in 1968 he became one of the two blacks to win election to the county commission and, for the first time, a black became a probate judge, the most important official at the courthouse. McCown had managed to construct a potent political organization that reduced black fears of participation and provided economic incentives to vote. His message appealed to black pride. "Instead of trying to change the heart of the lady at the welfare department," he declared, "it's better to get in a position to be her boss."

Severe tensions accompanied the transfer of power from whites to blacks, however. The Ku Klux Klan paraded through the streets on election eve, and assorted threats were hurled at black candidates. Once in office, McCown upset whites even further with his vigorous attempts to desegregate public schools and generate black economic development. In addition, McCown's abrasive manner offended whites, and in 1971 relations between the races plummeted to a new low in what was called "the Hancock County arms race." Sparta, the county seat with an all-white government, began to stockpile machine guns, allegedly to protect its residents. In response, the black-controlled county commission ordered its own cache of machine guns and sponsored the formation of a "hunting club." The confrontation ended only with the intervention of Governor Jimmy Carter, who negotiated an uneasy truce between the protagonists.

Nevertheless, verbal sniping continued for the next several years during which McCown was indicted for misusing federal funds. The turbulence finally ended after the outspoken McCown was killed in a plane crash in early 1976. A controversial figure was gone, but black political power remained. Even with McCown's tragic death blacks still controlled sixteen of eighteen positions in the government of Hancock County.

In other places blacks who gained political power found some whites willing to cooperate. In 1966, in Macon County, Alabama, the site of historic battles over black reenfranchisement, Lucius Amerson defeated the white incumbent for sheriff. Though Amerson won with solid grassroots black support, he declined to espouse the rhetoric of black power. Upon taking office, he received support from influential whites, including the probate judge and members of the Tuskegee City Council and County Commission. The chairman of the latter body, Allen Parker, helped promote interracial goodwill among officials and labored to enlarge county employment opportunities for blacks. "The public attitude...has changed

tremendously," Sheriff Amerson declared, "and has helped destroy
...the feeling that existed among Negroes as well as whites that a
Negro couldn't get cooperation from the white community."

The Macon County model pointed to the direction in which
black politics would head. Most black officials recognized the necessity of forming coalitions with whites to broaden their power
base. Only at the local level, where blacks were in the majority,
could they afford to ignore whites; and even there, the blacks had
to take whites into account to obtain needed economic resources.
The towns and hamlets where most black officials operated were
impoverished and depended on funds from state and national governments for internal improvements. Outnumbered in these arenas, as a fact of political life they needed to enter into alliances with
white lawmakers. Thus, black politicians who first obtained office
on the basis of appeals to racial pride nonetheless were compelled
to make common cause with whites to achieve their racial aims.

Black Mississippians were also torn between separatist and coalitionist tendencies. For them the civil rights struggle had meant a
way not only to secure the right to vote but also to obtain a fair
share of political power. Toward these ends, they had created the
Mississippi Freedom Democratic Party to stimulate voter registration and gain control of the instrumentality that dominated political
affairs in the state. Though interracial in conception—Ed King, the
white minister at Tougaloo College was one of its founders—in
practice the Freedom party reflected black consciousness and supported the election of black candidates whenever possible. "We
want to be on the ground level, where the decisions are made
about us," explained Bob Moses. "We don't want to [be] mobilized
every four years to vote. We want to be in the actual running of
things."

This strategy of encouraging independent black political action
clashed with the coalitionist approach of the NAACP. Since the
campaign to oust Theodore Bilbo from the Senate after World War
II, the NAACP had actively struggled to tear down the Magnolia
Curtain of racism draped across the state. During the 1950s and until his assassination in 1963, Medgar Evers, along with leaders like
Amzie Moore, Aaron Henry, and Hartman Turnbow, had kept
alive the voter registration efforts that SNCC and its allies would
build upon. The NAACP had collaborated with SNCC in launching
the MFDP and its 1964 convention challenge; however, after that

event the two groups drifted apart. Alarmed by the growing black power perspective of its rival, the older association chose to join with white moderates and labor leaders to seek national Democratic party recognition for their state's interracial coalition. In 1968, their protest proved successful, and a biracial Loyalist Democratic group supplanted the MFDP, which soon disbanded, as the chief vehicle for party reform among blacks and whites in the state.

The Democrats expanded black representation in party affairs not only in Mississippi but throughout the South. Wary of the formation of militant, predominantly black Democratic factions in Mississippi and Alabama, they sanctioned the claims of more moderate, interracial delegations, which pressed for seating at the 1968 convention. In addition, the party adopted far-reaching affirmative action guidelines that required "representation of minority groups on the national convention delegation in reasonable relationship to the group's presence in the population of the state." The results were striking. In 1972, at the Democratic presidential nominating meeting, 56 percent of the delegates from Mississippi were black, and in the delegations representing states covered by the Voting Rights Act, the proportion of blacks equaled or exceeded the percentage of blacks in the population.

Although they disdained political separatism, coalitionists tacitly supported their own version of black power as a form of voting power. Charles Evers, who succeeded his brother, Medgar, as the NAACP's field agent in Mississippi and who mounted several campaigns for political office in the state, urged blacks to "control the ballot of the county... control the entire county where we are predominant. We don't holler Black Power—but watch it." The NAACP and its black opposition did not disagree so much over ends—political parity for blacks—but over the means to attain it. Each side could have agreed with the view expressed by a black Mississippian who remarked: "Power is invested in the ballot, and that's why the white man worked like hell to keep you away from it."

Both the coalition and separatist courses significantly increased black office-holding in the years following adoption of the Voting Rights Act. In 1964, fewer than 25 black elected officials governed in the South, but by the end of the decade the figure had soared to nearly 500. In 1970, the number of elected blacks climbed still higher—to over 700.

Besides yielding these impressive gains, black ballots also helped elect more moderate white officials. In Dallas County, Alabama, shortly after the Voting Rights Act went into effect, newly enfranchised blacks remedied a long-standing political grievance and helped vote Sheriff Jim Clark out of office. In his place they installed Wilson Baker, the Selma law enforcement chief who had vainly tried to forestall violence against civil rights protesters in his city. In 1966, though blacks were not yet strong enough at the polls to beat the segregationist gubernatorial candidate, Lurleen Wallace, running as a surrogate for her husband, George, four years later blacks elsewhere joined with white majorities to elect moderate governors in Arkansas, Florida, Georgia, and South Carolina. Racist demagoguery in southern election campaigns was fast becoming a relic.

Despite these successes, southern blacks still encountered a variety of roadblocks to political equality. The formal impediments to voter registration had mainly disappeared, but white officials continued to devise techniques to hamper blacks who had managed to enroll for the suffrage. In 1971, white politicians in Mississippi ordered the reregistration of voters in approximately thirty counties, in many of which a large number of blacks had only recently enrolled. In other sections of the deep South, local registrars conducted business at inconvenient hours that failed to accommodate the schedules of working-class blacks, and they functioned exclusively at county courthouses too far away for many rural blacks easily to reach.

RACIAL POLARIZATION

As blacks reentered the political arenas of the South, mobilized their forces, and competed for office, the nation witnessed a sharp rise in racial polarization. Even at the height of the freedom struggle, many white Americans sympathized with black integrationist goals but disliked the movement's aggressive, confrontational tactics. In 1963, 64 percent of the whites polled in a nationwide survey had expressed the view that blacks were pushing too quickly for equality. The following year blacks rioted in the northern ghettos of Harlem, Rochester, Jersey City, and Philadelphia, and over the remainder of the decade violent uprisings spread to some 300 cities, involving a half-million blacks. The riots consumed millions of dollars in property damage and resulted in 50,000 arrests, 8,000 injuries, and 250 deaths, mostly of blacks. In 1967, in Detroit alone, 43 people were killed, 2,000 were wounded, and 5,000 were burned out of their homes.

The riots reflected both the reawakening of black consciousness and the continued awareness of unresolved grievances. Civil rights battles, while fought primarily in the South, inspired blacks everywhere to identify with the cause of liberation. Though rejecting nonviolence as a tactic, the rioters had taken pride in the willingness of their southern black brothers and sisters to stand up collectively to white racism. In the midst of the conflagration in Detroit, a looter explained what drove him into the streets. In words very much reminiscent of black protesters in the South, he explained that he was looking for "respect as a man, as a first-class citizen."

Outside the South, the law did not require segregation or promote disfranchisement; yet African-Americans faced systematic racial discrimination that deprived them of full equality. They had the right to vote and the right to enter public accommodations, but those who dwelled in squalid ghettos lacked decent housing, employment, and evenhanded police protection. Some notable economic improvements had occurred during the 1960s. Median black family income climbed to 61 percent of that earned by whites, the percentage of black families living below the poverty level diminished to 30 percent, and the unemployment rate for married black males dropped to 4 percent by mid-decade. However, these gains did not keep pace with rising black expectations stimulated by the civil rights struggle. Through rioting, many blacks sought to deliver a message of protest to white Americans that focused attention on the seriousness of their plight. They turned to extralegal methods because conventional political channels had failed to resolve their complaints.

The riots yielded mixed results. Many cities responded by seeking ways to relieve the miserable social conditions that fueled the disorders. They took out "riot insurance" by setting up programs to provide job training, recreational facilities, slum clearance, and more effective communication between police and the residents they served. At the same time, city and state governments also devised more punitive measures and put a good deal of their resources into riot control by beefing up their defense arsenals with expensive and powerful weapons.

This latter response mirrored the growing antagonism of whites toward black protest demands. Appalled by the violence and lawlessness, many whites called for a restoration of public order, severe punishment of rioters, and withdrawal of funding for poverty projects that appeared to reward antisocial behavior. Although civil rights leaders such as Dr. King and Roy Wilkins denounced violence, others like SNCC's Stokely Carmichael fanned the flames of discord. Carmichael and his black power associates were not responsible for the spontaneous eruptions that swept over American cities, but their inflammatory rhetoric scared and angered whites. "When you talk about black power," the SNCC chairman declared following a riot in Cleveland, "you talk of building a movement that will smash everything Western civilization has created." This type of provocative statement in tandem with the ghetto riots helped reinforce the menacing connotation that black power had assumed.

The rise of the Black Panther party (BPP) strengthened this image. Adopting the trademark of the Lowndes County Freedom Organization, Huey P. Newton and Bobby Seale, who had met each other in college, formed the organization in October 1966 in Oakland, California. In contrast to the LCFO, the Panthers were not a political party mainly interested in contesting elections. Along with Eldridge Cleaver, a thirty-one year-old ex-convict and writer who had spent most of his adult life in prison, they denounced capitalism and regarded the ghettos as an exploited colony within the United States. Blending black nationalism and Marxist-Leninist doctrines, the BPP considered itself as the revolutionary vanguard leading the urban masses in the destruction of "the machinery of the oppressor." In the ghetto this meant the police—"the military arm of our oppressors"—which residents frequently saw not as protectors but as the guardians of their misery and the agents of brutality. In fact, most of the summer riots had been sparked by incidents of excessive police force and charges of brutality. The Panthers responded by taking up arms for self-defense and patroling their neighborhoods to keep watch over the police. In 1967, a bloody confrontation between Newton and the police left one officer dead and the Panther founder wounded and placed under arrest. The next year, another shootout in Oakland killed a BPP official.

Often lost amidst this violence was the broader political program the Panthers advocated. In its original platform, the BPP demanded jobs for the unemployed, decent housing for the poor, and a greater voice for blacks in determining decisions affecting their communities. Working toward these goals, in Oakland and in cities such as Chicago, where they set up chapters, the Panthers instituted free breakfast and health care programs to improve neighborhood conditions. They conducted classes in black history and warned against the dangers of drug use, seeking to build racial pride in young black children and to instill confidence in their ability to reshape their lives.

Initially the Panthers put greater emphasis on community organizing than on electoral politics. Their battle cry of "power to the people" called for local control of economic and political institutions based upon armed struggle; nevertheless, by the late 1960s the Panthers had added the ballot as a weapon in its arsenal. Unlike some other black nationalist groups, the BPP formed alliances with white radicals and competed with them for political office in common cause against class as well as racial exploitation. By then, however, the militant actions of the party brought the weight of local, state, and federal governments upon the group, seriously damaging its efforts. Led by the FBI, whose director viewed the Panthers as "the greatest threat to the internal security of the country," government agents infiltrated the group, provoked internal dissension, and shot and jailed its followers. By the end of the decade, the police had killed over a score of Panthers and arrested some 750.

Meanwhile, such strife and the media attention it attracted had fueled a reactionary white backlash against additional civil rights reforms. No one played on the anxieties of whites better than did George Wallace. Having whipped up the antagonism of southerners against desegregation, the Alabama governor transported his racist messages to the North, where they received a favorable reception from those whites who feared that black progress came at their expense. Wallace exploited class as well as racial tensions. He catered to blue-collar workers and excoriated "left-wing theoreticians, briefcase totin' bureaucrats, ivory tower guideline writers, bearded anarchists, smart alleck editorial writers and pointy headed professors." The racial disturbances of the sixties propelled Wallace's presidential ambitions. In 1964, he tested out his antiestablishment, racist appeals by campaigning for the Democratic presidential nomination. His candidacy eventually fizzled, but not before he showed surprising strength among disgruntled white voters in Indiana, Maryland, and Wisconsin.

The increasing bitterness of racial tensions was reflected at every governmental level. In 1966, the Georgia legislature refused to seat Julian Bond as a duly elected representative from Atlanta. Bond had offended lawmakers by supporting SNCC's opposition to the Vietnam war and calling for alternatives to the military draft. A year later, Congress rejected the credentials of Adam Clayton Powell, who had easily won reelection from Harlem. Powell had embraced black power doctrines during the 1960s, but it was financial and ethical improprieties that got him into trouble. In each case, blacks saw white legislators as practicing a double standard of justice and acting unnecessarily harshly. The U.S. Supreme Court ultimately ruled in favor of Bond and Powell and restored their positions to them.

The politics of black power also aggravated racial discord in Ocean Hill–Brownsville, a section of Brooklyn, New York, populated by low-income, poorly educated African-Americans and Puerto Ricans. In 1967, under a plan sponsored by the New York City Board of Education in cooperation with the Ford Foundation, the United Federation of Teachers (UFT), and local community groups, Ocean Hill–Brownsville became part of an experimental project in school decentralization. Community activists had complained that the school system was failing to educate their children. Pointing accusing fingers at both insensitive bureaucrats and teachers, the overwhelming majority of whom were white, they called for sweeping educational reorganization to help address the needs of ghetto students. The proposal that was adopted fell short of their objectives, but it did establish school decentralization and called for the election of parents and other community residents to serve alongside teachers on a district governing board.

The experiment resulted in some positive achievements. Communitywide elections gave parents a powerful voice in their children's education that was used to introduce new programs emphasizing racial pride and instilling self-worth—two ingredients often absent from the classrooms and corridors of ghetto schools. As more minority teachers, parents, and paraprofessionals became involved in school affairs, students responded enthusiastically. One pupil recalled her excitement over seeing more black faces: "I mean you felt more accepted. You weren't an outsider in your own school. They were part of your environment. I mean they were Black. You can identify with them and they can identify with you."

However, the children soon got caught up in a power struggle between their parents, the teachers union, and the central school board. The Ocean Hill–Brownsville governing council, dominated by community residents, and the chief administrator of the district, Rhody McCoy, wanted greater community control over finances and personnel than the union and central board would allow. Albert Shanker, the president of the UFT, favored community participation, but demanded that teachers' job rights be protected. In the spring of 1968, the local governing agency unilaterally ordered the transfer of thirteen teachers and seven administrators out of the district, precipitating a confrontation with the union and central board over the issue of due process. When the matter was not resolved over the summer, the UFT took almost 54,000 teachers out on strike in September.

The controversy raged from Labor Day to the middle of November, driving a deep wedge between former allies in the civil rights coalition. Those like Shanker and his union followers who had supported the principle of school integration contended that the Ocean Hill–Brownsville experiment had deteriorated into black separatism. McCoy and his allies, many of whom were influenced by a growing emphasis on black consciousness, charged that the union constituted a racist obstacle to educational reform and black self-determination. Although the two sides did not divide strictly along racial lines—the community board hired a majority of white teachers as replacements for the strikers, and influential black activists such as Bayard Rustin supported the union—the conflict exacerbated racial tensions. The dispute turned even uglier and more divisive when charges of anti-Semitism surfaced. Most union members were Jewish, and they were angered by intemperate remarks made by some militants. After an inflammatory memo referring to Jews as "money changers," "bloodsucking exploiters," and "Middle East murderers" was distributed in two schools, the UFT made the already tense situation even worse by reprinting and circulating the missive to thousands of Jews throughout the city. For its part, the local governing board denied charges of anti-Semitism, pointing out that about half the teachers it hired were Jewish. Still, its measured response to the most vicious displays of anti-Semitism failed to settle the nerves of apprehensive Jews.

When the nearly two-month-old strike finally ended, the local school district was placed under state supervision and the union won reinstatement of the dismissed teachers and a new contract guaranteeing employee safeguards. At the same time, the state legislature enacted a measure that decentralized all New York City school districts, but it balanced local participation with limited autonomy for community governing boards. The educational establishment had prevailed, and had proved itself powerful enough to resist radical change. Overall, the political fallout from the dispute poisoned relations between blacks and Jews and between black power advocates and liberal labor leaders, and left the civil rights alliance and the electoral coalition behind it badly frayed.

Black militancy and white backlash also delayed passage of new civil rights legislation. In 1966, the Johnson administration proposed a package that attacked discrimination in housing and offered federal protection for civil rights workers. The former provision applied equally throughout the entire nation, thereby hitting whites in the North close to home. As the target of civil rights assaults expanded beyond the South, whites offered greater resistance. In 1966, a presidential aide complained "that it would have been hard to pass the emancipation proclamation in the atmosphere prevailing this summer." The hostile political atmosphere continued through the fall congressional elections, as Republicans increased their representation in the House by forty-seven seats.

Yet white backlash was not strong enough to kill the civil rights measure. Though President Johnson was deeply disturbed by the outbreak of riots and perceived them as the product of conspiratorial black nationalist forces, he did not retreat from supporting his latest civil rights proposals. He attempted to strike a balance between appearing not to reward the lawless actions of the rioters and backing measures that addressed what he considered to be the legitimate demands of traditional civil rights groups like the NAACP. In this way he could underscore, as one of his aides put it, that "law abiding citizens, black and white, should have and will have the safety and protection of their government." At the same time, he could strengthen the position of his moderate civil rights allies at the expense of their more militant critics. Joining with the NAACP and the Leadership Conference on Civil Rights, a coalition of reform lobbyists, the Johnson administration kept up the legislative pressure; in April 1968, Congress finally passed a civil rights act that featured the controversial fair housing provision. Reflecting the uneasy temper of the times, Congress also enacted a punitive antiriot measure aimed at prosecuting roving black agitators.

This hard-earned legislative victory could not restore unity to the civil rights forces. SNCC and CORE continued down their separatist paths and had little interest in a bill that aimed to promote integration. The SCLC continued to retain its interracial ideals, but broke with the President over his policy of escalating the war in Vietnam. In challenging the administration over this issue, Dr. King parted from his allies in the NAACP and Urban League, who remained loyal to Johnson. King's assassination on April 4, 1968, during the final deliberations on the Civil Rights Act, aided its passage as a tribute to the slain martyr, but also badly weakened the organization that relied heavily on his style of charismatic leadership. In addition to these internal strains that fractured the movement, the Johnson administration greatly accelerated its disintegration from without. The FBI had relentlessly investigated and harassed Dr. King and directed a clandestine counterintelligence program that succeeded in undermining black power groups such as the Panthers.

THE NIXON ADMINISTRATION AND BENIGN NEGLECT

While Johnson struggled to reinforce civil rights moderates at the expense of black radicals, the frustrations of military stalemate in Vietnam combined with antiwar protests at home prompted him not to run for another term as chief executive. The candidates who sought to succeed him guaranteed that African-Americans would remain faithful to the party of the President who had achieved more for civil rights than any of his predecessors. Johnson passed the Democratic standard on to his vice-president, Hubert H. Humphrey, the liberal stalwart who first led the charge, back in 1948, to swing Democrats behind a strong civil rights platform.

Humphrey's chief opponents did not offer black voters much of an alternative. Though once a firm advocate of the civil rights cause, the GOP nominee, Richard M. Nixon, had charted a political route that moved him away from the search for black ballots toward those of conservative white southerners. In this respect he had stiff competition from George Wallace, who ran on the American Independent party ticket and whose demagogic rhetoric and obstructionist actions had hampered black racial advancement.

Two black candidates competed as independents. Eldridge Cleaver, the Black Panther, was nominated by the Peace and Freedom party, a political formation of predominantly white leftists originating in California. The comedian Dick Gregory, who had assumed an active role in the civil rights movement, mounted a campaign that the political scientist Manning Marable concluded was "marked more by political satire than actual political content." Neither candidate had any chance of winning, but each served as an outlet for disaffected black nationalists and white radicals.

In his second bid for the White House, Nixon enthusiastically embraced a southern strategy that would ensure the victory that had narrowly eluded him in 1960. He pursued the same segment of white voters in Dixie that had backed Barry Goldwater in 1964. Besides resurrecting economic positions that attacked the big-spending social welfare programs of Johnson's Great Society, he played on the racial antipathies of conservative white southerners. Speaking out against busing to promote school desegregation, he voiced approval for freedom-of-choice plans that operated to retard full-scale desegregation. In obtaining the Republican nomination over another conservative aspirant, Governor Ronald Reagan of California, he associated himself with Senator Strom Thurmond of South Carolina, the 1948 Dixiecrat candidate, who had subsequently converted to the GOP. The alliance between the two was cemented by their agreement that, if elected, Nixon would slow down school desegregation and voting rights enforcement in the South.

In taking this stand Nixon hoped to undercut potential southern white support for Wallace. The Alabama governor delivered a populist message that echoed the economic and social discontent of working-class whites. To distinguish himself from Nixon and to appeal to a lower-income constituency than that attracted to well-to-do Republicanism, Wallace charged that there was not a "dime's worth of difference between the two major parties." He hammered away on the theme of "law and order," code words that expressed hostility toward black militants, antiwar demonstrators, and the liberal establishment that presumably "coddled" them.

Vice-President Humphrey represented that establishment, and only he actively campaigned for black votes. In a chaotic nominating convention racked by antiwar protests, the Democrats awarded unprecedented delegate representation to black southerners and ensured that their influence would expand even further in the future. On the campaign trail, Humphrey blasted Nixon and Wallace for exploiting "fear and tensions that grip significant portions of our

he was
right
✗

people." Instead of a society dedicated to "opportunity and justice," he warned that his opponents would usher in "a fractured and
separated society—black against white, rich against poor, comfortable against leftout."

As expected, Humphrey's rivals found a fertile field for their
views in the South. The Voting Rights Act had greatly expanded
the size of the black electorate in the region, but in the years immediately following its passage had also led to an upsurge in the
number of whites registering to vote. Whites constituted some 60
to 70 percent of the newly enrolled electorate. In addition, demographic shifts laid the foundation for white defections from candidates of the national Democratic party, who were considered too
liberal. The influx into the sunbelt of white northerners, many of
whom had previously voted Republican, boosted the constituency
for the growth of the GOP in the traditionally one-party South.
Furthermore, as the South became more urbanized, Republicans
drew increasing support from middle- and upper-class whites
whose economic interests tied them more closely to the GOP's outlook.

Neither in the South nor elsewhere in the nation were black
votes abundant enough to offset white abandonment of the Democrats. Though Humphrey received 88 percent of black ballots,
southern whites overwhelmingly lined up behind his opponents.
The Democratic candidate received only 31 percent of southern
votes, most of them blacks, a figure that was nineteen points behind Johnson's in 1964. Nixon and Wallace divided Dixie's white
electorate, each capturing five states and leaving Texas to Humphrey. The GOP contender obtained the support of 35 percent of
the region's electorate, a share only slightly larger than Wallace's
34 percent. The Alabama governor cut into Democratic support in
the North—working-class whites provided half his total votes—and
nationally Wallace obtained 13.5 percent of the ballots cast, the
strongest performance by a third-party contestant since 1924.
Overall, Democratic defections also helped propel Nixon into the
White House. The Republican winner garnered 301 electoral votes
and a plurality of 43.4 percent of the popular votes.

President Nixon attempted to deliver on his southern campaign
strategy. As Ethel Payne, a black journalist, noted shortly after his
election, "Mr. Nixon has no debt to pay black voters." He tried to
lift the burden of civil rights enforcement off the South by extend-

ing it to the North. The President told reporters, "we finally have in this country what the South has wanted and what the South deserves, a one nation policy." However evenhanded this approach sounded, it aimed to weaken civil rights implementation. The Justice Department's Civil Rights Division would be spread too thin with a staff insufficient in size to monitor and litigate against racial discrimination everywhere in the country. Moreover, many critics believed that in expanding civil rights coverage outside the South, Nixon strategists hoped that disgruntled northern politicians would join southerners in opposing strict enforcement of such controversial desegregation remedies as school busing.

Soon after entering the Oval Office, Nixon sought to reverse policy on school integration of fifteen years' standing. In 1969, for the first time since the historic *Brown* decision, federal lawyers appeared in court to support a southern state, Mississippi, in attempting to postpone the implementation of a desegregation plan. Subsequently, the chief executive affirmed his backing for "a truly desegregated public school system" through improvements in the quality of education, rather than by "buying buses, tires, and gasoline to transport young children miles away from their neighborhood schools."

At the same time, the Nixon administration looked to overhaul the provisions of the Voting Rights Act in order to relieve pressure on the South. Most of the important features of the statute were due for renewal after five years, and civil rights advocates favored a simple extension of the law. As with school integration, the President wanted to reshape the measure so that it would extend to the North. Consequently, his attorney general, John Mitchell, requested Congress to scrap the automatic triggering and preclearance sections and in their place authorize the Justice Department to initiate litigation against suffrage discrimination anywhere in the country. The attorney general would be empowered to seek suits halting the imposition of new voting restrictions and to send federal examiners to enforce court orders. Also, the law would suspend the use of literacy tests in the North as well as the South. "Voting rights is not a regional issue," Mitchell asserted. "It is a nationwide concern for every American which must be tested on a nationwide basis."

Civil rights supporters derided the proposal. They viewed the administration bill as a subterfuge to cripple a law that had proved successful. Having experienced the pitfalls of relying on courts to protect black voting rights, they vigorously opposed a return to the judicial approach. After five years, blacks still encountered suffrage problems in the South, and civil rights proponents wanted attention to remain focused on that region. Clarence Mitchell, the chief lobbyist for the NAACP, attacked the Nixon administration's offering as "a sophisticated, a calculated, incredible effort... to make it impossible for us to continue on the constitutional course that we have followed... in protecting the right to vote."

In general, the Nixon administration did not succeed in curbing civil rights advances. Though blacks had lost political clout within the White House, they still retained influence before the Supreme Court and in Congress. In 1969, the high tribunal rebuked the administration for stalling desegregation in Mississippi, and in *Alexander v. Holmes County Board of Education* it ordered an immediate end to dual school systems. Two years later, the justices sanctioned busing as a remedy for fashioning interracial schools in districts that had practiced segregation by law. Disappointed with the ruling in *Swann v. Charlotte-Mecklenburg Board of Education*, Nixon subsequently requested Congress to pass legislation limiting the use of busing, but the proposal failed. By the middle of the decade, southern schools surpassed those in the North as the least segregated in the country. In the South, 47.1 percent of black students attended schools with a white majority compared with 42.5 percent of northern blacks who did so.

With respect to political rights also, Congress and the courts checked the Nixon administration's racial options. In 1970, lawmakers renewed the Voting Rights Act with its original provisions intact. Literacy tests were again suspended for five years, though Nixon got his way in applying this to the entire country. In addition, the legislation extended the franchise to eighteen-year-olds. The following year when the attorney general tried to interpret the preclearance provision in a manner that narrowed its operation, Congress stepped in to frustrate him. In the meantime, the Supreme Court defined the scope of the Voting Rights Act very broadly. Beginning in 1969, it decreed that the statute was not only directed toward voter registration but was also meant to include "all actions to make a vote effective." In a series of decisions the judiciary empowered federal authorities to strike down electoral rules that had the purpose or effect of diluting the strength of black ballots. The conversion from single-member districts to at-large

gerrymander laws

elections, the expansion of municipal boundaries through annexation of largely white areas, and reapportionment plans that produced racially gerrymandered districts were regulations of this type.

Given the judicial mandate and under the watchful eyes of Congress, the Nixon administration satisfactorily fulfilled its constitutional obligation to protect black enfranchisement. Whereas White House policymakers may have wished to slow down implementation of the Voting Rights Act, career service lawyers in the Justice Department carried out their enforcement duties in a highly professional manner. Many, of these attorneys had held their positions since the Johnson era, and they took their cues from the court and the legislature. Consequently, as William E. Leuchtenburg has noted, "much of the positive activity under the Nixon Administration came not because of the enterprise of Nixon and his immediate aides, but rather from the momentum developed by the federal bureaucracy, a momentum no president can easily halt."

Congress also contained a sufficient amount of procivil rights strength to block the chief executive's attempt to appoint conservative southerners to the Supreme Court. In 1969, the Senate rejected the nomination of Clement Haynsworth from Strom Thurmond's South Carolina. A federal judge whose opinions in racial cases had aroused the concern of civil rights groups, Haynsworth was defeated after months of bitter and protracted debate. The next year, the President sent up the name of G. Harrold Carswell to fill the vacancy and was similarly rebuffed. The Florida jurist appeared much less qualified than Haynsworth, a judgment inadvertently rendered by one of his defenders. Even if Carswell "were mediocre, there were a lot of mediocre judges and people and lawyers," Republican Senator Roman Hruska of Nebraska declared. "They are entitled to a little representation, aren't they, and a little chance?" Hearing praise like this, a majority of lawmakers turned down the nominee.

In other areas affecting black advancement, the Nixon administration ranged between moderation and affirmative action. In 1970, one of Nixon's top counselors on domestic affairs, Daniel Patrick Moynihan, a former aide in the Johnson administration, advised the President: "The time may have come when the issue of race could benefit from a period of 'benign neglect'.... The forum has been too much taken over by hysteria, paranoids, and boodlers on all sides.

We may need a period in which Negro progress continues and racial rhetoric fades." Accepting this reasoning, the chief executive attempted to encourage economic self-help as the key to racial equality. In conservative fashion, Nixon promoted black capitalism as the cornerstone of black power. Cleverly expropriating his critics' rhetoric, he contended that despite their stridency and seemingly anticapitalist tones, the militants' ideas more clearly resembled "the doctrines of free enterprise than... those of the welfare thirties—terms of 'pride', 'ownership', 'private enterprise', 'capital', 'self-assurance', 'self-respect'."

To expand minority business opportunities, the President increased funding to the Small Business Administration and the Minority Business Enterprise in the Commerce Department. In 1969, minority firms received $8 million in federal contracts; four years later, they were getting $242 million. Similarly, during this period government aid to minority enterprises leaped from $200 million to $472 million. For the mass of blacks who were destined to remain employees and not employers, the President established the "Philadelphia Plan," which required construction workers' unions involved in federal contracts to sign up and retain a fixed proportion of black apprentices. Befitting his economic philosophy, Nixon's major innovative foray into the field of affirmative action shrewdly shifted the obligation of meeting equal opportunity guidelines away from management and onto organized labor.

BLACK CAUCUSES AND CONVENTIONS

By the end of Nixon's first term, blacks sought new ways to increase their influence. While the legislative and judicial branches of the federal government overrode the executive, black politicians organized to boost their leverage in Congress and shape the direction of public policy. In 1969, Representative Charles Diggs, Jr., a Detroit Democrat, organized the eight other black members of the House of Representatives into an informal committee to work with congressional leaders on civil rights and social welfare issues. Two years later, the Congressional Black Caucus (CBC) was officially formed, and functioned as a lobbying group along the lines of other special-interest blocs in the legislative branch. Though it made policy recommendations to expand benefits for blacks, the caucus succeeded mainly in joining with white liberal lawmakers in waging defensive actions to preserve strong enforcement of suffrage legislation and rescue civil rights programs from conservative assault. In addition, the formation of the CBC inspired black elected officials at the state and local levels to establish similar groups, such as the National Conference of Black Mayors, to present a black perspective on policy matters crucial to minorities.

Though not an official member of the CBC, which consisted solely of House lawmakers, Senator Edward Brooke of Massachusetts became its ally. At a time when the overwhelming majority of African-Americans preferred the Democratic party, Brooke was a Republican who belonged to the GOP's moderate-to-liberal wing. Elected in 1966, from a state with less than a 3 percent black population, the former state attorney general declared: "I can't serve just the Negro cause. I've got to serve all the people of Massachusetts." Nevertheless, as the nation's highest-ranking black elected official, Brooke attempted to press upon the White House his concern for civil rights and other items on the CBC agenda during the years his party held the presidency. He had actively campaigned for Nixon in 1968, but his enthusiasm waned as the President tried to put his southern strategy into practice. Consequently, Senator Brooke joined those of his colleagues who successfully thwarted much of Nixon's effort in that direction.

In the face of the Nixon administration's calculated retreat in many areas of civil rights, the most ambitious attempt to unite black political leaders came with the 1972 National Black Political Convention in Gary, Indiana. The meeting grew out of a call by the CBC for the development of "a national black agenda and the crystallization of a national black strategy for the 1972 elections and beyond." The caucus wound up not giving the conference its official endorsement, but individual members did attend. With some cracks in the foundation of unity already surfacing, convention planners emphasized the need for racial solidarity to "transform black political potential into power commensurate with the number of blacks in the United States." The more than 3,500 delegates who attended the sessions from March 10 to 12 adopted a comprehensive set of recommendations for black political and economic empowerment and created the National Black Political Assembly as an independent force for exerting pressure on white political institutions.

Stressing "unity without uniformity," the meetings were presided over by Diggs, Gary Mayor Richard Hatcher, and Amiri Baraka, the poet and black nationalist. The convention secured agreement on most of the items constituting a national black agenda. It approved resolutions calling for increased black congressional representation, community control of schools, a national health insurance program, and a guaranteed minimum annual income. Moreover, the delegates felt exhilarated by the very act of gathering together to shape a political course for African-Americans to follow. "I guess the strongest image I have about Gary," an organizer for the Mississippi Freedom Democratic Party remembered, "is the fact that black people were able to mobilize, black people from all walks of life, from all different states, to this one focal point."

However, the highly prized unity failed to last. The convention was torn by divisions between racial integrationists and cultural nationalists and between those who proposed forming a third political party and those who defended working within the existing two-party system. Tensions peaked, however, over the issues of school desegregation and support of the Palestine Liberation Organization, a revolutionary group opposed to Zionism and the state of Israel. When the convention voted to endorse black control of neighborhood schools instead of busing and its promotion of integration and to recognize the right of self-determination for Palestinians, integrationists and supporters of Israel vigorously condemned the resolutions. Succeeding meetings of the Black Political Assembly attracted progressively fewer delegates, black nationalists came to dominate them, and black elected officials abandoned them.

The attempt in Gary to forge black political unity collapsed under the weight of clashing political and ideological interests. Without solid support from established electoral leaders, Representative Shirley Chisholm of Brooklyn, New York, made a futile bid to compete in the Democratic presidential primaries in 1972. Her fellow members of the CBC, along with other prominent black Democrats, refused to line up behind her candidacy and instead chose to support the various leading white contenders for their party's nomination. Blacks played a large role at the Democratic National Convention, which nominated Senator George S. McGovern of South Dakota, the coauthor of the convention's newly reformed antidiscriminatory delegate selection rules.

In selecting the liberal McGovern, the Democrats infuriated

those who had found the candidacy of George C. Wallace attractive. The primary season had witnessed the explosive presence of Governor Wallace, who vowed to shake the "eyeteeth out" of the Democratic party. Running a staunchly antibusing campaign aimed at exploiting the white backlash, the Alabama governor defeated ten rivals for the Democratic presidential nomination to capture a victory in Florida with 42 percent of the vote. Wallace's win accurately gauged the mood of the white electorate, as Sunshine State voters passed a nonbinding referendum against forced busing. Fresh from this success, Wallace went on to pile up wins in the normally friendly southern states of Tennessee and North Carolina. The governor delighted crowds with his antielitist rhetoric: "If the pseudointellectuals think it is good to bus little children backwards and forwards...the average man doesn't, and there are more of them than there are [of] the pseudos." Northern voters also responded enthusiastically to this message, and Wallace triumphed in Michigan and Maryland and scored strong second-place finishes in Wisconsin, Pennsylvania, and Indiana. Tragedy struck while he was speaking in Maryland, as an assassin's bullet left him alive but paralyzed from the waist down. Unable to continue campaigning actively, the governor saw his powerful bid for the presidential nomination effectively come to an end.

Even without a Wallace candidacy, the results of the 1972 election suggested the sharpening polarization of the electorate along racial lines. Taking his cue from the Alabamian, the President repeated his own opposition to busing, called for a moratorium on additional court-ordered busing until July 1973, and vowed to "end segregation in a way that does not result in more busing." Winning 60.8 percent of the popular vote, Nixon attracted the vast portion of the southern white electorate that supported Wallace and collected the electoral votes of the entire South. Indeed, in his landslide victory, Nixon carried every state except Massachusetts and predominantly black Washington, D.C. Ironically, African-Americans demonstrated a high degree of the now seemingly elusive racial solidarity in giving the losing candidate more than 85 percent of their ballots.

From the vantage point of state and local arenas, black political progress appeared brighter. Although much remained to be done, following Nixon's reelection the number of black elected officials in the nation stood at over 2,600. Very impressively, the number of minority officeholders in the South climbed to nearly 1,200, up from approximately 875 a year earlier. The rate of increase in black electoral victories was slowing down, but some notable triumphs had occurred. In Selma, Alabama, the civil rights veterans Amelia Boynton and Frederick Reese led five blacks to win half the seats on the city council. Despite the continued existence of racism in more sophisticated forms, a local black leader contended that "by and large things have improved." Elsewhere in the South in 1972, two blacks, Andrew Young of Atlanta, Georgia, and Barbara Jordan of Houston, Texas, were elected to the U.S. House of Representatives. For the first time in seventy years blacks from the former Confederate states sat in Congress.

By the time the Watergate scandal pushed Richard Nixon into retirement, southern blacks had managed to make steady political gains within their communities. At the end of 1974, over 1,500 blacks held public office in the South. This figure included an additional congressman from Memphis, Tennessee, Harold Ford, and a growing number of black state legislators. Of the ninety-four who occupied legislative seats, about forty-eight were elected in 1974 alone, largely as a result of reapportionment ordered by federal courts and the Department of Justice. Birmingham, Alabama, once the most violently racist of all the major cities in the South, counted fifteen blacks in its state legislative delegation. In addition, black ballots continued to serve as an important element in the biracial Democratic party coalition that elected white Dixie moderates to governor's mansions and the U.S. Senate.

Reflecting the growing number of black elected officials, the Joint Center for Political Studies was founded in 1970 and has continued in operation to the present. According to Eddie N. Williams, its president since 1972, the Joint Center grew out of the assumption "that the civil rights movement as we knew it in the '60s was dead, that a new thrust was needed in the '70s, and that there was a great deal to be gained by developing that thrust along the lines of political participation by the citizen and the elected official." Working closely with the Congressional Black Caucus and associations of state and local black officeholders, the nonprofit, nonpartisan group conducts research on policy issues of special concern to black Americans and provides technical assistance to minority officials. The information gathered by this "black think tank" is disseminated largely through its monthly newsletter, *Focus*; a variety of research publications; workshops and educational seminars; and *The National Roster of Black Elected Officials*, which appears annually.

A decade after passage of the 1965 Voting Rights Act, black political influence was widespread but fragile. Renewed in 1970, the suffrage law was becoming a permanent fixture on the American scene. Under the vigilance of the federal government and civil rights groups, many of the impediments to black political participation were being eliminated. With registration of the majority of eligible blacks, attention shifted to making the most effective use of their ballots. Having won reenfranchisement, southern blacks strived to mobilize their communities in the competition for full electoral representation.

Chapter 5

The New Black Politicians: From Protest to Empowerment

CIVIL RIGHTS AND THE PROMISE OF ELECTORAL POLITICS

In February 1965, when demonstrations still constituted the central tactic of the freedom struggle, Bayard Rustin forecast the direction in which the civil rights movement would head. A seasoned veteran in the battle for racial justice, Rustin had participated in pioneering freedom rides challenging segregated transportation facilities in the 1940s, served as an adviser to Martin Luther King during the Montgomery bus boycott of the mid-1950s, and in August 1963, had helped organize the celebrated March on Washington for Jobs and Freedom. His civil rights activities had been built around protest, but looking ahead to the future he saw a shift taking place. "Direct action techniques," Rustin observed, "are being subordinated to a strategy calling for the building of community institutions or power bases." As the black struggle evolved from achieving equality of opportunity to obtaining equality of results, Rustin contended that political power, more than the moral force of nonviolent protests, would best fulfill the aims of the struggle.

Few civil rights proponents doubted the wisdom of organizing blacks to increase their political leverage. Although after the summer of 1964 militants increasingly questioned the value of forming coalitions with white liberals and labor unionists, as Rustin urged, they did agree with his premise that blacks needed greater power to reshape economic and political institutions that perpetuated their subordination, even after legal rights were attained. During the 1966 Meredith march through Mississippi, Stokely Carmichael emphatically told a crowd of blacks along the route: "If you don't have power, you're begging. We're going to take over and get black sheriffs and black tax assessors." SNCC, the group he led, had helped construct the Mississippi Freedom Democratic Party precisely for the purposes of gaining black control over political decisions affecting their own communities and influencing public policy in the South and the nation.

For different but related reasons, this preference for political solutions also appealed to white liberals. Presidential allies of the civil rights movement had expressed concern about the disruptive effects of demonstrations in provoking confrontations between the races. President Kennedy sought to steer black discontent off the streets and into courthouses, legislative halls, and voting booths. Along with his successor, Lyndon Johnson, he emphasized the right to vote as the chief instrument for blacks to resolve their grievances through regular electoral channels. As black protest took a violent course with the outbreak of urban riots in the mid-1960s, the Johnson administration prescribed the franchise and the election of black officials as an antidote to extremism. "There is more power in the ballot than there is in the bullet," the chief executive declared, "and it lasts longer." White House aides expected black officeholders to counteract the influence of "civil rights kooks" within their communities by offering responsible leadership.

Black elected officials also appealed to conservative whites. Although President Nixon had attempted to blunt enforcement of the Voting Rights Act, at the same time he recognized the value of the growing number of black officeholders who benefited from the measure. When a group of black elected officials visited the nation's capital in September 1969, the President ordered his staff to roll out "the red carpet" for the delegation. According to Leon Panetta (the chief civil rights officer in the Department of Health, Education, and Welfare), the Republican chief executive, like his Democratic predecessors, believed that "elected people were something special." Of all black leaders they "were most worth listening to" because they "clearly represented a constituency." Furthermore, some conservatives suggested that black involvement in government, either as voters or as officeholders, might help calm public unrest. John Patterson, who in the late 1950s had beaten George Wallace for governor of Alabama by outcampaigning him as a segregationist, a decade later came to see the merit of black political participation. "When you allow the nigra to participate in government," Patterson declared in 1966, "you can demand that he obey the law and stay off the streets, but deny him participation...and you can't make any demands on him at all."

In the post-Voting Rights Act era, blacks who competed for and obtained electoral positions understood the responsibility that had been placed upon them. As one officeholder succinctly put it, he and his elected colleagues represented "the last great white hope for peace in this land." As long as blacks sought to achieve their racial goals within the conventional political system, they conferred legitimacy on the ruling order and devalued other more disruptive tactics, from protest marches to riots. And as long as black candidates did not find their way unfairly blocked in seeking elective posts, they renewed faith in the possibility of minority advancement in peaceful and orderly fashion. But, if their bids for representation were thwarted, the black journalist Chuck Stone noted, "the comparative moderation of the political process will be increasingly disavowed by young blacks as a meaningless exercise in the quest for power."

However, African-Americans competed for political office for reasons other than defusing potential racial strife. Rather, they hoped to build upon the legal rights secured through the protest struggle and use them to continue the pursuit of first-class citizenship. "There's an inherent value in officeholding," a black political aspirant in South Carolina asserted. "A race of people excluded from public office will always be second class." Successful black candidates were expected by their constituents to close the gap between the promise of equality and the reality of the inferior conditions they still endured. "As the black politician returns to the scene of politics from years of deprivation," Fannie Lou Hamer declared, "he must restore the democratic principles of shared local control and responsiveness to human needs." From this perspective black elected officials were regarded as saviors of their people and, at the very least, they had the obligation to perform in a manner that advanced the material interests of the communities they represented.

The civil rights movement had served as a valuable training ground for the emergence of black politicians. John Lewis, a former chairman of SNCC, who later became a congressman from Atlanta, pointed out that, like himself, "a great many of the people that you see being elected are people that come from the civil rights movement." In the wake of passage of the 1965 Voting Rights Act most blacks who rose to office in Alabama and Mississippi had participated in some aspect of the freedom struggle. Whether through joining in a voter registration drive, marching in a demonstration, signing a petition, or housing a civil rights worker, black candidates had taken the first step toward political liberation. For those who engaged in such efforts, entry into the electoral arena constituted a natural extension of their commitment to toppling the hurdles to black equality. As they made the journey from protest to electoral politics, black officeseekers usually carried with them the same concern for helping the oppressed escape from poverty and injustice that had brought them into the movement in the first place. "Virtually every black candidate who runs in the South," one observer remarked, campaigns "with the hope of improving the lot of black people in his community."

In addition to the civil rights movement, President Johnson's Great Society programs paved the way for black electoral competition. Although the funds allocated to fight the "war on poverty" were insufficient to win an unconditional victory, they greatly increased the economic resources available for political organizing. Antipoverty agencies fostered the development of local leaders who gained valuable experience in exercising power and in establishing a political base from which to operate. Through the Economic Opportunity Act of 1964 blacks obtained representation on community governing boards, which furnished training in building necessary political skills, such as bargaining and negotiation. The Community Action Programs (CAPs) decreed that the poor have "maximum feasible participation" in designing and implementing policies directly affecting their welfare. Their presence on antipoverty governing boards, which allocated large sums of money, hampered the traditional control by white mayors over lucrative patronage rewards. Fighting back, the mayors managed to obtain a congressional cutback of the programs within a few years. Despite the controversy raised, the CAPs helped empower the previously disfranchised in many towns and cities in the South as well as the North. "The process of election and service on community poverty boards," the political scientist Robert C. Smith has concluded, "provided a useful socialization experience for blacks in urban politics."

One of the poverty program's recruits who successfully graduated to elective office was Johnny Ford of Tuskegee. The son of a VA hospital employee, Ford had grown up in the town during the heyday of the civil rights movement, before heading off to college in Tennessee. He wound up in New York City in the mid-1960s and found a job as a counselor in Brooklyn's impoverished Bedford-Stuyvesant ghetto. In 1968, he hopped aboard the presidential bandwagon of Senator Robert Kennedy as a staff member, and after the senator's assassination he decided to return to his Alabama hometown. "I've long felt that the South is the real frontier of this nation," he remarked about his decision to move back to Dixie. In 1969, the twenty-eight-year-old Tuskegee native became director of Macon County's Model Cities program, which garnered millions of dollars in federal revenue. From this position he campaigned for mayor and, in 1972, defeated the white incumbent, thereby becoming the city's first black to hold this top executive office.

For many others, however, making the adjustment from civil rights to electoral politics was neither automatic nor easy. The two activities involved different tactics and talents. Though demanding a substantial degree of organization, mass demonstrations depended a good deal on emotional appeals and highly charged targets to rally people. They tended to be episodic and often lapsed quickly after resolution of a particular crisis. In contrast, competition for public office, as a political scientist has observed, "is more mundane and requires both long-term political skills and the ability to consistently draw the black electorate." Candidates had to get elected by spending long hours trying to register voters, campaigning door to door, and shepherding large numbers of people to the polls. Robert Clark, the first black elected to the Mississippi legislature since Reconstruction, explained the challenge: "Just because some folks hear you talk at a rally don't mean they're gonna vote for you. You got to go campaign, talk to 'em, make 'em know you want *each* vote."

The transfer of black politics from the streets to city halls, county courthouses, and legislative chambers frequently had a moderating effect on its practitioners. Once elected, black politicians had to master the techniques of making deals and forging compromises, often settling for solutions hammered more out of pragmatism than principle. Despite the humanistic concerns they often brought to their jobs, black elected officials had to accommodate to the constraints imposed upon them by the traditional political system they entered. Illustrating the aphorism that "politics makes strange bedfellows," some black officials collaborated with powerful whites whose past record on civil rights had been deplorable in order to pry loose economic rewards for their communities. In this vein, during the 1970s Mayor Ford of Tuskegee supported George Wallace in exchange for the benefits that the Alabama governor could deliver. Ford explained the practical considerations that guided him: "It's business with me—no emotion. What you must do is penetrate the system and, once within the system, learn how it works. And then work it well."

Most blacks who successfully entered politics did not abandon their civil rights concerns, but their movement into the electoral mainstream weakened some of the radical impulses of the civil rights era. The experience of the Mississippi Freedom Democratic Party was a case in point. The organizers of the MFDP conceived of the group as representing economically dispossessed sharecroppers and domestic workers. In 1968, when the biracial Loyalist delegation from Mississippi gained the authorized seats at the national convention, moderate whites and blacks had replaced many of the original Freedom Democrats. Mrs. Fannie Lou Hamer "felt disgusted" with the newcomers because they "didn't know what suffering is and don't know what politics is about." By the end of the 1970s, this Loyalist faction traded its national recognition for incorporation with the mostly white Democratic regulars, who controlled the party apparatus in the state. Little remained of the original spirit or membership of the MFDP by the time of fusion. Although unity accorded blacks formal sanction as political partners within the Democratic party, the progressive vision of the early civil rights militants had been tempered in the process.

The admission of blacks into electoral politics in places like Mississippi and Alabama did not displace former civil rights activists so much as it elevated into greater prominence one layer of the black leadership strata. During the height of the freedom struggle, battle zones throughout the deep South had attracted the most radical elements in the movement to brave the dangers of brutal repression. Field-workers from SNCC and CORE had recruited leaders predominantly among poor blacks and built a strong lower-class following in the hope of changing both political and economic relations in the region. The success of the movement in restoring voting rights and in encouraging competition for office-holding cleared the way for the emergence of middle-class blacks to assume a larger role in electoral politics. Equipped with greater educational skills and financial resources, they had the necessary advantages to construct political organizations and wage time-consuming campaigns. The political scientist Lester Salamon, who studied Mississippi very closely, noted one important effect of the transformation of the civil rights crusade: "As the danger of Movement involvement has subsided, the leadership... has shifted from the sharecroppers and small farmers who spearheaded the battle for political rights to the black professionals and businessmen who generally stayed in the background until the ball got rolling."

This changing source of leadership should not obscure the positive consequences that the civil rights movement had on altering the structure of black politics. Before the era of reenfranchisement, black political leaders who represented their communities usually derived authority from prominent whites. "Clientage politics," as Martin Kilson termed it, linked blacks personally to powerful whites who delivered minimal welfare rewards within the rigid system of segregation. Considering the "overwhelming preponderance of political, social and economic power of the white majority," Everett C. Ladd concluded, "it is hardly surprising that the decision of influential whites as to which of the 'eligible' Negroes were to be leaders was accepted by Negroes themselves." The extension of the suffrage, the racial esteem that accompanied it, and the mobilization that followed it broke the stranglehold of whites over selecting black political leaders and setting their agendas. According to Louis Martin, the noted black journalist and adviser to Presidents Kennedy and Johnson, the Voting Rights Act ushered in a new breed of minority politician who understood "that political power is generated in the black precincts and does not come from the hands of the great white father."

OBSTACLES TO OFFICE-HOLDING BLOC VOTING

Blacks stood the best chances of winning election to office where they outnumbered whites, primarily at the local level. Because bloc voting generally characterized the conduct of elections between the

races, blacks needed to comprise a clear majority of the population
in order to triumph. The size of the black population was one of the
most important resources black communities possessed in electing
members of their race to represent them. As Albert Karnig and Susan Welch found, black candidates usually lost as the black population grew proportionately larger, winning only when it reached a
majority. Before that point, the growing percentage of blacks posed
a threat to whites, who closed ranks against minority-group candidates. Once blacks obtained a majority, they had the raw strength
to overcome white opposition.

Still, in many black-majority areas of the South, in order to win
blacks needed to comprise at least 60 percent of the population,
a figure that indicated an effective voting-age majority. In many
places, demographic shifts had resulted in a black population with a
disproportionate share of children and the elderly, the former not
old enough to vote and the latter less inclined to do so. Migration
from rural locales to the cities of the South and North had thinned
the ranks of the adults most likely to cast a ballot. Moreover, the
continued economic dependency of poor blacks on white employers
and creditors as well as the persistence of racial discrimination and
of fear and apathy meant that a simple population majority did not
always guarantee black electoral success. Old habits died hard and
some blacks could be expected to vote for whites because of the
deference they had paid them in the past, others may have done so
as a consequence of jealousies and rivalries within the black community itself, and some retained a reasoned measure of fear that
casting a ballot could still lead to reprisals.

In addition, blacks had to contend with electoral rules that diluted the power of their ballots and hampered them from electing
members of their own race. The most significant of these were at-
large election requirements. Such arrangements, in which candidates were chosen by voters throughout a wide jurisdiction, frequently resulted in the election of whites and the exclusion of
blacks. Even if blacks constituted 40 percent of the total population
of a municipality, for instance, in an at-large contest they almost
certainly failed to elect members of their race in proportion to their
numerical presence in the community. In switching to elections by
ward or single-member districts, black residents greatly enhanced
their opportunity to elect black candidates in closer approximation
to their strength in the overall electorate. Given the typical con-

centration of black residents in distinct subdivisions of a city, single-member district elections virtually assured that minorities could maximize their votes and select representatives of their own choosing.

Furthermore, with whites firmly in control of every state legislature, they could reapportion districts to weaken the black vote. Racial gerrymandering kept to a minimum the number of blacks who won election to state houses. For example, in 1971 three adjacent parishes [counties] in Louisiana each had a black population majority. However, when incumbent lawmakers redrew district lines for the state House of Representatives, they refused to form a black-majority district. Instead, they combined two of the black parishes with two predominantly white areas to form a white-majority parish and submerged the remaining black parish within a white-majority district. On the municipal level, white officials attempted to preserve their power by annexing adjacent territory in which a sufficient number of whites lived to once again put blacks in the minority. These sundry practices were often disguised as color-blind regulations, and indeed, at-large elections had first come into existence during the wave of Progressive reform at the turn of the century. Whatever their origins, their continued operation in the South, reinforced by the heritage of racial bias, deprived blacks of an equal opportunity to determine the outcome of elections.

This question of determining what constituted a fair share for minority representation proved especially controversial. Many white liberal allies of the civil rights movement were satisfied with a suffrage solution that removed unfair obstacles to minority registration and provided blacks with an equal opportunity to go to the polls and cast their ballots in a situation free from intimidation. They viewed the ballot from an individualistic perspective and rejected any notion that particular groups, however historically disadvantaged they might have been, were entitled to a share of representation proportionate to their percentage in the population. Accordingly, the federal government should do no more than protect individual black voters from invidious forms of discrimination rather than ensure that black ballots resulted in the election of black officeholders. Suffrage reformers had sought to make the black franchise equal in value to that of whites and then let blacks compete for political power in conventional ways. "If blacks...are able to form political alliances, to have their interests considered by elected officials through threat of political action, and are generally able to secure through their ballots the benefits of citizenship," one white observer remarked, "they are effectively participating in the political process."

Black leaders and their civil rights supporters generally saw the matter differently. They contended that the Voting Rights Act and the expanded registration accompanying it did not confer actual political equality or power. To them the ballot derived importance not principally as a color-blind instrument but as a race-conscious tool to advance the collective goals of Afro-American communities. Ultimately, blacks aimed to make government more responsive to their needs, and in theory it was possible to obtain greater influence over political affairs by backing white candidates who competed for their votes. However, in reality most blacks preferred representation by other blacks, who they believed reflected their aspirations. Feelings of pride and self-respect were also at stake. The civil rights struggle had succeeded in reawakening group consciousness among blacks, fostering the desire to see members of their own race attain positions of electoral leadership. Short of claiming a right to proportional representation, civil rights stalwarts considered the ratio of black officeholders to the percentage of minorities in the population as a convenient yardstick to measure political equality.

Although the 1965 Voting Rights Act dealt with the right to register to vote and not with the ability to win elections, it did recognize the plight of African-Americans in group-centered terms. The law addressed current black disfranchisement by locating its organic roots in the past, and attempted to remedy patterns of racial discrimination against a persecuted group rather than correct specific acts of bias suffered by individuals. The lawmakers devised a statistical formula that automatically identified the presence of racial bigotry and empowered the federal government to challenge the consequences of previously injurious practices. Employing a type of affirmative action, the statute compensated southern blacks for the discriminatory treatment they had received by suspending literacy exams and allowing blacks to register on the same basis as had whites in the past.

The federal courts helped resolve the issue by limiting the operation of at-large elections in the South. Holding back from declaring at-large contests constitutionally invalid, the judiciary nonetheless struck down electoral systems that hampered participation by minorities and constricted their possibilities for holding office. To gauge whether a particular at-large electoral plan was impermissible, judges considered a "totality of circumstances." They looked for a history of racial bias that had excluded blacks from gaining equal access to the electoral process and evaluated whether current electoral institutions perpetuated discriminatory practices of the past. To this end, the courts were less concerned about the original purposes behind the adoption of the election rules and were more interested in ascertaining the effect on black representation. This standard of judgment applied throughout the 1970s and boosted black officeholding in those jurisdictions mandated by the bench to discard their at-large procedures.

Cases from Texas and Louisiana, in 1973, established the precedents. In the Lone Star State blacks challenged the 1970 reapportionment of the state House of Representatives for creating multimember districts in Dallas and Bexar (San Antonio) Counties that diluted minority voting power. Only two blacks had ever been elected to the state legislature from Dallas and only five Mexican-Americans had represented Bexar County. In *White v. Regester*, the Supreme Court ordered the creation of single-member districts after examining a combination of factors that effectively reduced black electoral opportunities. Accordingly, it discovered a history of racial discrimination and black underrepresentation: the failure of the white-dominated Democratic party organization to nominate black candidates; the waging of racist campaigns; and the operation of electoral rules that handicapped African- and Mexican-Americans from winning at-large elections.

Following up this decision, a lower federal court overturned the at-large system of electing members to the school board and police jury in East Carroll Parish, Louisiana. Although constituting a majority of the population of this parish, blacks comprised only 46 percent of enrolled voters, having been barred from registering from 1922 to 1962. Though blacks had managed to win three of twelve contested seats since the initiation of at-large elections in 1968, the court found that the electoral system prevented Afro-American voters from achieving more effective representation. The judges acknowledged that barriers to black participation had been removed, but they concluded that "the debilitating effects of these impediments do persist." In rendering its opinion in *Zimmer v. Mc-Keithen*, the judiciary looked at the "totality of circumstances" in uncovering racial bias that denied blacks equal access to the political process. A governmental jurisdiction violated the rights of black voters if it consistently failed to slate blacks to run for office, if its elected officials declined to respond to the interests of their black constituents, and if it adopted procedures that heightened the effects of past racial bias by submerging black voters within large electoral districts and requiring that winning candidates receive a majority rather than a plurality of the votes cast. (Given the prevalence of racial bloc voting, the majority-vote rule hurt blacks particularly where they did not constitute a majority of registered voters.)

These rulings were reinforced by the Justice Department. Under the preclearance section of the Voting Rights Act, the attorney general possessed the authority to reject suffrage changes that had the purpose or effect of discriminating against blacks. This provision pertained only to electoral rules adopted or altered since November 1964. Challenges against procedures fashioned before that date required litigation and were adjudicated as discussed above. Nevertheless, the Civil Rights Division of the Justice Department took its legal cues from the judiciary and refused to sanction switches from single-member districts to at-large elections that weakened the potency of black votes. Along with the courts, Justice Department watchdogs scrutinized reapportionment, redistricting, and annexation plans that potentially minimized opportunities for black representation.

HIGH HOPES, LIMITED REWARDS

As the judicial and executive branches cleared sundry obstacles to minority political participation, southern blacks continued their slow but steady progress in winning public office. In 1976, blacks held 1,847 elected positions in the South, and four years later, the figure rose to 2,457. Despite these successes, blacks remained underrepresented in the proportion of offices they won. In 1980, of the more than 32,350 elected officials in the jurisdictions originally covered by the Voting Rights Act, about 5 percent were black. This share trailed far behind the proportion of the black population in

1980 - 2,500 Black Local officers
32,350 possible

the region, which ranged from 18.9 percent in Virginia to 35.2 percent in Mississippi. Moreover, in approximately one-quarter of the black-majority counties no blacks had been elected, a condition that also existed in nearly half the counties with a black population over 20 percent.

The substantial number of blacks who did triumph managed to reap important rewards for their constituents. Though the situation varied from place to place, from rural villages and towns to major urban areas, in general black elected officials delivered tangible benefits that had been long denied to their communities. Routine services, such as garbage collection, paved streets, police and fire protection, and recreational facilities, were upgraded and extended to black residents. Wherever possible, black public officials sought to increase the number of government jobs available through affirmative action programs that awarded contracts to minority businesses and employment to minority workers. They also avidly pursued and obtained federal government grants to fund capital investment for economic development and to expand the distribution of health care and social welfare projects in their locales.

The election of blacks pried open access to governmental structures that had been the exclusive domain of whites. Since the late nineteenth century, the disfranchisement of black southerners had made them the object of political attention; however, in regaining the ballot and recovering positions in government, they returned as active political agents. In so doing, black elected officials joined in the formulation and execution of policies, and brought to the attention of their white colleagues issues of special concern to blacks that previously had been ignored. To the extent that knowledge is power, black representatives gained vital information to help shape decision-making and protect the interests of their constituents. "No matter what happened," a black city council member in Florida declared, his white counterparts "knew I was listening to everything that went on."

In addition to these material improvements, blacks gained critical psychological advantages from their empowerment. The presence of black candidates and officeholders stimulated increased black political mobilization, as African-Americans turned out with pride to vote for one of their own. This revived sense of self-esteem was aptly voiced by Fannie Lou Hamer. When blacks still sat on the political sidelines, Mrs. Hamer remarked, "some white folks

...would drive past your house in a pickup truck with guns hanging up on the back and give you hate stares." This changed as blacks approached the center of the electoral arena, she pointed out, and "those same people now call me Mrs. Hamer, because they respect people who respect themselves." Furthermore, these feelings of respect and dignity were carried forth by black politicians, who served as valuable role models, especially for the younger members of their communities.

With political reemancipation came raised expectations of what black representatives could accomplish. Because they had been systematically excluded from political participation, southern blacks prized the ballot in the belief that it would advance the goals of their race as a whole and not merely benefit a few. The president of the Savannah, Georgia, branch of the NAACP explained: "Black officeholders...must be individuals who serve at the pleasure of the black community." Accordingly, black constituents placed demands on their representatives that exceeded the ordinary requirements of the job. Edith Ingram, elected the probate judge of Hancock County, Georgia, in 1968, described the myriad services she performed for the people who regularly came to her office, many of whom were on public assistance:

> I have to write checks for them, pay bills, buy groceries, take them to the doctors, balance checkbooks, certify them for welfare, make doctors' appointments, read letters, answer letters and fix loan papers for houses. A good 85 percent to 90 percent of the work that we do is non-office related work, but these people have no one else to depend on—they trust us, so we do it.[1]

Indeed, many black officials discovered what Richard Arrington found out when he became mayor of Birmingham: "There are the expectations of the black community that expects you to do more than you can do."

Though black officials exerted increasing influence and shared authority, their power was limited in a variety of ways. With a relatively small number of exceptions, black elected officials in most cities and counties of the South and the nation were in the minority

---

[1]Ingram is quoted in Lawrence J. Hanks, *The Struggle for Black Empowerment in Three Georgia Counties* (Knoxville: University of Tennessee Press, 1987), pp. 69–70.

and could not deliver political dividends without the cooperation of white colleagues. In such situations minority officeholders had to walk a delicate tightrope in balancing the concerns of their constituents with the need to bargain with their fellow white officials who represented opposing interests. Based on personal experience, State Senator Leroy Johnson of Atlanta stated the problem: "Your position in the black community has to take on a veneer of militancy, but...you have to be willing to negotiate, to compromise, in order to be effective."

Even in those areas where blacks came to control the majority of government posts, they often lacked the economic resources to affect significantly the material conditions of the impoverished population. Although the poverty rate among black families declined over the course of the 1970s, from 41 percent to 30 percent, the percentage of poor blacks was more than four times the white figure of 7 percent. At the end of the decade black families earned 57 percent of the income of that of whites. This represented a slight improvement over the economic situation that existed when the Supreme Court outlawed school desegregation in *Brown*, but marked a downswing from the 60 percent level that prevailed in the years immediately following Johnson's Great Society. Blacks also experienced a higher incidence of unemployment than did whites, and the joblessness of young black male adults reached depression-era levels.

Lowndes County, Alabama, highlighted the gap between political and economic power. Directed by LCFO, black political participation did improve living conditions, largely through the acquisition of outside federal and foundation grants and the election of a sheriff who attempted to dispense a more evenhanded brand of justice than in the past. But blacks continued to suffer from a disproportionate burden of economic distress. Their median family income rose slightly in comparison with that of white residents, from a ratio of 33 percent to 41 percent. However, their median family income of $7,443 lagged way behind the national average of $18,350 earned annually by whites. Expressing this predicament, the black Sheriff John Hulett remarked: "Until people become economically strong, political power alone won't do."

Though economic prospects remained as bleak for most blacks elsewhere throughout the country, a small but growing segment of African-Americans saw their fortunes rise. Expanding opportunities resulting from desegregation and affirmative action programs swelled the size of the black middle class. By the late 1970s, the share of black workers occupying middle-class positions stood at 33 percent, a jump from 13 percent in 1960. For two-income families in which both husbands and wives worked, blacks had just about achieved parity with whites. From this group, with its access to superior economic resources and educational skills, black political leaders emerged. Following reenfranchisement, the representatives of this class, more so than those of lower-income blacks, succeeded in penetrating the structures of electoral office-holding that traditionally had been reserved for whites.

The ascent to power of that class during the 1970s reflected a complex picture of black political development. Themselves only recently risen from the bottom rungs of the economic ladder, middle-class black politicians tended to identify with the plight of their less fortunate brethren. Moreover, the newly acquired wealth of black middle-class families was not fully secure because their prosperity rested more heavily than that of whites on the combined incomes of working wives as well as working husbands and on earnings derived from public sector jobs and those protected by affirmative action regulations. Consequently, they were vulnerable to downswings in the economy and fluctuations in the political climate, especially in a conservative direction. Under these circumstances and because they were products of the same emancipatory forces that shaped the racial consciousness of poor blacks, these middle-class leaders often shared with the former mutual concerns associated with race.

Yet the interests of these politicians also cut across racial lines and embraced concerns they held in common with their middle- and upper-class white colleagues. Urban black politicians, especially in cities that sought to attract economic investment on a large scale, joined with moderate white businesspeople and their representatives to promote lucrative downtown redevelopment projects that favored buildings over ordinary people. In the process, black businesspeople, professionals, and white-collar workers benefited from attempts to revitalize the economy of their cities, whereas poor residents gained little from the private-sector, low-wage service jobs that accompanied urban renewal, and often suffered dislocation as a result of "urban removal." As a result, the black middle class reaped substantial rewards, while considerable poverty persisted among a sizable portion of the black population, a situation that occasioned observers to speak of the appearance of a permanent black underclass.

The "new South" interracial coalition did produce progress, albeit unevenly. The alliance of middle-class black politicians with white corporate and financial elites made sense during the 1970s when American cities were suffering from internal decay and a shrinking tax base. The flight of middle-class whites to the suburbs left behind the poor, who required a large share of public services but who could not afford to fund them. In striking a partnership with influential white civic leaders, black politicians sought to plug the drain on the depleted treasuries they had inherited upon assuming office. They did manage to attract new industries and jobs, and at the very least their presence at the governmental helm assured that consideration would be given to black concerns as never before. The election of blacks to high public office, according to the political scientist Peter Eisinger, meant that "black interests, *as they are defined by black administrators*, have proved as central as the interests of white capital in the establishment of economic development goals" (emphasis in original).

BLACK WOMEN OFFICEHOLDERS

Although the majority of black elected officials were men, the 1970s saw a rapid rise of black women officeholders throughout the nation. In 1975, black women comprised 15 percent of all Afro-American elected officials, a total of 530 out of 3,503 officeholders. Four years later the proportion of all black elected officials who were female had jumped 59 percent, and black females held 882 of 4,607 positions. By comparison, the figures for black men elected to public office increased from 2,973 to 3,725, a growth rate of 25 percent. Like their male counterparts, black women were most likely to hold government posts at the municipal and county levels and to represent areas with a predominantly black population.

The growing number of black women politicians reflected the impact of the civil rights movement. Black women had played a crucial, though often unsung, role in the freedom struggle. The top leadership positions were usually held by men and individuals such as Martin Luther King, Roy Wilkins, and Stokely Carmichael were most easily identified by the public; but women both initiated and

provided grassroots support for the civil rights protests that transformed the South and the nation. Without the courage, commitment, and vision of Rosa Parks, Jo Ann Robinson, Ella Baker, and
Fannie Lou Hamer, to name a few, together with the legions of
ordinary housewives and workers who boycotted, marched, sat in,
and went to jail, a widespread freedom struggle could not have
been launched and sustained. As with men, in recruiting large
numbers of women to its ranks, the civil rights movement inspired
pride and encouraged standards of political participation that carried over to the electoral arena. Not coincidentally, by the end of
the 1970s a majority of elected black women (51 percent) resided in
the South, the primary battlefield and proving ground of the civil
rights struggle and the region in which grassroots female leadership
first flourished.

Black female politicians owed some of their success to the expanding opportunities generally available to women. Between 1975
and 1981, the number of all female officeholders soared from 7,089
to 16,585, with most of these positions concentrated in local government. The proportion of women holding seats on county governing boards more than doubled, from 456 to 1,205; and from 1971
to 1981, the number of women state legislators tripled, from 293 to
908. By the end of the 1970s, a thousand women were serving as
mayors of towns and cities throughout the United States. This
extraordinary growth spurt can be attributed in part to the very low
level of female office-holding at the beginning of the seventies.
Nevertheless, these electoral accomplishments also owed much to
the development of the feminist movement during the 1960s and
1970s. Itself influenced by the civil rights struggle, the women's
movement raised an awareness of gender discrimination, provided
an egalitarian ideology to challenge it, and stimulated women to
attack the barriers blocking their full and active participation as
citizens.

The relationship of black women to feminism was complicated
by race. Although sympathetic with its liberationist goals, black
women activists tended to identify more closely with black men in
the fight against racial oppression than with white women, whose
skin color was the same as the male agents of blacks' exploitation.
Whatever male chauvinism black women experienced within civil
rights ranks did not stop them from displaying their considerable
talents alongside men and developing their skills even further. The
importance of black women within the political culture nurtured by

the civil rights movement can be seen in the relative figures for black and white female officeholders. Black women constituted a higher percentage of black elected officials than did white women of white officials. In 1979, 18 percent of all black state legislators but only 10 percent of white lawmakers were female.

At the same time, these figures showed that neither black nor white women had reached parity with men. In recognition of both their growing achievements and the distance yet to be closed, women of the two races joined together within the National Women's Political Caucus. Formed in 1971, the group promoted racial and ethnic diversity in its membership, challenged racism as well as sexism, and worked for a broad range of political and social reforms of special interest to women.

The importance of the civil rights struggle in serving to empower black women can be glimpsed in the life of Unita Blackwell. A resident of Mayersville, Mississippi, a tiny delta town of 500 people, Mrs. Blackwell was a housewife in her early thirties when she first encountered SNCC workers in the area. Impressed with the group's dedication and concern for developing local leadership, she gravitated toward SNCC and heeded its message: "If you all go and register to vote this is the way to help yourself." It took Blackwell three tries before the county registrar allowed her to register in 1964, and by then she was actively engaged with SNCC in the Freedom Summer campaign and in the creation of the Mississippi Freedom Democratic Party. A member of the MFDP contingent that failed to win recognition at the 1964 Democratic National Convention, she returned four years later to gain a seat on the revamped biracial delegation from the Magnolia State. After Mayersville became incorporated in 1976, Mrs. Blackwell was chosen its first mayor. In 1980, she became cochair of the state Democratic party, the organization that had excluded her on account of race sixteen years earlier. Her success illustrates the connection between the civil rights movement and electoral politics, as well as the strength and perseverance of the black women who contributed to the freedom struggle.

BLACK MAYORS IN ATLANTA AND TUSKEGEE

While noteworthy breakthroughs were occurring among women and in small towns like Mayersville, perhaps more than any other major city in the South, Atlanta, Georgia, reflected the changing currents of black political development in the years following passage of the Voting Rights Act. Characterized by a tradition of electoral activity that succeeded in dismantling discriminatory suffrage obstacles and in stimulating voter registration, black Atlantans already enjoyed a significant measure of influence in municipal politics during the 1960s. This "black Mecca" of Dixie, with its distinguished churches, independent businesses, and institutions of higher learning, had attracted and nurtured a resilient black middle class that included the family of the Reverend Martin Luther King, Jr. Its economic, political, and religious chieftains had allied themselves with white business and civic leaders, who ruled the city with a combination of racial benevolence and paternalism. The kind of racist rhetoric that infected political discourse elsewhere in the South was kept to a minimum, as white candidates campaigned for black ballots to ensure their victories.

Nevertheless, white politicians did not consider the black electorate as an equal governing partner, and they made vital decisions affecting their city without consulting the black community or adequately taking into account the impact of decisions upon it. In 1968, when city officials failed to solicit black advice in the creation of a metropolitan rapid transit system, disgruntled minority voters helped defeat the proposal in a referendum. The plan subsequently passed, but only after blacks were included in a policy-formulating capacity. Furthermore, under white control, urban renewal had meant revitalization of the central business district at the expense of the needs of low-income black neighborhoods.

The transition from moderate black influence to substantial black power began to occur in 1969. That year, white civic leaders split in their choice for mayor, and black voters swung the election to Sam Massell by giving him over 90 percent of their ballots. (He received only a quarter of the white votes.) At the same time, blacks won the post of vice-mayor, four seats on the Board of Aldermen, and an additional two seats on the school board. Mayor Massell's administration subsequently fractured its black base of support. Shortly after taking office, the chief executive faced a disruptive strike by predominantly black sanitation workers. Massell upset black leaders, including his vice-mayor, Maynard Jackson, in settling the dispute to the disadvantage of the strikers. However, the mayor attempted to patch up his coalition by rehiring the workers and appointing a black to head the Sanitation Department.

During the remainder of his term, black politicians devoted their energies to obtaining an increased share of government services and benefits for their constituents and to ensuring that existing programs were administered fairly.

In 1973, black Atlantans were ready to exert a greater measure of control over their city and to reshape the biracial coalition that had governed in the past. They had demographic forces on their side. During the 1960s the composition of the population had shifted in favor of blacks. Over the course of that decade, the proportion of black Atlantans had increased nearly 37 percent, while that of whites had fallen by 20 percent. In 1970, blacks comprised a 51 percent majority of the city's residents, and three years later they used this numerical advantage to elect Maynard Jackson, who defeated Massell in a racially charged campaign to become Atlanta's first nonwhite mayor. Having guessed that the bulk of the black votes would go to his opponent, Massell reversed his previous campaign form to appeal for white support. Proclaiming Atlanta "Too Young To Die," he suggested that the city would decay under black rule. The *Atlanta Constitution* frowned upon this approach and commented that the incumbent appeared to be "running for mayor of a South African city which practices apartheid rather than the mayor of a fully integrated American city."

Massell's strategy misfired, and Jackson captured 59 percent of the total ballots cast. The heated battle lured to the polls a larger proportion of blacks (67 percent) than whites (55 percent). Jackson received an overwhelming 95 percent of the black vote and, although the electorate generally divided along racial lines, he received 17 percent of the white vote. Together with the mayor's post, blacks won half the seats on the city council and gained a slim one-vote margin on the school board. These victories followed the previous year's election to Congress of Andrew Young, a former assistant to Dr. King. Young had a reputation as a skillful peacemaker and conciliator, and in a district only two-fifths black, he obtained 53 percent of the vote. Nearly every black and about one-quarter of the whites who went to the polls supported the civil rights activist. The triumphs of Jackson and Young demonstrated the arrival of black elected officials as a dominant force in Atlanta politics, but they also indicated that whites still retained significant influence in shaping the outcome of electoral competition.

Only thirty-five-years old when he became mayor, Jackson belonged to a family of distinguished men and women. His relatives included politicians and preachers, a professor and a performer. His father was a Baptist minister who once ran for a seat on a local school board in Texas. His great-great-grandfather founded the Wheat Street Baptist Church in Atlanta, and his grandfather organized the Georgia Voters League. Jackson's mother had earned a doctorate in French and taught at Spelman College in Atlanta and North Carolina Central University in Durham. One of his aunts, Mattiwilda Dobbs, was a highly acclaimed opera singer. A graduate of Martin Luther King's alma mater, Morehouse College, Jackson obtained a law degree from North Carolina Central and returned to Atlanta to work as an attorney handling cases for low-income clients. The assassinations of Dr. King and Senator Robert F. Kennedy in 1968 helped persuade him to embark on a political career. "I decided the solution to the country's problems had to be in politics," he remarked, "not in violence." He aimed high in his first campaign in 1968, competing for the U.S. Senate seat from Georgia held by Herman Talmadge. Jackson lost by a wide margin, but his strong showing in Atlanta, where he outpolled the popular incumbent, encouraged him to run for vice-mayor in 1969. Four years later, he succeeded in capturing city hall.

Once in office as mayor, Jackson helped deliver important rewards. He reorganized the police department, appointed a black to head the new agency, and increased the number of Afro-American law enforcement officers. Subsequently, the city experienced a decline in black complaints of police brutality. The mayor also embarked on a vigorous affirmative action program that resulted in the black share of Atlanta's public work force climbing from 42 percent in 1972 to 51 percent five years later. During this period, the share of contracts awarded by the city to minorities jumped from 2 to 13 percent. In addition, Mayor Jackson instituted a plan giving black firms 25 percent of the contracts for work to expand Atlanta's international airport.

Though Jackson disturbed white business and civic leaders with many of these policies and with an aggressive personal style they found abrasive, he could hardly afford to ignore them. To promote urban redevelopment and economic expansion, the mayor needed the resources and expertise white corporate executives and financiers could provide. "Blacks have the ballot box," an Atlanta newspaper editor admitted, "and whites have the money." When a sanitation strike tied up the city in 1977, Jackson treated it even more harshly than had his white predecessor. In a move that could only have pleased influential whites, the mayor took a hard-line stance against the work stoppage for higher wages, rejected union demands, and fired the offending strikers. Before he became mayor, Jackson had supported striking garbage workers; however, as official head of the city he placed sound business management practices and fiscal responsibility ahead of the needs of poor wage earners. He also heeded white demands to remove his controversial law enforcement chief, and replaced him with a more acceptable black.

The assumption of political power by Mayor Jackson and other black officials improved the overall position of Atlanta's nonwhite population, though it left many nagging problems unsolved. As one scholar has concluded, these accomplishments "often in the face of considerable opposition...represent...a more equitable share for the black community within existing priorities." Still, black leaders did very little to restructure those priorities, which continued to place the poor at a disadvantage. By 1980, 6 percent of black households earned at least $35,000, and more black Atlantans had incomes in excess of $50,000 than was true for minority residents anywhere else in the South. At the same time, however, this premier

Maynard Jackson, smiling after his victory as Atlanta's first black mayor. (UPI/Bettmann Newsphotos)

city had a high incidence of black poverty—25 percent of black families earned less than $5,000 a year. Overall, one-third of black families lived below the poverty line, compared with 7 percent of whites. Indeed, the diversity of Atlanta's population, reflected in its class structure, sometimes made it difficult for blacks to unite on behalf of efforts to relieve severe impoverishment. For example, during the 1977 sanitation strike, moderate black leaders rallied around the mayor against the demands of workers. In cities like Atlanta, as black political affairs progressed, they became more complicated and pragmatic—pointing to the distance traveled since the height of the civil rights movement with its moral clarity and solidarity.

Much of this complexity can likewise be seen in the experience of Tuskegee, Alabama. During the 1970s, Mayor Johnny Ford pursued a vigorous policy of obtaining outside money for economic development. At a time when the Nixon administration was dismantling the apparatus of Lyndon Johnson's War on Poverty, the Tuskegee mayor managed to secure over $30 million in federal and state grants and an additional $30 million from other funding sources. Much of Ford's success as a fund-raiser derived from his pragmatic brand of politics. This former campaign aide of Senator Robert Kennedy endorsed Nixon's reelection in 1972, explaining that he wanted to back a winner and have access to power. "It's paying off," he remarked in 1973. "Other places may be losing Federal funds because of cuts, but not Tuskegee. I've prevented that."

The Ford regime directed its efforts to improving basic public services and generating local financial growth. His administration created a new sewage system and expanded police protection. Municipal officials designed an industrial park to attract firms into the area, to serve as the centerpiece of the town's economic revitalization, and to provide jobs for area residents. Plans were prepared for the construction of an oil refinery, a dog-racing track, and an experimental tomato farm.

Unfortunately, many of these efforts failed to produce the anticipated results. Only the racetrack scheme materialized, while the industrial park failed to lure necessary private capital from investors. Although Ford continued to work with willing white leaders, more than half the white population fled Tuskegee, taking with them valuable economic assets that potentially could have benefited the town's growth. In addition, charges of corruption involving black officials, though unproven in most instances, hampered their ability to carry out several of the projects. As in Atlanta, the economic gains flowed to the black middle class rather than to those at the lower end of the economic scale. In 1980, the median income of black families was $10,423, the highest in the black-belt section of the state. Yet the percentage of blacks living in poverty was three times greater than that of whites, and over the decade the median income level in comparison with that of whites had actually dropped from 63 to 60 percent. Black politicians had not found sufficient resources or fashioned an adequate agenda to meet the needs of Tuskegee's most impoverished residents.

These drawbacks notwithstanding, the fruits of black political office-holding in the 1970s cannot be gauged simply in quantitative terms. In Tuskegee, reenfranchisement had empowered blacks to secure a significant measure of control over their lives. No longer did they have to endure the humiliation inflicted by white officials who sought to keep them from registering and who arbitrarily devised gerrymandering plans to limit the effectiveness of their votes. Black Tuskegeeans and their Macon County neighbors experienced the pride that comes when the barriers to treatment as first-class citizens are shattered. A government that for generations had been directed by and for whites came to represent the majority of the people it ruled. Political equality did not necessarily translate into economic equality, nor did individual opportunity guarantee that all members of the exploited group would derive benefits equally. But Tuskegee blacks had unprecedented access to a government that had previously excluded them, they more easily identified with governing officials, and they no longer felt so restrained within the tight physical and psychological confines of white supremacy. This experience of liberation meant a great deal to a retired VA hospital worker who had spent most of his life under vastly different circumstances. "Everything's better," he explained. "In the old days, before black elected officials ran the county, most black people steered clear of white enclaves. They used to arrest you over there if you went through, but not anymore."

BLACK RULE IN CLEVELAND AND GARY

While southern blacks were expanding their political power and leverage, their northern counterparts also extended their influence within the electoral arena. These regional pursuits of political equality were both distinct and interconnected. Black northerners, many of whom had migrated from the South during the periods surrounding the First and Second World Wars, generally faced a less rigid Jim Crow system than existed in Dixie. The residential and school segregation they encountered usually was reinforced by custom rather than by explicit laws. This was particularly true following World War II, when northern whites responded to anti-Fascist democratic ideology and removed some of the racially biased obstacles blocking minority advancement. Discrimination unquestionably remained embedded in northern institutions and practices, but they operated more subtly than in the South.

At the same time, given the freer space that they found in urban centers above the Mason-Dixon line, black northerners had greater access to political representation than did disfranchised or partially enfranchised southern blacks. In cities like Chicago and New York blacks sat on municipal councils and represented their districts in state legislatures and Congress. When not electing candidates of their own race, blacks cast their ballots to shape the outcome of local and national elections that pitted whites against each other. This type of electoral clout had helped nudge presidents and lawmakers since Franklin D. Roosevelt's time to add civil rights to the national agenda.

Nevertheless, black northerners lacked fully developed political strength. Their votes counted and frequently served as the balance of electoral power, but they did not share with whites an equal voice in their governance. In northern cities, political machines advanced the interests of an assortment of white ethnic groups that had arrived there in large numbers before transplanted blacks did. Though political bosses organized blacks as a constituency within their machines, the bosses kept the blacks on the periphery of real power and did virtually nothing to tackle the problems of racism and economic deprivation that pervaded the ghetto. Black politicians served as intermediaries between party organizations and their communities, and occasionally delivered material benefits— patronage jobs, intervention with law enforcement officials, handouts of food for the holidays—but they reflected the unequal power relationships between the races. Even where blacks constituted an integral component of the political machine, such as in Chicago, their leaders provided representation without disturbing the entrenched political and economic structures that perpetuated black subordination.

This form of quasi representation, bereft of independent power, depended on white patrons as the source of authority and dispenser of rewards. Unlike generations of white ethnic groups that had penetrated and captured control of urban political machines as an integral part of their upward economic and social mobility, African-Americans faced unparalleled obstacles in taking the same route to success. Though immigrants also encountered discrimination from whites whose forebears had preceded them to these shores, the newcomers nevertheless shared, in common with the existing residents, the privilege of skin color that relatively quickly lowered barriers to acceptance and assimilation. Blacks, however, could claim no such bond, and by virtue of their race faced uncommon prejudice that kept them on the outside of dominant political institutions. They alone had to wage a fierce struggle merely to obtain the right to vote and other elementary features of citizenship that white Americans from many ethnic backgrounds took for granted.

The new politics that emerged after 1965 increasingly thrust blacks onto center stage as agents of social change and group advancement. Black northerners took pride in the valiant struggles of the southern civil rights movement, which prompted community leaders to turn their attention to the more subtle problems of political and economic discrimination. Civil rights battles in the North focused on securing adequate jobs, quality housing and education, and impartial police protection rather than on Jim Crow and disfranchisement; but, as in the South, black northerners demanded respect and equal treatment in practice as well as in theory. The emancipationist ideology of the freedom movement joined with the social welfare programs of Johnson's War on Poverty to heighten black consciousness of oppression and the possibilities for overcoming it. The Voting Rights Act inspired northern blacks, and after 1970 eliminated literacy tests in the region. More and more black northerners successfully exercised their electoral muscle as had other ethnic minorities before them.

Yet egalitarian ideals and government programs were not enough. With shifting demographic patterns on their side, the number of blacks in the populations of urban centers rose, and they became serious contenders for public office. In the 1950s and 1960s whites had moved out of the inner cities and into the surrounding suburbs to seek a more comfortable lifestyle, one "uncontaminated" by the presence of incoming black migrants. These pilgrimages produced a sharp upswing in the black proportion of the urban population. In those areas in which blacks approached or actually became a majority of the population they had the most success in dethroning whites from the leadership of dominant political organizations.

Events in Cleveland, Ohio, and Gary, Indiana, demonstrated the changing configuration and complexity of black political development in the North. Between 1930 and 1965, the city of Cleveland lost about 300,000 of its white residents, while the number of blacks increased by over 200,000. As a result of this reshuffling, blacks constituted 34 percent of the total population and composed a slightly higher 40 percent of the city's registered voters. Many of the newly enrolled blacks had signed up during registration drives sponsored by the Democratic party in preparation for the 1964 campaign against the conservative Republican, Barry Goldwater. Thus, although blacks remained a minority of Cleveland's electorate, they held a large enough portion of the ballots to position themselves to compete for the most important post of mayor.

Until 1965, black voters had thrown their support behind white Democratic mayoral candidates. In 1961 and 1963, they had helped elect Ralph Locher and gained ten of thirty-three seats on the city council. Black politicians usually posed little challenge to white rule and chose to consolidate their power within their own districts. They had not developed the idea of uniting black communities around common issues in order to advance the racial goals of their constituents throughout the city. This situation began to alter after the mayor and his administration angered black leaders in their handling of disputes concerning school desegregation, employment practices, and police-community relations. The efforts of local chapters of national civil rights groups, such as the NAACP and CORE, along with a local coalition known as the United Freedom Movement, managed to increase black participation in protest and electoral activities and to raise expectations about the possibilities of running a black candidate for mayor against Locher. Indeed, as William Nelson and Philip Merranto observed, black leaders began to view "electoral politics... as an extension of the movement; a shortcut to the civil rights goals of housing, education, welfare."

In 1965, Carl Stokes launched a challenge to the mayor that fell short of success but pointed up the chance for future victory. Stokes had grown up in Cleveland's black ghetto, served in the armed forces, and obtained a law degree. He entered municipal government in the late 1950s with an appointment as a city prosecutor, and he first won a seat to the Ohio House of Representatives in 1962. Three years later, after his reelection, Stokes ran for mayor against three white candidates, including the incumbent. Though black Democratic elected officials stuck with Mayor Locher, Stokes won a whopping 85 percent of the minority electorate. With black officeholders lined up behind the Democratic organization, Stokes depended on grassroots groups and volunteers to conduct his campaign. Though he lost, his presence as a candidate succeeded in boosting black turnout at the polls to a record high level. Within two years black participation at the ballot box had leaped from 57 percent to 72 percent.

Given the population figures, Stokes's solid base of support in the black community alone was not enough for victory. He needed white allies. In his losing bid, Stokes had garnered 3 to 5 percent of white votes, but he required considerably more to win. The black aspirant looked to white business leaders for backing, and they saw in him an opportunity to heal the city's worsening racial conflicts. In 1966, a bloody riot in the Hough section of the city left four dead and hundreds wounded. Mayor Locher reacted to the violence with a tough law-and-order policy that emphasized more police firepower than programs to deal with the underlying ills that had sparked the uprising. The mayor set the tone for his tough approach by refusing to meet with the visiting Martin Luther King, Jr., or with local black leaders. When Stokes decided again to challenge Locher in 1967, he not only had blacks behind him, but he also attracted white businesspeople who believed that his election might calm racial tensions that posed a threat to their long-range plans for economic development of the city.

In his second try, in 1967, Stokes emerged victorious to become the first black mayor of a major American city. He patched together a winning coalition consisting of the overwhelming majority of blacks and enough whites to put him ahead. The black candidate reassured whites that he wanted "to get the Negro question out of the way." Once that happened, he asserted, "then we can talk about issues. I'm telling the people my election would not mean a Negro takeover." At the same time, Stokes ran as a black candidate as well as a candidate who happened to be black. "In 1965 when I ran," he declared, "they whispered that I was a Negro. They don't have to whisper today. I am a Negro. I am proud of it. I intend to remain one."

This strategy paid off in the 1967 campaign. First, he defeated Mayor Locher for the Democratic nomination by winning 96 percent of the black vote and 15 percent of the white. This contest again brought out black voters in record numbers, and their turnout at the polls exceeded that of whites by 15 percent. Next, in the general election Stokes defeated his Republican opponent, Seth Taft, by a slender margin of 50.3 to 49.7 percent. Black turnout was even higher than it had been in the primary, and Stokes captured 95 percent of the votes cast. He also slightly increased his backing among whites by gaining 20 percent of their ballots. In doing so, he

**Carl Stokes campaigning for votes in downtown Cleveland.
(UPI/Bettmann Newsphotos)**

had the support of white business leaders, including the publishers of the city's major newspapers. In contrast, Cleveland's working-class ethnic voters deserted him, thereby abandoning their traditional Democratic allegiances in harsh response to the riots and with the feeling that the fruits of black protest came at their expense.

Stokes's victory gave blacks a unique sense of pride, much the same way as the civil rights struggle in the South had empowered disfranchised blacks. "Stokes was a symbol...for black progress," a city councilman recalled. "You would see old people walking to the polls and perhaps they never voted a day in their lives." He underscored further the stark break from the past that had occurred for blacks: "They considered politics a white man's business. We could have councilmen and judges, but they never dreamed that day would come when a black man would be mayor of the town."

Unfortunately, the hopes generated by the election of Stokes went largely unfulfilled. The mayor did deliver a variety of benefits to his black constituents. His administration built public housing for poor blacks, set up child-care centers and health facilities in minority neighborhoods, and provided funds to stimulate black business enterprise. However, his two terms in office witnessed continuous conflicts with whites, especially city workers, and ongoing fragmentation among blacks. A series of scandals rocked the administration, which was also plagued by several strikes by municipal employees that paralyzed the city and fostered discontent. Contrary to the expectations of his white backers, Stokes's installation in city hall was not sufficient to forestall further racial disturbances, though he did have a calming influence when violence again flared in 1968.

The end of his second term saw the black electorate fractured and whites united. The split among blacks was particularly disappointing, and in 1971, upon Stokes's retirement, this division resulted in the election of a white Republican mayor. The grassroots organizations that had united around Stokes to place him in office collapsed, greatly lowering black morale and political participation. During the 1970s, the number of registered black voters decreased by 20,000 and voter turnout declined drastically—from 75 percent to 48 percent. Blacks still had access to city government, and Carl Stokes's brother, Louis, represented them in Congress, but the promise of a reshaping of municipal politics along progressive lines withered.[2]

Meanwhile, in Gary, Indiana, black political development followed a similar pattern as in Cleveland but proved to be more durable. In this midwestern home of U.S. Steel, by the late 1960s blacks comprised about 55 percent of the city's population. As whites flocked to the suburbs during the previous decade, Gary's black population rapidly expanded into a majority. Nevertheless, in 1967, whites accounted for 52.3 percent of the city's registered voters compared with 47.7 percent for blacks. Up to that time, the black electorate had thrown its clout behind the local Democratic machine, keeping its leaders in office. For instance, in 1963, two-thirds of the mayor's votes came from blacks, leaving whites to make up only a third of the winning total. In return for this support, black machine functionaries obtained patronage and other spoils; however, the dire economic conditions of their constituents living in the ghettos showed little improvement.

As in Cleveland, civil rights protests of the early 1960s helped alter the structure of black politics in Gary. Community activists engineered direct-action demonstrations to challenge unfair racial practices that the dominant machine organization failed to address. These drives mobilized many blacks who previously had been politically inactive, especially those in lower-income brackets, and heightened their desire to use the electoral arena to advance racial objectives. Community leaders looked to loosen the hold of the machine on blacks and substitute in its place a political organization directed by blacks and aimed at raising the poor quality of housing, education, and law enforcement that plagued many inner-city neighborhoods.

The leadership for this assault on the established order came from Richard G. Hatcher. A lawyer and county prosecutor, Hatcher had been active in local civil rights efforts. He served as adviser to the NAACP youth group, provided counsel for a number of local protest associations, and in 1963, headed the Gary contingent to the march on Washington. That same year, he won a seat on the city council with the backing of the Democratic machine. He soon established his independence from party chieftains and lost the

---

[2]Not until 1989 did Cleveland elect its second black mayor, Michael Smith.

plentiful patronage plums they had for distribution to the party faithful. Hatcher also broke with tradition by using his position to promote the broad civil rights aims of the black community. In one of his major accomplishments, he directed the battle to obtain a pathbreaking fair housing law for the city.

In 1967, while Carl Stokes was mounting an insurgent campaign in Cleveland, Hatcher launched his own bid for mayor of Gary. Divorced from the machine, including those black politicians customarily in its service, he set up a dynamic, grassroots organization of volunteers. Crisscrossing black neighborhoods, Hatcher's workers played upon the racial pride that had been blossoming and delivered the message that the time had arrived to elect a black mayor. They waged an intense drive to boost black voter registration, and over a seven-month period succeeded in enrolling an additional 2,200 names. Though black registration still lagged slightly behind that of whites, the Hatcher candidacy and the hard work behind it managed to stimulate 3,000 more blacks than whites to turn out at the polls. In his Democratic primary contest against two whites, including the incumbent mayor, Hatcher won by capturing about 70 percent of the black vote, while the white electorate split its ballots between his rivals.

The black nominee also prevailed in the general election, where he faced a single white opponent, the Republican Joseph Radigan. Though the candidate of his party, Hatcher failed to receive the endorsement of the regular Democratic organization, which remained deeply suspicious of his independence. Machine leaders not only withheld their backing, but they orchestrated attempts to purge the voter registration lists of 5,000 black names. This chicanery was blocked by the intervention of the Justice Department and issuance of a federal court injunction restoring the names. On election day, Hatcher eked out a slim victory of 1,389 votes, approximately 51 percent of the total cast. He garnered an astounding 96 percent of the black electorate, and owed his triumph to the very high turnout of blacks at the polls. A greater percentage of blacks than whites participated, 76 percent to 72 percent, and in addition to his solid black base of support, he obtained 14 percent of the white ballots. Though opposed by most whites, Hatcher scored particularly well in predominantly liberal Jewish districts.

Both Hatcher's candidacy and the determined organizing efforts on his behalf contributed to the victory of Gary's first black mayor.

The campaign mobilized many blacks who had felt themselves outside of the electoral process. "People for the first time really began to see how important a vote was," a Hatcher supporter acknowledged, "and that they could control a way of life." Having obtained office, the mayor initiated programs directed at relieving long-neglected problems in the black community. His administration undertook to construct public housing, encouraged affirmative action hiring plans, and recruited blacks for government employment. These benefits underscored for many blacks the connection between electoral politics and minority-group advancement and promoted in Gary's black residents both pride and confidence in government authority. Moreover, unlike the experience in Cleveland, Hatcher succeeded in solidifying black organizational support behind him and won reelection throughout the next two decades.

Black mayoral candidates also fashioned winning coalitions elsewhere by combining solid black support with a small but sufficient minority of white backers. Such was the situation in Detroit. Though the Motor City had a history of racial strife dating back to the 1943 race riot, it also had a tradition of biracial labor activism, black militancy, and liberal reform. By 1965, Detroit counted two blacks, Charles C. Diggs, Jr., and John Conyers, in its congressional delegation, and one African-American sat on the city council. During much of the 1960s the city had been run by Mayor Jerome Cavanagh, a white liberal whose generally enlightened administration was tarnished by the explosion of racial violence in 1967. The urban rebellion helped contribute to white flight to the suburbs. By the end of the decade, blacks comprised 43 percent of Detroit's population. In 1969, Richard Austin, a black accountant and chair of the Wayne County Board of Supervisors, ran for mayor but narrowly lost to his white opponent by a margin of 1 percent. Nevertheless, three blacks were elected to the nine-member city council. (The following year, Austin won election as Michigan's secretary of state.)

In 1973, Coleman Young attempted to become Detroit's first black mayor. During World War II, he had served as a second lieutenant in the Army Air Corps. While in the military, Young was arrested along with 100 black soldiers for trying to integrate an officers' club in Indiana. On the heels of the publicity generated by the protest, the Army desegregated this establishment. After finishing his tour of duty, he returned home to work as a union organizer in the automobile industry. However, his left-wing sympathies during the 1940s and 1950s made him the target of both conservative politicians and the powerful, anti-Communist United Automobile Workers. Nevertheless, he demonstrated remarkable political resiliency. By the 1960s, Young had survived the anti-Communist postwar backlash and moved into the electoral arena as a Democratic state senator and party leader still championing liberal and labor causes.

By the time he ran for mayor, in 1973, Young had an advantage that was not available to Austin four years earlier: The number of black registered voters exceeded that of whites. In the nonpartisan primary, he competed in a field of nineteen candidates. No one received a majority, and Young finished second to John Nichols, the white police commissioner. In the runoff contest against Nichols, who symbolized law and order to whites and police brutality to blacks, Young insisted that he would not engineer a black takeover and pledged "to field a team that has balance—racially, ethnically and politically." From the 1.5 million people who went to the polls, he hammered out a slim winning margin of 14,000 votes by mobilizing the overwhelming majority of the black electorate and obtaining about 8 percent of the white ballots.

Though Afro-American mayors of major cities usually emerged when blacks approached or reached a majority of the population, the election of Tom Bradley in Los Angeles was a notable exception. In a city with only a 15 percent black electorate, Bradley defeated the longtime incumbent, Sam Yorty, in a contest filled with racial bitterness. A former UCLA track star, policeman, and lawyer, Bradley served as a city councilman during the 1960s, representing a district that was two-thirds nonblack. Having lost the Democratic mayoral primary to Yorty in 1969, four years later Bradley fashioned a "coalition of conscience" to triumph over his rival with 56 percent of the vote. In 1973, he captured city hall by gaining 95 percent of black ballots, a bare majority of the Chicano (Mexican-American) electorate, and nearly half the white vote—running particularly well among liberal Jews. A source of pride to the black community in a city that was predominantly white, Bradley succeeded in convincing the electorate that his election was a sign of racial progress and an alternative to black radicalism. "The American dream is often verbalized," he asserted, "but it would really have meaning all over the country if a black who believed in the system, who worked and prepared himself for new opportunities, was able to achieve that kind of victory."

THE NEW CHALLENGE

These victories along with those in Cleveland and Gary marked the dawning of a new era in black urban politics. For more than a decade after 1967, black mayors took control of city halls in prominent urban areas both in the North and the South. As municipalities acquired black majorities, constructed political organizations to rally the previously disfranchised portion of the electorate, and marshaled economic resources to wage effective campaigns, black candidates triumphed in Newark, Washington, D.C., Oakland, Birmingham, and New Orleans. The appearance of black mayors and other elected officials directly opened up government to African-Americans on a more equal basis than ever before. In 1974, 1,593 blacks occupied elected positions outside of the South; six years later the number jumped to 2,455. Although black political leaders made mistakes and problems of poverty seemed as intractable to them as to their white predecessors, black officials demonstrated that white monopoly control of public affairs could be broken. Henceforth, blacks in towns and cities throughout the nation staked their claim to an equal partnership with whites in governance.

They faced a difficult task, however. In many of the cities in which they ascended to power, blacks inherited a multitude of severe financial problems that limited their options for action. Much of the situation was beyond their command. During the 1970s, structural flaws in the economy produced both recession and inflation that drained tax revenues away from maintaining basic city services, let alone expanding them. Major urban areas teetered on the brink of bankruptcy and needed to be rescued by infusions of state and federal funds. Low-wage foreign competition in the production and distribution of manufactured goods hurt American industry and resulted in plant closings and unemployment in many of the urban locations dominated by black chief executives. Furthermore, the continued migration of whites to the suburbs and the parallel movement of a rising black middle class out of the inner cities left behind an increasingly poor population of blacks unable to contribute to the upkeep of their communities.

In addition, black mayors were hampered in other ways. Those seeking improvements for their constituents often found their efforts slowed by entrenched municipal government employees whose jobs were protected by civil service codes. As a result, changes in personnel to implement new directions in policy could occur only slowly at best and at worst could be thwarted by unsympathetic bureaucrats. Moreover, many issues could not be handled through local initiatives. Cities depended on state and federal governments for funds, but growing conservatism in the 1970s deprived them of political allies to fill crucial material needs. Into the void stepped large corporate investors and financial developers, who in return for their economic assistance steered many municipal projects toward enterprises that created jobs and housing for middle- and upper-class residents to the detriment of the poor.

Despite this sometimes dismal picture, African-Americans still found pursuit of electoral power worthwhile. Throughout the nation, a substantial segment of the black electorate benefited from the tangible improvements that increased political strength brought. After 1965, opportunities for public employment and distribution of municipal services had far less to do with skin color than at any time during American history. Furthermore, black empowerment meant much more than could be calculated in dollars and cents. It provided a source of political agency for blacks, breaking down habits of nonparticipation ingrained through generations of racial discrimination. To the extent that the members of any group of people, white or black, male or female, could exert control over their lives in an increasingly complex and technological society, African-Americans had joined the ranks of first-class citizens and helped shape the political landscape of the country.

Chapter 6

Progress and Poverty: Politics in a Conservative Era

The movement of blacks into positions of influence and power in local and state governments, however impressive the gains, was not enough to produce genuine racial equality. Many of the problems blacks encountered were national in scope and required national attention and resources to remedy. Furthermore, the laws placed on the statute books as a result of the civil rights struggle needed federal enforcement, and in the case of the Voting Rights Act, periodic renewal. The economic misery that plagued so many African-Americans demanded solutions beyond the purview of local politicians. The burdens inflicted by chronic unemployment, inflation, and inadequate housing and health care traversed municipal, county, and state boundary lines and became the responsibility of officials in Washington. Unless blacks and their white allies could shape public policy in the nation's capital to deal with these concerns, the benefits of political empowerment would remain incomplete.

As the fruits of black political mobilization began to ripen during the 1970s, they matured in a climate less nurturing to their continued growth. Black southerners had regained their right to vote with the flowering of liberal reform in the mid-1960s; yet within a decade the nation had moved in a conservative direction that posed serious threats to hard-earned civil rights and social programs and to the initiation of new ones. In the wake of disillusionment over the Vietnam war and racial strife in American cities, Richard Nixon and other conservatives had risen to prominence by deemphasizing racial justice, promising a return to law and order, and pledging economic retrenchment. In this gloomy environment, African-Americans looked to engage their foes in the national arena in which the vital policies affecting their welfare were forged. The preservation and expansion of electoral victories in local black communities throughout the nation depended on winning battles in Washington to sustain them.

While much needed to be done before blacks achieved the economic equality to accompany their recently gained civil and political rights, in an age of federal retrenchment they were largely forced to fight defensive operations. Although they did wage new skirmishes for racial advancement, civil rights proponents spent much of their creative energies guarding against rollbacks in existing programs. During the Nixon administration, civil rights advocates had successfully petitioned Congress and the courts to maintain strict enforcement of the Voting Rights Act and school desegregation decisions. A bipartisan coalition of moderate and liberal lawmakers, reinforced by determined civil rights lobbyists, ensured that landmark suffrage legislation remained intact and defeated administration-sponsored attempts to circumvent court-ordered busing. On the economic front, the Republican chief executive managed to terminate some of his predecessor's Great Society programs and trim others by turning funding over to the states. But even in this area, in 1973 Congress acknowledged the plight of the poor by adopting the Comprehensive Employment and Training Act (CETA), which provided public service jobs and manpower training to those out of work.

BLACK POLITICAL INFLUENCE AND THE FORD ADMINISTRATION

When the Watergate scandal forced Nixon to resign, in 1974, Vice-President Gerald Ford stepped in to serve out Nixon's term. A staunch conservative and a veteran of some twenty-five years in the House of Representatives, Ford had given qualified support to civil rights legislation. As a lawmaker from Grand Rapids, Michigan, Ford routinely voted for passage of civil rights bills extending the suffrage to blacks and challenging racial discrimination in public accommodations and housing. However, in compiling this record he had, like President Nixon, embraced those proposals only after making concerted efforts to soften their impact. As a congressman in 1970, he had lined up behind the chief executive in favor of replacing key provisions of the Voting Rights Act with a version that would have removed much of the weight of enforcement from the white South. His stance in opposition to school busing reflected Nixon's, as well as that of his white constituents who decried imposing this means of remedying racial imbalance in neighborhood schools.

Nevertheless, upon succeeding the disgraced Nixon on August 9, 1974, Ford assumed a conciliatory posture that was absent from his predecessor's final days in office. To restore confidence in the presidency and to bind the wounds inflicted by the Watergate debacle, he sought to reassure some of those who felt most estranged from the White House. These gestures followed earlier attempts "to clear the air" with black leaders while he was still vice-president. As Ford later recalled it, disturbed that "the Nixon Administration had closed the door to minorities, particularly blacks," he hoped they would see him as "point man...for dealing with the government; that there was at least one man in the Administration who would listen to them." Unfortunately, when he tried to follow up these meetings by submitting recommendations for action, Nixon's staff ignored him. Within a week of becoming President, he summoned to the Oval Office members of the Congressional Black Caucus, whose chairman, Charles Rangel of New York, called the conference "absolutely, fantastically good."

A short time later, President Ford had sufficient opportunity to show the sincerity of his intentions. Very much on the minds of black lawmakers and civil rights advocates was the upcoming renewal of the Voting Rights Act, whose key provisions were due to lapse in August 1975. For the third time in ten years, Congress had to debate the merits of federal protection of the suffrage and decide whether forceful supervision should continue into the future and for how long. Though southern blacks had taken notable strides in gaining entry to the electoral arena, their political strength was still fragile and depended on continued oversight from Washington to reach its full potential. Remembering the nation's abandonment of the freed slaves at the end of Reconstruction a century earlier, modern-day civil rights supporters worried about the harm that another premature federal withdrawal would cause to the Second Reconstruction's enfranchised blacks.

President Ford appeared to agree with their concern. He okayed the Justice Department's recommendation to extend the Voting Rights Act for an additional five years, thereby choosing not to repeat Nixon's unsuccessful attempt to fasten controversial amendments to it. Acknowledging that southern blacks had made great progress in the decade since passage of the law, the Ford administration noted that the number of black elected officials remained disproportionately low and that evidence of racial discrimination in registration and voting persisted. In taking this position, the chief executive further endeared himself to civil rights advocates by invoking the memory of Dr. King and linking it to the renewal campaign. On January 14, 1975, Ford commemorated the anniversary of the slain minister's birthday by recalling King's leadership in enacting the original suffrage law, which, he remarked, "has helped to open our political process to full citizen participation" and must be "safeguarded."

Boosted by the President and with solid bipartisan congressional backing, the renewal measure headed for sure passage. Compared with previous battles, the current deliberations took place in an atmosphere of relative harmony. Neither the administration nor the liberals disagreed over preserving what had become the most important provision of the statute—the section-five requirement for the covered states to clear changes in their electoral laws with the Justice Department before they took effect. There were differences over the length of time desired for extension—the White House favored five years and civil rights lawmakers advocated ten—and the President was reluctant to add to the bill a liberal-sponsored measure to grant language minorities the same protection guaranteed to oppressed racial groups. Nevertheless, unity rather than discord characterized the congressional proceedings. Joseph Rauh, the civil rights attorney who had pleaded the case of the Mississippi Freedom Democratic Party in 1964, summed up the feeling of reformers: "I guess one of the happiest things for us is the broad consensus that has grown up behind extending the Voting Rights Act."

Though southern lawmakers did not abandon their customary opposition to the suffrage bill, they lacked both the passion and strength to mount an effective challenge to it in 1975. Accepting the political reality that the legislation was going to pass in some form, they tried to revive the Nixon administration strategy of expanding coverage of section five nationwide. Moreover, opponents concentrated their energy on designing provisions to make it easier for the southern states to remove themselves from the act's penalties. Their arguments failed to persuade their legislative colleagues. A proposal for a ten-year extension sailed through the House, and the Senate displayed an unusual enthusiasm for agreement by voting to impose cloture to terminate debate even before southern legislators had the opportunity to wage a filibuster.

Despite this overwhelming show of support, the final outcome became unexpectedly enmeshed in controversy. While the Senate discussed the measure, President Ford suddenly backed away from his firm endorsement of the bill and suggested enlarging its scope to include the entire nation. In offering this last-minute proposal, Ford seemed to be heeding the calls of southern members of his party to take such action. With Republicanism on the rise in Dixie—Goldwater and Nixon had made significant inroads in the once solid Democratic South's presidential vote—the GOP leader looked to the region to help gain his party's nomination and win election in his own right in 1976. His about-face drew a barrage of criticism from civil rights supporters, Democrats and Republicans alike, who charged that his puzzling position confused the issue and put the entire bill in jeopardy. However, Ford's political calculation turned into an empty gesture as the chief executive once again reversed his field. Fearing that his intervention would stall passage of the bill's special provisions before their expiration, the President withdrew his objection to enactment of the original measure. As the presidential fog lifted from the Capitol, both chambers of Congress approved a modified seven-year extension by wide margins.

This victory demonstrated the increasing leverage of southern blacks upon their national representatives. The South's trio of black legislators, Barbara Jordan of Texas, Andrew Young of Georgia, and Harold Ford of Tennessee, were expected to cast their votes for the bill (as were the thirteen black lawmakers from the North); but it was a matter of considerable surprise that 69 of 105 of their white colleagues from the region joined them on the final tally. In the Senate, where Edward Brooke, the Massachusetts Republican, sat as the lone black, 13 of 24 southerners lined up behind the measure.

Reflecting the changing pattern of partisan affiliation in Dixie, the party of Abraham Lincoln and the party of Jefferson Davis were trading places. As conservative whites jumped to the Republicans and northern transplants brought their GOP allegiances to the region, Democrats in the South were coming to rely more heavily on the growing black electorate for support at the polls. Though southern Democratic lawmakers did not embrace liberal economic positions that would have benefited African-Americans, they had little difficulty in backing a suffrage law that created the very constituency they needed to help keep them in power. This shifting arithmetic led southern Democrats and Republicans to calculate differently. In the House, two-thirds of the southern Democratic bloc supported extension of the Voting Rights Act in contrast to nearly two in three Dixie Republicans who opposed it. A Louisiana lawmaker expressed the sentiments of his fellow Democrats: "We found that the sky did not fall under the 1965 Voting Rights Act, that things worked pretty well in the South, the deep South of the old Confederacy, which readjusted their [sic] patterns of voting, readjusted their attitudes toward all people."

In the end, the Ford administration chose to follow the new consensus on voting rights that had developed, but in the more controversial area of school busing the administration pursued the old course laid out by President Nixon. Supreme Court decisions sanctioning busing generated substantial opposition among whites in the North as well as the South. Building upon this hostility, in 1972 the Nixon administration had introduced congressional legislation instructing the judiciary to try to retain the neighborhood school concept and to use busing only as a last resort. The bill passed the House only to die in the Senate. The chief executive kept the measure alive during the remainder of his abbreviated term, and after Ford replaced him, Congress finally approved the proposal. This action delighted the new chief executive, who declared: "I have consistently opposed forced busing to achieve racial balance as a solution to quality education." Furthermore, these words gave encouragement to antibusing opponents such as those in Boston who militantly protested against court-ordered desegregation. Launching school boycotts, holding marches, and fomenting violence, these foes of busing succeeded in plunging the city into turmoil for several years during the mid-1970s.

These attacks notwithstanding, the practical effect of the legislative measure was minimal, because Congress did not have the authority to curtail courts from enforcing the constitutional rights of minority students through busing. In fact, during the Nixon-Ford years nearly 50 percent of black pupils attended desegregated schools in the South, a figure higher than that in the North. And, despite the resistance in Boston, the judiciary remained firm in enforcing its busing decrees. In addition, civil rights lobbyists and their congressional allies defeated a more serious threat to busing than the bill Ford had signed into law. They succeeded in turning back attempts to end court-ordered busing altogether by way of a constitutional amendment, passage of which would have required a two-thirds vote of Congress before ratification by the states.

Beyond salvaging the influential Voting Rights Act and retaining some degree of enforcement of school desegregation, African-Americans saw their efforts toward greater racial advancement stall. Blacks used political power to sustain their legal rights of citizenship, but they had far less success in shaping the agenda that would have addressed their economic needs. With fiscal conservatism emerging as the dominant theme in Washington and throughout the country, social programs to stimulate employment, extend health insurance, and furnish housing, which would have aided the working class and poor of both races, realistically did not stand much of a chance. Moreover, the growing inflationary spiral of the mid-1970s, together with rising unemployment—"stagflation," as economists labeled it—brought to a virtual halt the economic gains blacks had been experiencing since the heyday of the civil rights movement a decade before. In 1975, the median income of black families had inched up to 61 percent of whites', but having reached this peak, it immediately began sliding even further away from full equality. Without renewed federal commitment to tackling their economic problems, blacks managed only to fight a rearguard political battle to maintain the status quo.

THE ELECTION OF JIMMY CARTER

The presidential election of 1976 offered dim prospects for meaningful change. The Republican incumbent's performance in civil rights matters, after getting off to a good start, had come to disappoint blacks. Much of the goodwill Ford had created by supporting extension of the Voting Rights Act eroded in his clumsy handling of the bill at its final stage before passage. In addition to his antibusing stand, Ford's position against federal aid to rescue financially troubled cities from bankruptcy upset black activists. They criticized the President for his callousness in allowing major urban centers of the North, which contained substantial black populations, to cut back on municipal social services rather than helping them preserve these programs through an infusion of funds from Washington. In the wake of the riots in the late 1960s and the flight of whites to the suburbs, the cities had become associated increasingly with the presence of impoverished racial minorities whose problems white Americans preferred to ignore. After Ford rejected New York City's plea for relief in 1975, M. Carl Holman, a longtime civil rights advocate and director of the Urban Coalition, contended that many blacks believed New York "would never have been dealt with like that if it had been seen as a city of Wasps [white Anglo-Saxon Protestants]."

Nor had the Democratic presidential nominee identified himself closely with the cities and their black residents. The former governor of Georgia, Jimmy Carter had presided over a largely rural and small-town state. He brought a brand of New South progressivism to the statehouse in Atlanta that emphasized honesty and efficiency in government, streamlining the budgetary process, and upgrading the public education system, which ranked near the bottom in the country. Accordingly, this political and economic modernization fostered an environment hospitable to business investment and growth. In 1976, Carter secured his party's presidential nomination by effectively campaigning in the primaries as an "outsider" from Washington, an image that in the post-Watergate era garnered widespread appeal from an electorate disillusioned with national politicians. Weary of "imperial presidents," either of the activist Republican or the Democratic variety, Americans saw merit in the kind of low-expectation approach to government offered by Carter. A self-described conservative in fiscal affairs, the Georgian fit in well with the mood of economic retrenchment and frugality that voters wanted in the nation's capital.

Although Carter's record as governor did not hold out much promise for the extension of costly programs to reduce black poverty, his racial views provided a bit more encouragement for black advancement. However, the case in his favor was hardly clear-cut. Carter had been born and raised in Plains, Georgia, and returned there to live after completing a career in the Navy. During the 1950s and 1960s, he accepted the rigid segregationist practices and nearly total disfranchisement that characterized his home area in southwest Georgia. Never a negrophobe, he did not actively condone Jim Crow so much as he made very little effort to eradicate it. Yet unlike many of his neighbors, this peanut farmer refused to join the White Citizens Council or other states' rights groups opposed to desegregation, and on one occasion in the mid-1960s, he even waged a losing battle to open up his Baptist church doors to black congregants. Nevertheless, elected governor in 1970, he roundly criticized court-ordered busing and endorsed a constitutional amendment to prevent it. He also developed close ties with George Wallace, who he thought had the best chance of defeating Nixon in 1972, and when George McGovern instead of Wallace won the Democratic nomination that year, Carter unsuccessfully tried to extract a pledge from him to relax enforcement of the Voting Rights Act in the South.

While in office, the Georgia governor balanced these positions with others that won black support. In an era when black voters were becoming critical to the election of white Democratic party officials, new South politicians like Carter (and even some old-style segregationists like Wallace) discarded the racist rhetoric of the past and abandoned irresponsible opposition to the laws of the land that compelled desegregation. The changes wrought by the civil rights movement had made a distinct impression upon Carter, and he accepted them with both a "sense of relief" and "secret gratitude." In effect, the struggle for black equality had also freed many whites from the shackles of racism that kept the South locked into economic and political backwardness. In 1971, Governor Carter had proclaimed the start of a new day: "I say to you quite frankly that the time for racial discrimination is over. No poor, rural, weak, or black person shall ever have to bear the additional burden of being deprived of the opportunity for an education, a job, or simple justice." He matched the symbolism of his eloquent rhetoric with some substance. During his administration, the governor arranged to desegregate the walls of the state capitol by hanging a portrait of Dr. King alongside paintings of distinguished white Georgians, a ceremony that ended with the singing of the powerful civil rights anthem "We Shall Overcome." Moreover, Carter doubled the number of blacks working in state government, increased black appointments to middle-management positions, and signed into law the state's first open-housing measure.

This overall performance won Carter the staunch backing of Dr. King's family and some of the martyred civil rights leader's top associates. Congressman Andrew Young of Atlanta, a King confidant, became an early booster of the governor for the Democratic presidential nomination in 1976. He was joined by the Reverend Martin Luther King, Sr., who remarked that he had "never met a finer person than Governor Carter." Though other black civil rights leaders-turned-politicians, such as Julian Bond, declined to endorse him, Carter held on firmly to his King-Atlanta connections.

The strength of this attachment was sorely tested during the primaries. In Indianapolis, appearing before a largely white audience, Carter reiterated his opposition to racial discrimination at the same time as he defended those "who are trying to maintain the ethnic purity of their neighborhoods." He further stated his disapproval of the government's deliberately "trying to break down an ethnically oriented community...by injecting into it a member of another race." These comments smacked of the kind of rhetoric that George Wallace had skillfully employed as a presidential candidate in whipping up a white backlash among ethnic groups fearful that black advances would come at their expense. Carter survived this episode by apologizing for any misunderstanding his statement might have caused, which satisfied most black leaders. Representative Young and "Daddy" King rallied around Carter and forgave him for making "a slip of the tongue that does not represent his thinking."

This reaffirmation of support enabled Carter to attract the bulk of black votes in winning crucial primary contests, which carried him to the Democratic National Convention as the frontrunner. There he heard the stirring keynote speech of Representative Barbara Jordan of Houston, the first black to receive the honor of delivering this prestigious address. In 1967, as a first-term Texas state senator, Jordan had come to the attention of President Lyndon Johnson, who invited her to the White House to participate in a strategy session concerning fair-housing legislation. She impressed the President, as well as her colleagues in the Texas legislature, by combining a concern for civil rights with hardheaded legislative pragmatism. Elected to Congress in 1972, Jordan quickly rose to prominence as perhaps the most eloquent member of the House Judiciary Committee in its televised investigation of the Watergate-related impeachment charges against President Nixon. Chosen to rally the Democratic faithful at the 1976 nominating convention, she declared that her very presence on the podium showed "that the American dream need not forever be deferred." The assembled delegates who heard these words and who subsequently nominated Carter for President included 323 blacks comprising 10.6 percent of the convention members. (In contrast, blacks comprised only 3 percent of the GOP convention delegates who chose Ford as their candidate.) The Democratic reform initiative launched in 1964 was evidenced most vividly in the Mississippi contingent, which contained the highest ratio of blacks to whites of any delegation at the gathering.

Throughout the nomination process and in the subsequent general election campaign, Carter successfully reached out to blacks. A devout Baptist, he avidly cultivated black support by speaking in black churches and delivering a message his listeners could relate to. Churches had traditionally functioned as key institutions in the political life of black communities, and Carter knew how to tap into their emotional style and felt comfortable in the role of a preacher presenting a sermon. He stressed the themes of redemption and compassion, brotherhood and love, justice and equality, and linked them personally and directly to Dr. King. "I sometimes think that a Southerner of my generation," the Georgian remarked, "can most fully understand the meaning and impact of Martin Luther King's life. He and I grew up in the same South." As Carter's biographer, Betty Glad, concluded, more than any substantive program the candidate offered, blacks responded to him out of "nostalgia for the rhythms and religion of rural Christianity."

Indeed, black ballots proved pivotal in Carter's triumph over Ford. The Georgian eked out a very tight victory over the incumbent, gaining a bare 50 percent of the popular vote and capturing 297 electoral votes to Ford's 241—the closest margin since 1916. In patching together a coalition of states from his native South, the Midwest, and the Northeast, Carter secured a whopping 90 percent of the black vote. His strongest support came from the southern black electorate, which gave him 92 percent of its ballots. The

Representative Barbara Jordan of Texas delivering the keynote address at the 1976 Democratic National Convention. (AP/Wirephoto)

huge vote that Carter obtained from blacks helped him secure all but one state (Virginia) in the South, where Ford otherwise received about 55 percent of the total white southern vote. When Mississippi, which only a decade before had barred nearly all blacks from the franchise, swung into the Democratic column, Andrew Young gleefully declared: "I knew that the hands that picked the cotton finally picked the president." Nationally the governor piled up 5.2 million black votes, more than triple his slender popular vote margin of 1.7 million.

Blacks flocked to Carter for a variety of reasons. On a personal level, his southern Baptist religious fervor and regional heritage appealed to blacks not only in the South but also to those whose roots extended back to Dixie. Carter credited the civil rights movement with transforming both himself and the South, a message that earned him widespread support from former leaders of that struggle. The key endorsements of Reverend King and Congressman Young, Julian Bond noted, "made Carter legitimate in the eyes of blacks all over the country." Furthermore, Carter ran extremely well among blacks because of his party label. Polls revealed that the Georgian scored heavily with traditional Democrats, and no group exceeded the loyalty exhibited by black Democrats in recent presidential elections. The party of FDR's New Deal and LBJ's Great Society had even greater attraction in 1976, when the unemployment rate under the Republicans had risen to 8 percent and was substantially higher among adult black males.

The important contribution African-Americans made to Carter's triumph stood in sharp contrast to the mood of despair felt by many blacks in that bicentennial-year celebration of the Declaration of Independence. Carl Holman detected "a dangerous cynicism," especially among young blacks, who demanded more than the civil rights victories of the past that had brought liberty without equality. "There's a great feeling of being out of it—outsiders in your own country—which was a feeling they began to lose in the sixties," Holman asserted. "And it's come back double-barrelled now." Even before the 1960s ended, the country's urban ghettos had exploded as rioters violently expressed their bitterness in the streets rather than calmly at the polls. Between 1968 and 1972, the black turnout of eligible voters fell. The decline was especially pronounced in the North, where the ballot did not hold the same attraction for blacks as it did for those southerners who had fought a long, difficult struggle to regain the franchise. The traumas of Vietnam and Watergate had heightened this alienation, but the frustration of many African-Americans emerged even stronger from the unwillingness of political leaders to grapple with the continuing crises of joblessness, poor health, and substandard housing that gripped black communities. "There is," the political scientist Samuel D. Cook declared in 1976, "a groping for direction, issues, priorities, funds, organization, inspiration, affirmation, protest, and movement."

Yet such assessments did not tell the whole story, as many blacks showed signs that they were not ready to give up on the political system. Since 1972, the number of blacks registered to vote had grown by three quarters of a million. Civil rights groups such as the NAACP had joined with labor unions, the Democratic party, and the Voter Education Project to mount active enrollment campaigns to sign up new voters. In the South, blacks narrowed the registration gap between the races from over 40 percent in the mid-1960s to about 11 percent a decade later. Equally as impressive, registered blacks turned out for the 1976 presidential election in growing numbers. This contest brought to the polls about 64 percent of enrolled black voters nationwide, surpassing the 58 percent participating in 1972. The upswing in the rates of black registration and turnout as well as the impact of the minority vote in determining Carter's victory convinced many African-Americans that they were still heading in the right direction. No one was more optimistic than John Lewis, the former chairman of SNCC and director of VEP. "I wish—Lord, how I wish," he commented after the election, "Martin [Luther King] were alive today. He would be very, very happy. Through it all, the lunch counter sit-ins, the bus strike, the marches and everything, the bottom line was voting."

AFFIRMATIVE ACTION AND BAKKE

Having helped elect a President, blacks expected their faith in the electoral system to be suitably rewarded. Not only did they desire to obtain the traditional spoils of victory—jobs and appointments—but they also sought to influence the setting of a public policy agenda that recognized the special needs of their communities. In President Carter they acquired increased access to top-level government positions, but they fell short in steering his administration along a course that would lead to bold new programs.

The President recruited an impressive array of blacks to Washington. Patricia R. Harris, former ambassador to Luxembourg and chair of the Credentials Committee at the 1972 Democratic National Convention, entered the Cabinet as secretary of housing and urban development. An undergraduate at Howard University in 1943, Harris had participated in an early sit-in demonstration to desegregate a cafeteria in the District of Columbia. The chief executive staffed the Justice Department with Solicitor General Wade McCree, a Harvard-trained federal judge from Michigan, and Assistant Attorney General for Civil Rights Drew Days III, a Yale Law School graduate who had previously handled cases for the NAACP Legal Defense Fund. He chose Clifford Alexander, Jr., an adviser to President Johnson, as secretary of the Army. Carter, who on the campaign trail had showered praise upon the civil rights movement, appointed several individuals who had played significant roles in that struggle. He selected Andrew Young, one of Dr.

King's closest advisers in the SCLC, for the Cabinet-level post of ambassador to the United Nations. From SNCC the President tapped John Lewis to operate Volunteers in Service to America (VISTA), the domestic equivalent of the Peace Corps. (This agency was a division of ACTION, whose associate director was Mary King, a white SNCC organizer.) Named as assistant secretary of labor, Ernest Green twenty years earlier, in 1957, had been part of the courageous group of black students that defied a menacing mob to desegregate Central High School in Little Rock, Arkansas. By the end of Carter's term in office the list of his black appointees had expanded to include 15 ambassadors, 30 federal judges, over 50 sub-Cabinet officials, 110 members of advisory boards and commissions, and 25 members of the White House staff.

Aside from the recognition they conferred, these appointments did not produce bold initiatives in civil rights policy. The most challenging opportunity arose over affirmative action, and the Carter administration acted cautiously. This issue sharply divided the races. Most whites objected to any preferential treatment—reverse discrimination as they saw it—that placed them at a disadvantage in hiring and in admission into graduate and professional schools. They considered any program that established a fixed number of positions, or quotas, for minorities as a violation of the principle of equal opportunity. In stark contrast, the majority of blacks took the opposite position. African-Americans argued that on the basis of past discrimination, the effects of which still persisted, they were entitled to compensatory treatment. In their view, this meant the establishment of flexible goals, not quotas, to recruit qualified minorities until a level was reached that indicated they were competing equally. The controversy posed a thorny political hazard for Carter because it split two key elements of his electoral coalition: blacks and Jews. Victims of discriminatory quotas in the past, Jewish-Americans deplored any attempt to resurrect quotas even for the purpose of including, rather than excluding, certain groups of people.

The President attempted to walk a fine line on this matter. Having made earnest efforts to increase minority employment in his administration, the chief executive readily acknowledged that blacks suffered from the impact of racial bias, past and present, and pledged "to root out those last vestiges of discrimination in government and set a pattern for the private sector." He disapproved of quotalike regulations that limited access to employment, however, and believed that minorities would benefit in the long run from racially impartial hiring and admission standards.

In this respect, President Carter reflected the position of most white Americans. A 1972 survey had indicated that 82 percent of whites opposed affirmative action plans that favored blacks over equally qualified whites. Nevertheless, 77 percent of those polled approved of the creation of job-training programs for blacks. Like Carter, the overwhelming majority of respondents differentiated between "legitimate" compensatory programs that allowed minority groups an opportunity to compete on an equal level with whites and "unfair" policies that supposedly granted one group preferential treatment over another. These attitudes were hardened by the economic situation of the 1970s, which heightened competition for increasingly scarce jobs and spaces in graduate and professional schools. The decade's economic cycle of recession coincidental with inflation—that is, stagflation, as noted earlier—together with the outpouring into the marketplace of the postwar baby-boomers made whites much less hospitable to racial advancement than in the 1960s, when jobs and educational opportunities were more plentiful.

African-Americans generally considered affirmative action from a much different perspective. Having only recently regained their legal right to equality, blacks resented being told to forget their unfortunate history of racial discrimination and to make it on their own without due compensation from the government and the private sector. They refused to believe that such relief could be termed "reverse discrimination" when whites still retained firm control over economic and political power in society. Besides, to blacks racial bias was not so much an individual matter of discrimination as an institutional one allowing whites on the whole to continue to preserve their long-standing advantages. African-Americans argued that they would have a very difficult time in ever catching up to the mass of white Americans who had inherited the legacy of superior educational and employment benefits solely on the basis of their skin color. Thus, they contended that "benign" racial classifications were legitimate and proper.

Their arguments received some sanction in the courts. In 1971, the Supreme Court ruled in *Griggs v. Duke Power Company* that "neutral" employment tests were invalid if they perpetuated the effects of prior discriminatory employment practices. The justices found the results of such bias to exist when blacks failed to hold jobs in rough proportion to their percentage in the general population. Yet the issue was far from settled. In 1974, the high tribunal in *DeFunis v. Odegaard* had the opportunity to decide the fate of an affirmative action plan adopted by the University of Washington Law School that applied different entrance standards for blacks and whites. However, because the white plaintiff who charged discrimination had already been admitted to the law school while the suit was pending, the court declared the litigation moot, left the admissions plan intact, and managed to duck the controversial question for the time being.

The issue again surfaced at the medical school of the University of California, Davis, and forced the Carter administration to take action. The university had set aside a designated number of spaces for minority students in order to guarantee their selection. Alan Bakke, a rejected white applicant, sued to gain admission and overturn this procedure. After Bakke won in a lower court, the university appealed to the Supreme Court, where the Justice Department intended to file a brief in opposition to the school's affirmative action plan. Reflecting White House thinking, government lawyers premised their arguments on the principle that "racial classifications favorable to minority groups are presumptively unconstitutional."

Before the department could complete its brief, civil rights advocates inside and outside the administration managed substantially to revise the government's handiwork. Ironically, the original draft that critics found unacceptable had been written under the supervision of Carter's two top black attorneys, McCree and Days. In opposition stood Joseph Califano, the secretary of health, education, and welfare, who was white, and several black officeholders such as Ambassador Young and Eleanor Holmes Norton, the director of the Equal Employment Opportunity Commission. Taking their concerns to the President, they warned him, in Young's words, that the "Bakke case is perceived as a betrayal of the black community by the judicial system." At the same time, the Congressional Black Caucus applied additional pressure on the chief executive and informed him that the Justice brief "irretrievably undermined public and private affirmative action programs." In the wake of these maneuvers, Carter's lawyers, led by McCree and Days, redrafted the brief along lines suggested by its critics. The final version softened the department's antiquota position, supported university guidelines that took race into account for admission, and suggested that the case be returned to the California judiciary for rehearing. Although the Supreme Court agreed that racial criteria generally were a legitimate consideration in designing affirmative action programs, in this instance it upheld the claim of unfair discrimination and ordered Bakke's matriculation into the medical school.

This episode demonstrated the strengths and exposed the limitations of black political influence during the Carter years. Because the President had had the sensitivity and had felt a political obligation to appoint blacks to important posts in his administration, they were well-placed during the Bakke affair to correct Carter from making, what Califano called, "the most serious mistake... in domestic policy to date." Yet having helped shape this crucial policy matter, black officials and their white allies could not control the ultimate outcome of the decision. The Supreme Court took care of that, and its increasingly conservative orientation, reflecting appointments to the bench made by Nixon, confined affirmative action within narrow boundaries. Though civil rights sympathizers sat on the high tribunal, most notably Thurgood Marshall, the former chief counsel of the NAACP, they did not constitute a majority. Nevertheless, their presence on the court, like that of blacks in the Carter administration, modestly advanced civil rights goals so long as they did not stray too far from the center of the judicial and political spectrum.

The same situation applied in Congress. Throughout the late 1970s the Black Caucus and its white liberal allies made little progress with the majority of lawmakers who believed their constituents demanded fiscal restraint and would not tolerate massive spending to relieve economic distress. For example, the Black Caucus rallied behind a measure aimed at relieving the problem of unemployment, which was disproportionately high among blacks. Before Congress, in 1978, enacted a "full employment" bill sponsored by Senator Hubert Humphrey of Minnesota and Representative Augustus Hawkins, a black Democrat from California, conservative lawmakers had turned it into a hollow proposal.[1] Even worse, a national health plan offered by Senator Edward Kennedy of Massachusetts that would have been of great benefit to blacks went unpassed.

Given their optimistic expectations of President Carter, blacks had reason to feel disappointed with his performance. The President, who had campaigned for the White House as a Washington outsider, failed to establish effective relations in dealing with Congress. In this post-Watergate era, the task of leading lawmakers in a more activist, progressive direction would have severely challenged any chief executive, but Carter proved unwilling and unable to marshal his resources toward that end. He had promised the electorate competence, efficiency, and integrity—to restore character and decency to the Oval Office—not new programs for social reform. Further, the slimness of his victory did not furnish a mandate or provide him with the incentive to pursue bold domestic ventures. Still, he might have channeled some of the enthusiasm and energy he displayed in promoting his policy of human rights abroad into efforts at extending civil and economic rights at home. His liberal critics waited in vain for him to guide the nation morally and politically "to an understanding of the demands and subtleties of civil rights in the late 1970s and 1980s."

For black Americans Carter compounded his leadership difficulties by his handling of a controversy surrounding Ambassador Young. The outspoken delegate to the United Nations had become the most visible black representative in the Carter administration. To blacks the former civil rights leader and Atlanta congressman was a source of great pride, but to whites he demonstrated the inability of the chief executive to exercise his presidential authority firmly. The U.N. diplomat had received a great deal of publicity for his comments denouncing the racism both of America's friends and foes abroad as well as for extolling one of the nation's enemies, Cuba, for combating colonialism in Africa. Indeed, Young had served as a forceful advocate within the administration against apart-

---

[1]The original bill had called for a reduction of unemployment to 4 percent within five years and authorized the federal government to provide "last resort" jobs to reach this target. Instead, the final version relied primarily on the private sector to create jobs and attempted to set a brake on federal spending by establishing a goal of 3 percent inflation within five years.

heid in South Africa and for establishing closer ties with newly independent African states. In August 1979, after it became known that Young had held an unauthorized meeting with agents of the Palestine Liberation Organization (PLO), an action contrary to Carter's Middle East policy, the ambassador was forced to resign. The appointment of another black, Donald F. McHenry, to succeed Young only partially repaired the damage to Carter's image in the black community.

In addition, the Young incident once again inflamed tensions between two of the most loyal elements of the Democratic coalition: blacks and Jews. Despite their long history of cooperation within the civil rights movement, since the late 1960s issues concerning affirmative action and the Middle East had strained relations between the groups. Jewish organizations had thrown their considerable weight behind Bakke's challenge to racial quotas, and black activists had called for recognition of a Palestinian homeland, a position they held as an act of solidarity with nonwhite, exploited people and one which they regarded as even handed. Blacks considered support for Bakke's case as inimical to their economic advancement, and Jews viewed deliberations with the PLO as a threat to the security of Israel. Proponents from each side worked to defuse the hostility, but events such as those prompting Young's departure heightened the conflict. Shortly after the U.N. ambassador left his job, tempers again flared. When Jesse L. Jackson, the director of People United to Save Humanity (PUSH)[2] and a former colleague of Young's in the SCLC, met with and embraced Yasser Arafat, the leader of the PLO, he occasioned a barrage of criticism from Jewish organizations.

THE ELECTION OF RONALD REAGAN

Troubled by these political splits, African-Americans had even more to worry about in the hard times that had befallen many residents of their communities. Between 1975 and 1980, the median income of blacks compared with whites dropped three points to 58 percent. The proportion of blacks without jobs hovered around 14 percent, double the rate for whites. That figure was bad enough,

---

[2]The name was later changed to People United to Serve Humanity.

but the 40 percent rate of unemployment for black teenagers, more than twice that of white youths, was even worse. The incidence of poverty among blacks was also greater than for whites, and the situation was deteriorating. In 1980, 33 percent of blacks compared with 10 percent of whites were impoverished. Much of their plight stemmed from the rise of single-parent families headed by women. At the end of the decade, 40 percent of black families lived in such households, and half of them experienced poverty. These deplorable conditions were aggravated by the spiraling inflation of the late 1970s, and the suffering continued as Afro-American activists could get neither the President nor Congress to exert sufficient leadership to mount a forceful attack on black problems.

Nonetheless, blacks did not abandon their quest for political power. While stalemated in the national arena, they continued their efforts at the local level. The greatest progress came in the South, where the civil rights movement served as a catalyst for political change. By 1980, over 50 percent of all black officeholders, nearly 2,500, resided in Dixie. In 1979, Richard Arrington won election as mayor of Birmingham, the scene of some of the most vicious racial strife during the freedom struggle. In the North and West, black mayors occupied city halls in major urban areas such as Detroit, Gary, Newark, and Los Angeles; and in the nation's capital, Marion Barry, an early leader of SNCC, ran the municipal government. On the down side, the annual rate of increase in the number of black elected officials was on the decline, falling from 13.5 percent in 1977 to 6.6 percent three years later. Moreover, blacks held only about 1 percent of the available elected positions in the nation overall, though they made up over 11 percent of the population. In the Voting Rights Act states of the South, where the minority population reached as high as 35 percent in Mississippi, blacks composed only 5 percent of elected officials.

The prospects for improvement did not appear too bright as the presidential election of 1980 took place. The Democrats renominated Carter after he beat back a challenge from Senator Kennedy, but his chances had been severely damaged by the inability of his government to bring a halt to galloping inflation and to obtain the release of fifty-three American hostages held in Iran since November 1979. However limited the incumbent's accomplishments in civil rights, a Carter victory offered greater hope for black advancement than did a win by his Republican opponent. Ronald Reagan, the former governor of California and opponent of the 1964 Civil Rights Act, held the states' rights philosophy of the right wing of his party and promised to reduce the federal commitment to civil rights enforcement and the Great Society economic programs that had benefited blacks substantially. He launched his campaign in the South with an appearance in Philadelphia, Mississippi, the location of the murders of three civil rights workers during the 1964 Freedom Summer, by pledging to "restore to state and local governments the powers that properly belonged to them." These views reflected Reagan's close ties with southern Republicans who had replaced the Democrats in the region as the fiercest opponents of civil rights measures.

Unlike in 1976, the black vote did not save Carter from defeat. Though Reagan won only 51 percent of the popular vote, he overwhelmed his Democratic rival in the electoral column with 489 votes. The incumbent received 41 percent of the popular vote total, with most of the remaining 8 percent going to Congressman John Anderson of Illinois, a liberal Republican running as an independent. Blacks cast the bulk of their ballots for Carter (estimates ranged from 85 to 90 percent), but their votes could not overcome the GOP contender's margins of victory in key industrial states of the Northeast and Midwest and in every southern state except Carter's home territory of Georgia. In spite of their lopsided support for the Democrat, black enthusiasm for Carter had waned. Whereas the turnout of the total voting-age black population was almost 4 percent higher than in 1976, the turnout of eligible registered voters was lower by nearly 3 percent. Because the number of black registrants had increased over the past four years, the percentages meant that many of those who had signed up to vote chose not to cast their ballots (see Table 2).

The elections not only thrust a conservative Republican into the White House, but they also spelled defeat for several prominent liberal Democrats in the Senate. Control of the upper chamber shifted to the GOP, which secured a net gain of twelve seats for a total of fifty-three. Among the losers were Gaylord Nelson of Wisconsin, Birch Bayh of Indiana, Frank Church of Idaho, and George McGovern of South Dakota, all of whom had been counted on as civil rights supporters in the past. The new Senate included an additional four Republicans from the South, which mirrored the improved GOP fortunes in the region in presidential and statewide

Table 2   Estimated National Black Voter Registration and Turnout in 1976 and 1980 Presidential Elections

	1976	1980
Voting-age population	15,398,000	16,967,000
Number registered	9,024,800	11,400,000
Number of voters	5,784,872	7,000,000
Turnout of registered voters, percent	64.1	61.4
Turnout of voting-age population, percent	37.6	41.3

SOURCE: Joint Center for Political Studies, *The Black Vote: Election '76* (Washington, D.C., 1977), 11; and Eddie N. Williams, "Black Political Progress in the 1970s: The Electoral Arena," in Michael B. Preston, Lenneal J. Henderson, Jr., and Paul Puryear, eds., *The New Black Politics* (New York: Longman, 1982), 103.

elections. Perhaps as distressing to black reformers as the upsurge of conservatism in the Senate, the Republican majority resulted in the selection of Strom Thurmond of South Carolina as chair of the powerful Judiciary Committee. Though Thurmond had made some accommodations to the black electorate that had swelled in his state since his Dixiecrat bid for the presidency in 1948, he still favored a sharp curtailment in federal spending and a relaxation of civil rights laws in the South.

On a slightly more encouraging note, the elections saw a net increase of one member in the Congressional Black Caucus, bringing its total to eighteen. Losing one nonvoting delegate seat from the Virgin Islands, the caucus picked up two new representatives from Los Angeles and Chicago. Another two seats passed from one black to another, while the rest were retained by incumbents. (Two years earlier Senator Edward Brooke of Massachusetts had lost his reelection bid for a third term.) Overall, the Democrats kept their majority in the House, 243-192, though the Republicans gained thirteen new legislators. At state and local levels, black officeholders grew by 2.6 percent to 5,020, still a modest figure but markedly higher than the 1,185 officials who had held office in 1969.

THE REAGAN ASSAULT AND HARD TIMES

Reagan's first term witnessed an expected assault on the racial front. The President set the tone of his administration in his appointment policy. Although he selected a black, Samuel Pierce, to sit in his Cabinet as secretary of housing and urban development, the chief executive disappointed black Republicans by falling short of reaching the number of top-level minority appointments made under Carter. Not merely the quantity but the ideological bent of the appointments troubled civil rights proponents. In making selections the President picked individuals who shared his concern that civil rights programs be limited in scope and not be used to practice "reverse discrimination."

Signaling this shift in direction was his handling of the Commission on Civil Rights. He turned this respected, independent investigative agency, operating since 1957 as a strong advocate for bold racial policies, into an organization that trumpeted the administration's retreat from affirmative remedies to combat the effects of racial bias in employment and education. To preside over this change, Reagan selected Clarence Pendleton as chair of the commission. A black Democrat turned Republican, Pendleton had worked for the Model Cities Program and served as executive director of the Urban League branch in San Diego, California. Despite his background, Pendleton denounced the notion that "all minority progress comes out of a civil rights or social service gun." He opposed busing and affirmative action as "bankrupt" policies, and argued that the "only way for blacks to get a real piece of the action is to get out there and compete in the marketplace and not rely solely on handouts and political favoritism."

As a defender of the free enterprise system and an opponent of restrictive federal regulation, the chief executive sought to weaken government enforcement of affirmative action plans for hiring minorities. Though Reagan intensely disliked compensatory programs, the Supreme Court had upheld, with qualifications, the principle of affirmative action in *Bakke* and in a series of cases following it. As recently as 1980, the high tribunal sustained congressional legislation requiring that at least 10 percent of all federal funds for public works projects go to minority contractors in order to rectify past discrimination. The Reagan administration tried to confine the impact of such rulings. The administration narrowed the coverage of its affirmative action guidelines to exclude federal vendors with less than 250 employees whereas previously the regulations had applied to firms with a minimum of 50 workers. According to the secretary of labor, the new standard exempted 75 percent of federal contractors. In a similar vein, William Bradford Reynolds, the assistant attorney general in charge of the Civil Rights Division, signaled an even further pullback from the concept of affirmative action as a legitimate means of promoting the constitutional rights of exploited groups. Reynolds opposed policies that entitled blacks and other minorities to benefits strictly on the basis of their race. Under his direction, the Justice Department office chiefly responsible for civil rights enforcement sought to provide employment relief only to individuals who could prove they had personally suffered from discrimination.

The Reagan administration also damaged civil rights interests by attempting to reverse a long-standing policy concerning racial discrimination in education. Since the 1960s, private academies had sprouted in the South as a refuge for white students fleeing court-ordered desegregation of public schools. In 1970, after the judiciary refused to allow segregated private academies the benefit of a federal tax exemption, the Internal Revenue Service promulgated regulations to carry out that decree. However, in January 1982, the President instructed the IRS to restore tax-exempt status to private schools like Bob Jones University, a religious institution in South Carolina that admitted blacks but banned interracial dating between coeds. The President agreed with the university's claim that removal of the tax exemption interfered with the First Amendment freedom of the school to practice its religious beliefs. Reagan's order, which nonetheless smacked of racism, also stemmed from his conservative opposition to government interference with private enterprise and to the establishment of coercive guidelines for mandating racial quotas in schools. After influential lawmakers and civil rights lobbyists fired a heavy round of criticism against Reagan's proposal, the President backed off. The Supreme Court eventually decided the issue against Reagan's position by approving the original IRS ruling denying tax exemptions to private schools that engaged in racial discrimination even if the policy conflicted with their religious practices.

The major political battle between Reagan and his civil rights opponents occurred over renewal of the Voting Rights Act. For black Americans this landmark law had come to represent one of the last vestiges of federal commitment to racial advancement in an era of diminishing expectations, and they considered the measure essential for continuing to open up government to minority participation. As the Reagan administration slashed the budget with deep cuts in social programs, critics looked to the power of the ballot as a crucial means of challenging these reductions. "The only real safety net that minorities and the poor can rely on is their capacity to influence the political system," remarked Eddie N. Williams, the president of the Joint Center for Political Studies. Toward that end, the suffrage statute had effectively eliminated the major barriers to voter registration, but its enforcement machinery was still necessary to combat a new generation of obstacles—at-large elections, racial gerrymandering, discriminatory annexations—that diluted the strength of minority ballots cast at the polls.

With the act due for renewal in 1982, with Reagan in the White House, and with Republicans in control of the Senate, the bill's supporters took the precaution of starting their efforts a full year in advance. In addition to undertaking the customary fight to retain the special provisions requiring prior federal clearance of electoral changes and keeping designated jurisdictions from escaping coverage prematurely, the suffragists pursued a new challenge. In 1980, in a slim 5-to-4 decision, the Supreme Court ruled that in suits involving at-large election procedures, civil rights litigants had to prove that a municipality deliberately intended to weaken the vote of minorities. This opinion, in *City of Mobile v. Bolden*, posed a particular problem for blacks because most of the disputed at-large rules had been passed at the turn of the century, and their framers had usually couched their intentions in racially neutral language and in the spirit of reform. In contrast to this burdensome standard of proof, black plaintiffs and their attorneys wanted courts to judge the legality of at-large elections by their effect in permitting or denying blacks the opportunity to choose members of their own race to represent them. Thus, suffrage proponents wanted Congress to amend the Voting Rights Act to direct the judiciary to make discriminatory result as well as intent the standard for proving electoral bias.

The Reagan administration took a position on renewal that conformed with its opposition to race-conscious affirmative action remedies. In October 1981, after the House passed a ten-year-extension proposal containing a provision for an "effects" test in vote dilution suits, the President sought to persuade the Republican-dominated

Senate to modify it. The administration and its supporters charged that the bill's result-minded approach would promote proportional representation, which the President warned "would come down to whether all of society had to have an actual quota system" of minority elected officials. Echoing this view, the foes of "preferential treatment" portrayed themselves as standing for the true meaning of civil rights: the "color-blind ideal of equal opportunity for all."

Defenders of the measure denied any design to impose racial quotas on the electoral system. In contrast to the administration's, their view of equal opportunity allowed, indeed required, the government to take racial considerations into account in order to overcome the current effects of past discrimination. They believed that the Constitution safeguarded individual as well as group rights within the political process. The suffrage coalition, composed of the Congressional Black Caucus and civil rights, liberal, and labor groups, insisted that the bill did not sanction proportional representation or quotas, but only enabled the courts to consider whether certain rules had an unfair impact in lowering the chances for minorities to elect candidates of their own race. A civil rights attorney from Atlanta thought it inappropriate to raise the issue of proportional representation, "just as it is also pretty irrelevant to talk about any realistic opportunity within the existing electoral system because black voters had always been shut out, pure and simple."

From this clash of arguments, the Senate hammered out a compromise. Within the Republican majority, a contingent of racial moderates was not willing to abandon blacks, especially in their quest for something so basic to democracy as the right to vote. Led by Robert Dole of Kansas, the upper chamber agreed to an effect-oriented approach that permitted the courts to examine the "totality of circumstances" resulting in the denial of equal electoral opportunity for minorities. In practice, this reestablished the judicial standard in operation before the *Mobile* decision. At the same time, the lawmakers specifically rejected proportional representation as a valid remedy and affirmed their commitment to the Voting Rights Act by renewing it for another twenty-five years, the longest extension to date.

The final outcome illustrated that despite recent setbacks, blacks still commanded political influence in preserving hard-earned fundamental rights of citizenship. This was particularly ev-

ident in the South. With most southern senators refusing to join the
filibuster waged by Jesse Helms, a North Carolina Republican, the
obstructionist ploy failed miserably. Only four senators from Dixie,
three Republicans and one independent, steadfastly declined to approve the measure, and even Strom Thurmond saw fit to cast his
first vote ever in favor of a civil rights law. The expanded black
electorate in the South, which served as a crucial balance of power
in sending legislators to Washington, once again swayed the majority of the region's congressional lawmakers to stand behind the suffrage law. Given this overwhelming mandate, President Reagan
signed the bill, praising it as proof of "our unbending commitment
to voting rights."

Nevertheless, like Nixon before him, Reagan supported the
principle of enfranchisement while attempting to weaken its implementation. Though the Justice Department continued to enforce
the statute in conformity with the general policy outlines established by previous administrations, Assistant Attorney General
Reynolds interpreted his responsibilities narrowly in clearing electoral procedures submitted by the South. He attempted to raise the
standard for demonstrating racial discrimination and to shift the
burden of proving it from state and local officials onto the victims.
However, as was the case during the Nixon years, civil rights
activists successfully persuaded both Congress and the Supreme
Court to hold the Justice Department to strict enforcement of the
law.

The Reagan administration's policies had a more devastating
effect on the economic well-being of blacks than on their political
clout. During his first two years in office, Reagan adopted anti-
inflationary, budget-slashing programs that succeeded in bringing
prices under control at the expense of rising unemployment.
African-Americans suffered disproportionately. In 1982, over 17
percent of the black work force could not find jobs, compared with
8.6 percent for whites. The ratio of black families living in poverty
jumped from 32.4 percent to 35.7 percent, about three times the
figure for impoverished whites. Black poverty continued to be associated with female-headed households: 56 percent of black
women (compared with 36 percent of white women) who headed
families fell below the subsistence level. The last two years of
Reagan's first term brought a measure of economic recovery, but
blacks still suffered harshly. Unemployment fell to about 14 per-

cent, and the proportion of the poverty-stricken declined to just under 34 percent. These "improvements," however, did not enable black families to close the gap between their income and that of white families. By the mid-1980s, black families earned a median income of 57.6 percent of whites', a ratio about the same as at the beginning of the decade.

Although part of the deterioration in black material conditions could be attributed to structural defects affecting the American economy in general, the Reagan administration exacerbated the problems. Drastic cuts in or outright elimination of job programs like CETA; reductions in food stamp distribution, health services, and welfare eligibility; and the removal of guaranteed student loans punched holes in the "safety net" of federal assistance to low-income workers and the poor. For instance, rollbacks in educational support were reflected in the decline in black matriculation in four-year colleges from 10.4 percent in 1978 to 9.2 percent in 1984. Not surprisingly then, a 1982 public opinion survey revealed that 85 percent of blacks believed the Reagan administration was going too far in slicing government spending for social welfare programs. In contrast, only 37 percent of whites shared this view.

The President's fiscal policies also accentuated class divisions within the black community. During the 1970s, expanding opportunities arising from desegregation and affirmative action programs had swelled the size of the black middle class, at the same time as the number of poor black families increased. While the share of black families earning more than $50,000 annually nearly doubled—from 4.5 percent in 1970 to 8.8 percent—by the mid-1980s, the number of black households with incomes under $10,000 comprised 30.3 percent of the total, a leap of 11 percent. To achieve middle-class status, black families depended on two wage earners and employment in public-sector jobs to a greater degree than did white middle-class households. The recession and budget cuts of Reagan's first two years in office hurt both the poor who relied on declining welfare assistance and middle-class families dependent upon government employment. But the economic recovery after 1982 mostly aided middle-class blacks who had the skills and educational background to take advantage of the new job openings.

In stark contrast to the majority of African-Americans and their elected representatives, some middle-class black professionals and businesspeople endorsed Reagan's conservative brand of government retrenchment and free-market economics. Such notable intellectuals as Thomas Sowell, an economics professor at Stanford University, lent their voices to the attack on affirmative action and welfare programs. Like Reagan, they blamed the enduring poverty in black communities on New Deal–Great Society liberalism. According to their viewpoint, these programs reduced individual incentive to find jobs and fostered out-of-wedlock births and single-parent households. These black "neoconservatives" charged established black political and civil rights leaders with perpetuating this cycle of government dependency and called upon African-Americans to help themselves by adopting traditional values of individual initiative, competition, and hard work. Agreeing that black communities should do more to solve their own problems, their opponents responded to this criticism by accusing Reagan's conservative supporters of blaming the victims for the social ills resulting from generations of systematic racism and economic exploitation in the United States.

HAROLD WASHINGTON, CHICAGO, AND THE POLITICS OF RENEWAL

In the political arena, blacks had been struggling to gain greater electoral power in their communities since the early days of the civil rights movement. In the decade and a half following passage of the 1965 Voting Rights Act, black politicians had been striving to put into practice many of the goals of the freedom struggle. Much remained to be done. The damaging impact of the Reagan retrenchment helped reenergize blacks at the local level to seek to gain a fair share of the scarce economic resources available. At the same time, the black electorate looked forward to the possibility of challenging Reagan's reelection and moving the White House in a progressive direction more compatible with their interests and needs.

The city of Chicago provided an excellent opportunity for blacks to lead the way in revitalizing Afro-American politics. Since the New Deal, blacks had served as clients of the Democratic machine that ran the "Windy City," an arrangement that afforded them some influence in municipal affairs without any real power. Their elected leaders, such as Congressman William Dawson, had faithfully delivered the black vote for the organization's candidates and in return received the spoils of patronage and access to city hall. Their constituents obtained the benefits typically conferred by political machines, but these token rewards for their loyalty failed to make up for city officials neglect of widespread problems of poor housing, inferior education, and lack of police protection. In fact, black collaboration with the dominant white machine had not prevented Chicago's neighborhoods and schools from becoming among the most segregated in the nation.

For two decades following his election as mayor, in 1955, Richard J. Daley, the "Boss," displayed the power of the machine to manage black politics and stifle challenges to its rule. Daley, who had first won victory largely on the strength of black votes, operated a kind of "plantation politics" that treated blacks as subjects rather than equal ruling partners and placed white interests ahead of black concerns. One of his black critics who successfully broke from the machine described the mayor as a "plantation master ...who keeps his darkies loyal to him by doling out small political favors... [and] is playing the same old 'divide and conquer' game his forefathers experienced when they made some slaves 'house servants' and kept others out in the field." In the mid-1960s, when civil rights leaders launched a determined attack on racial discrimination in housing and education, Daley drew upon his black machine loyalists to help outmaneuver the insurgents. Even Martin Luther King, Jr., who, in 1966, had been invited by local civil rights leaders to direct the campaign against racism, proved little match for the "Boss" and his entrenched black political allies.

However, during the 1970s black Chicagoans showed increasing signs of independence from machine domination. In 1972, a disgruntled black electorate aided in the defeat of the incumbent state's attorney, Edward V. Hanrahan, a law-and-order candidate. A few years earlier he had authorized a raid against the militant Black Panthers that left two of their leaders dead and four wounded under questionable circumstances. Black voters also successfully challenged the Daley organization in several congressional and aldermanic contests. The greatest chance for blacks to declare their political independence came only after the death of Mayor Daley, in 1976. In a special election to choose Daley's successor, black voters lined up behind the machine-picked candidate, but three years

later over 60 percent cast their ballots for Jane Byrne, who ran
without the Democratic organization's backing against the incumbent.

These encouraging signs notwithstanding, blacks still remained
subject to the effects of machine rule. The organization had depended
on low levels of black participation so that its ward heelers and pre-
cinct captains could most effectively control those who bothered to
show up at the polls. Furthermore, by placing the party's interests
above the needs of the minority community, machine politicians discouraged many blacks from seeing how their electoral participation
might make a difference in improving their lives. In 1977, only 27.5
percent of eligible blacks turned out to vote for mayor despite the candidacy of an antimachine black, State Senator Harold Washington.
Two years later, the black turnout scarcely climbed to 34 percent. Racial polarization compounded blacks' problem. In elections that pitted
the races against each other, black contestants stood very little chance
of attracting white votes to achieve a winning margin.

For blacks the Byrne administration proved to be a severe disappointment. Once installed in power, the mayor made her peace
with the Democratic regulars and dashed any hope of reform. Instead, she tried to diminish the voting strength of blacks on the city
council, and replaced black appointees on municipal boards with
whites. Although blacks had contributed to her mayoral victory,
she calculated that her chances for reelection were greater if she
mobilized white ethnic voters, who had long supported the Democratic organization. These moves galvanized black activists to oppose the mayor. In June 1982, they mounted a well-publicized and
highly coordinated boycott of Byrne's ChicagoFest, a summer fes-
tival and exposition designed to promote local business. This successful display of unity encouraged blacks to transform their protest
activities into an electoral movement challenging the mayor at the
polls. One of the boycott's organizers, the Reverend Jesse Jackson,
of Operation PUSH, expressed the anger of blacks who felt ne-
glected by city hall politicians: "We are not bound by Chicago plantation politics. We must aggressively use our dollars and our
votes."

Merging protest and electoral politics, Chicago blacks struggled
for empowerment with a fervor reminiscent of the civil rights era.
As they had in the South during the 1960s, voter registration drives
rallied blacks around a common battle for freedom. The task was

much bigger than getting people to exercise their civic responsibility of voting; it aimed, as one black leader asserted, "to accomplish a dramatic shift in the political scales in favor of those who have been ignored, used, and abused for too long." Showing the way, an alliance of groups representing Chicago's poorest, most politically disfranchised neighborhoods emerged to conduct voter enrollment campaigns. People Organized for Welfare and Employment Rights (POWER), an organization originally established to protest cutbacks in state welfare funding, spearheaded the registration drives by operating in public assistance offices and unemployment centers. More than 200 community groups helped get their message across to congregations in black churches and to audiences listening to "soul" stations on the radio. Largely as a result of this impressive grassroots coalition, by the fall of 1982 around 150,000 blacks had added their names to the suffrage lists. Moreover, this community-wide campaign succeeded in bringing up the enrollment of eligible blacks to just over 86 percent, a figure that exceeded the 78 percent registration rate for whites.

This surge in enrollment placed blacks in a strong position to unseat Mayor Byrne in her bid for reelection in 1983. By this time, the black population had grown to 40 percent in the city; Hispanics constituted another 12 percent of its residents. As in other places with a large Afro-American population, black Chicagoans entertained serious hopes for electing a member of their race as mayor. Owing once again to a formidable display of community organizing and group solidarity, blacks chose a consensus candidate to compete for city hall. Under the direction of Chicago Black United Communities, over 30,000 blacks had participated in surveys to determine who they desired to run. From what amounted to a carefully planned but informal plebiscite, Harold Washington emerged as the top choice from over ninety prominent names.

Washington commanded respect for his extensive political experience. A graduate of Northwestern University Law School, he had served as a member of the Illinois legislature and as a representative in Congress. Once an ally of the Daley machine, he had broken away to establish strong credentials as an independent reformer who spoke out for liberal, consumer, and civil rights causes. Elected to Congress in 1980, he fought for extension of the Voting Rights Act and battled against the Reagan administration's spending cuts for jobs and welfare assistance. In 1977, Washington had

run in the Democratic primary for mayor, but with the black electorate poorly mobilized, he received only 11 percent of the total
vote. Heartened by the outpouring of new registrants in 1982 and
convinced that this time he had a chance to win, the congressman
agreed to run. In doing so, he reminded blacks that after years
of giving white candidates their votes without receiving an adequate share of power in return, the point had arrived when "it's our
turn." Though constructing his campaign on a solid black foundation, Washington fully realized that he needed progressive white
and Hispanic votes to win in a city where blacks composed a minority of the population.

Against all odds and predictions, Washington won a narrow victory in the Democratic primary against two prominent white contenders. In addition to Byrne, the congressman faced Richard M.
Daley, the son of the former mayor, who considered himself his fa-

Harold Washington campaigning for mayor of Chicago in 1983.
(AP/Wide World Photos)

ther's rightful successor. In this three-way contest, Washington captured 37 percent of the ballots to 33 percent for the incumbent and 30 percent for the heir of the "Boss." The white vote divided nearly evenly between Byrne and Daley, while the congressman garnered nearly 85 percent of the black votes. The victor benefited from the outpouring to the polls of newly registered blacks. In 1983, the turnout of blacks in the primary soared to 64 percent of the voting-age population, up from 34 percent in the previous Democratic mayoral race. Approximately 56 percent of Washington's black voters reported that they had registered during the massive enrollment drives of the year before. Though the white turnout rate had also grown since 1979, it had fallen five percentage points behind that of blacks. The winner also secured about 12 percent of the Hispanic and 4 percent of white ballots cast, but their combined votes amounted to slightly less than his margin of victory. Thus, Washington won on the strength of unprecedented support from blacks and the close split in the white vote for his opponents.

Customarily, the winner of the Democratic primary in Chicago was a sure bet to triumph over the Republican in the general election, but when that winner was black all wagers were off. As the earlier contest had shown, the electorate in Chicago voted mainly along racial lines. In a city where whites comprised over 53 percent of the registered voters, unless Washington made greater inroads among whites and Latinos than he had in the primary, he stood a good chance of losing. This was especially true in a showdown with a single white opponent around whom the majority white electorate could unite.

The Republican candidate, State Representative Bernard Epton, made Washington's character and race the dominant campaign issues. Hammering away at Washington's ethics, the GOP nominee attacked his rival's record, which included a conviction for income tax evasion and a suspension of his law license. By the usual standards of Chicago's political morality these indiscretions, for which Washington acknowledged his mistakes, were relatively minor. However, most whites were willing to abandon their party's nominee more so on the basis of his skin color than his ethical transgressions. One of the many Democratic officials who defected from Washington justified his decision in this way: "The people in my area just don't want a black mayor—it's as simple as that." Epton's campaign supporters fed on this racial animosity by adopting the slogan "Epton For Mayor. Before It's Too Late," and by passing out handbills warning in vulgar language that a takeover of city hall would spell doom for Chicago. These negative comments prompted Washington to respond in kind, and he attacked Epton's integrity, his cozy legislative relationship with private insurance companies, and his emotional stability. At the same time, the congressman took the higher road in urging reform-minded white voters to join his campaign assault against the Democratic machine.

On election day, Washington won with a fraction over 50 percent of the votes cast in the closest mayoral clash since 1919. As expected, the voting was polarized by race. The Democratic nominee owed his victory to the nearly unanimous backing (99.5 percent) he received from blacks, which accounted for approximately 77 percent of his total vote. Not only did Washington's candidacy attract solid black approval, but it also succeeded in mobilizing an extraordinarily high black turnout of 73 percent of the voting-age population, surpassing the white figure of 67 percent. In contrast, Epton obtained 95 percent of his ballots from whites, and the Republican candidate won over eight out of ten white Democrats. The victor scored poorly among the city's Irish, Italian, and Polish voters, the mainstays of the Daley machine, who deserted the black Democratic candidate in droves to back Epton. Their racial fears and animosities were strong enough to override their traditional ethnic allegiances to whoever triumphed in the Democratic primary. "They responded to Washington's race rather than to his partisan affiliation," Dianne Pinderhughes concluded. "They became whites, as opposed to Americans of European descent."

There were key exceptions to the racial division at the polls that helped cement Washington's slender 46,000-vote victory. The triumphant mayor-elect captured almost three-quarters of the Hispanic vote. The more than 45,000 votes marked a stunning jump six times greater than the number he had garnered in the primary. In addition, Washington won a small but sufficient portion of whites to his side. About 12 percent of those who participated provided more than double the number of white ballots cast for him in the Democratic primary. A large share of these votes came from liberal Jews who put race and religion aside (Epton was Jewish) and welcomed Washington's reform message.

Washington captured the mayor's office, but he did not immediately gain control over the city government. Democrats on the municipal council outnumbered Washington supporters and brawled them to a stalemate. These heated battles reminded one journalist of "Mississippi in 1964, where the Freedom Democratic Party challenged the segregationist regulars." After court-ordered redistricting left the pro- and anti-Washington factions at equal strength, the mayor was able to cast tie-breaking votes in his favor. Like other black mayors in major cities throughout the country, Washington recognized that he needed the cooperation of influential white civic leaders in order to govern, and he brought them into his ruling partnership with blacks, Latinos, and reformers to replace the old party stalwarts.

The mayor promoted the financial development of Chicago, which most profited the city's elites, while at the same time he did not neglect minority economic concerns. He initiated a vigorous affirmative action program in municipal hiring and in awarding government contracts, which aided black businesspeople and professionals. Also, he continued to work to relieve the plight of working-class and poor blacks, who had constituted the backbone of his candidacy and election. Though many problems lingered, the reform mayor took significant steps to increase the availability of low-income housing and provide such public services as health care and police protection more equitably than in the past.[3]

Much of the pattern in Washington's election was repeated in the victory of W. Wilson Goode as the first black mayor of Philadelphia, in May 1983. Goode had compiled a strong record as chair of the Pennsylvania Public Utility Commission and as managing director of Philadelphia. In a city in which blacks comprised 40 percent of the population, he competed in the Democratic primary against the former mayor, Frank Rizzo, the darling of the city's white ethnic groups, who had inflamed racial passions during his two previous terms in office. Surprisingly, this contest did not witness the bitter racial rhetoric of the Chicago campaign. In beating Rizzo with 53 percent of the votes, Goode did slightly better than Washington had against Epton. He galvanized black voters into

[3]In 1987, Mayor Washington won reelection to a second term, but shortly thereafter, he suffered a fatal heart attack. His death occasioned a power struggle in the city council to choose a successor. The black alderman Eugene Sawyer was selected, largely with white support, while the majority of black legislators favored another candidate, Timothy Evans. In 1989, the effects of this battle still divided the Sawyer and Evans forces within the black community, which led to the election of Richard M. Daley as mayor.

turning out in high numbers. He received 98 percent of their ballots, and secured a small but slightly higher proportion of white crossover support than his Chicago counterpart. Having won the mayoral nomination in this largely Democratic city, the black candidate went on to victory with 55 percent of the vote in the general election against two white candidates. Yet Goode encountered strong racial sentiment against him. The election returns indicated that white ethnic voters in the City of Brotherly Love were just as strongly opposed to Goode as were their ethnic cousins in Chicago to Mayor Washington.

The racial consciousness and solidarity tapped by Washington and Goode in their respective campaigns also were evident in the heightened efforts of blacks throughout the nation to become politically engaged. The victories in Chicago and Philadelphia convinced many blacks that their votes could make a difference. In addition to such positive reinforcement, African-Americans had an increased incentive to vent their negative feelings toward the Reagan administration at the ballot box. The success of the civil rights coalition in strengthening the Voting Rights Act against White House opposition focused renewed attention on the franchise as a key instrument in forwarding black interests.

Spurred on by anti-Reagan sentiments and rearmed with a powerful suffrage weapon, the NAACP, VEP, SCLC, and other organizations stepped up attempts to enroll additional black voters. The largest increases came in the South, where such intensive drives had taken place for over two decades. From 1980 to 1984, black voter registration in the region climbed by 14 percent, with the greatest gains occurring in the Voting Rights Act states of Alabama (37 percent), North Carolina (28 percent), and Mississippi (20 percent). Furthermore, throughout the country black political participation rose in response to active campaigning by black candidates for office and to heated state and local contests in which white politicians cultivated black votes. In the off-year congressional elections of 1982, minority turnout jumped by nearly 6 percent, a notable increase over the figure in 1978. Reflecting this revived spurt of interest, the number of black elected officials nationwide grew by 8.6 percent between 1982 and 1983, the steepest rise in seven years.

One of those winners, Harvey Gantt, became mayor of Charlotte, North Carolina, in 1983. He forged a coalition of blacks and whites to emerge victorious in this white-majority city. His career underscored the close connection between the civil rights struggle and electoral politics. As a youth in neighboring South Carolina, Gantt had participated in the early sit-in protests and become the first black student to desegregate Clemson University, where he received a degree in architecture. His generation, he remarked, is "the group now that are becoming the mayors." Though he had come to substitute negotiations for demonstrations as his preferred tactic, Gantt did not forget the lessons of his previous struggles. "I'm...a believer," the mayor affirmed, "in taking the benefits brought about by...all the other direct-action kinds of things and molding them into long-term, institutional changes that would occur, systematic changes that have occurred in our society."

This political reawakening stemmed from the desire of blacks to continue the process of empowerment that had begun with the emergence of the civil rights movement. As economic conditions deteriorated in the late 1970s and early 1980s, black communities mobilized to obtain a greater share of electoral power in order to meet the unfulfilled material needs of their residents. Though successful in many towns and cities across the nation, for the most part they had been unable to check the wave of political conservatism in national affairs ushered in by the Reagan administration. Blacks and their liberal white allies did hold onto many of their civil rights gains through victories in Congress and the judiciary. But as long as Reagan remained in office, the powerful institution of the presidency would continue to order priorities in a manner that limited advances toward racial equality. At a time when African-Americans were flexing their political muscles locally, the goal of capturing the White House and reshaping its agenda became as natural as it was essential.

Chapter 7

In Search of Legitimacy

In the four decades since the Second World War, African-Americans gradually, if not grudgingly, had won a considerable measure of acceptance for their reenfranchisement as full citizens of the United States. Where blacks gained public office, including those at the head of major cities throughout the country, whites generally endorsed the validity of their rule. Undoubtedly, the struggle for political empowerment produced legislative conflicts in Washington and fierce opposition both in the South and the North, as witnessed in Chicago, but, overall, white Americans acknowledged the principle of majority rule and the sanctity of free elections. Whites have largely recognized, that is, the legitimacy of black political representation as an extension of democratic values and the norms of fair play. Moreover, these basic tenets of the political culture received reinforcement from the nation's Cold War ideology, which contrasted American freedom with Soviet totalitarianism. Condemning the Soviet Union for stifling free elections abroad, the United States could not easily tolerate racist restrictions on ballot boxes on its own shores. Besides, federal enforcement of the Voting Rights Act kept in check the resistance of those whites who stubbornly refused to concede the legitimacy of black political power.

Both the considerable progress blacks had made in the electoral arena and their frustration with not having achieved a great deal more prompted black political leaders to focus their attention on the battle for the White House. Within the American political system perhaps nothing reflects the legitimacy of minority-group participation more than competition for the presidency. "The Presidential election is the centerpiece of the U.S. political process," the political scientist Mack H. Jones observed, "and therefore every discrete political faction should be expected to use the quadrennial election in some way to advance its interests." To the extent that American political leaders set out broad agendas and debate specific policy objectives, they do so during presidential elections. The chief executive, the nation's highest elected official, plays the key role in focusing attention on a problem, in identifying a course of action to address it, and in rallying legislative and public support behind efforts to solve it. Not since Lyndon Johnson had an occupant of the Oval Office assigned a high priority to the needs of blacks and other exploited groups. Unless the presidency once again became a platform for the cause of racial equality, African-Americans would continue to find it hard to catch up politically and economically with other citizens.

Previously, the black electorate had wielded considerable influence in presidential elections and contributed significantly to the winning margins of Democratic nominees, most recently in the election of Jimmy Carter in 1976. Still, no black candidate had mounted a strong challenge for the top office in the land. Representative Shirley Chisholm of New York had actively campaigned in the Democratic presidential primaries in 1972, but her effort attracted scant support. Not only a black, she was also a woman in a nation that simply was unprepared to cast aside considerations of race and gender in selecting its chief executive. Having won reenfranchisement scarcely a few years before, blacks did not constitute a large enough bloc of voters to turn Chisholm's hopes into a serious bid. However, since the early seventies black political muscle had developed sufficiently to elect mayors of major metropolitan areas as well as a growing contingent of county, state, and national lawmakers.

By the middle of Reagan's first term, the possibility of a black presidential challenge began to take shape. Upset by the President's economic policies, which disproportionately raised the level of black unemployment and poverty, influential blacks joined together to map out a strategy to combat those worsening conditions. After several months of discussions, on June 20, 1983, a group of elected officials, known as the Black Leadership Family, sponsored the idea of an Afro-American presidential bid. The mayoral victory of Harold Washington earlier in the year heavily shaped their thinking. His candidacy had served to mobilize the black electorate in record numbers and at the same time attracted enough Latinos and whites to form a winning coalition. "We've got to be involved in mainstream political activity," Washington declared. "That's what's happening here in Chicago. And that's the lesson that's going out across the country."

In striving for the presidency, blacks naturally looked to compete within the Democratic party. Though black voters had occasionally supported moderate-to-liberal Republican candidates in local and statewide elections, since the formation of FDR's New Deal coalition they stood firmly behind Democratic presidential nominees. In 1980, blacks had accounted for about one-quarter of the ballots cast for Jimmy Carter and remained the most loyal element within the Democratic fold. The party of Roosevelt, Truman, Kennedy, and Johnson opened its doors to increased minority representation after 1964; however, many black Democrats believed increasingly that their party had come to take their votes for granted. Given their overwhelming support for Democratic standard-bearers, they expected to obtain more decision-making positions within the party and to fashion programs that more forcefully addressed black concerns. They also worried that Democratic officials, in the hope of recapturing the votes of white conservatives who had become Reagan Republicans, were seeking to modify their position at the expense of the black faithful. Thus, by contending for the Democratic presidential nomination, blacks hoped to boost their leverage within the party and help pick the candidate most sensitive to their interests.

JESSE JACKSON FOR PRESIDENT

With these considerations in mind, the Reverend Jesse L. Jackson chose to launch his candidacy for the presidency. He received inspiration from the example of fellow Chicagoan Harold Washington. The mayor's come-from-behind victory, Jackson concluded, "demonstrated that while some will join us if we assert ourselves, without such aggressiveness no one else will lead our fight for equitable representation." He questioned whether Democratic leaders sufficiently appreciated the contribution blacks made to their party's fortunes. In the case of Washington, top national Democrats, such as Walter Mondale and Edward Kennedy, did not enter his corner until after he had beaten his white rivals in the primary and faced only a Republican hurdle to the city's highest office. Jackson believed that his candidacy would test whether white leaders were ready to accept blacks on an equal basis or whether blacks would continue to play a "Harlem Globetrotter" role, giving the Democratic party "its soul, its excitement, its rhythm, its margin of victory, and yet not be allowed to set any policy."

Jackson's foray into electoral politics grew out of his involvement in the civil rights struggle of the 1960s. As a student at North Carolina Agricultural and Technical State University in Greensboro in the early sixties, Jackson had led demonstrations in the city that spawned the sit-in movement. Subsequently, he became a staff member of the SCLC, and established his base of operations in Chicago after Dr. King directed a desegregation campaign there. He headed SCLC's Operation Breadbasket, a project that applied economic pressure on white-owned businesses to open up job opportunities for blacks, and on April 4, 1968, he was part of King's entourage when the civil rights leader was assassinated in Memphis. In the early 1970s, he broke with King's designated successor, the Reverend Ralph D. Abernathy, and created Operation PUSH as his own organization to carry on the work he had begun with the SCLC.

Though Jackson had not held public office in Chicago, he actively participated in its political life and supported the reform forces opposing the Daley machine. At the 1972 Democratic convention, he was a coleader of the interracial group that successfully challenged the credentials and unseated the delegation headed by the Chicago boss. From his base of operations at PUSH, Jackson initiated economic boycotts, held voter registration drives, furnished campaign workers, and conducted a weekly radio broadcast that publicized concerns voiced by the black community. By linking protest with electoral politics and mobilizing local communities to shape national agendas, he carried on the tradition of the civil rights movement.

A minister himself, Jackson also reflected the close relationship between the black church and Afro-American politics. During the civil rights movement clergymen had opened their churches to mass meetings and voter registration drives and preached sermons that combined the themes of personal redemption through Christ with social justice through protest. The church was a critical component of the black liberation battle because it was one of the few institutions exclusively under black control and capable of reaching a mass audience. The Reverend Jackson underscored the historic importance of the church in reminding blacks "that we were not brought from Africa to be white people's slaves. But perhaps [we] were sent here by God to save the nation." His political mission received the endorsement of the National Baptist Convention, the largest black religious body in the country, whose president, T. J. Jemison, had led a pioneering bus boycott in Baton Rouge in 1953.

More than an electoral campaign, Jackson's candidacy resembled a civil rights crusade. It attracted campaign staff such as the Reverend C. T. Vivian, who like Jackson had fought in the front lines of the freedom struggle during the 1960s. Many of those who worked on his behalf did so in recognition "of the unfulfilled objectives of Martin Luther King and the civil rights movement and to warn... that the movement's earlier gains were in danger." And the candidate clearly tied his current challenge to past civil rights efforts. Shortly before announcing his intention to seek the presidency, at a rally honoring Dr. King and commemorating the twentieth anniversary of the march on Washington, Jackson revived the spirit of that historic occasion by proclaiming: "Our day has come. From slaveship to championship... [f]rom the outhouse to the courthouse to the White House, we will march on."

Just as blacks once marched to recover the right to vote, they responded to Jackson's campaign by descending on courthouses and registration offices to sign up for the ballot. Jackson stirred memories of civil rights days by embarking on a "Southern Crusade" for voter registration that built upon the intensive local efforts of civic groups and civil rights organizations, such as the NAACP, to enroll additional blacks. He also took every available opportunity to prod the Reagan Justice Department to enforce the Voting Rights Act more vigorously, and he even succeeded in cajoling Assistant Attorney General William Bradford Reynolds to travel to Mississippi and witness suffrage violations for himself. In one notable instance, the persistent Jackson persuaded the usually reticent Reynolds to join him in singing "We Shall Overcome" at a rally. In the eleven southern states some 695,000 new black voters registered between 1980 and 1984, (see Table 3), with a considerable share of them lured out by Jackson's appeal. One survey indicated that 67 percent of recent registrants attributed their interest in enrolling to the Jackson campaign.

Jesse Jackson, on the right, leading the procession at the 1983 march on Washington. Next to him, from right to left, are Walter Fauntroy, the Washington, D.C., delegate to Congress; Coretta Scott King, widow of the slain civil rights leader; and Joseph Lowery, president of the SCLC. (Jim Wilson/New York Times Pictures)

His roots deeply sunk into the soil of civil rights, Jackson ventured to cultivate the field of presidential politics. According to a member of his campaign staff, Jackson's "genius lay in linking nonelectoral forms of political mobilization and protest with traditional electoral politics." The minister's charismatic personality, his ability to arouse masses of blacks at rallies and voter registration drives, and his support network in churches throughout black communities furnished him with valuable resources to attract a substantial following. By a wide margin over any other contender, 51 percent of African-Americans rated him the most important black leader in the United States. However, the ability to mount effective protests and deliver inspiring oratory would not translate into

Table 3   Black Voter Registration in the South, 1968–1984[a]

	1968	1976	1980	1982	1984
Alabama	56.7	58.4	55.8	69.7	69.2
Arkansas	67.5	94.0	57.2	63.9	60.9
Florida	62.1	61.1	58.3	59.7	55.5
Georgia	56.1	74.8	48.6	50.4	49.8
Louisiana	59.3	63.0	60.7	61.1	62.5
Mississippi	54.4	60.7	62.3	64.2	68.2
North Carolina	55.3	54.8	51.3	50.9	59.7
South Carolina	50.8	56.5	53.7	53.9	49.8
Tennessee	72.8	66.4	64.0	66.1	67.1
Texas	83.1	65.0	56.0	49.5	59.1
Virginia	58.4	54.7	53.2	49.5	50.7
Total	62.0	63.1	55.8	56.5	58.5

[a]Estimated percentage of voting-age blacks registered.

SOURCE: The 1968 figures are from David Garrow, *Protest at Selma* (New Haven, Conn.: Yale University Press, 1978), 189. The remaining figures are from U.S. Department of Commerce, Bureau of the Census, *Statistical Abstract of the United States*, annual (Washington, D.C.), 1976, 406; 1981, 495; 1982–1983, 488; 1985, 253.

real victories at the ballot box without a campaign that reached out to a broad segment of the Democratic electorate and brought large numbers of voters to the polls. Furthermore, as a civil rights organizer Jackson could devise novel tactics aimed at producing social change from outside the conventional political system, but as an aspirant for his party's nomination he had to operate within the confines of the Democratic organization and play by its rules. Ballots, not ballyhoo, counted in electoral victories.

Jackson acknowledged these political realities and sought to expand his base beyond the black community. He tried to fashion a "rainbow coalition" that attracted the dispossessed of all races—poor whites, Latinos, Native Americans, and Asians, as well as blacks. He hoped to draw upon those elements of the Democratic party that felt locked out of the process of decision-making. Intending to shift the ideological tilt of the party toward the left, Jackson argued that it could win against the conservative and popular Reagan only by gaining the backing of the millions of Americans who felt disaffected and no longer bothered to cast a ballot. In 1980,

198 - REAGEN
16 states
less than 5%
margin

Reagan had won in sixteen states by a margin of victory of less than 5 percent. A Democratic candidate who enticed higher percentages of ordinarily nonparticipating blacks and whites to the voting booths, he argued, could improve the party's presidential outlook in 1984.

Working with an assortment of civil rights activists, community organizers, antinuclear advocates, feminists, and others who championed progressive social causes, Jackson devised a "rainbow" agenda to incorporate into the Democratic platform. In the manner of Dr. King, he attacked a host of ills—racism, militarism, and materialism—that plagued not only blacks but all Americans. Making peace a priority, Jackson criticized Reagan's aggressive Cold War policies and called for stepped-up negotiations with the Soviets, a pledge from the United States not to deploy nuclear weapons in a first-strike capacity, a revamped approach toward the Caribbean that emphasized diplomacy instead of military might to resolve disputes, firm opposition to apartheid in South Africa, and a solution to Middle Eastern hostilities that recognized the Palestinian right to a homeland. The candidate envisioned that peace abroad would foster economic justice at home. By reducing the military budget 20 percent, Jackson claimed, the United States could reallocate its financial resources to create jobs and assist the poor. He would replace Reaganism, with its tax advantages for the wealthy and its deregulation of large corporations, with an economics of compassion that favored working people and the impoverished.

According to Jackson, the key to these changes came through political empowerment of alienated Americans. Notwithstanding that many of his proposals were considered too radical for mainstream Democrats, the candidate reflected the traditional liberal position that the remedy to social and economic problems rested in the ballot. In this vein, he made vigorous enforcement of the Voting Rights Act central to his campaign. An electorate that was expanded to include more blacks, Latinos, and poor people would presumably enhance the election possibilities of candidates sympathetic to progressive goals. If that happened, Jackson foresaw a chain of events producing sweeping reforms throughout society. For example, responsive elected officials would pass the equal rights amendment, and "since 70 percent of all poor children live in a house headed by a women where there is no man," Jackson contended, "to enfranchise women is to protect children." Furthermore, he envisioned women workers allying themselves with organized labor to end state right-to-work laws that hampered union organization. Thus, through beefed-up implementation of the Voting Rights Act, a measure originally crafted to help blacks, other exploited groups in society would ultimately gain protection and security.

Jackson's assault on the runoff primary fit in with this line of thinking. Used chiefly in the South, this procedure required that if no candidate received a majority of the vote on the first ballot, a second contest be held between the two top contenders to determine the winner. This system had come into effect at the beginning of the twentieth century during a period of one-party rule, when victory in the Democratic primary was tantamount to election. It was also part of a package of racially inspired laws that successfully disfranchised black southerners. After blacks regained the right to vote and began competing in Democratic primaries against a field of white candidates, they often found their path blocked by the majority runoff requirement. A black officeseeker might gain a plurality in the first election, especially if whites split their votes among several candidates, only to lose in a head-to-head contest with the remaining white opponent, as the electorate divided along racial lines. Where blacks comprised a minority of the voters their chances of winning a second primary were slim. Keeping in mind that candidates such as Harold Washington might not have won if they had had to survive a runoff primary, Jackson urged the elimination of this practice.

In addition, he wanted to change Democratic party rules that hampered minority contestants like himself in pursuing the presidential nomination. The Democrats required that primary candidates obtain at least 20 percent of the vote cast in a congressional district to gain a single delegate to the national convention. In only 86 of 425 congressional districts did the black population reach 25 percent of the total, barely enough to aid a black aspirant. Consequently, Jackson sought to convince Democratic leaders to lower the threshold requirement to no more than 15 percent, but they failed to agree. The unwillingness to revise this rule meant that a candidate might not achieve delegate strength approximating his or her primary vote. As it later turned out, Jackson obtained 18 percent of the popular vote, but his share of convention delegates amounted to only 10 percent.

Although the "rainbow" alliance had a distinctly black hue, Jackson's support among blacks was far from unanimous in 1984. A Gallup poll revealed that 59 percent of black Democrats preferred Jackson, but a hefty 34 percent favored Walter Mondale, Carter's vice-president, who had strong ties to the liberal-labor wing of the party. Those black politicians most closely linked to national Democratic affairs were less likely to back Jackson, the acknowledged outsider, than an established white candidate like Mondale, who had compiled a good record on civil rights as a senator from Minnesota. They believed that defeating Reagan was the most important goal in 1984, and that the quixotic Jackson certainly had no chance of doing so. Black mayors, such as Coleman Young of Detroit, Richard Arrington of Birmingham, and Andrew Young of Atlanta, along with the heads of national civil rights groups, declined to endorse the Chicago minister. "A black candidacy," the president of the Urban League declared, "would be a counterproductive retreat into emotional symbolism at the expense of realistic coalition efforts better suited to meeting black needs." In contrast, Jackson tended to generate greater enthusiasm from local black officials and community leaders who had few ties to the national Democratic party apparatus or the power brokers who ran it. Furthermore, he appealed most strongly to younger blacks, whose attachment to the Democrats did not date back as far as that of their elders.

Black opposition to Jackson also stemmed from issues of personality and power. The flamboyant candidate had a reputation for self-promotion, for failing to act as a team player while grabbing headlines to advance his own interests. A prominent black California legislator, Willie Brown, expressed the view of many of those who had doubts about him: "You can't teach Jesse anything. He never has been disciplined." Along with Andrew Young, many members of Dr. King's family and immediate staff refused to endorse their former SCLC associate, who, they believed, had rushed too quickly and indiscreetly to assume the mantle of leadership following the death of the martyred King. Moreover, some black officials who had successfully made the transition from civil rights to electoral politics resented Jackson's attempt to run for the presidency from outside an elected power base. They considered him an interloper, a shrewd protest leader, who threatened their hard-earned leverage within Democratic party circles and challenged their authority within their own electoral constituencies. Black politics had developed to the point at which its practitioners fought the same kind of "turf battles," as Adolph Reed calls them, as their white counterparts.

The rift among blacks was minor compared with the conflict between Jackson and Jewish voters. Next to African-Americans, Jews had been the staunchest supporters of Democratic presidential aspirants. Moreover, Jews had provided more support than the members of other white ethnic groups for black mayoral candidates, such as Carl Stokes, Richard Hatcher, and Harold Washington. Their devotion to liberalism and civil rights notwithstanding, since the late 1960s many Jews had broken with blacks over issues concerning affirmative action and the Palestinian-Israeli struggle (see Chapter 6). Unfortunately, Jackson's 1984 campaign damaged relations between these past allies even further. In an off-the-record remark to a black journalist, Jackson referred to Jews as "Hymies" and to New York City, the home of some 3 million of them, as "Hymietown." When his unguarded comments appeared in a news story in the *Washington Post*, the candidate first denied making them and then apologized, regretting any pain he may have caused and repudiating anti-Semitism.

Even had Jews been inclined to forgive Jackson's slip of the tongue, and most did not appear so willing, the substantive matter of Israel still troubled them. Jackson defended the survival of the Jewish nation, but he also called for the creation of a Palestinian state on territory Israel had captured in a war with its Arab enemies in 1967. This policy, which struck Jackson as evenhanded and essential for peace in the Middle East, was totally unacceptable to most Jewish leaders in its recognition of the radical Palestinian Liberation Organization. Extremists in the Jewish community viciously attacked Jackson for what they regarded as his anti-Semitic views, called him a "goddamn dirty Nazi," and picketed his appearances. Aggravating the situation, Minister Louis Farrakhan, the head of the Nation of Islam (the Black Muslims) and an outspoken Jackson defender, labeled Judaism "a gutter religion." Though Jackson denounced this inflammatory remark, he declined to repudiate Farrakhan himself. The candidate explained that he believed in the principle of redemption as embodied by Jesus and that he had tried to reach out and convert people with whom he disagreed, including white segregationists such as George Wallace and Orval Faubus.

"Isn't it better," he asked, to bring black militants "inside where we can at least talk to them, perhaps even change them?" Jackson knew that many blacks who were not Muslims, especially those living in impoverished urban ghettos, felt the same anger that separatists like Farrakhan expressed. Consequently, he attempted to walk a very fine political line between blacks and Jews in handling this emotional incident.

In effect, the candidate had to stick with his black base of support, his particular source of strength, whatever the risk of offending Jews and other whites. This fact of political life ensured him representation at the 1984 national convention, but guaranteed his defeat. Indeed, in a field crowded with seven white candidates, Jackson made a respectable showing by running third behind Mondale and Senator Gary Hart of Colorado. He won over 3.5 million primary votes, which included victories in Louisiana and the District of Columbia. He gained a plurality of the popular vote in South Carolina, his birthplace, and in Virginia, and carried forty-six congressional districts and seven major cities. In two of them, Atlanta and Philadelphia, Jackson triumphed without the backing of their black mayors, who endorsed Mondale. Ignoring the reservations of some of their political leaders, the overwhelming majority of blacks cast their ballots for Jackson. His figures among blacks ranged from a low of 50 percent in Alabama, where Birmingham Mayor Arrington supported Mondale, to a high of 87 percent in New York.

In contrast, the black candidate picked up only a fraction of the white electorate during the primaries. He averaged a slim 5 percent of the white vote, recording his greatest share, 9 percent, in California. Jackson tended to run slightly higher among whites in states containing the lowest percentages of blacks in the population—a clue that racial perceptions significantly affected voters. Although the evidence is fragmentary, it points to the conclusion that a hard-core one-fifth of whites were unwilling to vote for a black presidential candidate, and a substantial majority of the white electorate were not ready to support one as controversial as Jackson. Even many sympathetic white liberals refused to vote for him because they "felt left out." Believing that Jackson had not forged a true rainbow coalition, they faulted him for concentrating too heavily on solidifying his black support. A white Jackson adviser acknowledged that poor coordination and mistrust "inhibited the

campaign's ability to reach out beyond its black core." Nevertheless, Jackson did attract more than three-quarters of a million white
votes, which constituted about 22 percent of his total ballots. Given
the preponderance of the white majority in the electorate, this
showing fell far short of building the winning biracial coalition a minority presidential candidate needed.

Realistically, the black minister never had a chance of obtaining
the 1984 Democratic nomination. Though linking together a network of grassroots groups and a dedicated staff to guide their activities, Jackson lacked both an experienced national organization and
the funds to operate it. The candidate raised only about $4 million
in contributions, with an average donation of $27. This broke down
to an expenditure of 99 cents for each vote he won, compared with
the $3 per vote the more prosperous Mondale campaign could af-
ford to spend. Starved for adequate resources, Jackson did not have
the political capital necessary to defeat entrenched party leaders
with their access to superior sources of money and talent. These
deficiencies, in turn, reinforced the direction of his strategy. To
conserve expenses and deploy personnel efficiently, Jackson had to
focus on the black electorate, thereby reducing the possibility that
his message would get across to potential white supporters. Without this backing, the rainbow coalition appeared monochromatic.

Yet Jackson accomplished a good deal of what he had set out to
achieve. He succeeded in mobilizing unprecedented black political
participation. In the South alone, his candidacy sparked 150,000
blacks to add their names to the enrollment lists, and throughout
the country black registration reached the level of that of whites.
Nationally, about 20 percent of his supporters had decided to vote
for the first time in their lives, and in Dixie black voter turnout in
the Democratic primaries actually surpassed the rate for whites. He
also inspired other blacks to run for office, including a woman in
Dallas County, Alabama, who remarked that Jackson "made black
people feel they could make a difference." Having a black candidate as a serious contender for the presidency was a source of great
racial pride and revived some of the feeling of the civil rights movement that politics could be a tool for social change. "For those who
did not have an opportunity to participate in the 'March on Washington', or in Selma," the Reverend Jackson told his campaign followers, "God has provided you another opportunity."

Besides coaxing blacks out to the polls, Jackson's efforts opened the way for future presidential challenges. It brought large numbers of black activists into the electoral process and gave them an inside view of how to conduct a national campaign. They became intimately familiar with Democratic party rules and learned valuable lessons about fund-raising, media relations, and the myriad tasks of preparing a candidate to stump through the country in search of support. Drawing upon the metaphor of baseball, California Assemblyman Willie Brown concluded that Jackson had become the "Jackie Robinson of American politics," and predicted that "a whole lot of little leaguers in many cities and counties" would someday join Jackson in rising up to the political big leagues. The nomination contest had bestowed increased legitimacy on the notion of a black competing for the White House. Lucius Barker, a political scientist and Jackson delegate from Missouri, commented that "Jackson is the first black person to really become a *national political* leader in terms of national *presidential* politics" (emphasis in original). Jackson had communicated to white Americans that blacks were interested in and capable of contesting for the presidency and that they could offer leadership for millions of citizens distressed by the lingering problems of economic inequality, racial injustice, and Cold War hostilities exacerbated during the Reagan regime. "[W]e might have learned," the historian John Hope Franklin observed about Jackson's performance, "that it was conceivable that a black man had the qualities to be President." Though the Chicago clergyman had not triumphed in the usual sense, he did earn respect for himself and gained recognition for the political aspirations of African-Americans.

Despite these achievements, the Jackson forces had only a slight impact on the 1984 Democratic national platform. Blacks comprised 18 percent of the representatives in attendance and most of them were pledged to the Reverend Jackson. However, with Mondale firmly in charge, they proved no match for the majority of delegates who rejected the main planks of the "rainbow platform." They did manage to come away with one compromise, convention endorsement of affirmative action goals and timetables, but the convention remained silent on the subject of controversial quotas. Mondale easily won the nomination with 2,191 votes compared to 1,200 for Senator Hart and 465 for Jackson (higher than his actual number of delegates, which totaled 384). The former vice-president counted some prominent blacks on his side. Indeed, he tapped Mayor Andrew Young to speak against Jackson's proposal to curb runoff primaries, an action that engendered a barrage of boos and catcalls from most black delegates. Nor did the black contingent feel much better about the selection of Congresswoman Geraldine Ferraro of New York as Mondale's running mate. Jackson backers applauded the choice of a woman, but they regretted that a black female had not been seriously considered for the number-two spot.[1] Still, Jackson did gain a minor concession. The party agreed to establish a fairness commission to investigate complaints about the discriminatory operation of its rules on selecting convention delegates, and the group eventually dropped the threshold vote a candidate had to receive from 20 to 15 percent. (At the same time, it minimized the effect of this change by increasing the number of "superdelegates," party leaders chosen outside the primary and caucus system, who could attend the convention.)

Putting aside his disappointment, Jackson lined up behind the national ticket. Considerable sentiment existed among blacks for the Chicago minister to run as an independent, but he declined. Instead, he showed Democratic chieftains that he could play by the rules and abide by the outcome of party decisions. No longer a civil rights leader exclusively, Jackson had to act like a politician who needed to mend his fences in preparation to do battle another day.

He went a long way in that direction by delivering a stirring, emotional address to the convention. Affirming his political commitment to the Democratic party and to his social mission "to feed the hungry; to clothe the naked; to house the homeless; to teach the illiterate; to provide jobs for the jobless; and to choose the human race over the nuclear race," Jackson called for a coalition of "Red, Yellow, Black, and White" to join together in defeating Reagan in common pursuit of these goals. Toward this end, he attempted to heal the wounds of discord that had festered between blacks and Jews during the campaign. Recalling their mutual sacrifices sealed in blood in the civil rights era and their shared victim-

---

[1]Although white female delegates to the Democratic Convention were delighted with the choice of Ferraro, black female representatives were dismayed that no woman from their ranks came under consideration. In August 1984, they expressed their disappointment by forming the National Political Congress of Black Women as a means of exerting independent leverage.

ization as scapegoats throughout history, the Reverend Jackson denounced racism and anti-Semitism and urged Jewish-Americans and African-Americans to "turn to each other and not on each other, and choose higher ground." Without erasing all the bruised feelings, this powerful speech did have a soothing effect. Vic McTeer, a black delegate from Mississippi, where Fannie Lou Hamer and the Freedom Democrats had been denied representation twenty years before, felt much of his anger over the Democrats' treatment of Jackson subside after he saw white members of his delegation respond to the address with tears in their eyes and with hands reaching out to clasp those of blacks.

THE REAGAN LANDSLIDE AND THE STRUGGLE FOR BLACK POLITICAL SURVIVAL

Although Jackson's rhetoric touched deep emotions within Democrats at the convention and the millions watching on television, it could not save the party from defeat. Mondale chose not to assign Jackson a prominent role in his campaign, preferring instead to chase after the votes of traditional white Democrats who had defected to Reagan in 1980. Even the Mondale-loyalist Andrew Young griped about the neglect of blacks and called the candidate's advisers "smart-assed white boys and they think they know it all." Jackson dutifully made appearances for the ticket, but even if he had been used more heavily it would have made little difference. Surpassing his performance in 1980, the Republican chief executive won by a landslide. Reagan captured 59 percent of the popular vote and swept 525 of 538 electoral votes, taking every state except Mondale's home territory of Minnesota and the predominantly black District of Columbia. Losing 91 percent of the black ballots cast did not prove much of a handicap for the incumbent, because 66 percent of white voters, up from 55 percent in 1980, enthusiastically backed him. While Jesse Jackson had been mounting voter registration drives among blacks, the Republicans had been busily engaged in escorting new voters into their party. In fact, 60 percent of those citizens voting for the first time selected Reagan over Mondale.

The 1984 election returns indicated the enduring significance of race in determining presidential preferences. The polarization in black and white support for the two contenders continued a thirty-two-year trend. Starting with Eisenhower's victory in 1952, only one Democrat, Lyndon Johnson, had received a majority of white votes. This stood in sharp contrast to the mass of black voters who opposed every Republican challenger during that same period. Conventional wisdom attributed the polarization to Jackson; yet if the black minister's candidacy heightened it did not cause this racial divide. Though Jackson's campaign prompted some whites to jump to the Republicans, the large majority of them simply favored extending the term of a very popular chief executive whose administration had begun to restore economic recovery and national pride. Reagan's financial measures further split blacks from whites in making their presidential choices, as class reinforced racial concerns. Disproportionately harder hit by unemployment and poverty, and still trailing behind whites in average yearly earnings, most blacks found relatively little comfort in the Reaganomic policies aimed at boosting the fortunes of the middle and upper classes. Not surprisingly then, in the South, which had the largest income gap between the races, polls showed 57 percent of whites praising Reagan's economic performance and 87 percent of blacks objecting to it. Consequently, on election day over 70 percent of southern white voters cast their ballots for the Republican.

Despite the huge Reagan victory, blacks did not find the election completely discouraging. In the South, the black turnout rate grew by 5.3 percent from that of four years before. This increase reflected an even higher rise in the percent of blacks registered since 1980. Indeed, in Louisiana and Georgia the pace of black enrollment exceeded that of whites. Nationally, the upsurge in participation narrowed the differences between white and black registration (3.3 percent) and turnout (5.6 percent) to their lowest points in the post-World War II period. A higher proportion of the total voting-age black population in the country cast their ballots in this presidential election than in the previous one. On the down side, however, the percentage of those who were registered and actually voted had declined slightly. This situation suggested that the Jackson Democratic primary campaign had helped swell the pool of available voters, but that the subsequent contest between Reagan and Mondale dampened their enthusiasm. The President's conservatism and the challenger's failure to excite African-Americans kept many blacks at home.

Black participation produced mixed results. While Reagan retained the White House and the Republicans held onto their control of the Senate, the Democrats picked up one vote in the upper chamber and maintained their majority in the House. Black votes provided the winning margins for Democratic senators in Alabama, Illinois, and Michigan as well as for seven members in the House. Black candidates did not fare so well. Though the number of blacks serving in state legislatures increased slightly, the Congressional Black Caucus suffered a net reduction of one seat. In addition to this loss, six black congressional candidates who were considered as having a chance of winning went down to defeat. As usual, black officeseekers tended to run strongest at the local level. In 1984, the greatest annual increases occurred in the election of black county officials and mayors, especially in the South, the scene of Jackson's most intensive political efforts in mobilizing black voters. Yet, as Thomas Cavanagh, a political scientist and researcher for the Joint Center for Political Studies, suggested, "most of the black-majority districts may already have black incumbents, making future gains more difficult to achieve."

The second Reagan administration proved no more promising to Afro-American political advancement than did the first. Given the partisanship of the black vote, the President had little incentive to modify his previous course. Nevertheless, the Republican administration went further in antagonizing blacks than even its opponents had expected. In the aftermath of Reagan's reelection, the Justice Department indicted eight long-time civil rights activists in Alabama on criminal charges that were viewed as an attempt to roll back black political power. The government contended that the accused had engaged in vote fraud by improperly soliciting and casting absentee ballots in the heart of the state's black-belt area. Convictions on these felony charges could result in heavy fines and lengthy prison terms.

The cases originated in the region surrounding Selma, where blacks had encountered the greatest resistance to enfranchisement during the civil rights years. Through the efforts of such local leaders as Albert Turner of Perry County, a former SCLC staff member and an organizer of the historic 1965 suffrage march to Montgomery, and Spiver Gordon, a city councilman in nearby Greene County, blacks had won a total of 138 offices and gained control of five county commissions, five school boards, and nine towns. Though the Voting Rights Act had enabled blacks to constitute a majority of the electorate in those rural locations, whites managed to retain substantial influence. They continued to wield economic clout in those counties, which were among the poorest in the state, and they converted their superior financial resources into victories at the polls. Whites held onto the reins of government in five counties and in thirty-three towns and occupied the top positions of voter registrar, district attorney, and circuit judge. In the fierce political struggles that ensued, absentee ballots often counted as the margin of victory in determining the outcome of elections and thus had been a serious bone of contention for years. Each side charged the other with manipulating these ballots and with engaging in fraud by signing up people without their knowledge and voting in their names and those of individuals who no longer resided in the black belt.

Complicating this interracial conflict, blacks also divided among themselves. Increasingly, black candidates began to vie against each other for office, and in such instances the white minority played a balance-of-power role in deciding the winners. In this section of Alabama, with its history of bigotry and disfranchisement, black leaders eyed suspiciously white attempts to exploit rivalries between black factions. They charged that whites collaborated with disgruntled blacks as a subtle means of reasserting their political hegemony. As a matter of fact, John Kennard, the black tax assessor of Greene County, who had won election with white backing, initiated the complaints of absentee ballot fraud against his black opponents. Kennard, who had been in grade school during the heyday of the freedom struggle in the 1960s and had gone on to graduate from the University of Alabama, headed a group of young insurgents that sought to challenge the rule of blacks identified with the civil rights movement who had governed the county since 1970. Although as a youth he had joined in demonstrations and marches, he felt that the time had come for a change in leadership and strategy. "All this stuff about 'We Shall Overcome' was in the sixties," Kennard asserted and bluntly rejected the "philosophy among the old-line black leadership that there's something evil and demonic and a master plan in the white community to enslave us."

Conservative whites took advantage of these generational and ideological splits within the black community. Local white Alabamians joined Kennard in persuading the Reagan Justice Department to file charges against Albert Turner and his allies in Perry and Greene counties. The complainants were looking ahead to the upcoming 1986 elections, which featured the bid for another term by Senator Jeremiah Denton, a Republican who had opposed renewal of the Voting Rights Act in 1982. Involved in a close contest with his Democratic opponent, Representative Richard C. Shelby, Denton thought his chances would be stronger if black leaders came under attack and the black electorate felt discouraged from going to the polls. The Republican administration insisted that it was not acting out of political or racial motives and argued that it was merely seeking to punish one group of blacks for committing fraud against other blacks.

Federal prosecutors denied that they were deliberately intimidating black voters by bringing these suits, but the targets of these trials thought otherwise. They accused Washington of selective enforcement, pointing out that it had not responded in the past to similar complaints filed by blacks against whites. Furthermore, the "black-belt eight" contended that the federal government used heavy-handed tactics in investigating the cases, especially in rounding up for questioning those blacks who had signed the controversial ballots. Many of them were elderly and infirm, and their interrogation by federal agents revived memories of the not-so-distant past when blacks could not register to vote or paid a heavy penalty for doing so.

Ignoring cries of protest from civil rights organizations and the Congressional Black Caucus and their white allies, the Reagan administration persisted in its Alabama prosecutions but obtained only partial success. In the case of three defendants, including Albert Turner, an interracial jury failed to return a guilty verdict. Other trials resulted in hung juries, though several of the accused later pleaded guilty to lesser misdemeanor counts. Only in the case of Spiver Gordan did an all-white jury decide to convict, and even then he was acquitted on most of the charges. Whatever the intention of the Reagan administration, it failed to curtail the determination of Alabama blacks to exercise their franchise: in 1986, the latter won a measure of revenge by pouring out at the polls and contributing to the defeat of Senator Denton.

THE RESURGENCE AND RESHAPING OF THE CIVIL RIGHTS COALITION

Meanwhile, blacks had salvaged another victory against the Reagan administration shortly before the 1986 congressional elections. Blacks emerged triumphant as they once again bolstered electoral politics with protest to further their goals. Groups of blacks and

1986

their white supporters, many of them prominent individuals, took turns picketing the South African embassy in Washington for more than a year, which resulted in arrests on a daily basis. Their persistence and the surrounding publicity generated by the demonstrations had a positive impact on Congress. In mid-September, a bipartisan coalition of lawmakers passed a bill imposing moderate economic sanctions on South Africa. Later that month, President Reagan vetoed this popular legislative measure, which sought to apply punitive action against a nation whose institutions rested on racial oppression and minority rule. In doing so, the chief executive rejected this central item on the black political agenda, an expression of solidarity with a brutally persecuted people of color living on the continent to which African-Americans traced their roots. The civil rights movement had cracked the edifice of apartheid and disfranchisement that existed in the American South, and most Americans supported proposals to aid in overcoming these evils in southern Africa. Though the sanctions bill approved by Congress fell short of totally embargoing economic trade with and investment in the racist regime, it went too far for the President, who preferred to dismantle apartheid through a policy of "constructive engagement" that emphasized voluntary persuasion rather than coercion. On October 2, 1986, a month before the legislative elections, the Senate joined the House to register its disagreement with Reagan's approach and repass the bill over his veto. Representative Lynn Martin, an Illinois Republican, echoed the sentiments of more than two-thirds of her colleagues in overriding the President: "The vote matters not because of what it says about South Africa. It matters because of what it says about America."

This victory helped whet the appetite of disgruntled blacks throughout the South and the nation to use the off-year congressional elections to communicate their discontent with the White House. The existence of considerable Republican support for South African sanctions did not sufficiently offset general black hostility to Reagan's GOP administration. The Democrats recaptured control of the Senate by a margin of fifty-five to forty-five seats. According to the Joint Center for Political Studies, Democrats in California and Nevada gained only a minority of white votes but won by obtaining a huge share of black ballots. The same situation prevailed in four contests in the deep South—Alabama, Georgia, Louisiana, and North Carolina—where black voters tipped the winning balance in favor of Democratic challengers. In two other states, Florida and Maryland, blacks helped expand what otherwise would have been slight victory margins. They did so there by turning out to vote at a rate equaling or surpassing that of whites. Overall, blacks still lagged behind whites in turnout by 7 percentage points, but this marked a significant improvement over the gap of 11 percent in the 1982 off-year congressional elections.

Although the results of these elections demonstrated the rising strength of black political influence in the South since passage of the Voting Rights Act, they also indicated its limits. The triumphant candidates in Dixie gained the overwhelming portion of black ballots, between 80 and 90 percent, and a substantial minority of the white electorate, around 40 percent. Victory depended upon holding onto the bulk of the black electorate while at the same time luring enough white Reagan Democrats into a biracial coalition. Calculating this political arithmetic, successful southern Democrats ran as moderates, very carefully adjusting their messages to attract both liberal blacks and conservative whites. After winning his senatorial election, John Breaux of Louisiana pledged "to remember that he could never have won without the black vote." Nevertheless, the question remained of how responsive Democrats like Breaux would be to black concerns when they also had to consider the political risks of alienating their volatile white supporters. Many southern whites answered with caution. A Raleigh, North Carolina, newspaperman warned: "If black political leaders read too much into the returns of 1986 and do not fashion their agenda with an eye toward winning the next election, they could contribute to a rupturing of the Democratic coalition of which they are a vital part."

The election outcome also suggested that while blacks were continuing to advance politically, they could not afford to ignore the power of the white electorate. Though blacks secured four additional seats in the House of Representatives, pushing their total to a record high of twenty-three members, two of these gains were significantly shaped by the decisions of white voters. In Mississippi, Mike Espy became the first black candidate since Reconstruction to represent his state in Congress. The delta district Espy served contained a slight black voting-age majority, but on two previous occasions another black contestant, state legislator Robert Clark, had failed to win sufficient support from white voters and lost. In 1986, Espy defeated the incumbent Republican by generating a large black turnout in his behalf, nearly doubling his share of white votes to 12 percent, and keeping a significant bloc of whites from voting against him. Many whites who disliked his opponent but could not bear to cast a ballot for a black candidate simply stayed away from the polls, thereby indirectly contributing to Espy's slender 2.3 percent margin of victory.

In the case of the election of Congressman John Lewis from Atlanta, white voters played an even more direct role. This contest pitted Lewis, the former chairman of SNCC, against his old civil rights comrade, Julian Bond, in the Democratic primary. In this black-majority district, 87 percent of whites threw their support to Lewis, who triumphed while receiving only 40 percent of black ballots. This election reversed the traditional positions of each race at the polls. Previously, when blacks comprised a minority of the electorate, they had lined up behind the white candidate considered the most racially moderate in the field and swung the election in his or her favor. Now the white minority helped elect Lewis, who they perceived as more temperate than Bond. Elsewhere, in the black-majority city of New Orleans the winning black mayor, Sidney Barthelemy, also failed to win a majority of black votes, but clinched victory by capturing ample support from whites. These triumphant officials faced the delicate task of representing black concerns without offending the segment of the white electorate that had tipped the balance of power in their favor. At the same time, they had to repair splits within the black community that had opened from these intraracial clashes for power, which constituted a natural step in the evolution of black politics.

Although increased competition for public office sometimes proved divisive, blacks generally remained united in their unfinished goal of achieving racial equality. Despite the growing economic stratification within the black polity, middle-class black politicians still tended to identify with the plight of their less fortunate constituents from whom they were only recently removed. "Even those blacks who have 'made it' economically," Thomas Cavanagh reported, "are more likely to support the views of poor blacks than those of well-to-do whites." Having benefited from civil rights and affirmative action remedies, they most assuredly did not want to see those gains weakened or terminated. Public opinion surveys indicated that in contrast with whites most blacks favored compensatory federal programs to reverse the economic and social effects of past racial discrimination. Thus, so long as the United States had not become a color-blind society, race persisted as a crucial category for determining political choices.

Black solidarity, reinforced by expanding political clout, brought some notable legislative victories in the final two years of the Reagan era. With Democrats once again in control of both houses of Congress and with several newly elected senators owing their victories to blacks, the prospects for challenging the administration's conservative policies improved. This was especially true when issues involved basic civil rights matters and avoided controversial affirmative action or big spending measures. The defeat of Robert Bork's nomination to the Supreme Court vividly testifies to this point. A legal scholar and federal judge who had served as solicitor general during Nixon's final Watergate days, Bork had distressed blacks and their white allies by his long history of outspoken opposition to numerous pieces of civil rights legislation and accompanying liberal judicial opinions. Denying any racist motives, Bork had reached these judgments on constitutional grounds and propounded a conservative legal philosophy in harmony with the President's. Whatever the source of Bork's views, civil rights advocates contended that the nominee's ideas fell outside of the judicial mainstream, and they considered him a formidable threat to the advances so recently made. They further believed that his appointment to the high bench would forge a clear majority against extending any future benefits.

The administration and its opponents engaged in a vigorous lobbying campaign to rally public and congressional support for their respective sides. With Democrats having replaced Republicans in control of the crucial Senate Judiciary Committee, Bork's foes succeeded in using the hearings to generate resistance to the nomination. An interracial coalition of civil rights organizations, liberal and labor groups, and proabortion feminist organizations, all of which found Bork's positions detrimental to their respective causes, convinced the committee to issue a negative report on the candidate. The full Senate concurred with this recommendation, and the critical votes to deny the appointment came dramatically from southern Democrats. In a new version of the "solid South," fifteen of sixteen Democratic senators from the region voted against the judicial nominee. Though not entirely unsympathetic to Bork's legal reasoning, these moderate and conservative lawmakers were also mindful that this legal scholar aroused deep indignation from their black constituents. The 1986 elections had only recently underscored the political importance of the black electorate and the danger of ignoring its interests. "When the blacks stay with the Democrats," a senior Democratic officeholder in Mississippi remarked, "we can just about win, but when they leave, we can't." To many southern senators, the political risks of supporting the controversial Bork were too great, and they hesitated to stir up past racial animosities. As Senator Richard C. Shelby of Alabama, a moderate conservative who owed his election to black voters, declared: "In the South, we've made a lot of progress. We do not want to go back and revisit old issues."[2]

The revitalized civil rights forces in Washington won another important victory over the President's opposition that also reflected a concern with halting any retreat from hard-earned civil rights gains. Specifically, the One-Hundredth Congress reversed the President in his refusal to restore protections that had been recently whittled down by the Supreme Court in the case of *Grove City College v. Bell*. In 1984, the high tribunal had ruled that under the 1964 Civil Rights Act the federal government could not completely cut off funds to a college for practicing discrimination in some but not all of its activities. In other words, federal sanctions had to be applied on a selective basis specifically against an offending program without penalizing the entire educational institution. This decision represented a setback from the previously expansive interpretation of the law, and the Reagan administration heartily endorsed it. The case involved discrimination against women by Grove City College in Pennsylvania, but its legal reasoning also applied to racial minorities. Subsequently, civil rights and women's groups persuaded lawmakers to pass legislation restoring government authority to remove federal funds from institutions that permitted any discrimination under their auspices. After Reagan vetoed the bill, on March 22, 1988, moderate Republicans, as they had on the South Africa issue, joined the Democratic majority in furnishing the two-thirds vote necessary to override the President. In doing so, Congress expressed its broad agreement for preserving the full scope of the valued Civil Rights Act, which legislators had battled so hard to place on the books in the first place.

While blacks displayed their influence in Washington, they continued to flex their political muscle at the state and local levels. In

[2]This civil rights victory was diminished by the eventual confirmation of Judge Anthony M. Kennedy, a conservative considered to have a more flexible judicial temperament than Bork's but who nonetheless has consistently voted with the conservative bloc.

addition to playing significant roles in deciding the outcome of close elections between white candidates, they boosted the number of blacks holding office. In 1987, there were over 6,600 black elected officials throughout the nation, a rise of 4.1 percent from the year before. For the first time black politicians broke through the barriers that had kept governments lily-white in seventy-one locales. Among those significant victories was the election of a black candidate as a supervisor (commissioner) in Fannie Lou Hamer's Sunflower County, Mississippi; the election of the father of one of the young girls killed in the 1963 bombing of a church in Birmingham to a seat on the Jefferson County Commission; and further north, in Baltimore, Maryland, the election of a black as mayor. In addition, black incumbents triumphed as mayors in Atlanta, Birmingham, Chicago, Detroit, Los Angeles, and Philadelphia; and in cities such as Gary and Newark, black challengers defeated the reigning black chief executives.

Nationally, however, African-Americans still held only 1.5 percent of elected posts. Though minority office-holding continued to grow steadily, it did so very slowly. As blacks began to fill the available positions in places where they constituted a majority of the population, the opportunities to add to the total number of black officials diminished. There was room for some improvement as the judiciary ordered local governments to convert from at-large to single-member district elections, thereby creating new black-majority jurisdictions. Nevertheless, in many villages and towns in the rural South, blacks had yet to crack white political domination, which was reinforced through tradition and economic dependency. Furthermore, because they were a minority of the population in most cities, in every state, and throughout the nation, blacks needed to attract greater white support to expand their representation. As the 1980s drew toward a close, Afro-American candidates generally had failed to establish these winning biracial coalitions. Blacks did not occupy any state governor's mansion or hold any U.S. Senate seat, and only some thirteen held statewide offices.

JESSE JACKSON AND THE RAINBOW REVIVAL

With this mixed record in the background, Jesse Jackson once again sought to expand the horizon of black political opportunity by com-

peting for the 1988 Democratic presidential nomination. This time
he was less interested in the symbolism of merely running than
he was in actually obtaining the top prize. In this pursuit, he stood
upon an even firmer base of black support than in his previous
campaign. A poll taken a year before the Democratic convention
showed that 67 percent of blacks preferred Jackson as their first
choice for the nomination, whereas no more than 3 percent of those
surveyed favored any one of his potential rivals. Unlike 1984, there
was no white candidate in the field who had the liberal credentials
of a Mondale or his proven dedication to civil rights. Nor did any
aspirant have the former vice-president's close ties to the national
party establishment that pulled many black politicians away from
Jackson in his first campaign. Under these circumstances and given
the substantial backing Jackson commanded among rank-and-file
black Democrats, the Chicago minister experienced much less opposition to his candidacy from black leaders this time around. Most
notably, former opponents such as Mayor Richard Arrington of Birmingham; Willie Brown, speaker of the California Assembly; and
Congressman John Lewis hopped aboard his bandwagon. Some,
such as Mayor Coleman Young of Detroit, remained unconvinced,
but others, such as Andrew Young, though still not endorsing Jackson, at least stayed neutral.

Yet if Jackson had a realistic chance to improve his performance
in contending for the nomination, he had to do more than solidify
his black foundation of support. "It's very easy to finish third," Alan
Dershowitz, a Harvard Law School professor, said of Jackson's 1984
standing, "if you're black in America, and you're a black candidate
seeking a black constituency." To place second and especially first,
Jackson had to reach beyond the approximately 20 percent of the
Democratic electorate that was securely his. Accordingly, he attempted to broaden his appeal among whites and nonblack minorities, such as Hispanics and Native Americans, and draw a fuller
range of colors into his rainbow coalition than he had in 1984. He
moved in this direction by bringing in some experienced white
political consultants to serve alongside his trusted black confidants.
Bert Lance of Georgia, who had helped engineer Jimmy Carter's
successful 1976 campaign; John White, former chair of the Democratic National Committee; Ann Lewis, past head of the liberal
Americans for Democratic Action; and Jim Hightower, the agricultural commissioner of Texas, were among those Jackson relied on

for counsel. Underscoring his commitment to an expanded biracial coalition, he selected Assemblyman Brown to chair his national organization, and picked Gerald Austin, a white political operative who served as campaign manager for Governor Richard Celeste of Ohio, to oversee the organization's day-to-day affairs. The increased visibility of Austin and other nonblacks, Jackson calculated, "tells other people that *they* are welcome" and would raise "the comfort level" for whites.

Jackson aimed his message at diverse segments of the American electorate. He continued to trumpet many of the themes that identified him most closely with black and progressive white concerns: affirmative action, sanctions against South Africa, federally guaranteed full employment, opposition to Reagan's Central American policies, and support for evenhanded treatment of Israeli and Palestinian positions in the Middle East. However, he abandoned or downplayed other issues that had been associated with his previous campaign. No longer did he focus his attack on runoff primaries and party rules establishing a minimum threshold for winning convention delegates, procedures that had a disproportionately negative impact on black and other minority candidates. In general, he attempted to extend the appeal of his progressive agenda to moderate and conservative Democrats who, during the past two decades, had defected from the party or had been turned off to the political system altogether. Jackson explained: "Last time my rhetoric was sufficient to do what I had to do—open up the process, demand room for progressive-thinking people, register new voters. You know there's a right wing and a left wing, and it takes both to fly a plane. My concern is about 85 million voters in neither wing: they're in the belly of the plane."

Jackson raised economic and social issues designed to rally the disaffected behind him. He hammered away at Republican policies that cost factory workers their jobs and lost family farmers their mortgages. Speaking in the language, minus the racism, of white populists of the past, Jackson attacked the "economic violence" that wealthy corporations and their representatives in Washington had perpetrated on the economically disadvantaged. Addressing himself to black and white victims of financial privilege and corporate greed, he asked for the "small fish" to join against the "barracudas." He wrapped this message in a patriotic banner by calling for a "reinvestment in America" that would halt plant closings, stop foreclo-

Jesse Jackson, flanked by some of his rivals for the Democratic party
presidential nomination, appears at a candidate forum in October 1987.
From left to right stand Senator Albert Gore of Tennessee,
Congressman Richard Gephardt of Missouri, Jackson, Democratic party
chair Paul Kirk, Jr., Governor Bruce Babbitt of Arizona, Senator Paul
Simon of Illinois, and Governor Michael Dukakis of Massachusetts.
(**UPI/Bettmann Newsphotos**)

sures, and create domestic jobs. Furthermore, he highlighted his
long-standing concern with the danger of drugs ("Down with dope.
Up with hope."), a matter middle-class Americans felt extremely
worried about.

These themes struck some responsive chords among white voters. As he hopscotched around the country campaigning in the
Democratic primaries and caucuses, he wooed many whites who
would not have considered voting for him in 1984. In early April, a
USA Today poll revealed that 32 percent of whites were more willing to back Jackson on this occasion than four years earlier. Jim
Hightower of Texas noted the newfound appeal of Jackson as he espoused his brand of populism: "He is transcending the fact that he
is a black candidate. He is gaining white support... from the kind of

people who like Willie Nelson—the sort of redneck, lower middle-class constituency that is out there, and, since Bobby Kennedy and George Wallace, hasn't been voting that much." In one survey, taken in August 1987, 16 percent of rural whites selected Jackson as either their first or second choice for the top spot on the Democratic ticket. Furthermore, Jackson's approach encouraged his rivals for the nomination to shape their campaigns around similar issues dealing with drugs, education, health care, and protection for blue-collar workers threatened with layoffs and farmers endangered by foreclosures. Commentators observed that Jackson's popularity had risen as he moved into the party mainstream, but the Chicago minister could equally claim that he had pulled the Democratic center in his progressive direction.

Still, Jackson was stuck with several political liabilities that posed severe problems for him. His position on the Israeli-Palestinian conflict continued to cause him difficulties with Jewish-American voters. He tried to allay the fears of this important segment of the Democratic electorate by pledging to maintain strong U.S. support for the defense of Israel, whose security, he insisted, would not be jeopardized by carefully negotiating recognition of a Palestinian homeland. Jackson also avoided a repetition of the unfortunate "Hymie" incident, and he distanced his campaign from the controversial Muslim minister, Louis Farrakhan. This second time around, Jackson's attempts at reconciliation did bring some Jews into his camp. Indeed, his own campaign manager, Gerald Austin, was a Jew who had once been disturbed by the Hymie remark, but now had come to believe that Jackson meant no offense in using the term. However, most of Austin's coreligionists did not forgive Jackson so easily, and instead many apparently agreed with Mayor Edward Koch of New York City that Jews would be "crazy" to vote for Jackson.

Besides his specific problem with Jews, the Chicago civil rights leader generally had trouble convincing whites to endorse him. Whereas many of them thought that Jackson did not have sufficient political experience or that elements of his rainbow platform were too liberal, others indicated that they would not vote for him under any circumstance. Jackson was viewed unfavorably by 38 percent of Democrats, and even if he captured his party's nomination, polls showed him gaining only 27 percent of the total white vote. Personal perceptions and ideology undoubtedly influenced these views, but so too did the fact that Jackson was a black candidate and, therefore, to some extent unacceptable to many whites. The primary contest in West Virginia rudely demonstrated this point when a local resident bluntly informed reporters: "[I] ain't voting for no nigger." Most whites did not display such candor, and though it is difficult to disentangle racial concerns from other factors that generated opposition to Jackson, one may reasonably conclude that race came into play. As a black Jackson supporter lamented after New York's divisive primary: "In the South, if they didn't like you, they told you. In the North, they are just as racist, and just as prejudiced, but they're just a little smoother." Like his populist predecessors before the turn of the century, the black candidate had difficulty in forging an interracial alliance behind common class grievances.

In spite of these drawbacks, Jackson achieved some notable successes in the primaries and caucuses. He ran stronger than in 1984 among both black and white electorates and out of a field of six white candidates, including several state governors, U.S. senators, and a congressman, he finished second to Governor Michael Dukakis of Massachusetts. Gathering nearly 7 million votes, Jackson won over 1,200 delegates, three times the 1984 number. He scored impressive triumphs in the South by winning primaries in Alabama, Georgia, Louisiana, Mississippi, and Virginia, together with the caucus in South Carolina, his native state. In this region, blacks composed from 33 to 46 percent of the Democratic electorate, and they cast over 90 percent of their votes for Jackson. At the same time, the black candidate beat his rivals by lifting his share of the white vote to 10 percent, up from 4 percent in 1984. Overall, in the former Confederate states Jackson received 28 percent of the popular vote to edge out his closest competitors, Dukakis (27 percent) and Senator Albert Gore of Tennessee (25 percent). This showing was remarkable, particularly in a section of the country that until very recently had deprived its black citizens of the right to vote.

In the rest of the country (that is, outside of the South), where blacks generally constituted a smaller proportion of the population and the Democratic electorate, Jackson did surprisingly well. He astonished most political pundits and purveyors of conventional wisdom by winning the Michigan caucus. Forty percent of his total vote came from whites. In addition to capturing black-majority Detroit, despite the opposition of Mayor Young, he won in several predominantly white cities. In a state with a slumping automobile industry and strong blue-collar union membership, his condemnation of plant closings and corporate irresponsibility gained a large following. In this instance, his populist rhetoric was well-received. In addition, his personal magnetism, combined with a defense of old-fashioned values stressing the importance of family, upward mobility, and the danger of drugs, prompted many whites to shift, as Jackson put it, "from racial battleground to economic common ground and moral higher ground."

Elsewhere Jackson showed growing support among whites, as his share of the vote greatly exceeded the percentage of blacks in the voting-age population. He came in first in Alaska and Delaware, and finished second by gaining between 20 and 29 percent of the total vote in Connecticut, Indiana, Maine, Maryland, Minnesota, Missouri, Montana, Nebraska, New Mexico, Ohio, Pennsylvania, Vermont, and Wisconsin. He did even better in securing between 30 and 39 percent of the vote in Arizona, California, Colorado, Hawaii, Illinois, Kansas, New Jersey, New York, Oregon, and Washington. Although he finished second in the three-way, statewide contest in New York, Jackson triumphed in New York City with 46 percent of the votes and a coalition of blacks, Hispanics, and progressive whites behind him (see Table 4).

Nevertheless, Jackson fell considerably short of his goal. After peaking in Michigan, he lost in nearly all of the remaining primary and caucus elections. Following the bruising New York contest, Governor Dukakis emerged as the clear front-runner, and the field narrowed down to the Massachusetts governor and the Chicago clergyman. Jackson trailed behind his remaining rival in the ensuing head-to-head battles, especially as the white majority rallied around Dukakis. For all of his efforts over the previous four years in diminishing white opposition and even converting nonblacks to his candidacy, Jackson could not persuade a sufficient number of whites to back him. Whatever their racial views, many white Democrats appeared to harbor sincere doubts as to Jackson's electability. They believed Jackson's views were too far to the left of the political mainstream, and would not bring back to the fold conservative Democrats who had voted for Reagan. Anthony Lewis of the *New York Times* spoke for many of those who found Jackson appealing but a sure loser: "When I hear liberals talking about their exhilaration at the Jackson candidacy, their delight at its populist character, I worry. That sounds like the gushy liberalism that has

Table 4   Percentage of Votes Won by Jesse Jackson in Democratic Primaries, 1984 and 1988[a]

	Black voting-age population[b]	1984	1988
Alabama (p)	22.9	19.6	43.6[c]
Alaska (c)	3.4	10.6	34.6[c]
Arizona (c)	2.5	15.7	37.8
California (p)	7.1	19.6	35.2
Colorado (c)	3.2	4.2	33.6
Connecticut (p)	6.0	12.0	28.3
District of Columbia (p)	65.8	67.3[c]	80.0[c]
Georgia (p)	24.3	21.0	39.8[c]
Hawaii (c)	1.9	4.2	35.0
Illinois (p)	12.9	21.0	32.3
Kansas (c)	4.8	3.3	30.8
Louisiana (p)	26.6	42.9[c]	35.5[c]
Maine (c)	0.3	0.4	26.8
Maryland (p)	20.8	25.5	28.7
Michigan (c)	11.7	16.7	53.5[c]
Mississippi (p)	31.0	26.9	44.4[c]
Nebraska (p)	2.6	9.1	25.7
New Jersey (p)	11.0	23.6	32.9
New Mexico (p)	1.7	11.9	28.1
New York (p)	12.4	25.6	37.1
North Carolina (p)	20.3	25.4	33.0
Ohio (p)	9.2	16.4	27.5
Oregon (p)	1.2	9.5	38.1
Pennsylvania (p)	8.1	16.0	27.3
South Carolina (c)	27.3	25.0	54.8[c]
Tennessee (p)	14.2	25.3	20.7
Texas	11.1	16.4(c)	25.0(p)[d]
Virginia	17.5	26.7(c)	45.1(p)[c]
Vermont (p)	0.2	7.8	25.7[d]
Washington (c)	2.4	3.0	34.6
Wisconsin (p)	3.2	9.9	28.2

(p) represents a primary and (c) a caucus election.

[a]Primaries in which Jackson obtained at least 25 percent of the vote in either one or both years. Absent from the table is Puerto Rico, where Jackson won the primary with 29 percent of the vote in 1988.

[b]Percentage black of total voting-age population in 1980.

[c]Jackson victories.

[d]Texas and Vermont also had caucuses, and Jackson won both with 40 percent and 46 percent of the vote, respectively.

SOURCE: The Democratic primary election results are taken from *Congressional Quarterly Weekly* (June 16, 1984), 1443, and (July 9, 1988), 1894. The caucus totals, also, are from *Congressional Quarterly Weekly* (June 2, 1984), 1317, and (June 4, 1988), 1524. The figures on voting-age population are drawn from U.S. Department of Commerce, Bureau of the Census, *Statistical Abstract of the United States, 1984* (Washington, D.C.: Government Printing Office, 1984), 263.

got the Democratic Party out of touch with reality before: the reality of the need to win the center."

This hard-nosed perception of Jackson carried over to the decision not to select him as the vice-presidential candidate. Instead, Dukakis chose Senator Lloyd Bentsen of Texas as his running mate. In making this choice the Massachusetts governor sought to revive the "Boston-Austin axis" that had produced victory for John Kennedy and Lyndon Johnson in 1960. Bentsen was a moderate to conservative Democrat whose views on many domestic and foreign policy issues diverged from those of the more liberal Dukakis. In balancing the ticket geographically and ideologically, Dukakis hoped to forge a winning majority by prying loose Reagan Democrats and returning them to his column. Blacks decried this strategy because they believed that it took their votes for granted and it slighted the Reverend Jackson. They contended that the minister had earned a place on the ticket through his strong showing in the primaries. Jackson was similarly offended, but by the time the Democrats gathered at their convention in July, he had come around to endorsing Dukakis and Bentsen.

Although African-Americans did not get their first choice for either spot on the ticket, they did significantly increase their representation at the 1988 Democratic convention. Of those in attendance, 962, or 23 percent, were black. This constituted a one-third increase over the number of black delegates who had sat at the previous convention and comprised the highest number ever to participate in the party's quadrennial meeting. Together with Jackson's white delegates they succeeded in obtaining a few platform concessions on educational and health care issues as well as a pledge not to fund the military operations of antigovernment rebels in Central America. They also lent their support to Jackson in gaining a personal commitment from Dukakis to recruit additional blacks to his campaign staff and to policy-making positions within the party. Democratic chieftains also agreed to make some rule changes that Jackson had sought, including a reduction in the number of superdelegates chosen outside of the primary and caucus system.

The highlight for the Jackson delegates came with their candidate's prime-time television address to the convention and the nation. As he had in 1984, Jackson thrilled the audience with his vision of an America that "keeps hope alive" for all of its citizens, no matter how weak or humble, whatever their race, creed, or sex.

"We meet tonight at a crossroads, a point of decision," he remarked and went on to ask, "Shall we expand, be inclusive, find unity and power, or suffer division and impotence?" Jackson eloquently answered his own question by pointing out that Dukakis's Greek "foreparents came to America on immigrant ships. My foreparents came to America on slave ships. But whatever the original ships, we are both on the same side now."

Having failed in his bid for the nomination, Jackson nonetheless helped redefine victory. As the influential columnist David Broder noted: "For Jesse L. Jackson . . . 'winning' has meanings that cannot be captured in primary-election returns or exit-poll numbers." In a poignant illustration of the progress blacks had made, Jackson brought Rosa Parks with him onto the stage of the convention and introduced her to the thousands in the hall and the millions watching on television. Thirty-three years before, she had been arrested for challenging bus segregation in Montgomery, and now she stood beside a leading contender for the presidential nomination. Jackson also reminded the assemblage that only twenty-four years had passed since another group of Democrats had "locked out" Fannie Lou Hamer, Aaron Henry, and the Mississippi Freedom Democrats from taking their seats at the convention. Now Henry was listening to these words as a member of the Mississippi delegation, an interracial contingent headed by a black man, Ed Cole. Even the site of the meeting inspired thoughts of the momentous changes that had occurred. Jackson pointed out that this gathering in the capital of Georgia was taking place "in a state where governors once stood in school house doors." He further recalled that just over two decades before, in this city over which Andrew Young presided as mayor, the state legislature had barred the SNCC worker Julian Bond from assuming his seat in the legislature because of his objections to the Vietnam war. In this fashion, Jackson vividly connected his own journey as a legitimate contender for the presidency to the triumphs and sacrifices of the civil rights movement in scores of black communities across the nation.

In countless ways, Jackson had become a role model for young blacks who one day might also aspire to the nation's highest office. Certainly many African-Americans had dreamed that one day there would be a black president, but Jackson's candidacy gave new meaning to this hope. Shirley Chisholm's 1972 bid for the Democratic nomination had not attracted much support, even from

blacks, whereas Jackson's campaign had drawn a huge black following and considerable interest among whites. Although those who
were older might not see a black president in the White House in
their lifetime, they took great pride in what Jackson had already
achieved. "A five-year-old can look at the T.V. screen and see a
black man running for President and have it be credible," a Jackson
enthusiast explained. "Jesse has inspired a belief that nothing is un-
conquerable."

This contest also demonstrated that Jackson was more than a
candidate for blacks. His challenge helped transform the attitudes
of many whites, and sometimes in a startling manner. In Texas, for
example, a white man seeking to have his photograph snapped
alongside Jackson mentioned to the candidate that he had marched
in Selma. After Jackson retorted that it was nice to be with him
again, the fellow replied: "No, you don't understand. I marched
with the Klan. I just don't want to be on the wrong side of history
again." Although most whites did not experience a conversion this
dramatic, those marking their ballots for Jackson in some small way
reflected the changes that his candidacy represented. Not a winner
in the conventional sense, Jesse Jackson had taken a great stride in
gaining political acceptance for himself and for black Americans.

THE ELECTION OF GEORGE BUSH 1988

The 1988 presidential election did little to address, let alone pose solutions for, the chronic political and economic problems of African-
Americans. The Democratic standard-bearer, Michael Dukakis, appealed to voters to judge his competence as an administrator and
not his political ideology. Accordingly, for most of the campaign he
soft-pedaled his views as a liberal—the dreaded L word his Republican rival, Vice-President George Bush, hurled against him as an
epithet. Though Dukakis did appoint some blacks to his staff, including Ronald Brown, a Jackson campaign aide, and though he recruited Jackson to speak for him, especially in the last weeks of the
contest, he did not elevate the special concerns of the black community to the forefront of his political agenda. He set the tone early
when he delivered a speech in Philadelphia, Mississippi, mention-
ing civil rights in passing but omitting any reference to the three
Freedom Summer workers who were killed there a quarter-century

earlier. Taking note of this omission, *The New York Times* aptly commented: "Ignoring the South's often painful, sometimes proud progress in race relations is a peculiar way to profess leadership."

The GOP ticket of Bush and Senator Dan Quayle of Indiana offered no real alternative, as it pledged to extend Reagan administration policies that 79 percent of blacks found objectionable. In fact, blacks had comprised a scant 2.7 percent of the Republican National Convention delegates who chose their standard-bearers and the Reaganomic platform upon which they ran. If Dukakis could be faulted for sins of omission, Bush was guilty of premeditated racial assault. In shades of vintage George Wallace and Richard Nixon, Bush revived the theme of law and order by casting blacks in the image of criminals. Through highly provocative television ads, he attacked Governor Dukakis for granting a prison furlough to Willie Horton, a black inmate in Massachusetts, who escaped from the program and raped a white woman. The Republican candidate never referred to the color of Horton's skin, but he did not have to; the medium vividly conveyed this message for him. As Michael Kinsley, the editor of the *New Republic*, pointed out, whether Bush and his advisers were racially motivated was irrelevant. "Hortonism taps into a thick vein of racial paranoia that is a quarter-inch below the surface of the white American consciousness."

Given the choice of having Dukakis neglect them or Bush insult them, African-Americans chose to vote for the Democrat. Nearly 90 percent of the black electorate cast their ballots for the Massachusetts governor, about the same proportion supporting Democratic presidential nominees over the past two decades. Nevertheless, blacks appeared to approach the ballot box with slightly less enthusiasm than in recent years, as their turnout at the polls dropped by about 5 percent of those eligible to participate. (Overall, the white turnout also declined.) In major cities such as Chicago, Detroit, Cleveland, New York, and Philadelphia, the black vote fell an even larger 10 percent. While blacks continued to line up behind the Democratic hopeful, whites preferred the GOP contender. Bush received around 60 percent of white votes. Though he did not score as well as Reagan, the Republican President-elect won 54 percent of the popular votes and 426 electoral ballots.

Though blacks and Democrats failed to vault their candidate into the White House in 1988, they did better in extending their political power elsewhere. The Congressional Black Caucus added its first representative from New Jersey, and the Democrats gained five seats in the House and one in the Senate. At the state level, the Democrats increased their number by twenty-nine legislators, halting the trend toward the Republican party that was taking place throughout the 1980s. One of the black incumbents gaining reelection to the House, Mike Espy of Mississippi, did so in impressive fashion. Espy, who had triumphed with a bare 52 percent of the vote in 1986, walloped his Republican opponent by winning 65 percent of his district's electorate. He improved his performance by sweeping the black vote and obtaining an amazing 40 percent of the ballots from his white constituents. The House also saw Espy's colleague, William H. Gray of Pennsylvania, reach an important milestone in his selection as chairman of the Democratic Caucus. In securing this position, Gray became the first black representative to fill a prestigious leadership job in Congress. (The following year, he became House majority whip, ranking third in the Democratic chain of command in the lower chamber.) Moreover, after the election the Democratic National Committee selected Ronald Brown, who had steered Jackson's convention forces and later counseled Dukakis during the campaign, to the post of party head.

In addition, the election returns confirmed the continuing gains made by women of color. Although the annual growth rate was slowing down, between 1979 and 1988 the number of black female elected officials nearly doubled to a figure of 1,625. In the process, the gap between black male and female officeholders had narrowed. In 1979, there were about four times as many black men as women holding elected posts; a decade later the ratio stood at approximately three to one. Only one black woman, however, Cardiss Collins of Illinois, sat in the House of Representatives (a drop from a high of four in 1975). The majority of women still served in municipal governments and local school boards. Paralleling this upsurge in office-holding was the higher voter turnout rate of black females than males. Black women had not yet caught up with men in obtaining public office, but they had surpassed black males by about seven percentage points in going to the polls (see Table 5).

The 1988 elections underscored the difficulties and possibilities facing African-Americans. Staying exceedingly loyal to the Democrats and obtaining new bases of influence, they nonetheless felt that the party welcomed their presidential support but followed a

Table 5   Black Elected Officials in the United States, 1975–1988

	Number of males	Number of females	Percent male increase	Percent female increase
1975	2,973	530		
1976	3,295	684	10.8	29.1
1977	3,529	782	7.1	14.3
1978	3,660	843	3.7	7.8
1979	3,725	882	1.8	4.6
1980	3,936	976	5.7	10.6
1981	4,017	1,021	2.0	4.6
1982	4,079	1,081	1.5	9.7
1983	4,383	1,223	7.5	13.1
1984	4,441	1,259	1.3	2.9
1985	4,697	1,359	5.8	10.8
1986	4,942	1,482	5.2	9.1
1987	5,117	1,564	3.5	5.5
1988	5,204	1,625	1.8	3.9

SOURCE: Joint Center for Political Studies, *National Roster of Black Elected Officials* (Washington, D.C., 1988), 17.

strategy to attract conservative white voters. Surveys indicated that the strength of their partisan attachment to the Democrats was weakening, particularly among younger blacks coming of political age after the peak of the civil rights movement. At the same time, the Republicans showed some signs of trying to entice disaffected black Democrats to their ranks. Below the presidential level a number of Republicans had already fashioned winning coalitions with the black electorate. For example, New Jersey's governor, Thomas Kean, had won office with 60 percent of the black vote; and George Voinovich attracted 85 percent of black ballots in his victory as mayor of Cleveland. Even President Bush recognized the need to refashion the unflattering image left by his predecessor. Putting aside the offensive rhetoric from his campaign, he called for a "kinder and gentler America" and, in a highly publicized gesture, met with Jesse Jackson to discuss how to bring that about. Yet, until the Republicans offered more than soothing words and proposed meaningful alternatives to the policies of the Reagan administration, they had little chance of significantly improving their standing among nonwhite voters.

Chapter 8

Still Running for Freedom

KEEPING HOPE ALIVE

By the end of the 1980s, the future of black politics appeared unsettled. To an extent unfathomable in 1941, African-Americans exerted considerable influence in local and national affairs; yet old patterns of discrimination still lingered. The process of empowerment had moved ahead in many areas, but not at the same rate and often in a halting fashion. Furthermore, the increased measure of acceptance gained by Jesse Jackson in his presidential bids did little to wipe out opposition to black political equality in many places where racism had traditionally flourished and where it continued to operate, albeit in more subtle forms.

The notable achievements of the civil rights struggle often obscure the political dilemmas that continue to perplex African-Americans and their allies at the end of the 1980s. Unquestionably, blacks constitute a powerful force in the electorate. By 1988, they comprised 11.2 percent of the nation's registered voters, a figure comparable to the proportion of blacks in the nation's population; they had narrowed the enrollment gap between the races to a slight 1 percent; and their rate of turnout at the polls trailed that of whites by only 4 percent. Yet their political impact remained circumscribed. Holding a mere 1.4 percent of elected positions, blacks saw their chances for victory drop off as they competed for higher office. Although only 3 percent of whites declared themselves unwilling to vote for a black candidate in a local school board election, the figure jumped to 18 percent for a black presidential aspirant. Many blacks believed their electoral clout was further limited because the Democrats took them for granted and the Republicans virtually ignored them. They had loyally contributed around 90 percent of their ballots to Democratic presidential candidates since 1964, but as Dukakis's selection of Bentsen suggested, the party deliberately shaped its strategy with mainstream white voters, not blacks, in mind.

In addition, questions remained as to whether conventional electoral politics could resolve the fundamental economic problems experienced by blacks and other impoverished Americans. These were problems that resulted not from individual acts of bigotry but from the enduring presence of discrimination deeply embedded in fundamental institutions throughout the centuries.

Economic inequality imposed a heavy burden on African-Americans. Notwithstanding the gains achieved by the middle class, the majority of blacks had made little progress in catching up with whites. Twenty years after a presidential commission warned that the United States was "moving toward two societies, one black, one white—separate and unequal," the median family income of blacks relative to whites was heading downward. From 60 percent of the earnings of whites in 1968, the figure had dropped even lower, to 56 percent by 1988 (see Table 6). The proportion of blacks out of work was more than double that of whites, and the percentage of blacks living below the poverty line tripled that of whites. A visit to any of the inner-city ghettos that had experienced rioting in the 1960s revealed that little had changed since then; per-

Table 6   Median Family Income (current dollars), 1960–1987

	White	Black	Black-to-White Percentage
1960	$ 5,835	$ 3,230	55.4%
1965	7,251	3,993	55.1
1970	10,236	6,279	61.3
1975	14,268	8,779	61.5
1980	21,904	12,674	57.9
1985	29,152	16,786	57.7
1987	32,274	18,098	56.1

SOURCE: U.S. Department of Commerce, Bureau of the Census, *Statistical Abstract of the United States, 1989* (Washington, D.C.: Government Printing Office, 1989), 445.

haps conditions had even worsened. Scholars and journalists wrote increasingly about the phenomenon of the black underclass in those depressed areas, a growing group "that is slipping further and further behind the rest of society." People with little education, they no longer bothered to seek work, lived in poverty and despair, were hooked on drugs, and were virtually unaffected by the presence of blacks governing their city halls. This gloomy picture did not do justice to the millions of blacks in those communities who were working hard to raise their families, struggling to make ends meet, and striving to keep narcotics out of their neighborhoods. Nevertheless, the situation was desperate enough to alarm blacks and whites interested in achieving equality in fact as well as in law.

For Jesse Jackson or any other Afro-American leader seeking progressive social change, the challenge remains to develop black political resources and shape them into instruments to lessen economic disparities between the races. The success of the black middle class has heralded the breakdown of legal barriers to economic opportunity that accompanied desegregation, but the persistence of substantial black poverty and unemployment attests to the cleavage between electoral expectations and material rewards. By committing themselves to the ballot as a central tool for emancipation, blacks, implicitly if not explicitly, accepted the ground rules of the American political system. Consequently, black politicians have softened the more radical, communitarian side of reenfranchisement and empowerment, as envisioned by the Student Nonviolent Coordinating Committee. As a result, they have become part of the dominant political culture whose values have improved the lot of the black middle class while leaving the plight of lower-class blacks largely unaltered.

The increased legitimacy that Jesse Jackson gained for black political aspirations marked a new beginning and not an end. African-Americans could build on the political freedom they had so gallantly achieved during the second half of the twentieth century. They had learned the hard way that empowerment was an ongoing struggle and that genuine participation in community and governmental affairs involved more than the acquisition of formal constitutional rights. It also demanded collective action and the assertion of group pride to sustain the belief among ordinary people that they could exert greater control over their lives despite historic obstacles. The civil rights movement had reawakened racial consciousness, which in turn nurtured subsequent struggles for political power, such as those waged by the Reverend Jackson. Whatever else they obtained in the process, the quest for first-class citizenship revived in blacks feelings of self-respect and "somebodyness," qualities so essential in pursuing the struggle for freedom that will no doubt take many varied forms in the years ahead.

As blacks and their white allies looked toward the future, they could take some comfort from the past. Notwithstanding the limitations of the suffrage as an instrument of liberation, the political emancipation of blacks made a critical difference. The civil rights movement, combining protest with electoral politics, succeeded in transforming individuals and communities through collective struggle. It is inappropriate to figure black political advancement strictly on a cost-accounting basis, as a story recounted by SNCC's Bob Moses poignantly shows. He told of a woman he remembered working with in Mississippi, Mrs. Hazel Palmer, who had not been elected to any office or gained material success by objective standards. But that was beside the point. "[I]t didn't matter that she did not make it in any other way that society thinks people make it," Moses insisted. "But she had won something in her spirit that no one could take away from her." The Mrs. Palmers of the South became empowered to stand up in their communities and affirm their rights as first-class citizens and active political agents. This freedom of the mind will be difficult to take away and may serve as perhaps the most valuable legacy bequeathed to future generations of African-Americans in their attempt to obtain the unfulfilled promises of racial equality.

LOOKING TOWARD THE FUTURE

Disappointed with the performances of the two major parties in addressing their problems, African-Americans have been considering the option of pursuing an independent political course. A poll taken in 1986 revealed that 53 percent of blacks favored a black candidate like Jesse Jackson running for the presidency as an independent. Considering the structural biases of the political system in discouraging third parties and the danger of isolating blacks even further from the electoral majority, the prospect of a black-led party successfully competing for the White House appears remote. However, political theorists, such as Ronald W. Walters of Howard University, have suggested that while remaining within the two-party system, blacks could pursue an "independent-leverage" strategy. Based on group solidarity, collective interests, and the threat of withholding their votes, they would negotiate for increased programmatic benefits in return for their support. Such an approach would require a high degree of organizational cohesion and discipline not only from the mass of black voters but also from their leaders, many of whom are now tied into established political party structures. Nevertheless, it is clear that blacks must develop tough bargaining strategies to compete for power against the other interests arrayed in their partisan coalitions.

If blacks remain within the Democratic orbit, as they most likely would for the foreseeable future, they will have to forge coalitions that extend to them a greater share of political power. Along with progressive whites, Hispanics, and other minorities, they must find a way to broaden the party's foundation of support to include the millions of Americans who felt alienated from the system. The attempts of Mondale and Dukakis to outbid their conservative opponents for the same old votes did not work. Without an expansion of the electorate to embrace potential voters more inclined to favor government efforts against poverty and discrimination, the Democrats and their black supporters will probably continue to finish second in contests for the highest office in the land.

Blacks and their allies will also have to find a way to reconnect politics and protest, national and local struggles. The civil rights movement had made electoral progress possible, and without a revival of its energy and vision routine black political participation will not be sufficient to remove the blockades to genuine equality. The Jackson campaigns marked a start toward merging the forces seeking social change with the practitioners of conventional politics. The challenge ahead is to sustain this alliance and build a movement around it. The history of the civil rights struggle demonstrated that the quest for liberation arose not from any single individual but from collective action. Like Martin Luther King, the charismatic Jesse Jackson served as an agent for a larger network of blacks and whites pressing for freedom. Like their predecessors in the civil rights movement, African-Americans have to continue to organize their communities, devise innovative strategies to apply constant pressure on their representatives, and carry their demands from the towns and cities where they reside to the nation's capital, where power is ultimately wielded. The culmination of the civil rights movement in the achievement of political equality requires nothing less.

EPILOGUE

The entry of blacks into positions of political power has occurred relatively late enough to guarantee that the supply of victorious firsts will not be exhausted for some time. A year after Jesse Jackson's 1988 presidential run came to an end, the Democratic voters of New York City elected an African-American, David Dinkins, as their candidate for mayor. Because this triumph happened in the nation's largest city, the center of the media universe, it assumed greater significance than if it had come to pass virtually anywhere else. Yet surely as noteworthy as the event itself was the fact that it had taken New York more than twenty years to follow the examples set by Cleveland and Gary. In addition, since 1973, Los Angeles, the leading city on the West Coast, could brag about having an African-American mayor. In 1989, the city known as the Big Apple, which prefers to establish the fashionable trends, finally had caught up with its urban counterparts throughout the rest of the country.

Jackson's 1988 campaign had pointed the way toward victory. The civil rights minister, though losing the state to Governor Dukakis, carried New York City with slightly over 40 percent of the vote. In doing so, he exposed the vulnerability of Ed Koch, the incumbent mayor completing his third term. Elected in 1976, Koch confronted a desperate financial crisis and helped engineer the city's recovery. However, his administration was marred by a series of scandals involving close political associates, and his flamboyant personality offended many constituents. Among the most upset were blacks and other minorities who believed that the mayor's programs to restore the city's fiscal health ignored, or even aggravated, the condition of the most impoverished residents of their communities. To make matters worse, in 1988, Koch exacerbated tensions between blacks and the city's large Jewish population by attacking the Reverend Jackson as anti-Semitic, reminding voters that the presidential candidate had termed New York City "Hymietown" during the 1984 campaign. Despite the mayor's bitter opposition, Jackson managed to line up solid black support with sufficient backing from Hispanics and liberal whites to emerge ahead of his two opponents in the city. (Koch allied himself with Senator Albert Gore, who came in third.)

Encouraged by Jackson's strong showing, Dinkins, the president of the borough of Manhattan since 1985, challenged Koch's bid for an unprecedented fourth term. Born in Trenton, New Jersey, in 1927, Dinkins served in the Marines and, in 1950, graduated from Howard University with a degree in mathematics. A year later he moved to Harlem and decided to become an attorney. Following his graduation from Brooklyn Law School, in 1956, he pursued a career in politics and served as Democratic party district leader, state assemblyman, and city clerk, a position he held for ten years before winning election as chief executive of Manhattan. A pensive, soft-spoken individual, Dinkins had a talent for listening carefully before acting and for playing the role of conciliator. He would need to draw upon those skills to forge a winning coalition in a city where blacks constituted less than a quarter of the electorate. His critics called Dinkins indecisive, but almost all agreed that in the rough-and-tumble world of New York City politics, he remained a gentleman—"a political Bill Cosby," as one newspaper dubbed him.

Although neither Koch nor Dinkins sought to attack the other along racial lines, the Democratic mayoral contest took place against a backdrop of growing racial animosities. Trouble had been brewing for some time. The stress of daily life in a city as large as New York strained the limits of racial toleration. The twin problems of crime and drug abuse, nurtured by poverty, took on racial overtones and fostered mutual suspicion. In 1984, when Bernhard Goetz shot four black youths who he believed were trying to rob him on a subway train, many whites regarded him as a hero, a kind of real-life Lone Ranger. The situation grew worse as a number of disturbing incidents followed. On December 20, 1986, a gang of whites attacked three blacks after they entered a pizza parlor in the predominantly white section of Howard Beach, Queens. In trying to make his escape, one of the blacks was struck by a car and killed. A little more than two years later, in April 1989, a white female jogger running in Central Park was raped, beaten, and left for dead by a roving band of black and Hispanic teenagers. Racial friction again reached a peak during the primary campaign for mayor. On

August 23, 1989, four black youths ventured into the mainly white neighborhood of Bensonhurst, Brooklyn, to inquire about purchasing a used car. They were assaulted by a mob of whites, one of whom fired a gunshot that killed sixteen-year-old Yusuf Hawkins. Racial demonstrations followed this tragic incident.

Dinkins won the Democratic primary, but the outcome of the election reflected sharp racial cleavages. In a field of one black and three white candidates, Dinkins gained about 50 percent of the vote and Koch came in second with 42 percent. The nature of their support was markedly different. Blacks constituted 56 percent of Dinkins's total vote, while whites composed 34 percent, and Hispanics 8 percent. In contrast, 89 percent of Koch's vote came from whites, 7 percent from Hispanics, and only 2 percent from blacks. As expected Dinkins ran strongest in New York's minority communities. He captured more than 90 percent of black ballots and a slight majority of Hispanic votes. On the other side, 70 percent of whites stuck with Koch. One of his supporters from Bensonhurst, a community Koch carried by a margin of nearly seven to one, explained her vote for the incumbent: "I'm afraid to have a black mayor."

However, what impressed most observers was not the racial polarization of the electorate but the relative success Dinkins had in attracting white crossover voters. This minority of whites, about 30 percent, constituted a critical element of Dinkins's winning margin of victory. The Manhattan borough president scored twice as well among whites as Jesse Jackson had in 1988. His 25 percent share of Jewish votes was also an improvement over that of Jackson, and was noteworthy because it came against Koch, himself a Jew. Most whites believed that Dinkins would help heal the city's racial wounds, and according to one exit poll 60 percent of whites expected Dinkins to treat both races fairly. In sampling a cross section of the entire electorate, another survey reported that 91 percent said Dinkins displayed sensitivity to peoples' needs compared with only 7 percent who thought Koch did so. The impact of the Bensonhurst murder was difficult to measure precisely. Though most voters cited other issues as more important in making up their minds, the Bensonhurst killing probably encouraged a greater number of blacks to go to the polls and reinforced the feeling among whites that Dinkins could help defuse similar racial conflicts in the future. As one of his black supporters remarked: "Dinkins projects the kind of personality that's not threatening to whites and is acceptable to blacks."

Nevertheless, Dinkins had a tough battle in the general election. Successful in uniting Democratic party leaders, most notably Mayor Koch, behind him, Dinkins still had to keep the white Democratic rank and file in line. In a city where Republicans were outnumbered five to one, the Democratic nominee normally was a shoo-in. However, Dinkins's Republican opponent, Rudolph Giuliani, a former federal prosecutor, waged a fierce campaign to lure white Democrats away from their traditional fold. Besides attacking Dinkins for financial improprieties, Giuliani appealed to racial fears. Behind the moderate Dinkins, he warned, stood the more controversial figure of Jesse Jackson waiting to call the shots.

Dinkins won by a narrow margin of two percentage points—the closest mayoral election since 1905. Despite substantial defections by white Democrats, he held onto 30 percent of the white electorate, including between 33 and 40 percent of Jews. Dinkins ran extremely well among minority voters, gaining more than 90 percent of black ballots and nearly 70 percent of Hispanic votes. Notwithstanding this breakthrough victory, those figures showed the continuing role of racial considerations in determining electoral choices. Yet looked at from a different perspective, the results also demonstrated Dinkins's success in attracting a genuine multiracial coalition. Of the mayor's total vote, approximately 50 percent came from blacks, 30 percent from whites, and 17 percent from Hispanics—a "gorgeous mosaic," as Dinkins called it.[1]

If recent history can serve as an accurate guide, Dinkins will find his job as mayor a difficult challenge, filled with high expectations that may be difficult to satisfy. Most likely, African-Americans and Hispanics will receive more appointments to city government and minority businesses will obtain a greater share of municipal contracts. Mayor Dinkins already serves as a source of pride for

---

[1]Election Day also saw another landmark victory. L. Douglas Wilder, the Democratic lieutenant governor of Virginia, became the first black to be elected governor in the nation's history. In a contest characterized by negative campaigning, but in which the race issue remained in the background, Wilder defeated his Republican opponent by a mere 7,000 votes out of nearly 2 million cast. Race still mattered, however. Many whites who voted for the rest of the statewide Democratic ticket declined to support Wilder, accounting for the closest gubernatorial contest in Virginia's history.

**Campaigning for mayor of New York City, David
Dinkins stands under a statue of George
Washington on the steps of Federal Hall in lower
Manhattan. (AP/Wide World Photos)**

many black New Yorkers. "When Martin Luther King was alive we
had somebody to look up to," a resident of Brooklyn's Bedford-
Stuyvesant area declared. "Now the black community is lost. David
Dinkins will help a lot." At the same time, however, the plight of
the impoverished and the homeless and the problems of crime and
drugs will remain beyond the grasp of even the most compassionate
occupant of city hall to solve. The mayor will face an entrenched
municipal bureaucracy resistant to change, powerful corporate developers, tough-minded union leaders, and a shortage of revenue to
address issues that are national in scope. Furthermore, Dinkins will
have to strike the delicate balance of responding to the special

needs of minority communities without losing the necessary economic and political support of the white majority. Whatever solutions ultimately work, they must involve a readjustment of domestic priorities and a federal commitment that combines the economic realism of the New Deal's battle against the depression with the moral urgency of the civil rights struggle against racism.

Winning an election, especially for the first time, is rich in symbolism, but cannot be an end in itself. David Dinkins and other Afro-American elected officials, together with their nonblack allies, must somehow find ways to govern effectively and deliver the substantive benefits necessary to improve their constituents' lives. Otherwise, the promise of electoral politics as a means of achieving racial equality will remain unfulfilled.

Bibliographical Essay

The entries noted in the following pages are meant to be a select list of the works upon which this study is primarily based. A full citation appears only at the first referral to the source. My main purpose is to provide the reader with a guide to the available published literature and the themes that they raise; therefore, manuscript sources are omitted. I have made a few exceptions in noting unpublished doctoral dissertations and conference papers that were of particular help.

PREFACE

A very useful discussion that distinguishes between the civil rights movement and the black freedom struggle and calls for a focus on local communities is presented in Clayborne Carson, "Civil Rights Reform and the Black Freedom Struggle," in *The Civil Rights Movement in America*, Charles W. Eagles, ed., University Press of Mississippi, Jackson, Miss., 1986, 19–32.

CHAPTER 1

Two anthologies that furnish a background for the general study of Afro-American history and black politics are Darlene Clark Hine, ed., *The State of Afro-American History: Past, Present and Future*, Louisiana State University Press, Baton Rouge, 1986, and Michael B. Preston, Lenneal J. Henderson, Jr., and Paul Puryear, eds., *The New Black Politics: The Search for Political Power*, Longman, New

York, 1982. Useful surveys on the civil rights movement and on black politics can be found in Matthew Holden, *The Politics of the Black "Nation,"* Chandler, New York, 1973; Manning Marable, *Black American Politics; From the Washington Marches to Jesse Jackson*, Verso, London, 1985; Milton D. Morris, *The Politics of Black America*, Harper & Row, New York, 1975; Hanes Walton, Jr., *Invisible Politics: Black Political Behavior*, State University of New York Press, Albany, 1985; Lucius J. Barker and Jesse J. McCrory, Jr., *Black Americans and the Political System*, Winthrop, Cambridge, Mass., 1976; Harvard Sitkoff, *The Struggle for Black Equality, 1954–1980*, Hill & Wang, New York, 1981; and Rhoda Lois Blumberg, *Civil Rights: The 1960s Freedom Struggle*, Twayne, Boston, 1984.

W. E. B. Du Bois, *The Souls of Black Folk*, New American Library, Chicago, 1973, demonstrates the importance of the ballot as a key weapon for black liberation. On the influence of the New Deal on the development of black political strategies, there are two excellent monographs: Harvard Sitkoff, *A New Deal for Blacks*, Oxford University Press, New York, 1978, and Nancy J. Weiss, *Farewell to the Party of Lincoln: Black Politics in the Age of FDR*, Princeton University Press, Princeton, 1983. The impact of World War II is covered most extensively in Neil A. Wynn, *The Afro-American and the Second World War*, Holmes & Meier, New York, 1975, and in several surveys of life in general on the home front. Among them are Richard Polenberg, *War and Society: The United States, 1941–1945*, J. B. Lippincott, Philadelphia, 1972, and John Morton Blum, *V Was for Victory: Politics and Culture During World War II*, Harcourt, Brace, Jovanovich, New York, 1976. Richard M. Dalfiume, "The 'Forgotten Years' of the Negro Revolution," *Journal of American History*, 55 (June 1968): 90–106, is a seminal article on the origins of the civil rights struggle; Harvard Sitkoff, "Racial Militancy and Interracial Violence in the Second World War," *Journal of American History*, 58 (December 1971): 661–681, explores the moderating influence white liberals had on the development of black protest; Lee Finkle, "The Conservative Aims of Militant Rhetoric; Black Protest During World War II," *Journal of American History*, 60 (December 1973): 692–713, extends Sitkoff's analysis to the black press; and Peter J. Kellogg, "Civil Rights Consciousness in the 1940s," *The Historian*, 42 (November 1979): 18–41, notes the transformation of liberal thinking

toward support of racial equality. Dominic J. Capeci, Jr., has ex-
amined outbreaks of racial violence and the response of the federal
government in *Race Relations in Wartime Detroit: The Sojourner
Truth Housing Controversy of 1942*, Temple University Press,
Philadelphia, 1984, and "The Lynching of Cleo Wright: Federal
Protection of Constitutional Rights during World War II," *Journal
of American History*, 72 (March 1986): 859–887. Herbert Garfinkel,
When Negroes March, Atheneum, New York, 1969, investigates A.
Philip Randolph, the March on Washington Movement, and the
FEPC; and Allen M. Winkler, "The Philadelphia Transit Strike of
1944," *Journal of American History*, 59 (June 1972): 73–89, comments on the FEPC's efforts in resolving racial strife during a labor
dispute. Jervis Anderson, *A. Philip Randolph: A Biographical Portrait*, Harcourt Brace Jovanovich, New York, 1972, provides a flat-
tering account of the labor leader and protest innovator. Catherine
A. Barnes, *Journey from Jim Crow: The Desegregation of Southern
Transit*, Columbia University Press, New York, 1983, covers wartime challenges to segregated transportation and shows the continuity of those efforts with later civil rights struggles. Jules Tygiel,
Baseball's Great Experiment: Jackie Robinson and His Legacy, Vintage, New York, 1983, is a social history of the racial integration of
America's premier sport. August Meier and Elliott Rudwick,
CORE: A Study in the Civil Rights Movement, 1942–1968, Oxford
University Press, New York, 1973, details the emergence of a major civil rights group, which pioneered direct-action forms of protest that would become popular in the 1950s and 1960s.

The long legal struggle of blacks to topple the white primary as
a means of gaining access to the most meaningful elections in the
South is amply described in Darlene Clark Hine, *Black Victory:
The Rise and Fall of the White Primary in Texas*, KTO Press,
Millwood, N.Y., 1979, and Steven F. Lawson, *Black Ballots: Vot-
ing Rights in the South, 1944–1969*, Columbia University Press,
New York, 1976. The battles against the poll tax are discussed in
Hollinger F. Barnard, ed., *Outside the Magic Circle*, University of
Alabama Press, University, Ala., 1985, which is the autobiography
of Virginia Foster Durr, a leading southern white liberal reformer;
and in a scholarly study by Frederic D. Ogden, *The Poll Tax in the
South*, University of Alabama Press, University, Ala., 1958. The attempts of southern blacks and their allies to use their restored ballots in the postwar period were first chronicled by Henry Lee

Moon, *Balance of Power: The Negro Vote*, Doubleday, Garden City, N.Y., 1948, and more recently by Robert Korstad and Nelson Lichtenstein, "Opportunities Found and Lost: Labor, Radicals, and the Early Civil Rights Movement," *Journal of American History*, 75 (December 1988): 786–811, and by Patricia Sullivan, "The Voting Rights Movement in South Carolina during the 1940s" paper presented at meeting of the Southern Historical Association, Houston, Tex., 1985. Mississippi and the significance of the Bilbo episode are presented in James W. Silver, *Mississippi: The Closed Society*, Harcourt, Brace, & World, New York, 1966, and in Lawson, *Black Ballots*. Detailed studies of black politics in local communities are contained in C. C. Bacote, "The Negro in Atlanta Politics," *Phylon*, 25 (December 1955): 333–350; Everett Carll Ladd, Jr., *Negro Political Leadership in the South*, Atheneum, New York, 1969 [Winston-Salem]; Korstad and Lichtenstein, "Opportunities Found and Lost" [Winston-Salem]; and William H. Chafe, *Civilities and Civil Rights*, Oxford University Press, New York, 1981 [Greensboro]. Focused at the national level, Harvard Sitkoff, "Harry Truman and the Election of 1948: The Coming of Age of Civil Rights in American Politics," *Journal of Southern History*, 37 (November 1971), analyzes the pivotal balance of power wielded by northern black voters in Truman's presidential victory and its implications for the future.

CHAPTER 2

Historians are in general agreement that President Truman furthered the civil rights agenda of African-Americans, but they remain divided as to how effective and determined he was in achieving those goals. William Carl Berman, *The Politics of Civil Rights in the Truman Administration*, Ohio State University Press, Columbus, Ohio, 1970, and Barton J. Bernstein, "The Ambiguous Legacy: Civil Rights," in *Politics and Policies of the Truman Administration*, Barton J. Bernstein, ed. Quadrangle, Chicago, 1970: 269–314, take a critical view of Truman's performance and find fault with his leadership as well as with liberalism in general. A more favorable view of the President and his civil rights accomplishments is presented by Donald McCoy and Richard T. Reutten, *Quest and Response: Minority Rights and the Truman Administration*, University of Kansas Press, Lawrence, Kans., 1973, and by Robert J. Donovan, *Conflict and Crisis: The Presidency of Harry Truman, 1945–1948*, Norton, New York, 1977. For additional insights into the Truman presidency by a contemporary civil rights leader, see Walter White, *A Man Called White*, Viking, New York, 1948. Nancy J. Weiss, *Farewell to the Party of Lincoln: Black Politics in the Age of FDR*, and Harvard Sitkoff, "Harry Truman and the Election of 1948," both cited in Chapter 1, also offer judicious comments on the political dimensions of civil rights.

Postwar political developments in black communities are treated in Hugh D. Price, *The Negro in Southern Politics: A Chapter of Florida History*, New York University Press, New York, 1957; four works cited for Chapter 1 [Ladd, *Negro Leadership*; Moon, *Balance of Power*; Korstad and Lichtenstein, "Opportunities Found and Lost"; Chafe, *Civilities and Civil Rights*; and Bacote, "Atlanta Politics"]; Alton Hornsby, Jr., "The Negro in Atlanta Politics, 1961–1973," *Atlanta Historical Bulletin*, 21 (Spring 1977): 7–33; David J. Garrow, ed., *The Montgomery Bus Boycott and the Women Who Started It: The Memoir of Jo Ann Gibson Robinson*, University of Tennessee Press, Knoxville, Tenn., 1987; and J. Mills Thornton, "Challenge and Response in the Montgomery Bus Boycott of 1955–56," *Alabama Review*, 33 (July 1989): 163–235. The comments of William H. Chafe concerning the negative effects of anti-Communism on racially progressive labor unions appear in *The Unfinished Journey: America Since World War II*, Oxford University Press, New York, 1986. Adam Fairclough, "The Preachers and the People: The Origins and the Early Years of the Southern Christian Leadership Conference, 1955–1959," *Journal of Southern History*, 52 (August 1986): 403–440, notes the linkages between electoral and protest politics. Aldon D. Morris, *The Origins of the Civil Rights Movement*, Free Press, New York, 1984, offers a sociological perspective on the community structures that spawned black political protest. Doug McAdam, *Political Process and the Development of Black Insurgency*, University of Chicago Press, Chicago, 1982, also provides a sociological view, on a national as well as a regional scale, of the political resources that shaped the direction of the civil rights movement. The impact of the *Brown* decision in shaping racial politics in the South and the nation is beautifully chronicled in Richard Kluger, *Simple Justice*, Knopf, New York, 1975. The hostile reactions on the part of white political, economic, and social leaders in challenging the landmark opinion are dealt with perceptively by Numan V. Bartley, *The Rise of Massive Resistance*, Louisiana State University Press, Baton Rouge, 1970, and Neil R. McMillen, *The Citizens' Council: Organized Resistance to the Second Reconstruction, 1954–1964*, University of Illinois Press, Urbana, Ill., 1971.

A number of works have examined the impact of the accelerating civil rights struggle on national politics. Robert Frederick Burk, *The Eisenhower Administration and Black Civil Rights*, University of Tennessee Press, Knoxville, Tenn., 1984, offers a well-balanced, but ultimately unfavorable, portrayal of President Eisenhower's handling of civil rights matters, a view that is shared by most writers on the subject. One account that accords more credit to Eisenhower than has customarily been granted is Michael Mayer, "With Much Deliberation and Some Speed," *Journal of Southern History*, 52 (February 1986): 41–76. A sometimes fond but mostly harsh assessment of Eisenhower's role, written by one who served the administration, appears in E. Frederick Morrow, *Black Man in the White House*, Coward-McCann, New York, 1963. Roy Wilkins, with Tom Matthews, *Standing Fast*, Viking, New York, 1982, is the memoir of a prominent civil rights leader who found Eisenhower's leadership sadly lacking. The contrasts in style of the two most notable black politicians of this period, Adam Clayton Powell and William Dawson, are analyzed in James Q. Wilson, "Two Negro Politicians: An Interpretation," *American Journal of Political Science*, 4 (November 1960): 360–369. Gary W. Reichard, "Democrats, Civil Rights, and Electoral Strategies in the 1950s," *Congress and the Presidency*, 13 (Spring 1986): 59–81, traces Democratic party strategies toward black voters during the 1950s. Both regional and national assessments of the impact of the black vote on partisan politics at middecade are contained in a special issue of the *Journal of Negro Education*, 26 (Summer 1957), and in Chandler Davidson, *Biracial Politics: Conflict and Consensus in the Metropolitan South*, Louisiana State University Press, Baton Rouge, 1972. My own *Black Ballots* (cited for Chapter 1) also covers these issues.

The story of the Macon County and Tuskegee struggle, both patient and courageous, has found a historian worthy of its merit. Robert J. Norrell, *Reaping the Whirlwind: The Civil Rights Movement in Tuskegee*, Vintage, New York, 1985, carefully and sympathetically charts racial politics on both sides of the color line in this community identified with Booker T. Washington. Three earlier studies that provide useful accounts of the *Gomillion* case and the related boycott are Harry Holloway, *The Politics of the Southern Negro: From Exclusion to Big City Organization*, Random House, New York, 1969; Lewis Jones and Stanley Smith, *Voting Rights and Economic Pressure*, Anti-Defamation League, New York, 1958; and Bernard Taper, *Gomillion v. Lightfoot*, McGraw-Hill, New York, 1962.

CHAPTER 3

For nearly two decades after its publication, David L. Lewis, *King: A Critical Biography*, Praeger, New York, 1970 [republished as *King: A Biography*, University of Illinois Press, Urbana, Ill., 1978], was the standard interpretation of the nation's best-known civil rights leader. In the late 1980s, three enormously valuable studies appeared, which draw upon manuscript records that were not available to Lewis and on extensive interviews. David Garrow has written more thoroughly about King's career than any other contemporary scholar. His early studies, *Protest at Selma: Martin Luther King and the Voting Rights Act of 1965*, Yale University Press, New Haven, Conn., 1978, and *The FBI and Martin Luther King, Jr.*, Norton, New York, 1981, paved the way for the encyclopedic *Bearing the Cross: Martin Luther King, Jr., and the Southern Christian Leadership Conference*, William Morrow, New York, 1986. Adam Fairclough, *To Redeem the Soul of America: The Southern Christian Leadership Conference and Martin Luther King, Jr.*, University of Georgia Press, Athens, Ga., 1987, offers thoughtful interpretations of King, the organization he led, and the larger movement. Taylor Branch, *Parting the Waters: America in the King Years, 1954–1963*, Simon & Schuster, New York, 1988, places King within the larger black religious culture from which he emerged. Very helpful in discussing the Crusade for Citizenship program is Aldon Morris, *Origins of the Civil Rights Movement* (New York, 1984). The sketch of Fred Shuttlesworth was drawn primarily from Morris. Howell Raines, *My Soul Is Rested: Movement Days in the Deep South Remembered*, Putnam, New York, 1977, provides a revealing collection of interviews with prominent and not so well-known leaders and opponents of the civil rights movement. For additional interviews, along with a narrative of the freedom struggle that emphasizes the roles played by plain, though extraordinary, people, consult Juan Williams, *Eyes on the Prize: America's Civil Rights Years, 1954–1965*, Viking, New York, 1987. Other major civil rights groups that engaged in direct-action protests and political organizing in southern communities have also received detailed treatments. On SNCC, see the work of Howard Zinn, a historian who participated as an adviser to the organization, *SNCC: The New Abolitionists*, Beacon Press, Boston, 1964, and that of Clayborne Carson, *SNCC and the Black Awakening of the 1960s*, Harvard University Press, Cambridge, Mass., 1981, which is the most judicious treatment of the subject. The camaraderie born out of the fierce battles waged by this vanguard organization is reflected in the insightful accounts offered by three former staff members: James Forman (executive secretary), *The Making of Black Revolutionaries*, Macmillan, New York, 1972; Cleveland Sellers (program director), with Robert Terrell, *The River of No Return: The Autobiography of a Black Militant and the Life and Death of SNCC*, William Morrow, New York, 1973; and Mary King (assistant communications director), *Freedom Song: A Personal Story of the 1960s Civil Rights Movement*, William Morrow, New York, 1987. Joe Sinsheimer, "Never Turn Back: An Interview With Sam Block," *Southern Exposure*, 15 (Summer 1987): 37–50, furnishes a poignant firsthand account from a SNCC organizer from Mississippi. On CORE, see Meier and Rudwick, *CORE* (cited for Chapter 1), the standard work on the subject. James Farmer, *Lay Bare the Heart: An Autobiography of the Civil Rights Movement*, Arbor House, New York, 1985, provides a moving account of the organization and its operation from the perspective of one of its founders. The NAACP still has not been the focus of a scholarly monograph for the years since World War II. However, this period is seen through the eyes of its executive director, Roy Wilkins, in his memoir, *Standing Fast* (cited for Chapter 2).

The performance of the Kennedy administration is rated very highly in Carl Brauer, *John F. Kennedy and the Second Reconstruction*, Columbia University Press, New York, 1977. Another favorable study of Kennedy, by his chief civil rights adviser, can be found in Harris Wofford, *Of Kennedys and Kings: Making Sense of the Sixties*, Farrar, Straus & Giroux, New York, 1980. A sensitive portrayal, it describes the difficulties a civil rights advocate close to

Martin Luther King, Jr., faced in trying to shape government policy. Much more critical of the Kennedy administration are Victor Navasky, *Kennedy Justice*, Atheneum, New York, 1971, a trenchant analysis of the Justice Department, and Pat Watters and Reese Cleghorn, *Climbing Jacob's Ladder: The Arrival of Negroes in Southern Politics*, Harcourt, Brace, & World, New York, 1967, which finds Kennedy's implementation of voting rights programs sadly lacking. A balanced and mildly critical assessment of the Kennedy administration's handling of the desegregation of interstate transportation appears in Barnes, *Journey from Jim Crow* (cited for Chapter 1). A comparison of the styles and accomplishments of Kennedy and Johnson in furnishing presidential leadership is offered by Tom Wicker, *JFK and LBJ: The Influence of Personality Upon Politics*, Penguin, Baltimore, 1970. The political maneuvering behind the enactment of the 1964 civil rights law is detailed in Charles Whalen and Barbara Whalen, *The Longest Debate: A Legislative History of the 1964 Civil Rights Act*, New American Library, New York, 1986. I have previously reviewed the literature and historiographical opportunities for research on Johnson's civil rights policies in "Civil Rights," in *Exploring the Johnson Years*, Robert A. Divine, ed. University of Texas Press, Austin, Tex., 1981: 93–125.

The struggle of black Mississippians for political liberation is best analyzed by John Dittmer, "The Politics of the Mississippi Movement, 1954–1964," in *The Civil Rights Movement in America*, Charles W. Eagles, ed. University Press of Mississippi, Jackson, Miss., 1986: 65–93. The same volume includes comments on Dittmer's essay by Neil McMillen as well as essays and commentaries on various aspects of the freedom struggle. Joseph Sinsheimer, "COFO and the 1963 Freedom Vote: New Strategies for Change in Mississippi," *Journal of Southern History* 55 (May 1989): 217–244, perceptively discusses community organizing and political development surrounding the conduct of symbolic mock elections. These activities set the stage for the 1964 Mississippi Freedom Summer. The events of that campaign and its impact on the volunteers is analyzed from a sociological perspective in Doug McAdam, *Freedom Summer*, Oxford University Press, New York, 1988. The strains placed on black and white workers are described by Allen J. Matusow, "From Civil Rights to Black Power: The Case of SNCC, 1960–1966," in *Twentieth-Century America: Recent Interpretations*, Barton J. Bernstein and Allen J. Matusow, eds., Harcourt,

Brace, Jovanovich, New York, 1972: 494–519. Elizabeth Sutherland, ed., *Letters from Mississippi*, McGraw-Hill, New York, 1965 compiles the writings of the highly reflective summer participants. The challenge at the Democratic convention, which climaxed Freedom Summer, is documented and analyzed in Leslie Burl McLemore, "The Mississippi Freedom Democratic Party: A Case Study of Grass-Roots Politics," Ph.D. diss. (University of Massachusetts, 1971). For a listing of a variety of works on the same subject, see Jennifer McDowell and Milton Loventhall, eds., *Black Politics: A Study and Annotated Bibliography of the Mississippi Freedom Democratic Party*, Center for the Study of Political Science, San Jose, Calif., 1971. The legal response by the Johnson administration to the widespread brutality against the summer workers, including the murder of three of them in Philadelphia, Mississippi, receives critical treatment in Michal Belknap, *Federal Law and Southern Order: Racial Violence and Constitutional Conflict in the Post-Brown South*, University of Georgia Press, Athens, Ga., 1987. The strategy of President Johnson and the Democratic party in dealing with the black vote in 1964 is the topic of an unpublished essay by Mark Stern of the political science department of the University of Central Florida: "The 1964 Presidential Election: Partisan Shifts and the Southern Black Vote," in my possession.

The continuing story of the Tuskegee struggle appears in Robert J. Norrell, *Reaping the Whirlwind* (cited for Chapter 2). Some useful data on Birmingham is furnished by Harry Holloway, *Politics of the Southern Negro* (cited for Chapter 2). The diverse relationships between civil rights activists and southern white business leaders in fourteen communities are discussed in original essays prepared for a volume edited by Elizabeth Jacoway and David R. Colburn, *Southern Businessmen and Desegregation*, Louisiana State University Press, Baton Rouge, 1982. Colburn has also written a book-length study that ably traces the origins of a community's struggle and the impact the civil rights movement had upon it in *Racial Change and Community Crisis: St. Augustine, Florida, 1877–1980*, Columbia University Press, New York, 1985.

CHAPTER 4

The voting rights struggle in Selma is detailed in Garrow, *Protest at Selma*; Fairclough, *To Redeem the Soul of America*; Forman, *Mak-

ing of Black Revolutionaries; Zinn, *SNCC*; and Clayborne Carson, *In Struggle* (all cited for Chapter 3). The local actors and politics of the Selma movement are fleshed out in Charles E. Fager, *Selma, 1965*, Charles Scribner's Sons, New York, 1974; J. Mills Thornton, "Municipal Politics and the Course of the Civil Rights Movement" (paper delivered at the Conference on New Directions in Civil Rights Studies, University of Virginia, May 1988); Stephen L. Longenecker, *Selma's Peacemaker: Ralph Smeltzer and Civil Rights Mediation*, Temple University Press, Philadelphia, 1987; Sheyanne Webb and Rachel West Nelson, *Selma, Lord, Selma*, University of Alabama Press, University, Ala., 1980; and from interviews contained in Williams, *Eyes on the Prize*, and Raines, *My Soul Is Rested* (cited for Chapter 3). The legal precedents leading to passage of the Voting Rights Act and the legislative battle itself are discussed in Charles V. Hamilton, *The Bench and the Ballot: Southern Federal Judges and Black Voters*, Oxford University Press, New York, 1973; Lawson, *Black Ballots* (cited for Chapter 1); and in President Lyndon B. Johnson's memoirs, *The Vantage Point: Perspectives of the Presidency, 1963–1969*, Holt Rinehart Winston, New York, 1971. For similar conclusions about the federal government's caution in implementing the 1965 law, see my *In Pursuit of Power: Southern Blacks and Electoral Politics, 1965–1982*, Columbia University Press, New York, 1985, and Howard Ball, Dale Krane, and Thomas P. Lauth, *Compromised Compliance: Implementation of the 1965 Voting Rights Act*, Greenwood Press, Westport, Conn., 1982. Mary King's *Freedom Song* (cited for Chapter 3) notes the nontangible rewards of political organizing.

The development of black power and its theoretical application to electoral strategies in the South appear in the classic work of Stokely Carmichael and Charles V. Hamilton, *Black Power: The Politics of Liberation in America*, Vintage Books, New York, 1967. Matusow, "From Civil Rights to Black Power" (cited for Chapter 3), places the issue in historical perspective and offers a critique of the approach. Joyce Ladner, a sociologist and SNCC veteran, offers very useful insights into different conceptions of black power in "What Black Power Means to Negroes in Mississippi," in *The Transformation of Activism*, August Meier, ed. Aldine, Chicago, 1970: 131–154. For examinations into the effects of racial awareness on black voting behavior, see Sidney Verba, Norman Nie, and Jae-on Kim, *Participation and Political Equality*, Cambridge University Press, Cambridge, Engl., 1978, and Richard D. Shingles, "Black Consciousness and Political Participation: The Missing Link," *American Political Science Review*, 75 (1981): 76–91. The Meredith march, during which the slogan of black power was first publicized, is treated in Milton Viorst, *Fire in the Streets: America in the 1960s*, Simon & Schuster, New York, 1979; Cleveland Sellers, with Robert Terrell, *The River of No Return*; Carson, *In Struggle*; David Garrow, *Bearing the Cross: Martin Luther King, Jr., and the Southern Christian Leadership Conference* (all cited for Chapter 3); and Lawson, *Pursuit of Power*. Martin Luther King, *Where Do We Go from Here?: Community or Chaos*, Harper & Row, New York, 1967 offers a sensitive account by one of the central participants in the march about the controversy over black power. The comment of Malcolm X on the use of the ballot is quoted in Manning Marable, *Race, Reform, and Rebellion: The Second Reconstruction in Black America, 1945–1982*, University Press of Mississippi, Jackson, Miss., 1984, which provides a provocative and informative synthesis of the larger black freedom struggle.

Case studies of black power in operation in southern politics are found in works dealing with Lowndes County, Alabama, and Hancock County, Georgia. For the former see Hardy T. Frye, *Black Parties and Political Power: A Case Study*, G. K. Hall, Boston, 1980; Andrew Kopkind, "The Lair of the Black Panther," *New Republic*, 155 (June 18, 1966): 10–13; Kopkind, "Lowndes County, Alabama: The Great Fear Is Gone," *Ramparts*, 13 (April 1975): 8–12; and John Corry, "A Visit to Lowndes County, Alabama," *New South*, 27 (Winter 1972): 28–36. On Hancock County, see the critical account by John Rozier, *Black Boss: Political Revolution in a Georgia County*, University of Georgia Press, Athens, Ga., 1982, and the more favorable scholarly appraisal by Lawrence J. Hanks, *The Struggle for Black Political Empowerment in Three Georgia Counties*, University of Tennessee Press, Knoxville, Tenn., 1987. Firsthand accounts of the efforts of black candidates to gain office are compiled in Julian Bond, ed., *Black Candidates: Southern Campaign Experiences*, Voter Education Project, Atlanta, Ga., 1968. William M. Simpson, "The 'Loyalist' Democrats of Mississippi: Challenge to a White Majority, 1965–1972," Ph.D. diss. (Mississippi State University, 1974), describes the transformation of the insurgent movement in the Magnolia State. For case studies of successful black political organizing and campaigning in Mississippi, see Minion K. C. Morrison, *Black Political Mobilization: Leadership, Power, and Mass Behavior*, State University of New York Press, Albany, 1987. The efforts of the Democratic party to increase minority access to its affairs are detailed in William J. Crotty, *Decision for the Democrats: Reforming the Party Structure*, Johns Hopkins University Press, Baltimore, 1979, and Byron E. Shafer, *Quiet Revolution: The Struggle for the Democratic Party and the Shaping of Post-Reform Politics*, Russell Sage Foundation, New York, 1983.

The subjects of black power, the ghetto explosions, and the white backlash are dealt with in Joe R. Feagin and Harlan Hahn, *Ghetto Revolts*, Macmillan, New York, 1973; James W. Button, *Black Violence: Political Impact of the 1960s Riots*, Princeton University Press, Princeton, N.J., 1978; and Marshall Frady, *Wallace*, New American Library, New York, 1975. Robert H. Wiebe, "White Attitudes and Black Rights from *Brown* to *Bakke*," in *Have We Overcome?*, Michael V. Namorato, ed., University Press of Mississippi, Jackson, Miss., 1979: 147–171, discusses the changing shape of white public opinion during this period. The story of the Black Panther party from the perspective of its leaders is told in Huey P. Newton, with J. Herman Blake, *Revolutionary Suicide*, Harcourt Brace Jovanovich, New York, 1973; Bobby Seale, *Seize the Time*, Random House, New York, 1970; and Robert Scheer, ed., *Eldridge Cleaver: Post-Prison Writing and Speeches*, Random House, New York, 1969. The Ocean Hill–Brownsville controversy is detailed in Diane Ravitch, *The Great School Wars*, Basic Books, New York, 1974; Robert G. Weisbrot and Arthur Stein, *Bittersweet Encounter: The Afro-American and the Jew*, Negro Universities Press, Westport, Conn., 1970; and Jonathan Kaufman, *Broken Alliance*, Charles Scribner's Sons, New York, 1988. Henry Hampton and Steve Fayer with Sarah Flynn, *Voices of Freedom*, Bantam, New York, 1990, contains an oral history of the school crisis. Allen Matusow, *The Unraveling of America: A History of Liberalism in the 1960s*, Harper & Row, New York, 1984, and Todd Gitlin, *The Sixties: Years of Hope, Days of Rage*, Bantam, New York, 1987, comment on the influence of the Panthers on white radicals. Philip S. Foner, ed., *The Black Panther Speaks*, Lippincott, Philadelphia, 1970, provides a documentary collection of the organization. The complex history of the Detroit uprising is told in painstaking detail and in balanced fashion in Sidney Fine, *Violence in the Model City: Race Relations, the Cavanagh Administration, and the Detroit Race Riot of 1967*, University of Michigan Press, Ann Arbor, Mich., 1989. On the efforts against Julian Bond and Adam Clayton Powell, see John Neary, *Julian Bond: Black Rebel*, Morrow, New York, 1971; Andy Jacobs, *The Powell Affair, Freedom Minus One*, Bobbs-Merrill, Indianapolis, 1973; Kent M. Weeks, *Adam Clayton Powell and the Supreme Court*, Dunellen, New York, 1971; and P. Allan Dionesopoulos, *Rebellion, Racism, and Representation: The Adam Clayton Powell Case and Its Antecedents*, Northern Illinois University Press, De Kalb, Ill., 1970.

The election of 1968 is covered in Lewis Chester, Godfrey Hodgson, and Bruce Page, *An American Melodrama*, Dell, New York, 1969, and William L. O'Neill, *Coming Apart: An Informal History of America in the 1960s*, Quadrangle, New York, 1971. The changing outlines of southern politics, especially the drift toward presidential Republicanism, are portrayed in a number of impressive works by political scientists. See Earl Black and Merle Black, *Politics and Society in the South*, Harvard University Press, Cambridge, Mass., 1987; Alexander P. Lamis, *The Two-Party South*, Oxford University Press, New York, 1984; and Harold W. Stanley, *Voter Mobilization and the Politics of Race: The South and Universal Suffrage, 1952–1984*, Praeger, New York, 1987. Two historians who have provided a sophisticated examination of evolving political trends in Dixie are Numan V. Bartley and Hugh D. Graham, *Southern Politics and the Second Reconstruction*, Johns Hopkins University Press, Baltimore, 1975. Each of these works owes a great debt to V. O. Key's classic, *Southern Politics in State and Nation*, Vintage Books, New York, 1949. Monroe Lee Billington, *The Political South in the Twentieth Century*, Charles Scribner's Sons, New York, 1975, is a useful text for historical background on the changes that have taken place. Jody Carlson, *George C. Wallace and the Politics of Powerlessness*, Transaction Books, New Brunswick, N.J., 1981, analyzes the Wallace campaigns for the presidency from 1964 to 1976.

On the Nixon administration, consult the President's own account, *RN: The Memoirs of Richard Nixon*, Grosset & Dunlop, New York, 1978, as well as the work of one of his chief political aides who dealt with the South, Harry S. Dent, *The Prodigal South Returns to Power*, John Wiley, New York, 1978. More negative assessments of Nixon's performance are found in Richard Harris, *Justice: The Crisis of Law, Order, and Freedom in America*, Dutton, New York, 1970; Leon E. Panetta and Peter Gall, *Bring Us Together: The Nixon Team and the Civil Rights Retreat*, Lippincott, Philadelphia, 1971; William E. Leuchtenburg, "The White House and Black America: From Eisenhower to Carter," in *Have We Overcome?* Namorato, ed., 121–145; and my *In Pursuit of Power* and "E Pluribus Unum: Civil Rights and National Unity," in *American Choices: Social Dilemmas and Public Policy Since 1960*, Robert H. Bremner, Gary W. Reichard, and Richard J. Hopkins, eds. Ohio State University Press, Columbus, Ohio, 1986: 35–73. Gary Orfield, *Congressional Power: Congress and Social Change*, Harcourt Brace Jovanovich, New York, 1975, offers a sharp appraisal of the 1970 Voting Rights Act extension.

The efforts to form independent black political interest groups have received some treatment. Marguerite Ross Barnett, "The Congressional Black Caucus: Illusions and Realities of Power," in *The New Black Politics: The Search for Political Power*: 28–55, Preston, Henderson, and Puryear, eds. (cited for Chapter 1), offers a useful overview of the operation of black congressional lawmakers. A wide variety of organizational attempts are described by Martin Kilson, "The New Black Political Class," in *Dilemmas of the New Black Middle Class*, Joseph R. Washington, ed. (n.p., 1980): 81–100. The Gary convention is discussed in Marable, *Race, Reform, and Rebellion*; Vincent Harding, *The Other American Revolution*, Center for Afro-American Studies, University of California, Los Angeles, 1981; and Ronald W. Walters, *Black Presidential Politics in America: A Strategic Approach*, State University of New York, Albany, 1988. The early years of the Joint Center for Political Studies are recounted by Alex Poinsett, "'The Joint': D.C. Center for Political Studies Backs Up Elected Officials," *Ebony*, 28 (April 1973): 124–132.

CHAPTER 5

Bayard Rustin's challenging analysis appears in "From Protest to Politics: The Future of the Civil Rights Movement," *Commentary*,

39 (February 1965): 25–31. On the transition of blacks from protesters to candidates, see my *In Pursuit of Power* and Bond, *Black Candidates*, which are cited for Chapter 4; Ladd, *Negro Leadership* (cited for Chapter 1); Albert K. Karnig and Susan Welch, *Black Representation and Urban Policy*, University of Chicago Press, Chicago, 1980; Chuck Stone, *Black Political Power in America*, Dell, New York, 1970; Jason Berry, *Amazing Grace: With Charles Evers in Mississippi*, Saturday Review Press, New York, 1973; Leonard A. Cole, *Blacks in Power: A Comparative Study of Black and White Elected Officials*, Princeton University Press, Princeton, N.J., 1976; Lester M. Salamon, "Leadership and Modernization: The Emerging Black Political Elite in the American South," *Journal of Politics*, 35 (August 1973): 615–646; Robert C. Smith, "The Changing Shape of Urban Black Politics, 1960–1970," *The Annals of the American Academy of Political and Social Science*, 439 (September 1978): 16–28; Paul Jeffrey Steckler, "Electing Black Candidates to Office in the South," *The Urban Lawyer*, 17 (Summer 1985): 473–487; Jack Bass and Walter DeVries, *The Transformation of Southern Politics: Social Change and Political Consequence Since 1945*, Basic Books, New York, 1976; Bette Woody, *Managing Crisis Cities: The New Black Leadership and the Politics of Resource Allocation*, Greenwood Press, Westport, Conn., 1982; and Martin Kilson, "Political Change in the Negro Ghetto, 1900–1940's," in *Key Issues in the Afro-American Experience*, vol. 2, Nathan I. Huggins, Martin Kilson, and Daniel Fox, eds. Harcourt Brace Jovanovich, New York, 1971: 167–192. The politics of the Community Action Program of the War on Poverty are discussed in Matusow, *The Unraveling of America* (cited for Chapter 4). For a profile of Tuskegee's Johnny Ford, see Marshall Frady, *Southerners: A Journalistic Odyssey*, New American Library, New York, 1980.

The best overview of the issue of at-large versus single-member district elections is provided by the essays contained in Chandler Davidson, ed., *Minority Vote Dilution*, Howard University Press, Washington, D.C., 1984. The Washington Research Project, *The Shameful Blight: The Survival of Racial Discrimination in Voting in the South*, Washington Research Project, Washington, D.C., 1972, catalogues the sundry forms of franchise abuse that persisted after passage of the Voting Rights Act. For the argument that the federal government has exceeded statutory and constitutional boundaries in seeking to maximize minority voting strength by applying affirmative action principles, see Abigail M. Thernstrom, *Whose Votes Count? Affirmative Action and Minority Voting Rights*, Harvard University Press, Cambridge, Mass., 1987, and Katharine I. Butler, "Denial or Abridgement of the Right to Vote: What Does It Mean?" in *The Voting Rights Act: Consequences and Implications*, Lorn S. Foster, ed. Praeger, New York, 1985: 44–59.

The performance of black elected officials is discussed and evaluated in Hanks, *Black Empowerment* (cited for Chapter 4); Margaret Edds, *Free At Last: What Really Happened When Civil Rights Came to Southern Politics*, Adler & Adler, Bethesda, Md., 1987; Peter K. Eisinger, *The Politics of Displacement: Racial and Ethnic Transition in Three American Cities*, Academic Press, New York, 1980; Rufus P. Browning, Dale Rogers Marshall, and David H. Tabb, *Protest Is Not Enough: The Struggle of Blacks and Hispanics for Equality in Urban Politics*, University of California Press, Berkeley, Calif., 1984; James W. Button, *Blacks and Social Change*, Princeton University Press, Princeton, 1989; and Paul Jeffrey Stekler, "Black Politics in the New South: An Investigation of Change at Various Levels," Ph.D. diss. (Harvard University, 1982). The black middle class has received extensive treatment in L. Bart Landry, *The New Black Middle Class*, University of California Press, Berkeley, Calif., 1987, and the underclass has been analyzed by William Julius Wilson, *The Truly Disadvantaged: The Inner City, the Underclass, and Public Policy*, University of Chicago Press, Chicago, 1987.

There remains to be written a systematic study of the role of black women in the civil rights movement and electoral politics. The best place to obtain data on black female officeholders is the Joint Center of Political Studies, *The National Roster of Black Elected Officials*, published annually. The center started keeping statistics on black women officeholders in 1975. Other sources of useful information are Susan M. Hartmann, *From Margin to Mainstream: American Women and Politics Since 1960*, Knopf, New York, 1989; Paula Giddings, *When and Where I Enter: The Impact of Black Women on Race and Sex in America*, Bantam, New York, 1984; and Sara Evans, *Personal Politics: The Roots of Women's Liberation in the Civil Rights Movement and the New Left*, Vintage, New York, 1980. For a discussion and analysis of Unita Blackwell, see Minion K. C. Morrison, *Black Political Mobilization* (cited for Chapter 4).

Mack H. Jones, "Black Political Empowerment in Atlanta: Myth and Reality," *The Annals of the American Academy of Political and Social Science*, 439 (September 1978): 90–117, offers a critical assessment of the impact of black mayors in Atlanta; and Edds, *Free At Last*, and Eisinger, *The Politics of Displacement*, provide more favorable evaluations. For background on Maynard Jackson, see Fred Powledge, "Profiles: A New Politics In Atlanta," *New Yorker*, 49 (December 31, 1973): 28–40, and Peter Ross Range, "Capital of Black-Is-Beautiful," *New York Times Magazine*, April 7, 1974, 28–29, 68–78. Edds, *Free At Last*, and Robert J. Norrell, *Reaping the Whirlwind* (cited for Chapter 2) offer complementary and balanced views on Tuskegee and Macon County. The discussions of Cleveland and Gary are based largely on the thorough case study by William E. Nelson, Jr., and Philip J. Meranto, *Electing Black Mayors: Political Action in the Black Community*, Ohio State University Press, Columbus, Ohio, 1977. For additional information on Cleveland, see Kenneth G. Weinberg, *Black Victory: Carl Stokes and the Winning of Cleveland*, Quadrangle, Chicago, 1968. On other victorious mayors, see Wilbur C. Rich, *Coleman Young and Detroit Politics*, Wayne State University Press, Detroit, 1989, which is a favorable if uneven treatment. It can be supplemented by Fine, *Violence in the Model City* (cited for Chapter 4); Eisinger, *The Politics of Displacement*; and Korstad and Lichtenstein, "Opportunities Found and Lost" (cited for Chapter 1). Tom Bradley has yet to find a scholarly biographer, but background information can be compiled from the sketch in *Current Biography* (1973): 53–55. Appearing too late to be helpful in this study but nonetheless useful for others to consult is Jimmie Lewis Franklin, *Back to Birmingham: Richard Arrington, Jr., and His Times*, University of Alabama Press, Tuscaloosa, 1989.

CHAPTER 6

President Ford offers his version of his efforts to work with blacks in *A Time to Heal*, Harper & Row, New York, 1979. He does not, however, explain his maneuvering on the Voting Rights Act extension. I examine the renewal of that legislation in my book *In Pursuit of Power* (cited for Chapter 4). Jack Bass and Walter DeVries, *The Transformation of Southern Politics*, as cited for Chapter 5, provides valuable data on the shift in southern Democratic support for the suffrage act. A thorough review of various aspects of the busing controversy is furnished by Gary Orfield, *Must We Bus? Segregated Schools and National Policy*, Brookings Institution, Washington, D.C., 1978. A comprehensive and eloquent treatment of the Boston struggle from the perspective of three diverse families is J. Anthony Lukas, *Common Ground*, Knopf, New York, 1985. In contrast with Boston, efforts to desegregate the schools through busing went more smoothly in Charlotte, North Carolina, and this story is chronicled in Frye Gaillard, *The Dream Long Deferred*, University of North Carolina Press, Chapel Hill, N.C., 1988.

On the 1976 presidential election and the political mood of African-Americans, see Elizabeth Drew, *American Journal: The Events of 1976*, Random House, New York, 1977; Samuel DuBois Cook, "Democracy and Tyranny in America: The Radical Paradox of the Bicentennial and Blacks in the American Political System," *Journal of Politics*, 38 (August 1976): 276–294; Kandy Straud, *How Jimmy Won: The Victory Campaign from Plains to the White House*, Morrow, New York, 1977; Jules Witcover, *Marathon: The Pursuit of the Presidency, 1972–1976*, Viking Press, New York, 1977; and the Joint Center for Political Studies, *The Black Vote: Election '76*, Joint Center for Political Studies, Washington, D.C., 1977. Barbara Jordan relates her story in her memoir coauthored with Shelby Hearon, *Barbara Jordan: A Self-Portrait*, Doubleday, Garden City, N.Y., 1979. President Carter defends his policies in *Keeping the Faith: Memoirs of a President*, Bantam, New York, 1982. On his gubernatorial record, see the laudatory account of Gary Fink, *Prelude to the Presidency: The Political Character and Legislative Leadership Style of Governor Jimmy Carter*, Greenwood Press, Westport, Conn., 1980. For the presidential years, Betty Glad, *Jimmy Carter: In Search of the Great White House*, Norton, New York, 1980, offers a favorable, but well-balanced, contemporary assessment. Louis Martin, the veteran black journalist, Democratic party operative, and Carter aide offers a glowing comment in "Carter Accomplishments in Civil Rights," *Focus*, 8 (December 1980): 7–8. A highly critical portrayal of Carter's civil rights performance, especially compared to Lyndon Johnson's, from a man who served both presidents is Joseph Califano, *Governing America: An Insider's Report from the White House and the Cabinet*, Simon & Schuster, New York, 1981. The Carter administration's twists and turns on the *Bakke* case are described by Califano and in studies by J. Harvie Wilkinson III, *From Brown to Bakke: The Supreme Court and School Integration 1954–1978*, Oxford University Press, New York, 1981, and Alan P. Sindler, *Bakke, DeFunis, and Minority Admissions: The Quest for Equal Opportunity*, Longman, New York, 1978. Relations between blacks and Jews receive historical treatment in Robert Weisbrot and Arthur Stein, *Bittersweet Encounter* and Weisbrot's *Israel in the Black American Perspective*, Greenwood Press, Westport, Conn., 1985. Jonathan Kaufman, *Broken Alliance* (cited for Chapter 4), is a sensitive work by a journalist focusing on the people involved in several of the episodes that heightened tensions between the two groups.

The rise of Ronald Reagan to the presidency is lucidly portrayed by the *Washington Post* columnist Lou Cannon in *Reagan*, Putnam, New York, 1982. Details of black voting in the 1980 elections are furnished in Milton Morris, "Blacks and the 1980 Presidential Election," *Focus* (October–November 1980): 3–4, 8. Critical evaluations of the Reagan administration's performance on equal opportunity and affirmative action programs are contained in Harrell R. Rodgers, Jr., "Fair Employment Laws for Minorities: An Evaluation of Federal Implementation," in *Implementation of Civil Rights Policy*, Charles S. Bullock III and Charles M. Lamb, eds. Brooks/Cole Publishing, Monterey, Calif., 1984: 93–117; Hanes Walton, *When the Marching Stopped: The Politics of Civil Rights Regulatory Agencies*, State University of New York Press, Albany, 1988; and Tinsley Yarbrough, "The Reagan Administration, the IRS, and Discriminatory Private Schools" (paper presented at Southern Political Science Association annual meeting, Birmingham, Ala., 1983). The Eddie Williams quote on the importance of the vote to counteract Reagan's budget-slashing effects on the poor appears in "Perspective," *Focus*, 9 (May 1981): 2. I trace the events surrounding renewal of the Voting Rights Act in 1982 in my *In Pursuit of Power*. For different views of the Reagan administration's enforcement of the landmark suffrage law, compare Frank Parker, "Retreat on Voting Rights?" *Focus*, 14 (May 1986): 4–5, 7, and Abigail M. Thernstrom, "Voting Rights' Trap," *New Republic*, 193 (September 2, 1985): 21–23, as well as her *Whose Votes Count? Affirmative Action and Minority Voting Rights* (cited for Chapter 5). The economic crisis among blacks and the growing class distinctions are reviewed in "The State of the Union: One Nation or Two?" *Focus*, 10 (March 1982): 6; Andrew F. Brimmer, "Black Economic Progress," *Focus*, 13 (April 1985): 6, 8; and Andrew Hacker, "American Apartheid," *New York Review of Books* (December 3, 1987): 26–33. A discussion of black neoconservatives appears in Salim Muwakkil, "New Issues Reviving Dominant Arguments," *In These Times* (November 13–19, 1985): 3, 6. Thomas Sowell, *Race and Economics*, D. McKay Co., New York, 1975, and his *Civil Rights: Rhetoric or Reality?*, Morrow, New York, 1984, are two of the most notable works that reflect the thinking of black conservatives.

The Chicago mayoral election has already captured a good deal of scholarly investigation. For a background of black politics in Chicago, see the classic, James Q. Wilson, *Negro Politics: The Search For Leadership*, Free Press, New York, 1965. A more recent account that challenges Wilson's model of black political behavior is Dianne M. Pinderhughes, *Race and Ethnicity in Chicago Politics: A Reexamination of Pluralist Theory*, University of Illinois Press, Urbana, Ill., 1987. David Garrow, *Bearing the Cross: Martin Luther King and the Voting Rights Act of 1965* (cited for Chapter 3), and Alan B. Anderson and George W. Pickering, *Confronting the Color Line: The Broken Promise of the Civil Rights Movement in Chicago*, University of Georgia Press, Athens, Ga., 1986, offer accounts of Martin Luther King's campaigns for open housing and the grassroots struggle for racial equality in Chicago during the 1960s. William J. Grimshaw, *Black Politics in Chicago: The Quest for Leadership, 1939–1979*, Center for Urban Policy, Loyola University, Chicago, 1980, briefly surveys black politicians and their changing relationship to the Democratic political machine. A first-hand account by an opponent of the Daley machine appears in Anna R. Langford, "How I 'Whupped' the Tar Out of the Daley Machine," in *What Black Politicians Are Saying*, Nathan Wright, Jr., ed. Hawthorn Books, New York, 1972: 3–31. On the election of Harold Washington, the most reliable account is Paul Kleppner, *Chicago Divided: The Making of a Black Mayor*, Northern Illinois University Press, De Kalb, Ill., 1985. Other useful works on this subject are Abdul Alkalimat, "Mayor Washington's Bid for Re-election," *Black Scholar*, 17 (November/December 1986): 2–39; Alkalimat and Doug Gills, "Black Power vs. Racism: The Election of Harold Washington," in *The New Black Vote: A Look at Four American Cities*, Rod Bush, ed. Synthesis Publications, San Francisco, 1984: 55–179; Michael Preston, "The Election of Harold Washington: Black Voting Patterns in the 1983 Chicago Mayoral Race," *PS*, 16 (Summer 1983): 486–488; Twiley W. Barker, "Political Mobilization of Black Chicago: Drafting a Candidate," *PS*, 16 (Summer 1983): 482–485; Manning Marable, "Harold Washington and the Politics of Race in Chicago," *Black Scholar*, 17 (November/December 1986): 14–23; Thomas E. Cavanagh, "How Washington Won Chicago," *Focus*, 11 (May 1983): 3, 7–8; David Moberg, "Washington Learns that Reform Comes Slowly," *In These Times* (January 28–February 3, 1987): 12–13; and Gerald McWorter, Doug Gills, and Ron Bailey, "Black Power Politics as Social Movement: Dialectics of Leadership in the Campaign to Elect Harold Washington Mayor of Chicago" (Afro-American Studies and Research Program, University of Illinois, June 1984). A very handy compilation of newspaper clippings and other sources related to the election can be found in Peoples College Press, *Black Power in Chicago: A Documentary Survey of the 1983 Mayoral Democratic Primary*, Chicago, 1983.

On the upsurge in black voter participation in the early 1980s, see Gracia M. Hillman, "Operation Big Vote: Crusade '82 Begins," *Focus*, 12 (January 1984): 8; "Largest Increases in BEOs Since 1976," *Focus*, 12 (January 1984): 8; and Adolph L. Reed, Jr., *The Jesse Jackson Phenomenon: The Crisis of Purpose in Afro-American Politics*, Yale University Press, New Haven, Conn., 1986. Harvey Gantt details his career and political philosophy in Laura Haessley, "We're Becoming the Mayors," *Southern Exposure*, 14 (March/April 1986): 44–52.

CHAPTER 7

The issue of legitimacy is discussed in Peter K. Eisinger, *The Politics of Displacement* (cited for Chapter 5). The importance of the presidency as a symbol of political legitimacy is noted from a critical perspective by Mack H. Jones, "A Black Presidential Candidate in

1984: More of the Same," *PS*, 16 (Summer 1983): 495–496, and from a more positive viewpoint by Lucius J. Barker, "Black Americans and the Politics of Inclusion," *PS*, 16 (Summer 1983): 500–507. Shirley Chisholm, *Unbought and Unbossed*, Avon Books, New York, 1971, is an autobiographical account of the Brooklyn lawmaker's political career before her unsuccessful campaign for the presidency, which she writes about in *The Good Fight*, Harper & Row, New York, 1973. On that race, see Stephan Lesher, "The Short, Unhappy Life of Black Presidential Politics, 1972," *New York Times Magazine*, June 25, 1972, 12–22. It is still too soon to have a first-rate biography of Jesse Jackson, but until one appears there are several helpful works on the subject. Unfortunately, most of these reflect the highly charged views that divide opinion about him. Barbara A. Reynolds, *Jesse Jackson: The Man, the Movement, the Myth*, Nelson-Hall, Chicago, 1975, offers much detail about Jackson's life and generally portrays the minister in an unflattering light. However, the author's negative conclusions apparently underwent modification in the wake of Jackson's bid for the presidency. Reynolds republished the book with a different title, *Jesse Jackson: America's David*, JFJ Associates, Washington, D.C., 1985, and although the text remains the same, she added a new introduction much more sympathetic to her subject. Thomas H. Landess and Richard M. Quinn, *Jesse Jackson and the Politics of Race*, Jameson Books, Ottawa, Ill., 1985, draws heavily on the Reynolds account to reach unfavorable conclusions about Jackson personally and professionally. A more scholarly but no less critical analysis of Jackson's attempt to jump from protest to electoral politics is presented by Adolph L. Reed, Jr., *The Jesse Jackson Phenomenon* (cited for Chapter 6). A more balanced account, by two reporters who covered Jackson's 1984 campaign, appears in Bob Faw and Nancy Skelton, *Thunder in America*, Texas Monthly Press, Austin, 1986. Elizabeth O. Colton, Jackson's press secretary, who resigned during the campaign, offers an inside account of the 1988 presidential bid that is critical of the candidate's personality but recognizes the importance of his cause [see *The Jackson Phenomenon: The Man, the Power, the Message*, Doubleday, New York, 1989]. The most sympathetic treatments of the Jackson bid are found in the wide-ranging work of a campaign aide, Sheila D. Collins, *The Rainbow Challenge: The Jackson Campaign and the*

Future of U.S. Politics, Monthly Review Press, New York, 1986, and of a scholar–Democratic convention delegate, Lucius J. Barker, *Our Time Has Come: A Delegate's Diary of Jesse Jackson's 1984 Presidential Campaign*, University of Illinois Press, Urbana, Ill., 1988. The participation of black voters in the primaries and general elections is analyzed in a series of publications sponsored by the Joint Center for Political Studies, Washington, D.C.: Thomas E. Cavanagh, *The Impact of the Black Electorate* (1984); Thomas E. Cavanagh and Lorn S. Foster, *Jesse Jackson's Campaign: The Primaries and Caucuses*, (1984); and Thomas E. Cavanagh, *Inside Black America: The Message of the Black Vote in the 1984 Elections* (1985). Hardy T. Frye, "Jesse Jackson and the Rainbow," *Socialist Review*, 17 (March-April, 1987): 55–80, and Marguerite Ross Barnett, "The Strategy Over a Black Presidential Candidacy," *PS*, 16 (Summer 1983): 489–491, provide an understanding of the divisions within black leadership circles on support for Jackson. The most recent collections of scholarly analyses of the Jackson campaign and its impact are Robert P. Steed, Laurence W. Moreland, and Tod A. Baker, eds., *The 1984 Presidential Election in the South: Patterns of Southern Party Politics*, Praeger, New York, 1986, in which see especially Harold W. Stanley, "The 1984 Presidential Election in the South: Race and Realignment," 303–335, for a summary conclusion; Laurence W. Moreland, Robert P. Steed, and Tod A. Baker, eds., *Blacks in Southern Politics*, Praeger, New York, 1987; and Lucius J. Barker and Ronald W. Walters, eds., *Jesse Jackson's 1984 Presidential Campaign: Challenge and Change in American Politics*, University of Illinois Press, Urbana, Ill., 1989.

The Reagan administration's prosecution of the voter fraud cases in the Alabama black belt is discussed in Margaret Edds, *Free At Last* (cited for Chapter 6); Sheila D. Collins, "Justice Department Undermines Act," *In These Times* (July 10–23, 1985): 5, 22; Allen Tullos, "Voting Rights Activists Acquitted," *Nation* (August 3, 1985): 78–80; and "Vote Fraud on Trial," *Newsweek* (November 25, 1985): 10. The results of the 1986 congressional contests are analyzed in Linda Williams, "1986 Elections: Major Implications for Black Politics," *Focus*, 14 (November-December 1986): 5–7, and Bill Minor, "Congressman Espy from Mississippi," *Southern Changes*, 8 (December 1986): 1–3. The effect of the black electorate on reshaping southern white Democratic politicians is discussed in Earl Black and Merle Black, *Politics and Society in the South*, and Alexander P. Lamis, *The Two-Party South* (both cited for Chapter 4). The increasing competition between black candidates for office and the pivotal balance of power role played by whites is discussed in a paper by Monte Piliawsky and Paul J. Stekler, "The Evolution of Black Politics in New Orleans: From Protest to Powerbrokers," in possession of author.

Information on Jackson's 1988 presidential bid was compiled concurrently with the campaign. Given the contemporary nature of the event, I had to rely on available newspapers and periodicals. Of particular importance in tracking this contest was *Focus*, published by the Joint Center for Political Studies, particularly the section called "Political Trendletter." In addition, from the popular press the following articles are worth noting explicitly: Doug Foster, "Interview with Jesse Jackson: He Thinks He Can Win," *Mother Jones* (October 1987): 27–45, and "Jackson's White Organizers," *Newsweek* (February 8, 1988): 26. In the *Village Voice*: "Jackson's Message" (March 21, 1988): 23–24; "Jackson's Big Takeoff" (April 11, 1988): 22; and Thulani Davis and James Ridgeway, "Jesse Jackson's New Math" (December 22, 1987): 20–25. Also, Joyce Purnick and Michael Oreskes, "Jesse Jackson Aims for the Mainstream," *New York Times Magazine*, November 29, 1987, 28–31, 34–36, 58–61; E. J. Dionne, "Black Residents of New York See a Campaign Tinged with Racism," *New York Times*, April 21, 1988, 12; Anthony Lewis, "The Jackson Reality," *New York Times*, March 31, 1988, A27; David Broder, "Jackson Becomes an Agent for Change," Raleigh *News and Observer*, May 2, 1988, 13A; Andrew Kopkind, "Is Jesse the Great White Hope?" *Nation* (December 26, 1987/January 2, 1988): 773, 790–791; Kopkind, "Jesse's Movement," *Nation* (April 2, 1988): 448–489; "For Jesse Jackson and His Campaign," *Nation* (April 16, 1988): 517, 519–522; and "Bad," *New Republic*, 198 (April 18, 1988): 7–9. The implications of the Willie Horton issue are discussed by Michael Kinsley, "GOP Knew Symbolic Value of a Black Rapist," *Tampa Tribune*, November 5, 1988, 15A. For an academic study published before the Jackson candidacies that is pessimistic about the possibilities of a biracial coalition of the dispossessed in the South to unite politically, see Robert Emil Botsch, *We Shall Not Overcome; Populism and Southern Blue-Collar Workers*, University of North Carolina Press, Chapel Hill, 1980.

CHAPTER 8

The Moses statement comes from a speech to the organizers training center (San Francisco, Calif., June 5, 1987), a copy of which was kindly furnished to me by Joseph Sinsheimer. For a similar point of view by a movement veteran and scholar, see Vincent Harding, *The Other American Revolution* (cited for Chapter 4). For suggestions on options open to black politicians and the electorate in the future, particularly concerning an independent strategy, see Ronald W. Walters, *Black Presidential Politics in America* (cited for Chapter 4); and Lorenzo Morris and Linda F. Williams, "The Coalition at the End of the Rainbow: The 1984 Jackson Campaign," in *Jesse Jackson's 1984 Presidential Campaign*, Barker and Walters, eds. (cited for Chapter 7).

Index

Abernathy, Ralph David, 78, 225
Affirmative action, 140, 161, 167, 211
  and *Bakke* case, 199–200
  and Carter administration, 197–198
  cutback of, 206–207
  views of, 198–199
  and voting, 154–155, 208–209
Afro-American, 104
Alabama, 48–49, 115
Alabama Christian Movement for
    Human Rights, 92
Alexander, Clifford, Jr., 197
*Alexander v. Holmes County Board of
    Education*, 138
Allen, Ivan, 95–96
Amerson, Lucius, 124–125
Amsterdam News, 10, 62
Arafat, Yasser, 202
Arkansas, 127
Arrington, Richard, 159, 203, 231, 233,
    248
Atlanta (GA), 26, 43, 67, 70, 75, 95, 244
  and black mayors, 165–169
Atlanta Constitution, 166
At-large elections, 138–139, 153,
    155–157
Austin, Gerald, 249, 251
Austin, Richard, 179

Baker, Ella, 70–71, 73, 74, 163
Baker, Wilson, 110–111, 127
Bakke, Alan, 199, 200
Baltimore Afro-American, 7
Baraka, Amiri, 142
Barker, Lucius, 235
Barnett, Ross, 94
Barry, Marion, 203
Barthelemy, Sidney, 244

Baton Rouge (Louisiana), 46n, 67, 226
Bayh, Birch, 204
Bell, Griffin, 77
Bensonhurst (Brooklyn), 267, 268
Bentley, Herman, 61
Bentsen, Lloyd, 255, 262
Bilbo, Theodore, 17, 23–25, 34
Birmingham (Alabama), 22, 67, 70,
    144, 247
  demonstrations in, 91–95
Black church, 66–67, 193, 225–226
Black elected officials, 147–149, 187
  barriers to, 152–157
  benefits of, 122, 158–159, 167, 169,
    176, 179, 181, 182
  and civil rights movement, 149,
    151–152, 173
  problems of, 150–151, 159–161,
    167–170, 176, 181–182
  statistics on, 122, 126, 143–144,
    157–158, 162, 163, 181, 203,
    205, 239, 247, 259, (table) 260,
    261
  and women, 162–164, 259, (table)
    260
Black income, 128, 161, 169, 170, 189,
    203, 210–211, (table) 262
Black Leadership Family, 223
Black middle class, 161, 211–212, 244
Black migration, 19, 31–32
Black Muslims (*see* Nation of Islam)
Black nationalism, 3, 118–121, 126,
    129, 131–133, 142, 232
Black Panther Party (BPP), 129–130,
    213
Black power, 117–121, 126
*Black Power: The Politics of Liberation
    in America*, 120

Black representation, 154–155
Black suffrage, 42. *See also* Black
    elected officials, and Voter
    registration
Blackwell, Unita, 164
Block, Sam, 88–89
Bob Jones University, 207
Boggs, Hale, 115
Bond, Julian, 120, 131, 192, 195, 244,
    256
Bork, Robert, 245–246
Boston (MA), 189
Boynton, Amelia P., 108–109, 112,
    144
Bradley, Tom, 180–181
Brady, Tom, 50
Brauer, Carl, 76, 80
Breaux, John, 243
Broder, David, 256
Brooke, Edward, 141, 187, 205
Brown v. Board of Education, 28, 47,
    73
Brown, Lloyd, 7
Brown, Ronald, 257, 259
Brown, Willie, 231, 235, 248, 249
Brownell, Herbert, 56
Burk, Robert F., 51
Bush, George, 257, 258, 260
Busing, 138, 142, 188, 189
Byrne, Jane, 214–216, 218
Byrnes, James F., 41

Caldwell, Arthur, 55
Califano, Joseph, 199–200
Carmichael, Stokely, 118–120, 123,
    129, 147. *See also* Student
    Nonviolent Coordinating
    Committee (SNCC)
Carswell, G. Harrold, 139
Carter, Jimmy, 124, 223, 224
    assessment of, 201
    background of, 190–191
    as governor, 191–192
    as president, 193–195, 196–202
    and reelection attempt (1980),
        203–204
Case of Martin Luther King, The, 78
Cavanagh, Jerome, 179
Cavanagh, Thomas, 239, 244
Chafe, William H., 44, 73
Chaney, James, 99
Charlotte (North Carolina), 220
Chicago (IL), 171–172, 212–219

Chicago Black United Communities,
    215
Chisholm, Shirley, 142, 223, 256
Church, Frank, 204
City of Mobile v. Bolden, 208, 209
Civil Rights Act (1957), 56–58, 62
Civil Rights Act (1960), 63–64
Civil Rights Act (1964), 95, 99, 246
Civil Rights Act (1968), 133
Civil Rights Division, 56, 58
Clark, James G., 107–112, 127
Clark, Robert, 150, 243
Cleaver, Eldridge, 129, 134. *See also*
    Black Panther Party (BPP)
Clement, Rufus E., 43
Cleveland (OH), 173–177
Clifford, Clark, 35, 36
Cobb, Charles, 86
Cold War, 27, 34, 44, 222, 229. *See
    also* Communism
Cole, Ed, 256
Collins, Cardiss, 259
Collins, LeRoy, 113
Communism, 27, 38, 39, 44, 77, 180.
    See also Cold War
Community Action Programs, 149
Comprehensive Employment and
    Training Act (CETA), 184, 211
Congress of Industrial Organizations
    (CIO), 17, 27, 39, 43–44
Congress of Racial Equality (CORE),
    80, 82, 90, 104, 151, 173
    and black power, 118, 121
    creation of, 9
    demise of, 133
    and voter registration, 82, 84
Congressional Black Caucus (CBC),
    140–142, 144, 185, 200–201, 205,
    209, 241, 259
Connor, Eugene "Bull", 91–93
Conyers, John, 179
Cook, Samuel D., 195
Council of Federated Organizations
    (COFO), 90–91, 99–100
Cox, William Harold, 85
Crusade for Citizenship, 70–72. *See
    also* Southern Christian
    Leadership Conference (SCLC)

Daley, Richard J., 213
Daley, Richard M., 216–218, 219n
Dallas County (Alabama), 105, 107,
    109, 116, 127, 234

Dallas County Voters League (DCVL), 108–110, 114. *See also* Selma (Alabama)
Davis, Benjamin O., 13
Dawson, William, 32, 52, (photo) 53, 76, 212
Days, Drew, III, 197, 199, 200
DeFunis v. Odegaard, 199
Democratic party, 193, 230, 265
  and black support, 30, 106, 126, 224, 243, 260
  and defeat of Bork, 245–246
  and presidential election (1948), 36–37
  and presidential election (1956), 54
  and presidential election (1964), 100–104
  and presidential election (1984), 233–236
  and presidential election (1988), 251–253, (table) 254
  and South, 188
  and voter registration, 196
  and white primary, 14–16
  and white voters, 238
Denton, Jeremiah, 240–241
Dershowitz, Alan, 248
Detroit (MI), 128, 179–180
Devine, Annie, (photo) 103
Dewey, Thomas, 37, 38
Diggs, Charles, Jr., 140, 142, 179
Dinkins, David, 266, (photo) 270
  background of, 267
  election of, 269
  expectations of, 269–271
  primary campaign of, 268–269
Dirksen, Everett, 115
Dittmer, John, 102
Doar, John, 90
Dobbs, Mattiwilda, 167
Dole, Robert, 209
Double V, 8. *See also* World War II
Douglas, Paul, 62
Drew, Charles, 6
Du Bois, W. E. B., 1–3, 38
Dukakis, Michael, (photo) 250, 251, 253, 255, 257, 258, 262, 265, 266

Eastland, James, 54, 56, 84, 85, 101
Eisenhower, Dwight D., 77, 78, 104
  assessment of, 51, 64–65
  and Civil Rights Act (1957), 55–58

Eisenhower, Dwight D. (*Cont.*):
  and Civil Rights Act (1960), 63
  and desegregation, 51–52
  election of, 40, 54
  and Prayer Pilgrimage, 68–69
  racial views of, 41, 51
Eisinger, Peter, 162
Elections:
  1940, 13–14
  1944, 14
  1948, 35–39
  1956, 53–55
  1960, 75–79
  1964, 100–104
  1968, 134–136
  1972, 142–143
  1976, 193–196
  1980, 204, (table) 205
  1984, 237–238
  1986, 241, 242–243
  1988, 257–258
Ellender, Allen, 24, 25
Engelhardt, Samuel M., Jr., 61
Epton, Bernard, 217–218
Espy, Mike, 243–244, 259
Evans, Timothy, 219n
Evers, Charles, 126
Evers, Medgar, 26, 95, 125

Fair Employment Practice Committee (FEPC), 9, 12–13, 31
Fairclough, Adam, 68
Farrakhan, Louis, 232, 233, 251
Faubus, Orval, 65n, 232
Fauntroy, Walter, (photo) 227
Federal Bureau of Investigation (FBI), 83, 84–85, 99, 110, 130, 134
Ferraro, Geraldine, 236
Fifteenth Amendment, 15, 16
Florida, 49, 127, 158
Focus, 144
Foner, Eric, 1
Ford, Gerald, 190
  as president, 184–189
  and reelection attempt, 193
Ford, Harold, 144, 187
Ford, Johnny, 150, 151, 169. *See also* Tuskegee (Alabama)
Forman, James, 89, 110. *See also* Student Nonviolent Coordinating Committee (SNCC)
Fourteenth Amendment, 14
Frankfurter, Felix, 62

Franklin, John Hope, 235
Freedom rides, 80–81
Freedom summer (1964), 98–99, 118, 257–258
Freedom vote (1963), 90–91, 98

Gallup Poll, 39–40, 115, 231
Gantt, Harvey, 220–221
Garvey, Marcus, 3
Gary (Indiana), 141, 177–179
Georgia, 17, 115, 127, 159. *See also* Atlanta; Hancock County
Georgia Council on Human Relations, 123
Glad, Betty, 193
Goetz, Bernhard, 267
Goldwater, Barry, 100, 103, 104, 106, 135, 173
Gomillion, Charles G., 59–60, 62, 97. *See also* Tuskegee (Alabama)
Gomillion v. Lightfoot, 62
Goode, W. Wilson, 219–220
Goodman, Andrew, 99
Gordon, Spiver, 239, 241
Gore, Albert, (photo) 250, 252, 267
Gray, Victoria, (photo) 103
Gray, William H., 259
Gregory, Dick, 135
Green, Ernest, 197
Greene County (Alabama), 123, 239–240
Greensboro (North Carolina), 72–74
Greenwood (Mississippi), 87–90, 118
Griggs v. Duke Power Company, 199
Grove City College v. Bell, 246
Grovey v. Townsend, 15
Guiliani, Rudolph, 269
Guyot, Lawrence, 86, 88–89

Hamer, Fannie Lou, 86, 101, (photo) 103, 148, 151, 158–159, 163, 237, 247, 256
Hamilton, Charles V., 2, 120
Hampton, William, 73
Hancock County (Georgia), 123–124, 159
Hancock County Democratic Club, 123
Hanrahan, Edward V., 213
Hare, James A., 107
Harlem Renaissance, 3
Harris, Patricia R., 196
Hart, Gary, 233, 235

Hartsfield, William, 43
Hatcher, Richard, 142, 177–179, 232
Hawkins, Augustus, 201
Hawkins, Yusuf, 268
Haynsworth, Clement, 139
Helms, Jesse, 210
Henry, Aaron, 91, 98, 100, 101, 125, 256
Highlander Folk School, 45
Hightower, Jim, 248, 250
Hill, Lister, 19
Hine, Darlene Clark, 16
Hinton, James, 18
Holman, M. Carl, 190
Hood, James, 94
Hoover, J. Edgar, 56. *See also* Federal Bureau of Investigation (FBI)
Horton, Willie, 258
Houston, Charles, 15, 32, 38
Howard Beach (Queens), 267
Howard Law School, 15
Hruska, Roman, 139
Hulett, John, 123
Humphrey, Hubert, 36, 58, 101, 134–136, 201

Ingram, Edith, 159

Jackson, Jesse, 214, (photo) 227, 237, (photo) 250, 260, 261, 263–265
　background of, 225
　importance of, 256–257
　and Jews, 202, 232, 251, 266
　and presidential race (1984), 224, 226–237
　and presidential race (1988), 247–257, 266–268
　and racial polarization, 238
Jackson, Jimmie Lee, 111
Jackson, Maynard, 165–168
Jemison, T. J., 46n, 226
Jenkins, Timothy, 85
Jews, 132, 133, 142, 178, 197–198, 202, 218, 268, 269
　and Jesse Jackson, 202, 232–233, 237, 251, 266
Johnson, Frank M., 64, 107, 113
Johnson, Lyndon B., 100, 104, 149, 223, 238
　and Civil Rights Act (1957), 57
　and Civil Rights Act (1964), 99
　and Civil Riaghts Act (1968), 133
　and presidential election (1960), 77

Johnson, Lyndon B. (*Cont.*):
  and presidential election (1964),
    100–102
  and Selma campaign, 111, 113
  and views on suffrage, 106, 147
  and Voting Rights Act (1965), 107,
    112–115
Joint Center for Political Studies,
  144–145
Jones, Mack H., 222–223
Jordan, Barbara, 144, 187, 192–193,
  (photo) 194
Justice Department, 81, 109, 178, 226
  and enforcement of voting rights,
    89–90, 157
  and federal protection, 99
  and voter registration, 81–86
  and voting fraud cases, 240–241

Karnig, Albert, 153
Katzenbach, Nicholas, 94, 109
Kean, Thomas, 260
Kennard, John, 240
Kennedy, Edward, 201, 203, 224
Kennedy, John F., 104, 147
  and appointment of federal judges,
    85–86
  and Birmingham, 93
  and civil rights strategy, 76, 79–81,
    94, 95
  and presidential election (1960),
    75–79
  and voter registration, 81
Kennedy, Robert, 78, 80, 83, 84, 150,
  167, 169
Kilson, Martin, 152
King, Coretta, 77, (photo) 227
King, Ed, 91, 100, 101, 125
King, Lonnie, 75
King, Martin Luther, Jr., 81, (photo)
  96, 104, (photo) 119, 134, 146,
  166, 167, 174, 186, 191, 193, 213,
  225, 226, 229, 265
  appeal of, 67
  and Birmingham campaign, 92–93
  and black power, 120–121
  and Eisenhower, 51, 68–69
  and Montgomery bus boycott, 45–46
  philosophy of, 67–68
  and Prayer Pilgrimage, 69
  and presidential election (1960),
    75–79
  and riots, 129

King, Martin Luther, Jr. (*Cont.*):
  and Selma campaign, 105, 108, 110,
    111, 113, 114
  and SNCC, 74, 75, 102
  and voter registration, 70–71, 82
  and Voting Rights Act, 112. *See also*
    Southern Christian Leadership
    Conference (SCLC)
King, Martin Luther, Sr., 26–27, 75,
  78, 192, 195
King, Mary, 116, 197
Kinsley, Michael, 258
Kluger, Richard, 48
Koch, Edward, 251, 266–269
Korstad, Robert, 44
Ku Klux Klan, 48, 99, 124, 257

Ladd, Everett C., Jr., 27, 152
Lance, Bert, 248
Lawson, James, 74
Leadership Conference on Civil
  Rights, 133
LeFlore County (Mississippi), 87–90.
  See also Greenwood (Mississippi)
Leuchtenburg, William E., 139
Lewis, Ann, 248
Lewis, Anthony, 253
Lewis, John, 96, 111–112, 119, 149,
  196, 197, 244, 248. *See also*
  Student Nonviolent Coordinating
  Committee (SNCC)
Lewis, Rufus A., 45
Lichtenstein, Nelson, 44
Literacy tests, 22, 99*n*, 114, 138
Little Rock (AR), 64–65, 197
Liuzzo, Viola, 113
Locher, Ralph, 173–175
Los Angeles (CA), 180–181
Louisiana, 49, 115, 156
Lowery, Joseph, 117, (photo) 227
Lowndes County (Alabama), 123, 160
Lowndes County Freedom
  Organization (LCFO), 123, 129,
  160
Loyalist Democrats of Mississippi, 126,
  151

McCain, Franklin, 72
McCown, John, 123–124
McCoy, Donald, 38
McCoy, Rhody, 132
McCray, John, 18
McCree, Wade, 196–197, 199, 200

McGovern, George, 142, 205
McHenry, Donald F., 202
McKaine, Osceola, 18, 27–28
McKissick, Floyd, (photo) 119
McMillen, Neil R., 98
Macon County (Alabama), 58–64, 124–125. *See also* Tuskegee
Macon County Democratic Association, 97
McTeer, Vic, 237
Malcolm X., 118, 121
Malone, Vivian, 94
Marable, Manning, 135
March on Washington (1963), (photo) 96
March on Washington Movement (MOWM), 8–11. *See also* Randolph, A. Philip
Marshall, Burke, 84, 93
Marshall, Thurgood, 15, 200
Martin, Louis, 76, 77, 103–104, 152
Martin, Lynn, 242
Massell, Sam, 165, 166
Massive resistance, 48, 71
Memphis (Tennessee), 70
Meranto, Philip, 173
Meredith, James, 94, 118
Meredith march, 118–120, 147
Miller, Dorrie, 2, (photo) 3
Mississippi, 115, 158
  black politics in, 125–126, 151
  changes in, 122
  and voting discrimination, 23–25, 127
  and voter registration, 86–91
Mississippi Freedom Democratic Party (MFDP), (photo) 103, 125, 147, 164
  and black power, 117
  creation of, 100
  decline of, 151
Mississippi Progressive Voters League, 23, 24
Mitchell, Clarence, 54, 138
Mitchell, John, 137
Mitchell, William P., 60, 62–64
Mondale, Walter, 101, 224, 231, 233–237, 265
Montgomery (Alabama), 44, 65, 67, 70, 80–81
Montgomery bus boycott, 45–47, 117, 146
Montgomery Improvement Association, 46

Moon, Henry Lee, 42–43
Moore, Amzie, 87, 88, 125
Morrow, E. Frederic, 77
Moses, Robert Parris, 82–83, 86, 87, 91, 98, 107, 125, 264. *See also* Student Nonviolent Coordinating Committee (SNCC)
Moynihan, Daniel Patrick, 139–140

Nashville (TN), 67, 74
Nation of Islam, 232
National Association for the Advancement of Colored People (NAACP), 3, 8, 34, 39, 44, 67, 69, 73, 90, 92, 133, 173, 177
  attack on, 48–49
  and Civil Rights Act (1957), 58
  and Mississippi, 102, 126, 127
  and opposition to Bilbo, 23–25
  and other civil rights groups, 71, 82, 98
  and poll tax, 17
  and voter registration, 26, 27, 49, 82, 116, 196, 220, 226
  and white primary, 14–16, 18
  and World War II, 7, 9, 10. *See also* Wilkins, Roy
National Black Political Assembly, 141, 142
National Black Political Convention, 141–142
National Committee to Abolish the Poll Tax, 16–17
National Council of Negro Republicans, 39. *See also* Republican party
National Political Congress of Black Women, 236*n*
National Roster of Black Elected Officials, The, 145
National Women's Political Caucus, 164
Nelson, Gaylord, 204
Nelson, William, 173
New Orleans (LA), 244
New York City, 32, 131–133, 251, 253, 266–270
New York Times, The, 258
Newton, Huey P., 129. *See also* Black Panther Party (BPP)
Nixon, Edgar D., 44–45. *See also* Montgomery bus boycott
Nixon, Richard M., 75–76, 183, 184

Nixon, Richard M., *(Cont.)*:
    and black elected officials, 147, 169
    as president, 136–137, 138, 139–140
    and presidential election (1960),
        75–79
    and presidential election (1968),
        134–136
    and presidential election (1972), 143
    as vice president, 51, 54, 69
    and Voting Rights Act, 137–138
Nonviolent Action Group, 118
Norfolk (Virginia), 95
North Carolina, 115
Norton, Eleanor Holmes, 200

O'Brien, Lawrence, 103
Ocean Hill-Brownsville (Brooklyn),
    131–133
Operation Breadbasket, 225
Operation PUSH, 202, 225

Palestine Liberation Organization, 202,
    232
Palmer, Hazel, 264
Panetta, Leon, 147
Parker, Allen, 124
Parks, Rosa, 45, (photo) 47, 163, 256
Patterson, John, 76, 148
Peace and Freedom party, 134
Pendelton, Clarence, 206
People Organized for Welfare and
    Employment Rights (POWER),
    215
People United to Save Humanity
    (PUSH). *see* Operation PUSH)
Perry County (Alabama), 111
Philadelphia (Pennsylvania), 12–13,
    219–220
Philadelphia Plan, 140
Pierce, Samuel, 206
Pinderhughes, Dianne, 218
Pittsburgh Courier, 8, 20–21, 22, 40
Plessy v. Ferguson,, 48
Poll tax, 16–17, 23, 32, 41, 115
Powell, Adam Clayton, 32, 52, (photo)
    53, 69, 76, 131
Prayer Pilgrimage, 68–69
President's Committee on Civil Rights,
    33–34
President's Committee on Government
    Contract Compliance, 51, 76

Quayle, Dan, 258

Radigan, Joseph, 178
Rainbow coalition, 228, 229, 231, 248.
    See also Jackson, Jesse
Randolph, A. Philip, 3, 8, 34–35,
    (photo) 37, 68. *See also* March on
    Washington Movement (MOWM)
Rangel, Charles, 185
Rauh, Joseph, 101, 102, 186
Reagan, Ronald, 135, 228, 229
    black opposition to, 221, 223, 238
    as first-term president, 206–212
    as second-term president, 239–242,
        245–246
    and presidential election (1980), 204
    and presidential election (1984),
        237–238
Reeb, James, 113
Reed, Adolph, 232
Reese, Frederick, 108, 111, 144
Republican party, 56, 193, 224
    black support of, 260
    and presidential election (1948), 37, 39
    and presidential election (1952), 41
    and presidential election (1956), 54
    and presidential election (1984), 237
    and presidential election (1988), 258
    and South, 136, 187, 188, 205
    and white voters, 238
Reuther, Walter, 101
Reutten, Richard T., 38
Reynolds, William Bradford, 207, 210,
    226
Richmond (Virginia), 26, 43
Riots, 127–129, 174, 179
Rizzo, Frank, 219
Robeson, Paul, 38
Robinson, Jackie, 5–6, 21–22
Robinson, Jo Ann, 45, 163. *See also*
    Montgomery bus boycott
Rogers, Grady, 63
Roosevelt, Eleanor, 3–4, 11
Roosevelt, Franklin, 3, 4, 30, 31, 104
    and black electorate, 13–14
    and black protest, 8–9, 12
    racial views of, 11–12
    and white primary, 19
Rustin, Bayard, 68, 102, 132, 146–147

Salamon, Lester, 152
Sawyer, Eugene, 219n
Schwerner, Michael, 99
Seale, Bobby, 129. *See also* Black
    Panther party (BPP)

Selma (Alabama), 144, 239. *See also*
    Dallas County (Alabama)
    demonstrations in, 105–113
    description of, 107–108
Seward, Herbert W., 20
Shanker, Albert, 132
Shelby, Richard C., 241, 246
Shuttlesworth, Fred, 92, 93
Sit-ins, 72, 75
Sitkoff, Harvard, 11
Smith v. Allwright, 14–16, 27, 31
Smith, Michael, 177n
Smith, Robert C., 150
South Africa, 202, 229, 242
South Carolina, 17, 49, 115, 127
South Carolina Progressive Democratic
    Party, 18
Southern Christian Leadership
    Conference (SCLC), 90, 123, 225
    background of, 66–67
    and Birmingham campaign, 91–94
    decline of, 134
    and Meredith march, 118
    and other civil rights groups, 71, 74,
        82
    and Selma campaign, 108, 110–112
    and voter registration, 70–72, 82,
        220
    and Voting Rights Act, 114. *See also*
        King, Martin Luther, Jr.,
Southern Conference for Human
    Welfare (SCHW), 26, 28
Southern Regional Council, 82, 116
Sowell, Thomas, 212
Sparkman, John, 40
Stennis, John, 25
Stevenson, Adlai, 40, 54
Stokes, Carl, 173–176, 232
Stokes, Louis, 176
Stone, Chuck, 148
Student Nonviolent Coordinating
    Committee (SNCC), 90, 104, 107,
        118, 123, 151, 263
    and black power, 118, 121
    creation of, 74
    demise of, 133–134
    and freedom rides, 80
    and freedom summer, 118
    impact of, 164
    and Mississippi Freedom Democratic
        Party (MFDP), 100, 102, 147
    and other civil rights groups, 75, 82,
        98

Student Nonviolent Coordinating
    Committee (SNCC) (*Cont.*):
    and Selma campaign, 108–110, 113
    and Vietnam, 131
    and voter registration, 82–84, 86–91,
        125. *See also* Moses, Robert
        Parris
*Swann v. Charlotte-Mecklenburg
    Board of Education*, 138

Taft, Seth, 175
Tallahassee (FL), 67
Talmadge, Herman, 167
Tampa (FL), 95
Texas, 14–16, 156
Thornton, J. Mills, 47
Thurmond, J. Strom, 37, 135, 205, 210
Till, Emmett, 56, 88
To Secure These Rights, 33
Truman, Harry S., 104
    background of, 32–33
    civil rights proposals of, 33–34
    and Cold War, 34–35, 39
    and presidential election (1948),
        38–39
Turnbow, Hartman, 125
Turner, Albert, 111, 239–241
Tuskegee (Alabama), 13, 59–64, 120
    black election victories in, 97, 124,
        150, 169–170.
    See also Macon County (Alabama)
Tuskegee Civic Association, 60–62, 97

United Federation of Teachers (UFT),
    131–132
United Freedom Movement
    (Cleveland), 173
United States Commission on Civil
    Rights, 56, 58, 62–63, 71, 107, 206
United States Supreme Court, 14–16,
    29, 46, 62, 81, 139, 199, 207, 208,
    245–246
Urban League, 82, 134
USA Today, 250

Valeriani, Richard, 111
Vandiver, Ernest, 77
Vietnam, 131, 134, 183, 195
Virginia, 49, 115, 158, 269n
Vivian, C. T., 226
Voinovich, George, 260
Voter Education Project, 81–84,
    116–117, 196, 220

Voter registration, 17, 70–71, 81–86
   in Mississippi, 86–91
   obstacles to, 49–50, 60, 127
   statistics on, 27, 29, 84, (table) 85,
      105, 196, 220, 226, (table) 228,
      238
Voting Rights Act (1965), 172
   and affirmative action, 155
   enforcement of, 157, 226
   impact of, 115–116, 123, 136
   judicial interpretation of, 138–139
   origins of, 106–107
   passage of, 114–115
   renewal of (1970), 137–138
   renewal of (1975), 185–188
   renewal of (1982), 207–210, 240

Wallace, George, 94, 110, 127, 148,
      151, 191, 232
   as presidential candidate, 130,
      134–136, 142–143
   and Selma, 113
Wallace, Henry, 33, 35, 36–38
Wallace, Lurleen, 127
Walters, Ronald W., 265
Warren, Earl, 54
Washington, Booker T., 1, 59
Washington, Harold, 219, 220, 223,
      224, 230, 232
   background of, 214–216
   and election as mayor, 217–219
Washington Post, 232
Weiss, Nancy J., 30, 38
Welch, Susan, 153
White Citizens Council, 48–50, 191
White, John, 248

White primary, 14–16
White v. Regester, 156
White, Walter, 8
Wilder, Douglas L., 269n
Wilkie, Wendell, 13
Wilkins, Roy, 26, 51, 54, 55, 68, 69,
      116, 129. *See also* National
      Association for the Advancement
      of Colored People (NAACP)
Williams, Eddie N., 144, 208
Williams, Hosea, 111
Williams, Kenneth, 27
Wilson, T. R., 23
Winston-Salem (NC), 26, 27, 43–44
Wofford, Harris, 76–78, 83
Women's Political Council, 45
Woodward, Isaac, 33
World War II:
   black criticism of, 7
   and black economic gains, 13
   black support of, 7
   and black veterans, 21–22
   impact of, 2, 17, 20, 28–30
   and racial discrimination, 4–6, 10
   and white liberals, 11
Wright, Cleo, 2

Yorty, Sam, 180
Young, Andrew, 144, 166, 187,
      200–202, 237
   and Jesse Jackson, 231, 236, 248
   and Jimmy Carter, 192, 195, 197
Young, Coleman, 179–180, 248, 252

Zimmer v. McKeithen, 157
Zinn, Howard, 110